fP

ALSO BY ANN RULE

Heart Full of Lies
Every Breath You Take
. . . And Never Let Her Go
Dead by Sunset
Everything She Ever Wanted
If You Really Loved Me
The Stranger Beside Me
Possession
Small Sacrifices
Kiss Me, Kill Me
Without Pity
Last Dance, Last Chance
Empty Promises
A Rage to Kill
The End of the Dream
In the Name of Love
A Fever in the Heart
You Belong to Me
A Rose for Her Grave
The I-5 Killer
The Want-Ad Killer
Lust Killer

ANN RULE

GREEN RIVER, RUNNING RED

The Real Story of the Green River Killer—

America's Deadliest Serial Murderer

Free Press

New York London Toronto Sydney

*f***P**

FREE PRESS
A Division of Simon & Schuster, Inc.
1230 Avenue of the Americas
New York, NY 10020

FREE PRESS *and colophon are trademarks of Simon & Schuster, Inc.*

For information about special discounts for bulk purchases,
please contact Simon & Schuster Special Sales:
1-800-456-6798 or business@simonandschuster.com.

Designed by Karolina Harris

Manufactured in the United States of America

10 9 8 7 6 5 4 3 2 1

Library of Congress Control Number: 2004056338
ISBN 0-7432-3851-6

*In memory of all the lost and murdered young women
who fell victim to the Green River Killer,
with my profound regret that they never had the chance to
make the new start so many of them hoped to achieve.*

Cast of Characters

The Victims, in Order of Their Disappearance
Wendy Lee Coffield, Debra Lynn Bonner, Cynthia Jean Hinds, Opal
Charmaine Mills, Marcia Faye Chapman, Giselle Lovvorn, Terry
Rene Milligan, Mary Bridget Meehan, Debra Lorraine Estes,
Denise Darcel Bush, Shawnda Leea Summers, Shirley Marie Sher-
rill, Colleen Renee Brockman, Rebecca Marrero, Kase Ann Lee,
Linda Jane Rule, Alma Ann Smith, Delores LaVerne Williams,
Sandra Kay Gabbert, Kimi-Kai Pitsor, Gail Lynn Mathews, Andrea
M. Childers, Marie Malvar, Martina Theresa Authorlee, Cheryl
Lee Wims, Yvonne Shelly Antosh, Constance Elizabeth Naon,
Carrie Ann Rois, Tammy Liles, "Rose," Keli Kay McGinness, Kelly
Marie Ware, Tina Marie Thompson, Carol Ann Christensen, April
Dawn Buttram, Debora May Abernathy, Tracy Ann Winston,
Maureen Sue Feeney, Mary Sue Bello, Pammy Avent, Patricia Anne
Osborn, Delise Louise Plager, Kimberly Nelson, Lisa Lorraine
Yates, Cindy Ann Smith, Mary Exzetta West, Patricia Michelle Bar-
czak, Patricia Yellow Robe, Marta Reeves, Roberta Joseph Hayes,
Jane Doe C-10, Jane Doe D-16, Jane Doe D-17, Jane Doe B-20.

Victims Later Eliminated as
    Green River Killings
Leann Wilcox, Virginia Taylor, Joan Conner, Theresa Kline, Amina
Agisheff, Angelita Axelson, Patty Jo Crossman, Geri Slough,
Oneida Peterson, Trina Hunter.

The Investigators: 1982 through 2004
Green River Task Force Commanders: Dick Kraske, Frank
Adamson, Jim Pompey, Bob Evans, Mike Nault, Jim Graddon,
Bruce Kalin, Terry Allman.
    Green River Investigators: Sheriff David Reichert, Lt. Greg
Boyle, Lt. Jackson Beard, Lt. Dan Nolan, Sgt. Harlan Bollinger,

Sgt. Rupe Lettich, Sgt. Frank Atchley, Sgt. Bob "Grizzly" Andrews, Sgt. Ray Green, Sgt. Ed Streidinger, Sgt. D. B. Gates, Sue Peters, Tony McNabb, Bob Pedrin, Bob LaMoria, Fae Brooks, Ben Colwell, Elizabeth Druin, Larry Gross, Tom Jensen, Jim Doyon, Bruce Peterson, Ralf McAllister, Nancy McAllister, Spence Nelson, Pat Ferguson, Ed Hanson, Chuck Winters, John Blake, Carolyn Griffin, Mike Hagan, Rich Battle, Paul Smith, Rob Bardsley, Mike Hatch, Jerry Alexander, Ty Hughes, Randy Mullinax, Cherisse Luxa, Bob Gebo, Matt Haney, Kevin O'Keefe, Jake Pavlovich, Raphael Crenshaw, Katie Larson, Jon Mattsen, Denny Gulla, Cecil Ray, Norm Matzke, Robin Clark, Graydon Matheson, Ted Moser, Bill Michaels, J. K. Pewitt, Brent Beden, Malcolm Chang, Barry Anderson, Pat Bowen, Rick Chubb, Paul Griffith, Joe Higgins, Rick Jackson, Gene Kahn, Rob Kellams, Henry McLauchlin, Ross Nooney, Tom Pike, Bob Seager, Mick Stewart, Bob Stockham, Walt Stout, John Tolton, David Walker.

Evidence Specialists
Tonya Yzaguerre, Cheryl Rivers, Terry McAdam, George Johnston, Chesterine Cwiklik, Jean Johnston, Beverly Himick; Skip Palenik, microscopist, Microtrace; Marc Church; Kirsten Maitland.

Other Police Jurisdictions
Investigators from Washington State: Des Moines Police Department, Tukwila Police Department, Kent Police Department, Thurston County Sheriff's Department, Snohomish County Sheriff's Department, Pierce County Sheriff's Department, Tacoma Police Department, Spokane Police Department.

Oregon: Portland Police Department, Multnomah County Sheriff's Office, Washington County Sheriff's Office, Clackamas County Sheriff's Office.

California: San Diego Sheriff's Department, San Francisco Sheriff's Department, San Francisco Police Department, Sacramento Police Department.

Nevada: Las Vegas Police Department.

Medical Examiners
Dr. Donald Reay, Medical Examiner, King County; Bill Haglund, Ph.D., Chief Investigator, King County Medical Examiner's Office; Dr. Larry Lewman, Oregon State Medical Examiner.

The Prosecutors
Norm Maleng, King County Prosecutor; Marilyn Brenneman, Al Matthews, Jeff Baird, Bryan McDonald, Ian Goodhew, Patricia Eakes, Sean O'Donnell.

The Defense Team
Tony Savage, Mark Prothero, Fred Leatherman, David Roberson, Suzanne Elliott, Todd Gruenhagen, James Robinson.

Interested Observers
Barbara Kubik-Patten, psychic; Melvyn Foster, unofficial consultant; Cookie Hunt, spokesperson for the Women's Coalition; Dale Wells, public defender in Spokane.

Task Force Consultants
Pierce Brooks, former Homicide captain, Los Angeles Police Department, former police chief in Lakewood, Colorado, and Eugene and Springfield, Oregon, serial murder expert; Robert Keppel, Ph.D., serial murder expert; Dr. John Berberich, psychologist; Chuck Wright, Washington State Corrections probation and parole supervisor; Dr. Chris Harris, forensic psychiatrist; Dr. Robert Wheeler, psychologist; Betty Pat Gatliff, forensic artist; Dr. Clyde Snow, forensic anthropologist; Linda Barker, victims' advocate; Prof. Fio Ugolini, soil scientist; Dee Botkin, phlebotomist.

F.B.I. special agents: John Douglas; Dr. Mary Ellen O'Toole, Behavioral Science Unit; Gerald "Duke" Dietrich, Paul Lindsay, Walt LaMar, Tom Torkilsen, John Gambersky, Ralph Hope, Bob Agnew.

INTRODUCTION

As I Began this most horrifying of all books in my long career as a true-crime writer, I found myself faced with the same dilemma I encountered some twenty-five years ago. In the early 1970s, I worked as a volunteer at the Crisis Clinic in Seattle, Washington. Two nights a week, I worked an all-night shift with a young male psychology student at the University of Washington as my partner. Together we fielded calls from suicidal and distraught people. I hadn't published a book yet, but by 1975 I had a contract to write one if the nameless killer of at least seven young coeds in Washington and Oregon was ever caught. As many readers know, that murderer turned out to be my partner: Ted Bundy. By the time I learned that, however, he had left the Northwest and continued his murderous rampage in Utah, Idaho, and Colorado. Convicted of attempted kidnapping in Utah, Ted was extradited to Colorado in 1976 to await his murder trials for eight victims in that state, but he escaped from two jails, making his way to Florida after his second—successful—escape on New Year's Eve, 1977. There he took the lives of three more young women and left another three for dead in Tallahassee and Jacksonville before he was finally arrested, convicted of murder in two trials, and sentenced to death. After nine years of appeals, Ted was electrocuted on January 24, 1989, at Raiford Prison.

How many women did Ted Bundy kill? No one really knows for sure, but when Florida detectives told him that the F.B.I. believed his toll was thirty-six victims, he said, "Add one digit to that, and you'll have it." Only he knew if he meant 37, 136, or 360.

Throughout his years of imprisonment, Ted wrote dozens of letters to me, and sometimes made oblique statements that could be construed as partial confessions.

Initially, I tried to write the Ted Bundy saga as if I were only an observer, and no part of the story. It didn't work because I had been part of the story, so after two hundred pages, I started over on *The Stranger Beside Me*. There were times when I had to drop in and out of the scenario with memories and connections that seemed relevant. *Stranger* was my first book; this is my twenty-third. Once again, I have found myself part of the story, more than I would choose to be in some instances. Many of the men and women who investigated these cases are longtime friends. I have taught seminars at law enforcement conferences with some of them and worked beside others on various task forces, although I am no longer a police officer. I have known them as human beings who faced an almost incomprehensible task and somehow stood up to it and, in the end, won. And I have known them when they were relaxed and having a good time at my house or theirs, setting aside for a short while the frustrations, disappointments, and tragedies with which they had to deal.

Was I privy to secret information? Only rarely. I didn't ask questions that I knew they couldn't answer. What I did learn I kept to myself until the time came when it could be revealed without negatively impacting the investigation.

So, the twenty-two-year quest to find, arrest, convict, and sentence the man who is, perhaps, the most prolific serial killer in history has been part of my life, too. It all began so close to where I lived and brought up my children. This time, I didn't know the killer, but he, apparently, knew me, read my books about true homicide cases, and was sometimes so close that I could have reached out and touched him. As it turned out, varying degrees of connection also existed between his victims and people close to me, but I would learn that only in retrospect.

There were moments over the years when I was convinced that this unknown personification of evil had to appear so normal, so bland, that he could have stood behind me in the supermarket checkout line, or eaten dinner in the restaurant booth next to mine.

He did. And he had.

 Looking back now, I wonder why I cut a particular article out of the *Seattle Post-Intelligencer.* It wasn't headline news, and it was so brief that it would have been easy to miss. By the summer of 1982, I had moved on from covering six to eight homicide cases for *True Detective* and four other fact-detective magazines every month and was concentrating on writing books. I was under contract to do a novel at the time and I wasn't even looking for true-crime cases to write about. But the short item in the "Local News" section was

very sad: Two young boys had found the body of a young woman snagged on pilings under the Peck Bridge on Meeker Street in Kent, Washington. She had floated in the shallows of the Green River, her arms and legs entangled in a rope or some similar bonds.

The paper wasn't specific about the cause of death, but police in Kent suspected that she had been strangled. Although she had been in the river for several days, no one had come forward to identify her.

The woman was white, estimated to be about twenty-five years old, and at five feet four, she weighed about 140 pounds. She had no identification on her body, and she wore unhemmed jeans, a lace-trimmed blue-and-white-striped blouse, and white leather tennis shoes.

Her clothing wasn't distinctive, but King County medical examiner Dr. Don Reay noted that she had five tattoos on her body: a vine around a heart on her left arm, two tiny butterflies above her breasts, a cross with a vine around it on her shoulder, a Harley-Davidson motorcycle insignia on her back, and the unfinished outline of a unicorn on her lower abdomen. The delicacy of four of the tattoos warred with the motorcycle-gang mark, but Kent detectives still thought that it might be the likeliest lead they had in finding out who she was—*if* any members of local motorcycle organizations would admit to knowing her.

I clipped out the coverage of the woman's death, being careful to save the upper margin of the page with the date. It was published on July 18, 1982. She had actually been found on Thursday, July 15.

The victim hadn't drowned; she had been dead when she was placed in the river. When a description of her tattoos was published in area papers, a tattoo artist recognized his work and came forward to identify the victim. She wasn't a grown woman at all; she was much younger. He knew her as Wendy Lee Coffield. "I think she lives in Puyallup with her mother," he added. "She's only sixteen."

Detectives located her mother, Virginia Coffield. Although she appeared to be in shock, the woman murmured, "I kind of expected it." She explained that she suspected Wendy had been working as a prostitute and might have been attacked and killed by a "john."

"I know that was the kind of life she chose for herself," Virginia Coffield said with a sigh. "We taught her the best we could."

Wendy Lee's mother said her daughter had been a good little girl when they were living in the country, but that her "trouble" had started when they moved to Auburn and Kent, both of which were still very small towns compared to Seattle and Tacoma.

Wendy and her mother never had much money as Virginia struggled to support the two of them after Virginia and her husband, Herb, divorced; they lived in one low-rent apartment after another. There had even been times in the warm summer months when they had to live in a tent, picking blackberries to sell so they could buy food.

"Wendy dropped out of school—way back in junior high," her mother said wearily.

She didn't say, but Wendy had been caught in an all too familiar vicious circle. Virginia herself was only thirty-six, worn and discouraged beyond her years. Her own childhood had been a miserable time where many of the adults who were supposed to be caring for her were more interested in the fuzzy escape of alcohol. She had come from "a big family of drinkers."

Virginia had become pregnant at sixteen and given that child up for adoption. Then she spent two teenage years at Maple Lane, Washington's juvenile corrections facility for girls. "I felt like I was a misfit; nobody understood me. She [Wendy] was seeking help just like I did, but they put her out [of juvenile detention] when they should have given her supervision. She just needed a couple of years off the street to grow up."

By mid-1982, Virginia and Wendy were living in another rundown apartment in downtown Puyallup. Photographs of Wendy showed a smiling girl with a wide, open face. She could have passed for eighteen or nineteen, but she was only a few years past childhood. After she stopped going to junior high, she had been enrolled in Kent Continuation School in the hope that she could catch up. But she was a chronic runaway, perhaps wanting to leave behind a home where she wasn't happy, or simply looking for excitement out in the world—or both.

Her mother had lost control of her. "Wendy just started having trouble," Virginia Coffield said, explaining that her daughter was known to police for minor offenses in both King and Pierce Counties. "The last thing she did was she took $140 in food stamps from one of our neighbors."

One night, when Wendy was fourteen or fifteen, Virginia recalled, she had come home disheveled and upset. "She said some guy raped her while she was hitchhiking. That's the way she got around. *Hitchhiking*. I told her that's what happens."

Wendy changed after that and her problems grew. Her theft of the food stamps landed her in Remann Hall, the Pierce County juvenile detention center in Tacoma, and then into a foster home. She became a runaway from there on July 8 when she didn't return from a twenty-four-hour pass to visit her grandfather.

Wendy and her mother had lived a hardscrabble existence, and neither seemed to have met the other's expectations. Fathers drift away and single mothers despair of ever making enough money to keep going. Rebellious teenage daughters make it more difficult as they act out of their own pain. And so it continues. Wendy Lee got caught in the centrifugal force of it. She wanted the things she didn't have and she took terrible chances to get them. Somewhere along the way, she had met someone who was angry enough or perverted enough to consider her survival in the world insignificant.

Since Wendy's body had been found within the Kent city limits, her murder would be investigated by the Kent Police Department. Chief Jay Skewes said that the last time anyone had seen Wendy alive was shortly after she had slipped out of Remann Hall, a week before her corpse was discovered in the Green River. She had been listed as a runaway, but no one had been actively looking for her. There were so many runaways that it was hard to know where to start.

And now Wendy's sad little life was over before it really began. Her blurry photo appeared over and over in the media as the story of her murder was updated and details added. She was an attractive blond-haired girl, and I had written about hundreds of homicide cases in the dozen years before Wendy was killed, a number of them about pretty blondes who had been strangled.

But she was so young, and I learned she had been violently choked with her own panties. I had teenagers myself, and I remembered the girls I'd known when I was in college and worked summers as a student intern at Hillcrest, the juvenile girls' training center in Salem, Oregon (a facility once known as a reform school). The Hillcrest residents ranged in age from thirteen to eighteen, and they tried to act tough, although I soon realized just how frightened and vulnerable most of them were.

Maybe that's why I saved the clipping about the girl in the Green River. Or maybe it was because Wendy's body had been found close to where I lived in the south end of King County, Washington. At least a thousand times over the forty years I've lived here, I've passed the very spot where someone threw her away.

To reach this stretch of the Green River from my house, I had to cross Highway 99 and head about four miles down the long curving hill that is the Kent–Des Moines Road. The Green River coursed south from Eliott Bay and the Duwamish Waterway, irrigating the floor of the Kent Valley. In the days before the Boeing Airplane Company expanded and the Southcenter Mall mushroomed, the valley was known for its rich loamy soil and was home to family farms, many of which supplied produce to Seattle's Public Market, or who simply put up their own stands along the road. When my children were small, I took them every summer to one of the U-Pick strawberry patches that abounded in the valley. We often took Sunday drives through Kent, Auburn, and Puyallup.

I had also driven along Frager Road on the Green River's western bank in almost total darkness any number of nights, coming home from dinner with friends or from shopping at the Southcenter Mall. The lights of the huge mall faded within minutes as the road became indistinguishable from the river.

North of the Meeker Street Bridge, Frager Road and the rushing river frightened me a little at night because there were hardly any houses nearby, and winter rains made the Green River run so deep that it nudged the shoulders of the road. Drivers under the influence or inexperienced or reckless often missed turns on the narrow road and sailed into the river. Few of them survived. Sometimes they floated in the depths for a long time, because nobody was aware that their cars and bodies waited there beneath the surface.

In the moonless dark, the lonely road along the river seemed somehow sinister, although I could never come up with a good reason why I felt that way. It was just a river in the daytime, running past fields, tumbling-down farmhouses, and one tiny park that had two rickety picnic tables. There were usually a few dozen fishermen huddled in little lean-tos made of scrap wood, angling for steelheads along the river.

Despite my foreboding, I often took Frager Road home after midnight because it was a shortcut to my house on S. 244th Street. When I came to S. 212th, I drove away from the river, turning right and then left up a hill, past the "Earth Works Park," which was not really a park at all but a huge pile of dirt that had been bulldozed into oblique ascending levels and then thinly planted with grass. The City of Kent had commissioned it as an art project. It wasn't pretty, it didn't seem like art and it, too, was faintly threatening as it loomed beside the secluded road that wound up a hill that became steeper and steeper.

I was always relieved when I reached the top and crossed Military Road onto S. 216th. Highway 99—the SeaTac HiWay—where the lights were bright again, was only two blocks ahead and I was almost home.

I rarely had occasion to drive on Frager Road between S. 212th and Meeker Streets, and Wendy's body had drifted south of where I always turned off. In the summer months when she was found, the water wasn't deep beneath the Meeker Street Bridge. She would have been in plain sight of anyone who drove across it into Kent. Kent was a small town twenty-two years ago, without the block after block of condos and apartment houses it has now. The place in the river where Wendy's body floated didn't abut a golf course or a joggers' trail two decades ago because they hadn't been built yet. Kent's city council hadn't voted in 1982 to make the city's entrance picturesque.

Kent was mostly a blue-collar town and Seattle comedians were quick to make jokes about it. Bellevue and Mercer and Bainbridge Islands were the white-collar bastions, but Kent, Auburn, and Tukwila were fair game. Almost Live, the most popular local comedy show, even coined a euphemism for sexual intercourse, calling it "Going to Tukwila" after a local couple claimed the championship for "making love the most times in one year."

Close to where Wendy's body was left, there was a restaurant called The Ebb Tide that had moderately good food and served generous drinks in its smoke-filled lounge. A block or so east of that was a topless dancing spot, a two-story motel, and a handful of fast-food franchises.

The Green River was running low in July 1982, and much of the rocky shore with its reedy grasses was exposed. It wouldn't have been difficult for a man—or men—to carry Wendy from a vehicle down to the river, but it would have had to be done in the hours of darkness. Someone pushing a bike or walking across the bridge, or anyone driving along Frager Road, could have seen what was happening. No one had. At least no one came forward to report any sightings.

The chances were good that the person—or persons—who had murdered Wendy Lee Coffield would never be found. She had quite probably met a deadly stranger who had no ties that might link the two of them with physical or circumstantial evidence. Stranger-to-stranger homicides are traditionally the most difficult to solve.

Even so, I saved the small pile of newspaper articles about Wendy. I drove to the Green River and stood at the spot where she had been found, wondering how she had come to get in a car with the worst person possible. Had it been someone she knew and trusted not to hurt her? Homicide detectives always look first at a victim's friends, co-workers, and family. If Wendy Coffield had known her killer, the Kent police had a reasonable chance of finding him. If she had encountered a stranger with violence in mind, her case might very well end up in the unsolved files.

ALONG WITH THE NEWSPAPER clippings I saved, I began to receive letters from women with terrifying memories to share.

I don't remember what month it was, or even what season. I do remember that it was in 1982 or 1983. I was nineteen, maybe even twenty at the time. It's hard for me now to be sure because it's been a really long time ago. I was "working," because I didn't have much choice—I had a big hassle with my mother and I didn't have a place to live or a way to eat except to be on the streets. In those days, I pretty much worked in downtown Seattle and my street name was "Kim Carnes"—I got that from the song about "Betty [sic] Davis Eyes"—because, you know, none of us liked to use our real names. We knew we'd be out of "the life" pretty soon and we didn't want any connection to . . . you know . . .

This particular john picked me up at the Greyhound bus depot on Eighth and Stewart. He was driving kind of a clunker of a car. I'm pretty good on details 'cause it was safer I figured to pay attention. It was a light blue Ford sedan with four doors, and it had vinyl seats. He told me that he was taking me to a party, and I believed him and said that was okay, but I knew that it was a "date" for money.

He got on the I-5 Freeway right there close to the Greyhound station and headed south, but it seemed like we were going a long, long way. I mean, I knew the south end of the county pretty good because I'd had this job where I delivered parts to Boeing at the plant out in the Kent Valley. I was starting to get a little bit suspicious. I kept asking him where we were going, and he seemed like he was getting nervous. He just said we'd be there "Soon—soon."

I was trying to make conversation, but he was getting really antsy. One time he pointed kind of over toward the east and he told me that he worked over there "across the river." That would have been the Green River and I thought he meant he worked in Kent.

I kept asking him how far the party was and he started to get angry and he was rude to me. But then he turned off on the Orilla Road South exit that's just past Angle Lake and it goes down to the county dump there, and on down the hill into the valley. I thought that was where we were going, but then he made a turn and we were going up a hill, and through some streets where there were a lot of houses. I figured that's where the party was supposed to be, but he didn't stop—not until we came to this field or maybe it was just a big vacant lot. It was really lonesome out there with trees all around it. You couldn't see any lights, only the moon.

I was really scared by this time because we were so far from the freeway and we weren't near any houses, either. On the way out, I'd been memorizing everything I could about his car and I'd noticed that the glove box didn't have a lock on it—only a button. He reached over me and popped it open and I saw that there was a stack of Polaroid pictures in there. He made me look at them. The first one was of a woman with red lingerie wrapped all around her neck and her face seemed kind of swollen. She looked scared. The thing I remember about all the pictures was that the girls in them had the same look in their eyes, like they were trapped. I didn't ask him who they were because I was too afraid.

By this time, I knew I had to think really fast and not let him know I was scared, so I pretended that we were just out there to have sex and didn't give him any fight because it wouldn't have done any good, anyway. I asked him what his name was, and he said it was Bob, but didn't give me his last name. He reached in the back seat and pulled out a brown paper bag—like a grocery bag. I could see it was stuffed with all kinds of women's underwear, like you can buy at Victoria's Secret. He held up the bras and panties and stuff and lots of the things were torn or dirty. He wanted me to put some of it on and I said I couldn't do that.

I don't know where he got it from, but he was holding a gun. It was a "short" gun, like I guess you call a hand-gun. He held it up against my head behind my ear. He made me give him a blow-job. I didn't want to because he had these weird bumps or something all over his penis, but he kept the gun to my head all the time I was trying to get him off. It seems like it was forty-five minutes that I kept trying, but I kept gagging because of the bumps. That made him real angry.

I was sure he was going to shoot me. He never lost his erection and he didn't ejaculate. Finally, I just started talking as fast as I could and somehow I convinced him to take me back to Seattle. I told him I had this friend who *was really lonely and that she had been looking for a guy just like him and she would be a perfect date for him and he wouldn't have to pay her or anything. I gave him her phone number, but it wasn't really her number—I just made it up.*

All the way into town, I kept talking and talking, because I was afraid he was going to pull off someplace and try again, but he took me back to the bus station. I didn't call the police because I didn't trust them. One time I got arrested for prostitution and this one cop opened up my shirt and just looked down at my breasts, and there was no reason for him to do that. So when this happened to me, I decided I wasn't going to tell them anything. I wasn't hurt and I wasn't dead.

The nightmares didn't go away, though, for a long time. See, when I was younger, my stepfather fooled around with me and then he raped me. I told my mother but she wouldn't believe me. I found out then that nobody believes you when you tell the truth. Especially the cops. I just kept it to myself for all these years. I'm in a straight life now and I have been for a long time. I've got a good husband, and I told him what happened. When I saw this guy's picture in the paper, I recognized him. I knew that I had to tell somebody.

What did he look like? Pretty average. Not too tall. Not too heavy. Just a guy. But I still feel that I came this close to getting killed, and the funny thing is that when I got into his car, I had him pegged as harmless. . . . I never would have believed that he could murder all those girls.

Diantha G. [To the Author]
December 2, 2001

PART ONE

1

FOR DECADES, Tukwila, Kent, Auburn, Des Moines, and Federal Way depended on the Pac HiWay for their commercial sustenance, entertainment, and transportation to either Seattle or Tacoma. The road, like the river, has changed continually over sixty years. It began as Highway 99, and then it was "Old 99" when the I-5 Freeway opened. Some spots are called Pacific Highway South, except where it passes the Seattle–Tacoma International Airport, where it has become International Parkway. Despite the newly sophisticated name, fancy street signs, and the median planted with shrubs and bulbs, this part of Pac HiWay remains the "SeaTac Strip" to many King County residents.

Heading south from Seattle for the twenty-six miles to Tacoma, the highway was two lane in the 1930s and 1940s, a pleasant drive out of the city on Saturday nights to dance at the Spanish Castle, gamble at a permanently anchored ship on the Duwamish River, or eat fried chicken at Rose's on the Highway.

There were little motels, which were referred to as "cabin camps," decades before the Hiltons, Sheratons, and Doubletrees, before the Super-Eights and Motel 6's, and even before the Ben Carol, the Three Bears, and the Legend motels. And, of course, 99 was the only highway to take to Portland and on to California, passing through the center of towns along the way.

Roads age and change the way people do, so subtly that nobody notices the first faint wrinkles and loss of rosy innocence. Often, the good things are just gone one day and few remember when they disappeared. The Spanish Castle and Rose's burned down in unexplained fires. Manca's In-and-Out hamburger drive-through went out of business. The Midway Drive-in, said to be the first outdoor theater in America, stopped showing movies at some point and became a thriving weekend swap meet.

The marginal hotels and motels became seedier, a club called Dandy's that featured topless dancers and male strippers took over Pepo's Gourmet Hungarian Restaurant at the corner of Pac HiWay and 144th, and then Pepo himself died while still in his forties.

"Pepo's corner" became the center point for something else entirely.

In the old days, sections of Seattle where love for sale was commonplace were far from the SeaTac Strip because it was much too remote from downtown. The airport was hardly a draw because it wasn't all that large. Instead, undercover cops watched for prostitutes and pimps along downtown's Pike Street and out on Aurora Avenue in the north end of the city.

Over time, the Pac HiWay became a tunnel of contrasts. In 1954, the airport was a single structure with no jetways and no underground trains, but it morphed into a huge spiderweb of gates, jetways, and ramps with two runways. Indeed, today's SeaTac Airport is one of the nation's hubs, and the King County Port Authority Commission foresaw the need for more and longer runways. Through its power of eminent domain, the commission bought up whole neighborhoods of little postwar houses with perfect lawns, whose occupants had long since grown used to the roar of jets directly over their roofs. The Port paid fair-market prices and scores of homes were loaded onto trucks, leaving behind many miles of wasteland both north and south of the airport. The grass grew tall around the houseless foundations and the neglected trees and shrubs left behind. The trees still blossomed and bore fruit, although no one was left to appreciate them.

By the early 1980s, the whole ambience of Highway 99/Pac HiWay/International Parkway had been transformed. Serious motorists raced along the I-5 Freeway a mile to the east, and the strip became a local roadway, full of businesses that catered to those who flew in or lived and worked nearby, some of them long-standing, some new: fast food, overnight lodging to fit any budget, locksmiths, bicycle repair shops, hot-tub sales, one stupendous gourmet supermarket—Larry's—and any number of 7-Elevens. The Little Church by the Side of the Road was still there and so was The Pancake Chef and the Lewis and Clark Theater, but its once magnificent single auditorium was sliced into a utilitarian multiplex. Don the Barber, who shares his shop with his twin brother, Dick, has cut hair at Pac HiWay and S. 142nd for decades, and they still have hundreds of "regulars" who stop by to joke with Don or have serious conversations with his more taciturn twin.

Drug deals became commonplace as pimps and their girls moved to the area. Certainly, there were homicides and lesser crimes along the Pacific Highway. One Chinese restaurant has had two fatal shoot-outs in as many years, but next door, families still flock to Angle Lake State Park to picnic and swim in the summer, and no one could have foreseen that the deadliest killer of all would choose a ten-mile stretch of this roadway as his personal hunting ground.

He was like a wolf watching his quarry from the woods, almost invisible as he crouched where the leaves have turned to faint brown and gray, virtually hidden by protective coloration. No one really saw him, and if anyone did, they wouldn't remember him. More than any other serial killer in the annals of crime, he could quite literally hide in plain sight.

Disasters often begin silently with an almost imperceptible shift in the way things are expected to be. Rockslides start with a pebble or two plinking down a mountain, and avalanches with the first tiny jar beneath pristine snowbanks. A small hole in a dike. A crack snaking along the hull of a ship. Rocky plates far beneath the ground shift and a gigantic earthquake topples tall buildings above. By the time human beings find themselves in the path of destruction, it is all too often too late to save them.

Except for the people who had known and loved her, and the Kent Police Department, Wendy Coffield's murder didn't make much of a blip on the awareness of people who lived in King County, Washington. Locals in the south end *were* afraid that summer of 1982, but not because of Wendy Coffield's murder; they were frightened because two people in Auburn had died suddenly and agonizingly the month before of cyanide poisoning after taking Extra-Strength Excedrin capsules purchased in Kent and Auburn stores. Investigators from the U.S. Food and Drug Administration were sweeping thousands of pill bottles off store shelves for testing. A lead investigator warned against taking *any* capsules until all the seized painkillers had been tested.

It was a scary time, but, sadly, not because of one teenager whose defiant nature and habit of hitchhiking had probably ended her life. Various police departments in the greater Puget Sound area had unsolved murders and missing persons cases involving young women, but there didn't seem to be any pattern among them.

In the next few weeks, the Green River rolled on, and fishermen sometimes talked about the body found in the river, but teenagers didn't swim in the Green River, anyway, and few of them had even known Wendy Coffield. The river's current was too swift for swimmers, and Lake Fenwick was close by. It was dangerous, too, because there were no lifeguards on duty, but it was still a popular spot for keggers.

AND THEN THE EARTH SHIFTED and more stones bounced quietly down a mountain of catastrophe. It was another Thursday, August 12, 1982, four weeks after Wendy's body was found, when what had appeared to be an isolated tragedy began to take on a horrific pattern. Another woman's body floated in the Green River about a quarter of a mile south of where Wendy had been discovered. The second body was found by a worker from the nearby PD & J Meat Company. It was difficult to determine where she had gone into the river, but her corpse, unclothed, had been trapped in a net of tree branches and logs. Where her killer had met up with her, no one knew. It was unlikely that she had drowned accidentally.

There was no question that the body had been found inside the boundaries of King County, so the case was assigned to Detective Dave Reichert, who was next up to be lead detective on a homicide. Reichert, a detective for only a few years, was about thirty, although he looked much younger and the investigators he worked with usually called him "Davy." He was a handsome man with bright blue eyes and an abundance of wavy brown hair. Reichert was a family man with three small children and a strong Christian ethic. Like a lot of King County deputies and detectives, he had grown up in the south end of the county. He was totally familiar with the area, where he and several brothers had roamed as kids.

That summer of 1982 had been devastating for the King County Sheriff's Major Crime Unit, particularly for Dave Reichert. They had lost one of their own in a senseless shooting. Sergeant Sam Hicks would surely have been working alongside Reichert. They were very close friends, not really "hot dogs," but imbued with the enthusiasm of youth and the belief that they could track down almost any bad guy they were looking for.

Hicks was a tall, broad-shouldered man, slightly balding, always smiling, whose desk sat in the middle of the Major Crimes office. But on June 17, Hicks and Officer Leo Hursh approached an isolated farmhouse near Black Diamond to question Robert Wayne Hughes, thirty-one, about the murder of a south Seattle rock musician. Bullets zinged at them from somewhere inside a barn as they crouched, unprotected, in the open—they had had no forewarning that Hughes might be dangerous. As Hughes fired at them from his secure position, Sam Hicks was killed and Leo Hursh injured.

Hicks's funeral procession was many miles long and south-end residents, many of them with their hands over their hearts, lined the route in tribute, tears running down their cheeks. Captain Frank Adamson, Reichert's commander, saw how Hicks's death had crushed him and he'd considered reassigning him until the enormity of his grief had passed. But he thought better of it. Reichert was sensitive, but strong, and he was managing to cope. He wasn't likely to take things into his own hands if he encountered Hicks's killer.

Only three weeks after Sam Hicks's funeral, Wendy Coffield's body was discovered. And now another dead woman. Hicks was gone. One of the best homicide detectives the department had ever had wouldn't be there to help solve her case. But Reichert, if anything, would work as hard as two men now.

The woman floating in the Green River wasn't just a case to him—he cared about all human life. He was a high-energy optimist who waded into the water, expecting that he would find out what had happened to her, and that he would quickly ferret out who had done it. Years later, Reichert would recall that the slender hand of the woman in the river seemed to be reaching out to him for help. The only way he could do that was to help convict whoever had killed her.

It was easier to identify this "floater" than it had been in Wendy Coffield's case; her fingerprints were in police files. Debra Lynn Bonner was twenty-two years old, and she had lately made a precarious living on Pacific Highway South, working as a prostitute. In the thirty days before Debra's body was found, she had been arrested twice for offering sex for money.

Reichert and Detective Bob LaMoria learned that the last time Debra had been seen alive was on July 25, eighteen days before. She left the Three Bears Motel, located on the corner of Pac HiWay and 216th, telling friends that she hoped to "catch some dates." But she never returned, and her room was cleaned and rerented. It was only a short drive east from the Three Bears Motel to the Green River, down the winding road past the Earthworks Park.

At most, it was two or three miles to the riverbank. In life, Debra had been a slender, exotic-looking woman. She grew up in Tacoma, along with two younger brothers. Like Wendy, she had dropped out of school—in Debra's case two years before graduating. With little education, she'd had trouble finding jobs. She had been excited about taking a test to join the navy, but she didn't pass. Still, she planned to get her GED (high school equivalency certificate) and start a different kind of life.

But Debra fell in love with a man who was only too happy to let her support him. The only way she could do that was to work the streets. At first, her life with him was exciting. Max Tackley* treated her like a queen, he had a newer model Thunderbird and they traveled a lot. They also experimented with heroin. Once in the life, Debra found it hard to get out.

Detectives learned that she had told her friends that she was "freelancing," working the "circuit" from Portland to Tacoma to Seattle to Yakima and Spokane on the east side of the Cascade Mountains and back again. But Debra had been trying to turn her life around, and she was meticulous about paying $25 a week on a $1,000 fine she owed to the Municipal Court in Tacoma, the seat of Pierce County. Fines were the cost of doing business for girls on the street, but Debra wanted no reminders of her old life. Week by week, she had whittled her debt down to $775 by the summer of 1982. Wherever she was, Debra was faithful about calling home, and her folks always accepted her collect calls. Her dad had an eye operation scheduled for July 20, and she called a few days later to see how he was and to tell him she loved him. That was the last time she phoned.

Debra had sounded cheerful in that call, but she was actually running scared. She had confided in a bartender that she was being stalked by her boyfriend/pimp. All the sweet-talking was over and she said that Tackley claimed she owed him several thousand dollars. "She was crying and upset," the woman recalled. "She didn't know how she was going to pay him."

Debra probably had reason to be afraid. Twelve years earlier, her lover had been convicted of manslaughter (lowered from second-degree murder) in the shooting death of a man he'd known since childhood—and that was over a $25 debt. His sentence was only five years in prison. He'd also been charged with two counts of assault in different confrontations over drug deals gone wrong, and received a ten-year sentence, but one that ran concurrently with his first sentence. He was out in seven years. If Debra really owed him

* The names of some individuals in this book have been changed. Such names are indicated by an asterisk (*) the first time they appear.

thousands of dollars, it was likely he would collect it one way or another.

During the seventies, when the approach to rehabilitation was extremely lenient, Tackley was one of the recipients of a scholarship to the University of Washington. A number of parolees benefited from the educational experience, but some of them didn't change. Tackley's rages continued unabated and he got into fights. Heretofore, however, he had never been known to hurt women.

King County sergeant Harlan Bollinger acknowledged that they were focusing on Max Tackley, at least for the moment. As far as anyone knew, Debra had no links to Wendy—nothing more than their final resting place. It was even possible that two murders four weeks apart could be grim coincidence.

None of the homicide investigators made the mistake of using tunnel vision. In a week, they talked to almost two hundred people, most of whom worked in the areas where Wendy and Debra spent their days and nights—in Tacoma and along the SeaTac Strip. They questioned motel and hotel workers, taxi drivers, bartenders and cocktail waitresses. They contacted police and sheriff's detectives in both Portland and Spokane to see if they might have unsolved cases involving young women who worked the circuit. None of them had, making it less likely that a "pimp war" might be under way.

But something was happening. Three days later, there was no question at all that a bleak pattern was emerging. It was a warm Sunday, and a local man was in a rubber raft drifting along the Green River looking for antique bottles or anything else of value that someone might have thrown into the murky waters. Previously, he had found bottles so old that they had "applied lips"—their tops added after the rest came out of a mold, embossed by old-time companies, with the lavender patina created by a century of being left out in the elements. Bottles like that could bring hundreds of dollars apiece.

There were, of course, other things in the river not as desirable: garbage and junked cars and things people were too lazy or too cheap to take to the nearby county dump on Orilla Road. In the summer's heat, the river was shallower than it would be in winter, but there were still deep holes. Looking for treasure, the rafter found horror instead.

He squinted, trying to see through the hazy water, and drew back suddenly. Two still figures floated beneath the surface, their unseeing eyes staring blindly at the sky. They looked, at first glance, like dolls or store dummies, but he knew they were too detailed and lifelike to be only facsimiles.

The treasure hunter paddled frantically for the bank. There were no cell phones in 1982, so he had to signal passersby and ask them to call the King County Sheriff's Office.

The officer responding realized at once that the female forms were human, but oddly, something held them close to the river bottom.

Dave Reichert and Patrol Officer Sue Peters responded first to the scene when they were summoned by the sheriff's dispatchers. Reichert had been at the river when Debra Bonner was found, but Sue Peters had had her own patrol car for only a week. Neither Reichert nor Peters could have imagined then that they were stepping into a nightmare that would grip them for more than two decades, and undoubtedly haunt them for the rest of their lives. Each would remember that warm Sunday with crystalline detail, the way all humans recall a moment that suddenly alters the direction of their lives.

Major Dick Kraske, commander of the Major Crimes Unit for the sheriff's office, would remember, too. His pager sounded as he stood talking to a neighbor, balancing grocery bags. The Radio Room directed him to the river site. "In a way, I knew it was something big," Kraske said. "I had the same feeling—some call it your illative sense, where you know something big is happening—when I was a lieutenant and my boss, Nick Mackie, called me out to Issaquah because they'd found Bundy's victims. He told me to put on a tie and a sport coat and meet him out there. This time I put on my tie and my sport coat and went out to the Green River alone."

Kraske always thought the Ted Bundy murders would be the worst he'd see in his career, but he was wrong. He got to the riverside a few minutes after Reichert and Peters. Search and Rescue (SAR) was on the way already, and Reichert was photographing the riverbank while Peters was recording what was happening.

Reichert half slid down the bank—it was very steep, at least a seventy-degree angle. The grass and reeds were as tall as the six-foot Reichert, and Peters disappeared completely in it when she followed him down. The grass closed like curtains behind them when they reached the river.

Someone had gone to a great deal of trouble to keep the women's bodies hidden, and he had chosen this spot well. From the road it was almost impossible to see the bodies down in the river. The thick vegetation assured that. Now Reichert and Peters could see that both victims were weighted down by large rocks placed on their breasts and abdomens. The near-boulders were clearly designed to keep them from surfacing, as all bodies eventually do when decomposition gases form and make them buoyant.

Fixated on that, Dave Reichert suddenly slid on the slippery grass, only to look down at something that lay on the edge of the river. He tumbled backward to avoid it. He had almost stepped on yet another female corpse. Either the killer had been too exhausted to carry the third victim all the way into the water, or he had been spooked by someone approaching and dropped his burden.

This girl looked quite young, in her midteens, apparently. She had a paler complexion, although she was severely sunburned, probably after death. She looked to be of mixed racial heritage, and it was obvious she had been strangled by ligature, with her own blue shorts or slacks.

Whoever the killer was, he was almost certainly a very strong man. It would have been no easy feat to carry the three bodies from a vehicle and down the steep bank and its slippery grasses. The river bottom was silt, slick as grease, and yet he had somehow maneuvered the huge rocks into place. It would be even more difficult for investigators to carry the dead women back up, but they would have more manpower.

Deputy Mike Hagan of SAR and the Marine Unit arrived with a strong line. Police diver Bob Pedrin checked the river around the corpses, then maneuvered them closer to the river's edge.

King County medical examiner Dr. Don Reay had also responded to the scene, as the man detectives called "Doc Reay" always did. Sadly, there was no hurry now, and they waited for him to nod and say that it was all right to move the victims. The onerous task of lifting the dead girls from the Green River and up its bank began. Not only did the investigators, divers, Reay and his deputies have to hoist what was literally deadweight up the precipitous riverbank, they had to preserve as much possible evidence as they could while they did so. Kraske and Reay stood side by side with the others, heaving to keep the rope from slipping. Still, they were all aware that the heedless river had undoubtedly washed away much of what would have helped them the most. If the victims had been raped, semen traces were probably gone now.

As the three bodies were being put into the M.E.'s baskets, Kraske noticed that someone had mixed up the tags that noted the sequential extraction identification. It mattered which girl had come out of the river first—and last. Knowing that a mistake now could cause all further records to be faulty, he ordered a slowdown until the tags were corrected.

He had also called for radio silence while his investigators worked beside the Green River. The one thing they didn't need was a full bombardment from the media, which always monitored police calls for interesting incidents. He hoped to buy time until the next day when he knew reporters would descend on him like flies.

The two women who had floated beneath the surface of the river itself had ebony skin and were clearly African American. The girl on the bank could be either white or black. Along with Wendy Coffield and Debra Bonner, their names would become indelibly etched in the minds of the investigators, the news media, and anyone who lived in the Northwest. For the moment, however, they had no names. Hopefully, someone had reported them missing; they had been in the river for more than two days.

It wouldn't be easy to take their fingerprints because of the skin slippage caused by long immersion in warm water and decomposition. As the body decomposes, hand and finger skin loosens so much that it can be slipped off like a glove. In order to transfer prints, pathologists sometimes have to sever the skin at the wrist, then slip their own hands into the "glove" and press the crinkled tips onto an inked pad.

 MARCIA FAYE CHAPMAN was identified first, and it was through her fingerprints. She was thirty-one when she died, an attractive woman with symmetrical features and a lush mouth, so petite that she was known as "Tiny" by her friends. She had lived on the Strip with her three children, aged eleven, nine, and three, and she mainly supported them through prostitution. She had left her apartment on August 1, 1982, and failed to return.

The other woman in the river and the girl on the bank were still unidentified. Police sketches of how they might have looked in life were published in area papers, and the public was asked to respond if anyone recognized them. One was five feet three and a little chubby; the other was five feet five and very thin. The first girl had medium-length hair that had been dyed from black to red; the second had a cluster of short ringlets and a chipped front tooth.

One woman in the river had been completely nude; the other two still wore bras that had been yanked above their breasts and twisted around. They had all been strangled by ligature.

Although the medical examiner's staff knew that the cause of death in the four latest victims was strangulation—just as in Wendy Coffield's death—they refused to release that information. High-profile cases that receive a lot of publicity bring out compulsive confessors in droves. The more details police agencies can keep secret, the better their chance to weed out those who get a perverted thrill out of confessing to crimes they never committed. The cause and manner of death are difficult to conceal, but medical examiners and detectives try. It is absolutely essential not to reveal more specific information.

The two women in the river itself had been "raped" symbolically by their killer, perhaps after a true rape. He had inserted triangular-shaped stones into their vaginas so tightly that they had to be surgically removed. That might mean he had been unable to achieve an erection, and in his fury, the rocks were a crude substitute. It might be his way to denigrate the victims. It could even mean that a woman was the killer. But, for the moment, and for years to come, this information about the three-sided rocks would be guarded carefully.

When the last two victims were identified, one of them fit the profiles of Wendy Coffield, Debra Bonner, and Marcia Chapman. Cynthia Hinds was only seventeen, a vibrant and pretty girl who went by the name "Cookie." She also made her living on the street. She had felt safe working the SeaTac Strip because she had a male "protector"—in reality, a pimp. He told detectives he had seen Cynthia last on August 11. Near the Pac HiWay and S. 200th, he had watched surreptitiously as she got into a black Jeep with a male driver, but he hadn't written down the license plate and he couldn't describe the driver. Like most pimps, he had offered her very little security. The moment Cynthia was alone with a stranger, she had no protection at all.

 CYNTHIA had never been arrested for soliciting.

2

Dave Reichert had almost tripped over the girl who lay in the reedy grass on the bank of the Green River, and he had to stand there, motionless, while measurements were taken for triangulation. He would never forget her—a petite, slightly chubby girl, with reddish hair.

 After sketches of her face in death were published, her traumatized family realized why she hadn't come home. At the King County Medical Examiner's Office, they identified her as Opal Charmaine Mills. She was barely sixteen. Opal had a mother and father and a big brother who cared deeply about her. They lived on the East Hill outskirts of Kent.

Opal's mother, Kathy Mills, told investigators that the last time she had seen Opal was three days before her body was found—on August 12. Opal had told her that Thursday morning that she was going to "work," and called home again in the early afternoon, saying she was at a phone booth in Angle Lake State Park.

For Opal, work didn't mean prostitution. She was excited because she was going to be painting houses with her friend Cookie.

Kathy Mills barely knew Cookie, and didn't know her real name. She was a new acquaintance of Opal's, and she had been to the Mills home only once. Cookie was, of course, Cynthia Hinds, whose body was found so close to Opal's.

While it was true that Opal sometimes stayed away from home for a day or so without checking in with her family, and she had even run away once, there was no indication that she was involved in peddling sex on the highway. Her best friend, Doris Davis, had known Opal since they were both in fourth grade and they saw each other every day. She was appalled that anyone would link Opal to streetwalking. She had never mentioned prostitution to Doris. "That's why I couldn't believe it. She always shared her problems with me."

From the time she was a toddler, most people called her "Little Opal," because Opal Charmaine was always petite with chipmunk cheeks and a bright smile. She had put on a few extra pounds lately, but she still wasn't much over five feet tall.

Opal's mother, Kathy, was once a farm girl in Missouri, a pretty strawberry blonde with pale skin and a tendency to burn if she was out in the sun too long. Her mother was only fourteen when Kathy was born, and she would eventually give birth to fourteen more children, but the family decided she was too young to raise Kathy. The baby girl was given to her uncle Herbert to raise. Herbert Gardner, a milkman, and his wife became her "real parents," although they were not her birth parents. She knew her birth mother, however, because her extended family lived within blocks of one another. The Gardners were a proud family, able to trace their ancestors back many generations.

Kathy was a tomboy who loved wearing cowboy boots and riding horses on the farm. She was an intelligent little girl, raised as an only child. She married in 1955 when she was in her late teens, and she and her husband moved to Denver. But in the early sixties, Kathy's marriage was winding down. And shortly thereafter, she met someone whom the Gardners considered a most unlikely mate for her: Robert Mills. His sister, Irma, lived across the street from Kathy in Denver and invited her to a party. Mills was there—as dark and thin and tall as she was fair and plump.

Back in Missouri, her adoptive father, Herbert, and the rest of her southern family found Robert Mills to be the last possible man they would have chosen for Kathy. To begin with, he was too old for her—seventeen years older. For another, he had been married before.

Worst of all for a family steeped for generations in the prejudices of rural Missouri was the fact that Robert Mills was black. Although he was talented and charismatic and Kathy was thrilled when he paid attention to her, her family let her know that she would be as good as dead to them if she continued to associate with a black man.

Maybe she didn't really believe they meant what they said, or maybe Kathy was too much in love to break her romance off—in any case, she and Robert Mills decided to get married. However, Colorado had long-standing statutes against marriage between partners of different races. As archaic and shocking as those laws are today, they are not as remote in America's history as we would like to believe. Even in the sixties, miscegenation (marriage between two different races) was listed as an "immoral act" under the vagrancy statutes in Denver. Any couple who defied this law *and* anyone performing the wedding ceremony would be fined between $50 and $500 and sentenced to anywhere from three months to two years in jail.

"All marriages between Negroes or mulattoes of either sex and white persons are declared to be absolutely void" was the wording in the 1864 Territorial Assembly law that governed most of Colorado. Amazingly, the Colorado State Supreme Court found this law constitutional in 1942 and it stayed on the books—at least for part of Colorado. The part that had once been Mexico had no miscegenation law, so it didn't apply to anyone living south or west of the Arkansas River or on the other side of a line drawn north from the river's source at Climax.

Kathy and Mills gave up the idea of getting married in Denver. Instead, they traveled to Yakima, Washington, where Kathy's grandparents had been assigned as missionaries for their church. They, at least, were speaking to Kathy.

Washington was one of only fifteen states with no miscegenation laws at the time. Kathy and Robert got married there. She was twenty-eight; Robert was forty-five. From that moment and over the next three decades, the Missouri branch of Kathy's family cut off all ties with her. She sent them letters regularly, but they never responded. She would have felt even worse had she realized that during all those years her letters were tossed into a box, unopened.

Robert Mills worked as a warehouseman, and Kathy in a luggage store. Together, they made a good living. In 1963, they had their first child, Garrett, who was born with a hole in his heart and one of his heart valves on the wrong side. He would need surgery in the years to come if he was to survive.

Finally, when he was six, they could wait no longer. Garrett was scheduled for corrective surgery at Seattle's Children's Orthopedic Hospital. He had a close friend, a boy with very similar heart defects. "He had the surgery first," Garrett recalled. "And he died. When I heard that, I decided they weren't going to cut my heart open. I ran away from home, but I only got a few blocks. You know the old story: I wasn't allowed to cross the street alone. So I came back, and I was lucky. My surgery worked."

"I was to be 'The Hope,' " Garrett would remember, as he explained that his father expected him to become everything that he himself had failed to achieve. It was to be a great burden for Garrett, and Robert Mills used his own brand of tough love that often seemed to have no love at all behind it.

Little Opal Charmaine was born in Seattle's Harborview Hospital on April 12, 1966. "She was the 'Princess,' " Garrett said fondly. "From the time she was born, my main job, always, was to look after Opal and keep her safe."

He knew why his parents, particularly his father, were so adamant that Opal stayed safe. She was named after Robert Mills's sister, Opal, who had been murdered in Oakland, California. The older Opal's killer was never caught, and her death left a heavy burden on Mills.

Her big brother didn't mind looking after Opal. Garrett loved her and he'd always been in charge of her, so he didn't question that he was both her brother and her main babysitter. Kathy went back to work as soon as possible, and they were latchkey kids. Garrett was in charge of the house keys. "I would always pick Opal up from school and walk her home," he said. "We played in our yard or in the woods, sometimes in the park."

Garrett remembered Opal's face shining with excitement as she carried what she called her "Hair Bear Bunch" lunch box on the first day of kindergarten. "She was a tiny little 'Peanut' with baby fat and her hair braided into pigtails."

Wherever Garrett went, he had to take Opal along. The boys he hung out with in elementary school didn't mind; they all knew Opal was part of the deal. Even when he grew old enough to date, Opal was always there in the backseat at the drive-in movie. She was his responsibility and he accepted that.

The Millses lived in a nice home east of Kent on the way to Maple Valley. There were flowers in the yard, along with a miniature windmill and a brightly painted totem pole. They attended the Church of God in Christ on Capital Hill in Seattle several times a week. The services were four or five hours long, and Garrett and Opal often grew restive and bored. "We weren't allowed to move. We had to just sit there," Garrett said. After that, they were very active in the Assembly of God church in Kent.

Elementary school at Cedar Valley was a pretty good time for Garrett and Opal. Their closest friends from the fourth grade on were their neighbors' children—Doris Davis for Opal and Eugene Smith for Garrett. The families sometimes took each other's children on trips, and the Mills children were always welcome next door. Robert Mills owned campers over the years and they explored the western states for their vacations. Being mixed-race wasn't really an issue during Garrett and Opal's Cedar Valley school years.

In 1973–74, Robert Mills was a den father for Boy Scouts and Kathy a Brownie mother. Garrett and Opal had their picture in the *Kent Journal* after they raised close to a thousand dollars in a Variety Club benefit to help pediatric heart patients.

Early on, Opal had an optimistic view about the future. She told Garrett about all the kids she planned to have. "Naively, she would say, 'And they will all be happy!' Opal planned to be rich so she could take care of our mother, and she was going to buy her a big house someday," Garrett recalled. "Even when she was seven, she struck me as someone who cared about others more than herself."

Outwardly, the Millses seemed to be a happy family. In fact, Robert Mills was probably the most popular man in their neighborhood. He was the "go to" guy who was always willing to help everyone who lived there. He was friendly and charming, easy to get along with. He could fix things, and he could get people good deals when they were looking to buy something. He had a lot of charisma.

"And he could sing," Garrett remembered. "He looked and sounded like Nat King Cole, so close that when I was younger, I thought he *was* Nat King Cole!"

But Garrett Mills's life at home was extremely difficult, and things were not what they seemed to be. Once the front door closed, the father whom the neighbors admired and looked up to was a man full of rage.

"It's hard to describe," Garrett said. "In one way, my dad was the coolest person in the world, and I wanted to be like him. But I was also frightened of him. He always said, 'People are rats!' and if he thought I even looked the wrong way with my eyes, he'd hit me. He called me Whispering Smith because I was afraid to talk around him. He could never remember people's names so he called them some celebrity's name and they liked that."

Mills wanted Garrett to become a doctor or a famous saxophone player like Seattle's renowned Kenny G. But Garrett wasn't particularly adept at science, and he was only an average saxophone player, even though his father bought him the best instrument available. He took lessons for years and played in the school marching band, but Garrett just wasn't musically talented. His dad could sing but he couldn't.

"My father was bitter and he was mean," Garrett said. "But he wanted us to have everything material that we could—the best of everything. And we did, although he was very bad at handling money. He always had a job, except the one time he was fired after he saw one of his managers reading a 'Klan' magazine. He was so mad he went after the guy with a crowbar."

Robert Mills went to the union and appealed his firing on the grounds that it had come about because of racial prejudice, and he won. He was back on the job.

Although his family had a nice house and furniture, and he drove fancy cars, Mills's children never knew what would set his temper off. "He was always strict with us. But when he didn't take his blood pressure medicine," Garrett said, "he'd do things like shake down our bedrooms at one AM. We weren't doing anything wrong, or hiding anything, but he'd just get these ideas, come in and wake us up and start searching for whatever."

Robert Mills never hit Opal, although he used cruel words with her. He did use physical punishment with Garrett, hitting him with everything from a belt to a hammer. Most of his verbal abuse bounced off Opal. She was happy, bubbly, and full of mischief.

"We both were kind of mischievous," Garrett remembered. "We were home alone so much that we'd get bored. My parents had a hard time getting babysitters for us because we had a reputation, but not for anything really bad. We did stuff like dragging lawn sprinklers to the front of a babysitter's door—she lived in our cul-de-sac—and we'd turn it on so it would get her wet when she opened the door. Or we'd coast downhill in a grocery cart. Once, our cul-de-sac had a meeting about our pranks and what should they do with us?"

The only times that Garrett grew annoyed with his little sister was when Opal tattled on him for something. She was something of a snitch, often telling on her father, too, when he drank too much or flirted openly with other women.

"I was never supposed to hit Opal," her brother said. "But she could do anything she wanted to me, and sometimes she pushed it. If I got mad, she'd call my dad at work and I'd have to move out of the house for a couple of days."

Most of the time, however, Opal and Garrett were there for each other. Their mother had no power to stop her husband from his cruel punishments, which became more frequent after he had a series of little strokes. Although Garrett wanted her to leave his father, he knew she always held on to her belief that things were going to get better, that everything would turn out all right.

In the early years of their marriage, the Millses had had a lot of dogs—chows for Robert and collies for Kathy. But as the years passed, Robert's rage grew and he was no longer a kind pet owner. Asked if he and Opal had pets when they were children, Garrett shook his head and mumbled so softly that he was almost inaudible. "No . . . he'd get mad and kill them—so after a while, we didn't try."

While he bought the biggest TV sets and a series of cars for Garrett, the elder Mills sometimes thought his children ate too much, so he locked up the food cupboards and the refrigerator. He complained that their showers used up too much hot water, so they often went next door to eat and to use Doris and Eugene's folks' bathroom.

"I didn't feel like I was abused," Garrett said. "I didn't know anything different from the way it was for us."

While Garrett grew more quiet and tried to stay out of his father's way, Opal seemed happy. She always had "weird collections," said her brother. "One time, she papered one wall of her room with candy bar wrappers. Another time, it was posters from some movie she liked. She kept every doll she ever had, and she made up stories about all of them—really complicated stories because she had a great imagination.

"I remember us going to school, hours before anyone else, to dance in the school cafeteria with the jukebox. For those few hours we were free to be happy, free from ridicule and worry. We would tire out and sit and talk about the future as usual, and all her big dreams."

Opal and her friend Doris Davis would dance together at parties; Garrett laughed, remembering, "Opal couldn't dance at all!"

And so they lived with a nurturing mother, a father who was growing increasingly bitter, and had good friends. Things got much worse as Garrett went to junior high school. Kent was very different in the seventies than it is now. There were only twenty-five minority students in the entire Kent school system, and Garrett found himself a target for bullies.

"I was goofy-looking with a small head and big glasses. I was so skinny that my chest caved in. First, they called me 'gay' because there was this gay guy on *Soap*—the TV show that was popular then. Then, with the Iran war, they called me Sand Nigger, and then Kunta Kinte after *Roots*."

It was a very hard time for him. He tried out for football, but "I just didn't understand it."

Robert Mills urged Garrett to use violence to strike back at the students who teased him, and he put crowbars in his son's car to encourage him to do that. But Garrett didn't feel that was the answer to anything. He was not a fighter.

It got worse when Opal moved up to junior high. "Opal, Doris, Eugene, and I were the only black students in the school," Garrett said. "I tried not to let Opal see how I was treated. She would want to fight back and stand up for me."

Opal had always been feisty as well as fun, and she couldn't stand to see anyone mistreat her big brother. "When people picked on me for being multiracial, the Klan jokes, chasing me, shutting me out of everything, I didn't want her to be ashamed of me, but she never was. Opal would say, 'That's my brother and you better shut your mouth or get a knuckle sandwich!'

"Her face would get red and she'd put her tiny fist up and be ready to square off."

In their last year in school together, the new principal was also African American, and she really tried to help. She took them to see Jesse Jackson and encouraged them to be proud of who they were. The irony was that both Opal and Garrett were paler than many of the Italian or Slavic kids; they looked as though they had really good tans—the kind people lie in the sun to achieve—but they were just different enough to be singled out for derision. It seemed to roll off Opal's back, probably because her brother was always there to shield her from the worst of it, but it made his school years a nightmare.

By the time Garrett moved on to high school, he admitted that he had a "major chip" on his shoulder, but he'd put on weight, and he wasn't bullied any longer. He'd still pick Opal up from junior high school, but he moved away from home when he was sixteen, unwilling to endure his father's attitude any longer. Almost anything he did annoyed Robert. His father bad-mouthed any girl he dated—even before he met her.

"I lived with my friends Eugene and Glen on Capital Hill, but I was still pretty young," Garrett recalled. "I came home to visit my mom and Opal, and to have dinner and do my laundry. Glen was really big and tall. My dad called him Fat Albert."

Opal was fifteen, still best friends with Doris Davis, and still a terrible dancer. She had songs she liked: Tina Marie's "Square Biz" and "I Heard It on the Grapevine," the instrumental version. Her favorite was a slow song, "Love Begins with One Hello." They would play that song at her funeral.

At about fifteen, Opal started to put on weight and tried so hard to slim down. To remind herself that she had to diet, she plastered their refrigerator with her drawings and warnings. She was quite talented as an artist. She wrote: "Flat stomach!" "Size 5," "Skinny," "Drink Your Water!" "Tight Jeans," and "Short Shorts," illustrating them all before she taped them to the refrigerator. It was a struggle for her, though. Her mother had always had to fight weight, and Opal took after Kathy instead of Robert, who never seemed to gain an ounce. Although he was no longer skinny, Garrett was like his father.

In April 1982, Opal turned sixteen. Garrett was living away from home, but they were in touch and he still felt responsible for her. She was "kind of engaged" to his roommate Glen, and really seemed to care about him, but she was too young to consider marriage seriously. Garrett knew she was spending time in Tacoma with friends there—a change from her having a best friend who lived right next door.

In truth, Opal was what used to be called "boy crazy." Where she had once collected candy bar wrappers and movie posters, now she collected male names and telephone numbers. She'd made up stories about her dolls' lives, and now she fashioned fictional adventures about herself. She wanted to impress her friends, and sometimes she even copied names from the phone book—men or boys she didn't even know—and showed her lists to her girlfriend. She was "engaged" lots of times, but only in her own mind. She developed almost instant crushes on boys she did know.

Opal did date Glen, Garrett's roommate, quite often. They went to drive-in movies and on typical teenage dates. Opal didn't have access to a car, and she had to take a bus wherever she wanted to go unless her parents drove her.

She also fancied herself going steady with a man a few years older than she was, even though he was dating another girl far more often than he saw Opal. She wrote him a very dramatic and angry letter, but she didn't send it. Later, detectives found it among her belongings and tracked the man down.

He was bewildered about why she would be so upset with him, but then he shrugged and said, "She was just *fascinated* with writing letters to people. I did date her, and she got mad when I wouldn't drive from downtown to the East Hill of Kent to come see her. She'd be upset when she had to take a bus to come and see me. It's possible that she saw me with my other girlfriend—I don't know. But I was dating the other girl a long time before I dated Opal, and after she was murdered, too."

In many ways, Opal had one foot in childhood and one foot on a dangerously adult track. She tried marijuana, but didn't smoke it more than a few times. She was probably sexually active. She dropped out of school and was transferred to a continuation school in Renton, where she met older, more worldly, girls who were working toward their GEDs.

But Opal still loved to do the silly things she'd done as a little girl. "About a week before Opal disappeared, we had a 'me and her day,' " Garrett recalled. "She came up to Broadway where I lived and we were just goofing around. We went to Dick's for hamburgers, and we walked around. We swiped a grocery cart and rode downhill—just like we were seven or eight. I think we both realized it was kind of the end of an era."

Less than two weeks after that last day they spent together, Garrett Mills went with his parents to identify Opal's body. Because she had been strangled by ligature, her face still bore the mask of her final agony. Robert Mills told a reporter that he could identify her only by her slightly crooked toes.

Garrett had nightmares for years after. He had promised Opal when they were children that he would never leave her, and that he would never let anyone hurt her. He felt that he had failed her when she needed him most.

As the media showed Opal's picture over and over, rumors and lies "took on a life of their own," Garrett remembered. But no one who went to school with them truly understood what a tightly bonded relationship Garrett and Opal had, two children growing up in a very difficult world.

"Dave Reichert questioned me for four hours," Garrett said. "I realized that I was a suspect. The thing that pains me the most is that some people thought I actually had something to do with the killings."

A school official told a reporter that "Opal's pimp" picked her up at school, but it wasn't her pimp; it had been her big brother, seeing that she got home safely, as he always had. Some gossip painted Garrett as a drug dealer and said that the police were following him everywhere, long after he was cleared of any suspicions.

"All the while, I was just a gangly insecure kid who played the saxophone and had two guinea pigs," he said sadly.

His father had come home from identifying Opal's body and killed one of his pets in his rage and grief. Even so, Garrett moved home to help his parents face the tragedy as much as he could. He stayed about six months, but it didn't work. His father drank before; after Opal was murdered, he sank into alcoholism. Nine years later, Robert Mills died.

Was Opal about to become a prostitute? That is a question no one can answer. She loved attention and romance and excitement, and despite her voluptuous figure, she was emotionally immature. Even her brother didn't know how much influence her new friends from Renton and Tacoma had over her.

She would have been extremely guileless if a slick and persuasive pimp promised her freedom, money, and adventure.

Having her killer go unpunished made losing Opal all the more painful. There was no ending to it. Not for them, and not for any of the other families.

3

DICK KRASKE had been wise to keep as much information from the media about the five bodies in the Green River as he could. "They hammered us from day two and never let up," he remembered, wincing. "Throughout the rest of my time in this investigation, my attitude was you should not get into a pissing contest with a skunk—or anyone who buys ink by the barrel. There were times when I thought it wouldn't have been a bad idea to go across the street and apply [for a job] at the Fire Department."

The press and local television investigative reporters were anxious to link the victims by concluding that they had all worked the highway stroll. It made natural headlines. Prostitutes being murdered suggested a titillating story. Moreover, citizens, living in nice safe houses, whose wives and daughters were never alone on the streets could be reassured. *Their* female family members weren't offering sex for money, and they had no tattoos or drug habits, so they could conclude that a roving killer was no danger to them.

DICK KRASKE had wasted no time. On Monday, August 16, he organized the initial Green River Task Force with twenty-five investigators from King County, the Seattle Police Department, the Tacoma Police Department, and the Kent Police Department. It was a prescient decision. No one could have even imagined what lay ahead.

They didn't know at that point how many killers they were looking for. It was possible there was more than one. Killing partners were not unknown. In the early eighties, Henry Lee Lucas and Ottis Toole were boasting of over three hundred victims in their deadly travels around America, and Kenneth Bianchi and his cousin Angelo Buono had racked up a tragic toll of young female victims in Los Angeles before Bianchi moved to Bellingham, Washington, and committed more murders on his own. Two men working together and obsessed with killing wasn't unheard of, but it *was* unusual. One man, bringing a single body, day after day, to this river hiding place was a more likely scenario. Perhaps he even had a vehicle large enough to hold more than one of his victims, all of whom needed to be hidden as soon as possible.

With the discovery of the last three bodies in a secluded site along the river, the consensus was that probably all five of the victims had gone into the Green River at that point. But Wendy Coffield's and Debra Bonner's bodies had drifted downstream until they were caught on something.

The investigators had no doubt that the killer had watched the nightly news, realized his mistake at not weighting the dead girls down, and rectified that with the rocks and boulders. He was crafty, obviously unafraid to take five victims in one month, but smart enough to hone his technique to evade the detectives who were now stalking him. But his "dump site" had been discovered and he couldn't go back there now.

4

PEOPLE who lived in King County, Washington, weren't afraid. Yes, there were five unsolved murders in the county, and it might even be true that the deaths were in all likelihood connected to a common killer or killers. But the backgrounds of the victims, soon manipulated and smoothed and shaped into a single image by the media, showed them to be young female prostitutes who hitchhiked. Every one of them had died within a month, as if some deadly tornado had swept through the Kent Valley, a faceless killer who had destroyed them and then moved on. The lay public wanted to believe their murderer was a drifter who had already left the area.

The girls who were still out on the streets were working because most of them had no other way to survive. They *were* a little anxious, and a lot of them tried to get a gun, or they carried a knife in their shoes. Outreach workers advised them to "Stay in groups. Don't go out on 'dates' unless you've known them before. If you get a negative feeling, don't get in the car. Follow your intuition."

But they weren't dealing with Girl Scouts or students on a school trip. How often would young prostitutes know the men who stopped to pick them up? They had to take chances.

"We even tell them to get off the streets," one of the more naive social workers said. "But that's a joke to them. They think they can handle anything."

And some of the working girls believed they could, while others worried about what to do. Many relocated to Portland, finding Seattle too scary. One teenage prostitute shook her head and said, "Even Portland isn't safe. They think a 'trick' maybe killed all those girls. Well, just like we travel, tricks do, too. You never know whether he is here today or will be here tomorrow."

Needing rent or food or drug money, most of the girls returned to their regular haunts. The weather was warm in late August and it was light out until nine or so. They knew other people whose world was the Strip and they began to feel safe again.

The rest of August 1982 passed without incident. The bad times were probably over. At least everyone wanted to believe it was over, something frightening that had touched them briefly but hadn't really interfered with their lives.

Still, what had happened was not nearly as isolated as it first seemed to be. Looking at those hellish weeks in July and August was like walking into a movie in the middle. Maybe the summer of 1982 was not the first chapter of horror after all.

There were some similar cases in the Greater Seattle area from early in 1982 that troubled those who remembered them—cops and reporters and families who had lived through them. Adding to a faint sense of dread was the phenomenon that occurs in slow news periods. Columnists and TV news producers look for crime statistics or murders that might be connectable to scare up a story. Way back on Valentine's Day, popular columnist Rick Anderson filled an entire page of the Sunday *Seattle Times* with the details of the deaths of three young women.

Leann Wilcox was sixteen in October 1981, and she was a lovely-looking girl, but from the moment she entered puberty, she changed from an agreeable child to an incorrigible thirteen-year-old who was placed in a group home in Spokane when her mother could not control her. By the time she was sixteen, she was familiar with the street life and had four arrests for prostitution. She came home occasionally and vowed to change her life. But nothing lasted. Leann left for good on October 17, 1981.

Her mother's final phone conversation with her was typical of the acrimony that marked their struggles with each other. Leann said she wasn't going back to school and she wouldn't be home for Christmas either.

Exhausted and frustrated, her mother said something she would always regret: "Leann, my door has always been open to you; you know that. But as long as you live like you are, then I don't want you home anymore."

Leann hung up on her. A month later, on January 21, 1982, two men found her body facedown in a weed patch at S. 380th and Military Road South. Friends had seen her only two days before. With her wine-colored jacket thrown over her, she seemed almost to be sleeping, but she was dead, beaten and strangled.

On January 29, 1982, Virginia Taylor, eighteen, headed for a bus in southwest Seattle. It would take her to her job as a dancer in a peep show on the seediest section of First Avenue. Virginia had visualized her life as so much happier than it was. She was a bride, but her groom slept alone on a prison bunk, serving five years for theft. Virginia's job, where men sat in booths and dropped quarters into a slot to raise the curtains so they could watch half-nude girls gyrate and strip behind a glass wall, didn't pay that well. But it sure paid more than taking orders in a drive-through burger joint. Virginia hated her shifts in the booth. She was more modest than most of the girls at the peep show, so she wasn't a favorite of the patrons. And the piles of quarters weren't worth stripping all the way or accommodating requests from kinky customers.

Despite her job, Virginia was generally cautious, yet she occasionally hitchhiked. Nobody saw her get on the number 20 bus that January day, and nobody remembered seeing her beyond two blocks from her sister's house.

Schoolchildren found her body later that day in a muddy field. She was fully clothed and she had been strangled. The only suspect was a girl Virginia's own age who had threatened her in a silly feud over a stolen coat, and that had been a year before her murder. It was unlikely that a female would have had the strength to choke Virginia to death.

Joan Conner, sixteen, had lived with her mother in a small house in the far north end of Seattle. On Thursday morning, February 4, 1982, her mother left a bus pass for Joan and suggested it was a good day for her to look for a job. Joan had dropped out of school, and she hadn't worked since she left McDonald's employ the previous fall.

"Okay, Mom," she said. "But I'm going to try to sell some Campfire mints, too."

Joan belonged to the Campfire Horizon Club for teenagers, and she had no ties at all to prostitution or First Avenue. But she encountered someone infinitely dangerous. Joan was found dead later that day. She had been beaten and strangled and her body thrown out of a car on Fremont Street near the Ship Canal. Her purse, her identification, her GED certificate were all missing.

Joan Conner's mother, who had worried all Thursday night when her daughter failed to come home, was nervously watching the noon news the next day. She saw a young woman's body being placed in the medical examiner's van and she knew in her heart it was Joan. "That's Joan. That's Joan," she gasped to a friend, not knowing how she knew, but feeling ice in her veins as she saw only the form in a body bag.

Tragically, she was right.

The three victims hadn't known each other. They shared only their youth and the manner of their deaths. The public had well-nigh forgotten them by August 1982, but the detectives who worked to find their killer or killers remembered them. The question was: Were they connected to the Green River murders?

Perhaps they were, but their cases were not initially considered to be part of the Green River puzzle.

In any city of considerable size, there are always open homicide cases. Detectives work those cases they call "losers" more avidly than laymen ever realize. They do it quietly and with great determination, but they know too well the falsity of the old adage "There is no such thing as a perfect murder."

If you use the criteria that some killers are never caught, then there are countless perfect murders. Strangers who kill strangers and move on are the most likely to evade detection. However, if they continue to kill, the chance that they will leave behind clues that can be traced back to them grows. But computers were not generally in use in most homicide units in the eighties; they were expensive, complicated, and not considered to be of much value in investigations.

Furthermore, nobody voiced a concern in 1982 that a serial killer might be loose in King County. As widespread as they are today in movies, books, and on television, serial killers were virtually unrecognized as such by the general public and by most members of law enforcement. Few had even heard the term *serial killer*. Certainly, Ted Bundy, with more than three dozen young female victims, was a serial killer. But when he was sentenced to death in 1979 and again in 1980, the media referred to him as a "mass murderer."

The concept of a serial murderer—someone who killed similar victims one after another after another—had bloomed years before in the thought processes of one of the greatest homicide detectives of them all: Pierce Brooks. Confident that he was on to something way back in the fifties, Brooks did his research by visiting libraries when he was off duty, looking through old newspaper files for multiple-murder cases all across America. I remember his telling me, "Ann, there weren't any computers for cops then. It would have taken all of L.A.P.D. headquarters just to hold one of those first computers."

Once captain of the Homicide Unit in the Los Angeles Police Department, and later police chief in Eugene and Springfield, Oregon, Brooks wondered if criminologists had failed to recognize this kind of killer, for which he coined the term *serial killer.*

In March of 1983, Brooks would be responsible for a gathering of eagles among the top ranks of law enforcement to consider the problem of killers whose victim tolls rose into the double digits. He enlisted special agents in the Behavioral Science Unit (B.S.U.) of the F.B.I. and the U.S. Justice Department, along with top cops from cities, counties, and states all over America to confer at Sam Houston State University in Huntsville, Texas. Most of the B.S.U. special agents agreed with Brooks's theory that there was a unique and terrifying kind of killer roving just beneath the level of our awareness across the United States.

But this was August 1982, and the first five victims found in the Green River were still deemed to be the prey of a "mass murderer." They were not. They had, almost certainly, been killed by a serial killer, and within months, that would be understood.

The arena of forensic science has expanded again and again since 1982, and as Dick Kraske's task force began to pencil in a rough list of young female murder victims who might be connected, they suspected that they were dealing with a force of evil far greater than the general public realized. It didn't matter that only five young women had been found in the river, all the subsequent victims would be attributed ever after to "The Green River Killer."

IT WAS APRIL 1982, when Theresa Kline, twenty-seven, was last seen alive in Windy's Pub at Aurora Avenue N. and 103rd. She was a very pretty woman with long auburn hair, and people remembered her. She had planned to visit her boyfriend, a professional gambler, who was playing poker in a cardroom several blocks away. Theresa asked her friends in Windy's if any of them were heading north after closing hours, but they all shook their heads. She smiled and said she would catch a bus or hitchhike if she had to. It was 12:35 AM when she left the tavern. Five minutes later, one of her girlfriends walked outside, headed for a nearby gas station to buy a pack of cigarettes. Theresa was gone.

Less than three hours after that, Theresa's body was found in an alley eleven blocks away. She had been manually strangled.

Theresa was a divorcée with one son and her ex-husband had custody, although she visited her little boy often. She had been very happy the night she was murdered, and she was definitely headed to meet her boyfriend. She wasn't selling sex, even though Aurora Avenue was the north end Strip. Theresa wanted very much to have her son back with her, but she knew she couldn't do that until she had a job, and she had started a new job the night before. Things were suddenly looking up for her.

So far, Theresa's murder was unsolved.

Patricia Jo Crossman, fifteen, was a chronic runaway who had been arrested three times for prostitution. On June 13, she was found dead of stab wounds in the Garden Villa Apartments on S. 204th Street near the city limits of Des Moines. These apartments were near what was considered the southern tip of the SeaTac Strip.

Angelita Bell Axelson, twenty-five, had not been seen since sometime in the spring of 1982. No one kept very close track of her, and witnesses could remember only that she'd been with an unidentified man in a downtown Seattle transient hotel. Her body, badly decomposed, was found on June 18. She, too, had been strangled.

Unsolved cases involving young women were not peculiar to Seattle and King County. Snohomish County detectives, who worked in the county just north of King County, had their share, and so did Pierce County to the south. In fact, Snohomish County had a case somewhat similar to the Green River cases. It dated back to February 1982. Oneida Peterson, twenty-four, had last been seen as she waited for a bus to Marysville, Washington. Her strangled body was found on February 8, off the rural Sultan Basin Road. She had never been involved in prostitution.

Some of the women killed in early 1982 went on the Green River Killer victim list, and some did not. It was impossible to know if all the crimes were attributable to a single killer. Their ages and manner of death were alike, but their lifestyles differed. Ominously, the list grew longer. The entries may or may not have been correct. Some experts felt the range was too wide; others thought it wasn't inclusive enough.

In March 1982, several girls who made their living on the streets reported a weirdo to the Seattle Police Department's Sex Crimes Unit. A man had threatened them, using his Doberman as a weapon. He told them that he would command "Duke" to bite them if they didn't get into his 1967 Mustang. Those who obeyed him were raped, and then subjected to a bizarre lecture. The rapist warned them that they were going to hell if they didn't change their ways.

Those reports sounded as if a kinky-sadistic-religious psycho was out there preying on any woman he could find alone and either force or entice into his vehicle.

It was too early in a killing spree to look at the total number of murdered women throughout 1982 and see them as unknown and interchangeable entities who could very well be Green River victims. Many of the photos that accompanied the news coverage of the girls who were dead or missing were mug shots from prostitution arrests. There could have been many different killers. The victims all looked tired and sad and a little defiant, but more resolved to the life they were caught in. Some of their faces were tearstained, and they all looked years older than they really were. Those mug shots instantly separated them from the college girls and young women who lived in dorms or nice apartments in middle- and upper-class neighborhoods—Bundy's classic victims of eight years earlier.

The five victims whose bodies had floated in the heedless Green River were lumped together because of where they had been found, but they weren't really that much like one another, even though it was easy to infer that they had all met the same killing machine of a man.

Amina Agisheff, thirty-seven, was one of the first names on the extended Green River list even though she didn't fit into any of the predictable categories. She was twice as old as many of the dead girls, she was not a prostitute, she didn't hitchhike, she was a Russian immigrant, and she had a stable loving family, a loving boyfriend, and young children. She was a hard worker who couldn't afford a car.

On July 7, 1982, Amina left her mother's apartment after a visit and was waiting for a bus on Fourth Avenue in downtown Seattle. And she simply vanished, leaving her family to agonize over where she might be. When her picture appeared in the news alongside other presumed Green River victims, Amina always looked out of place. Perhaps she was added to the grim roster because she disappeared a week before Wendy Coffield's body was found.

5

FOR THE GREEN RIVER Task Force, it was akin to playing a game with no rules. There may have been many victims already, or was it possible that there were only five? There was no telling how many suspects they were looking for. With victims whose lives were peripatetic, moving from city to city or from one motel or apartment after another, it was difficult to know if they were truly missing. Many women on the streets lost touch with their families, who were spread out across America. In such cases, they might not be reported as missing until they hadn't called home for two Christmases in a row or for Mother's Day. They might be dead, but no one knew that except their killers.

When college girls vanish, their roommates or housemothers or families have great difficulty waiting the forty-eight hours required to make an adult "Missing" report. When runaways and kids on the street disappear, all too often there is no one to sound the alarm that they are gone.

For the initial Green River Task Force, it seemed more likely that the women found in the river were the only victims, that it was over, and the man who murdered them had either moved on or stopped killing. Now, looking at it with the twenty-twenty vision of hindsight, the pattern of multiple murder is crystal clear.

But it most definitely was not in the months that passed from August 1982 to November 1983. Validating disappearances and identifying true victims was as difficult as finding beads from a broken necklace, dozens of them rolling on the floor and becoming lost in crevices and under desks and cabinets. Who could ever know how many there had already been, or how many were yet to be found and restrung into a strand that connected them all?

 GISELLE LOVVORN was seventeen in the summer of 1982. She had no ties to the Seattle area, but earlier that year her boyfriend had persuaded her to leave California with him. Jake Baker,* known as "Jak-Bak," was several years older than Giselle. He had street savvy and had pulled enough bunco ploys in California that a move was beneficial—even urgent—for him. He figured he should start over in new territory. He got a job driving a cab on the SeaTac Strip.

Giselle was the youngest child of an upper-middle-class family in the San Fernando Valley, where her father had his own insurance business. She was an unhappy girl who had begun to run away from home when she was only fourteen, and she dropped out of school in the tenth grade. She had been miserable in California, ever since the family moved there from New Orleans a few years earlier. Her father wondered if it was because the district they lived in bused students to inner-city schools. Out of place ethnically, looking so different from her classmates, Giselle had been beaten up and robbed of her lunch money. It seemed impossible for her to make friends or to fit into any group in school, and she was lonely.

Whatever the reason, she refused to go back to school. Her parents certainly weren't happy to see her with Jak-Bak; he was too old for Giselle, and he wasn't the kind of man who would encourage their daughter to finish her education. That was a tremendous loss because Giselle was very intelligent; she read constantly and her I.Q. had tested at 145, well above genius level on some tests. She was a voracious reader and her favorite book was Colleen McCullough's *The Thornbirds*.

In her perfect longhand, Giselle wrote out McCullough's description of a songbird who was born to seek out the thorn tree, find the sharpest, longest thorn to impale itself upon—so that it might sing one high perfect note as it died.

Many of Giselle's thoughts were dark, and she appeared to find themes of death somehow romantic, even though she seemed sunny and upbeat on the surface. Like thousands upon thousands of other fans, she idolized Jerry Garcia and The Grateful Dead, and was proud to follow their concerts, considering herself a devout "Dead Head."

Giselle also liked the Charlie Daniels Band, and she collected antique Jack Daniel's whiskey labels. She wasn't very different from other young women of the late seventies–early eighties in her wardrobe, wearing long peasant skirts whose hems came undone because they swept the rough ground; tight, long-sleeved cotton shirts, without a bra, of course; and little makeup.

But she was more rebellious than most. Her parents could only hope that she would outgrow the wanderer streak that had taken her around the country with only a backpack to hold all her possessions. Sometimes Jak-Bak went with her, but she often traveled alone, calling him or calling home for money orders when she was broke. She sometimes landed in places like Fargo, North Dakota, or Cut Bank, Montana, or Eugene, Oregon, as she followed the Grateful Dead concerts. Western Union records showed that Giselle was at a truck stop in West Fargo, North Dakota, on June 3, 1982, to pick up a fifty-dollar money order that Jak-Bak had sent her.

Giselle's family was actually relieved when she traveled to Seattle for what they believed would be the final time before she turned her life around. She assured them that she was only going to pick up some possessions that Jak-Bak was holding for her, and then she was coming home to settle down and go back to school.

But within a week she changed her mind and decided to stay in Seattle. Jak-Bak was a master at persuasion, and he had evidently sweet-talked her into staying with him.

Giselle was a small girl whose thick blond hair tumbled down her back. She had freckles and looked wholesome and young, but she was soon working the SeaTac Strip. Her appearance appealed to certain males cruising the Strip—the ones who liked the "schoolgirl look."

Giselle was strolling along the highway in mid-1982, looking for tricks. Jak-Bak knew it and didn't stop her even though he later told detectives and reporters that he cared deeply for her and had done his best to talk her out of prostitution. He insisted that their living arrangement was merely platonic.

More likely, theirs was a typical relationship between an opportunistic man and a girl who didn't seem to question that if the man who was "protecting" her really loved her, he wouldn't allow her to sell herself to complete strangers. By the time most girls figured that out, it wasn't easy to break the ties.

But Giselle had some happy times in Seattle. On July 13, she got to see a Charlie Daniels concert. Four days later, Giselle left their apartment at one in the afternoon. It was a Saturday, and, according to Jak-Bak, she planned to turn three or four tricks. He said he'd asked her not to go but she'd been adamant about her plans.

If she had read local papers that week, she would have seen the coverage about the bodies in the Green River, and the murders were all over the news on television, too. But Giselle wasn't familiar with Seattle, and she really knew only the area around the airport. She probably didn't even know where the Green River was.

Afternoon became evening and Giselle didn't come back to the apartment. Not that night. Not on Sunday. Everything she owned and the only person she really knew in Seattle, everything that mattered to her, was in the little apartment on First Avenue South and S. 180th.

Jak-Bak soon warmed to the glow of media attention and gave many interviews. He recalled that he had tried to report Giselle missing right away, but the police wouldn't take him seriously. That wasn't true. They *had* listened to him, and Giselle had officially gone on their missing persons list on July 17.

Jak-Bak said he'd met Giselle in a Los Angeles–area restaurant a year earlier and they had become best friends. "We weren't intimate," he said sadly, "but we were really, really close." He and Giselle had shared their Seattle apartment with another man. He told reporters that he had continued to look for Giselle on the Strip, at truck stops, motels, and bars, but he never found her. She had left everything behind, even her treasured backpack; all she took with her was her California I.D. card, which falsely listed her age as nineteen, not seventeen.

Jak-Bak said Giselle's plan was to establish a regular clientele so she could have a career as a call girl and not have to stroll the highway. He had urged her to get a job in a delicatessen or some other straight employment, but she was headstrong and believed that she could take care of herself.

Perhaps. Or perhaps she was following a plan he had outlined for her.

IN MID-SEPTEMBER, the *Seattle Post-Intelligencer* published a "blind" story that quoted King County lieutenant Greg Boyle as saying the task force was investigating the possible disappearance of two more young women who fit the "profile" of the Green River victims. One was Giselle Lovvorn, although her name was not mentioned. The other was Mary Bridget Meehan, eighteen. Her boyfriend, Ray, reported that he had last seen her on September 15 as she left the Western Six Motel just off the Strip. He said she had planned to walk to the Lewis and Clark Theater that day. It was a two-mile walk, a long way for a girl who was eight months pregnant. Bridget and Ray hadn't come to the Strip from very far away; they'd both lived in Bellevue, just across the floating bridge from Seattle, all their lives.

"Was she working?" detectives asked Ray.

He shook his head, seemingly confused. "I don't know."

KING COUNTY detectives had now talked to almost three hundred people as they looked for connections between the first five victims and witnesses who might have seen or heard anything unusual. They had made a request of the Behavioral Science Unit of the F.B.I., asking for as thorough a profile as they could come up with on the man, or men, they were looking for.

The task force knew now that Wendy Lee Coffield and Opal Mills had attended the same continuation school in Renton, but there was no indication that they had known each other or been seen together at the end of their lives. And Debra Bonner and Cynthia Hinds had patronized the same bar in Tacoma. It was probable that they had been at least acquainted, although no one at the bar could remember ever seeing them come in together. It was an intricate pattern that the investigators would find again and again; people whose lives revolved around the Strip often knew each other, if only tangentially.

As for the two missing girls, they might come home again. Or they might be dead.

The first Green River suspect to merit headlines was Debra Bonner's lover/pimp, Max Tackley. By August 21, the thirty-one-year-old former University of Washington student was being held for questioning while three detectives searched his small house in Tacoma. Tackley had given his permission for the search, and Detective Bob LaMoria, Detective Dave Reichert's partner, remarked, "We either have to prove him innocent or prove him guilty."

It was not so much a case of Tackley's being a truly likely suspect in the death of all five women, it was more that the detectives had so little to go on. "We have not been able to develop enough evidence to develop a suspect," Major Dick Kraske said. "Consequently this [Tackley] is the focal point of our investigation."

However, Kraske came up with the first short profile of whom they might be looking for. He figured that the killer probably lived in either the south part of King County or in the Pierce County area, and he was apparently quite familiar with the Green River. He had picked a convenient turnout off Frager Road to dump the last three bodies, a spot most people wouldn't be aware of.

But so many possible victims in a month? They knew they weren't looking for an ordinary killer—if, indeed, there is such a thing. Lieutenant Greg Boyle commented that "This guy is more than just a 'john.' "

Would he go back to the Green River with more victims? If he did, it would be a pretty stupid choice. The whole area of Frager Road was being monitored by police, although they didn't publicize that.

THE so-called Green River Killer would soon prove he wasn't stupid. He apparently abandoned the river as the means to rid himself of his victims. On September 25, a trail biker was zipping around the empty streets of the ghost town left behind by the Port Authority's buyout when he became aware of a cloying, sickening odor. Seeking the source, he honed in on some overgrown bushes. There, he discovered a female body, in an advanced state of decomposition, half-hidden in the brush of an abandoned yard. She was nude except for what appeared to be a pair of men's socks that were tightly cinched around her neck.

The man backed away, sick to his stomach. It had been a warm September. No one would be able to identify the dead woman visually.

The acres of overgrown yards, trees, and cement front porches extended both north and south of the airport. Except for passengers in the planes coming in for a landing, few people were even aware it was there. The body's location was more than three blocks from the nearest street and it was six miles from the Green River, but it wasn't very far from where Giselle Lovvorn had last been seen— maybe two or three miles.

Now, there were six. This female body, who apparently was Caucasian, would only be absolutely identifiable using dental chart comparisons, although detectives suspected that she was Giselle. Jak-Bak had described a small bird tattoo on her right breast when he reported her missing, and despite postmortem changes, the bird tattoo was still visible in the same place.

The task force, accompanied by German shepherd search dogs, moved through the acres of isolated land, looking for more bodies or some physical evidence connected to the blond girl who had lain there for more than a month. They could see that this would be an opportune spot for a killer. Planes landing to the north at SeaTac were almost close enough to reach up and touch, and their engines screeched as they prepared to touch down. The screams of a hapless woman, crying out for help, would be swallowed up by airplane noise. And, certainly, nobody was going to drive by; the roads had long since been barricaded blocks away. A killer wasn't likely to be caught unawares as he dumped a body. Dirt-bike riders would signal their approach with the buzz of their loud motors.

Dental records confirmed that the petite blond victim was, indeed, Giselle Lovvorn. Her "best friend" Jak-Bak continued to talk to the press, explaining that he had taken a lie detector test and passed. He had his own opinion of who had killed Giselle. "The word I got on the street was that it was a pimp named Peaches who put the grab on her and was trying to break her spirit and work her out of a hotel or something."

Reporters' interest in Jak-Bak waned as his information grew more and more grandiose. And so did the task force's. He seemed like nothing so much as a con man coming across like a sanctimonious hero. In general, pimps lied to police, anyway.

Why? Why? *Why?* Whoever was killing the girls from the highway, there had to be a reason. Some motive that drove the faceless killer. Two days after Giselle's body was discovered, Pat Ferguson, who spoke for the Green River Task Force, admitted that none of them knew why. He said the detectives had speculated on many theories. Maybe the killer was a sexual psychopath, killing for the sake of killing. Maybe he was some kind of fanatic trying to rid the highway of prostitutes. Maybe it *was* a pimp war with the men who lived off women protecting their territory. They were even considering that it had something to do with narcotics traffic, or that somehow the girls were murdered to cover up another kind of crime.

6

SEPTEMBER NIGHTS began to turn chilly, and Mary Bridget Meehan was still missing. Ray, the boyfriend with whom she had been staying, and her family were very worried, more so because she was heavily pregnant. It didn't make any sense that she would suddenly decide to leave; she never had. She had spent all of her eighteen years in King County, Washington, in touch with her family even when she wasn't living at home.

Mary Bridget was the youngest child of four, adopted, as was her brother Timothy, shortly after her birth on May 16, 1964, by an Irish Catholic couple who lived in Bellevue, Washington. Patricia and John Meehan had two birth children, but they wanted a larger family and found Mary Bridget and Tim through the Catholic Charities Organization.

That Mary Bridget should one day vanish from a seedy section of highway twenty miles from Bellevue was almost unbelievable. Bellevue wasn't a place where terrible things happened, especially not to children of families who loved them so much.

After World War II, the building boom in Bellevue metamorphosed hundreds of acres of farmland and blueberry bogs into neighborhoods with ramblers and split-level homes. Many midwestern families were drawn to the Seattle area by the plethora of jobs available at the Boeing Airplane Company. Lake Hills was first, and then Robinswood, Robinsglen, Spiritwood, and every possible combination of rustic-sounding names for subdivisions that popped up like dandelions. The commute to Seattle seemed a long way then, but few new houses sat empty for long.

It didn't seem to matter if they were Lutheran or Methodist or Catholic; most families had four children in the fifties and sixties. The Meehans had a girl, Maeve,* first, and then Dennis two years later. Tim and Mary Bridget fit into their family perfectly with Tim a year younger than Dennis, and Mary Bridget two years behind Tim. Her family recalled that she liked to be called Mary, while friends she met later said she hated the name and insisted upon being called Bridget.

"Mary was her street name," Dennis said sadly. "She liked to call herself that when she was little."

The Meehans lived in a small house near the center of old Bellevue, the little town it had been before the building boom. The couple were very strong Catholics and saw to it that each of their children was baptized and went through the First Communion rituals. All four children attended Sacred Heart School through grade school, and then began going to public school in the seventh grade. They went to Ashwood and Chinook for junior high and then Bellevue High School.

The elder Meehans were highly educated and intelligent people. Her mother was in her midforties when Mary Bridget was adopted and her father was around fifty. John Meehan was a chemist who worked in the dairy industry, but later he started his own business with a former fraternity brother. They were responsible for developing the powder used to manufacture epinephrine, a very important lifesaving drug that is routinely used to jolt a heart into sinus rhythm in extreme cardiac distress cases, the "epi" that ER doctors call for.

Meehan sold his business in 1975 and soon his financial fortune plummeted. He worked in Alaska in quality control for a year, and later drove a van for Metro, Seattle's transit service.

Patricia Meehan was a bookkeeper before her marriage, working for the U.S. Foreign Service in Mexico and for the Great Northern Railroad. After she was married, she often did bookkeeping work on a temporary basis for doctors' offices. They were—except for John Meehan's remarkable achievements in chemical research—an average Bellevue family. They weren't rich, but they had enough to raise their children and send them to private school.

Mary Bridget was a sparkling little girl with shiny dark hair. As a toddler she was "standoffish" with men, but she came to adore John Meehan. Her childhood was happy and sheltered. She loved animals but she couldn't have any pets beyond fish because she and other family members had allergies. She railed at this.

"She would bring home stray cats all the time," her brother Dennis remembered. "And hide them in her room. And sure enough, we'd start sneezing and coughing. We'd find them, and my mom would say, 'You can't keep them—see how everyone is sneezing?' And Mary would say, 'But I *want* them! I want them!' "

In an attempt to find a middle ground, the Meehans got Mary a parrot. "It didn't really work," Dennis said. "She still went out and brought more cats home."

Mary Bridget had a great big smile and a sometimes fiendish sense of humor. She was talkative and outgoing and when she began to tease her brothers or her older sister, "She wouldn't back off." Her humor wasn't mean, but she could be relentless, as many youngest children are.

Mary Bridget suffered from a hearing misperception that made some subjects in school difficult for her. When she was around ten, her grades dropped. But she was a very talented artist. More than twenty years later, her drawings still turn up unexpectedly in the Meehans' house in Bellevue. Her "Christmas Mouse" sketch will one day soon be printed on holiday cards her siblings create and send. As different from her mother as most daughters claim to be, they were both artistic and interested in crafts, and probably would have found more in common as the years went by.

On the other hand, she and her brother Tim were often "partners in crime," getting into things, breaking rules. Mary Bridget and her five-years-older sister were very different. Maeve almost always did the right thing, while Mary Bridget would balk and question why she had to obey.

It was when she hit puberty that her rebellious side made her question her parents' rules and beliefs. She "discovered boys," her mother recalled, "in junior high."

She began to play hooky. Her parents would drive her to school and watch her go through the front door. What they didn't see was Mary Bridget walking down the hall and out the back entrance. They found out later, from her report card, that she was often absent and close to failing a number of classes. Still, it was hard to be angry with her.

"She was always outgoing, and very dramatic," her brother Dennis said. "She could work a room and get your attention. She could be very loud."

Mary Bridget couldn't have been more than fourteen or fifteen when she met Jerry,* a guy even his friends called "a rat." Bridget—she was Bridget now—was entranced with him, and her parents' disapproval only made him more attractive. His father was a highly respected community leader, but Jerry hadn't followed his example.

Bridget's world revolved around Jerry, and her grades dropped even more dramatically because studying didn't seem important if it meant she couldn't be with him. The Meehans set a curfew for Bridget so she would be home at a reasonable time and study. It didn't work. Bridget either didn't come home on time or she snuck out of her window late at night to meet Jerry.

Hoping that tough love would make her realize that she was risking her education and her future over a boy who was nowhere near good enough for her, Bridget's parents gave her an ultimatum. If she didn't obey the family rules, she would have to leave. And they stuck to this decision. At fifteen, she found the door locked one night when she came home late.

Bridget acted as if she didn't care, but she was shocked to learn that she couldn't go home again. She loved her family, but she was stubborn, too. She had virtually no street smarts. She got frostbitten toes when she tried to sleep outside.

Soon, she moved in with Jerry, who was initially glad to have her there. But twice Bridget became pregnant, and that wasn't anything Jerry had planned on.

Bridget Meehan wouldn't even consider an abortion. She was a devout Catholic and she wanted the baby. She miscarried the first pregnancy spontaneously. She wasn't sixteen yet when she conceived again. Bridget told Jerry that she would never kill this baby, and he kicked her out of his apartment. She either couldn't or wouldn't go home to her parents, who were shocked and saddened by her behavior.

Instead, Bridget moved from one friend's house to another, but she miscarried her second baby, too. The loss of the babies was so traumatic for her that she could never really talk about it beyond saying that she had lost a baby. She couldn't bring herself to say that she'd miscarried *two*. She felt that she had failed.

But Bridget Meehan had such an appealing personality and she usually fought down the sadness that gripped her. There were a number of young men who wanted to date her. She didn't trust them. She had lost her center, and she had trouble believing in anyone. Still, she needed someone to talk to, someone who would listen to her and help her figure out where her life had teetered and slid down into an abyss.

One of the young men who loved her from a distance was named Andy. He lived with his mother in Enetai, one of the more desirable addresses in Bellevue. She agreed to let Bridget live with them in her house in the spring of either 1979 or 1980, but Bridget wasn't intimate with Andy. She was too bruised emotionally. Andy accepted her terms; he was happy just to have her around. His best friend Dave was a constant visitor, and he, too, found Bridget a wonderful, if fragile, girl. She had a presence that drew people to her, a kind of glow and appreciation for life, even while she insisted that she had already accepted failure.

"The first time I met Bridget," Dave recalled, "she came up real close to me and studied my face. Finally she announced, 'You're Irish.' And I was, but I'd never thought much about it before."

It was Dave who fell so totally in love with Bridget that he would have trouble talking about her more than two decades later, still angry that she had been put into a position where someone could hurt her, and frustrated that he could not save her. In an era where so many teenagers were lost and doing drugs, a lot of Bellevue parents were trying to rescue them. If their own children would not listen to them, they often reached out to other teens. It was commonplace for parents whose own teenagers railed against them to give shelter to kids from other families. They were all buying time, hoping that maturity would bring reconciliation.

Dave already had a girlfriend, and his mother had taken her in. After he met Bridget, he moved out of his own home to avoid a confrontation with either his girlfriend or his mother. He simply wanted to be with Bridget Meehan. "I became voluntarily homeless to spend more time with her," he recalled. "I guess she really liked me, too, but she had been out of her house for some time when I met her and was already a little bit crazy from it."

It was 1980, and Bridget still lived at Andy's house, and Andy and Dave were best friends, and they both loved her. There could have been open hostility, but there wasn't. She wasn't interested in sex and she was particularly afraid that she might become pregnant again.

Mostly, Dave and Bridget boasted to each other that they could deal with their own demons if they just explored them enough. Bridget told him that she had never suffered from any physical or sexual abuse in her home, but she claimed to have felt emotionally lost because her parents had been cold and distant with her for as long as she could remember. In her version, she was suddenly asked to move out and her parents had refused to let her ask questions or to give her another chance.

Dave *had* been abused at home, but he found Bridget's story "the saddest I'd ever heard."

As dramatic as many teenage girls can be, Bridget outdid them. She was being very dramatic then. In truth, she was not as estranged from her family as she told Dave. She called home every week or so. Her parents loved her devotedly. If she had agreed to the house rules, she was welcome to come home. But, with Dave, and with Andy, Bridget insisted she could not go home again.

"We talked forever," Dave remembered. "She really needed someone to talk to and I was in love with her, but there was reserve and distance on my part because she was so darn unstable and she theoretically knew I had a longer-term relationship still pending. I wanted to help her get her life together, which, in retrospect, seems ridiculous because I was a total mess myself.

"All of us smoked pot and took LSD occasionally," Dave recalled of the spring and summer he spent with Bridget. "But Bridget and I used to take it and spend hours in hideous self-dissections, examining our inner workings, our worst fears, our problems. I suppose it was narcissistic . . . but we thought we spared ourselves nothing and sort of reveled in seeing ourselves in the worst possible light. We thought we were being honest."

The marijuana made their hazy dreams for the future seem possible. They drifted through the spring and summer on the fantasy that they would move to Arizona with Andy in September, when he started college there, even though they knew that wasn't going to happen. They had no money to travel, and Andy's grade point average was too low to get into college.

"Andy's parents finally laid it out for him only a few days before he was due to go to Arizona," Dave said. "He ended up going to mechanics' school and then joining the navy. The last I heard of him, he was married and living in California."

Bridget filled a lot of her days by going to a group in Bellevue called Youth Eastside Services—or Y.E.S., set up to help homeless teenagers. Dave thought it was pointless to go there. There wasn't anything to do but hang out all day and play backgammon. When the sun went down, savvy teens knew they could score drugs at another group allegedly meant to help street kids. Dave found the "counselors" there creepy and didn't feel they were a positive influence on Bridget.

"I'd meet her there to rescue her by going for walks with her for hours. She said some of the counselors had made fairly sleazy advances, but, of course, her self-esteem was so low that she thought it was something she had done that made them do that." When the place was investigated for suspicion of sexual abuse and drugs, it was closed down.

Bridget sometimes went to a kind of hobo jungle in an overgrown lot close to downtown Bellevue. Teens would gather there and live in their cars. She also hung out at a Bellevue bowling alley where aimless dropouts gathered.

Bridget maintained a brittle, tough facade most of the time.

"She had a fearless nihilistic quality that I really admired at the time," Dave recalled. "Now, I see that we were both just scared of life and it wasn't going very well for us. We were accepting failure as a given and then going from there. There is strength in facing the worst and not caring, because it couldn't hurt you if you've been hurt enough already."

Bridget was far from morose or depressing to be around. "She was 'up' almost all the time, and she had a quick and clever way about her. She wasn't afraid to speak plainly, so she was refreshingly 'no B.S.' "

But Dave realized there were things that could really hurt her. Bridget mentioned something to him once about having a baby, and he shot back, without really thinking, "Oh, you'd be an awful mother!" Her face crumpled as she answered, "That's a terrible thing to say!" And she began to cry. It was the first and last time he saw her cry. He panicked when he remembered that she'd said she'd lost a baby, and apologized. She seemed so tough most of the time that he thought she had no nurturing qualities at all, and he was too young to realize how tender she was behind her mask.

"Well, look at your own mother," he countered. "She did a lousy job with you." Bridget nodded and calmed down.

"I never met a funnier girl—or one more in pain. Sometimes, when she would knock on my window at night, I would ask 'Who is it?' as if I didn't know, and she would say 'My mother' in a funny voice. God, she was funny."

He didn't know that she had had two mothers—her birth mother, and Patricia Meehan who had raised her lovingly.

Dave heard Bridget call home once to ask if she could come by and take some things she needed from her old room, and was apparently told that she couldn't.

"I took the phone away from her," Dave recalled. "I screamed at her mother that they were treating their daughter like shit and that they should be ashamed of themselves. She hung up on me."

There were several aspects of Bridget's life that Dave was unaware of. The Meehans had become wary of having their two youngest children come to the house when they weren't there. Bridget, and sometimes her brother Tim, would take things from their parents' home to sell for cash: coins and other collectibles.

"It was typical teen attitude, I think," Bridget's brother Dennis said. "They figured that anything in the house belonged to them."

One day, Bridget convinced Dave to go with her to her house when she knew no one would be there. They went to the neat home in a good neighborhood, and Bridget opened a window she knew would be unlocked, then she let Dave in through a side door. He saw that the house was tidy and the objets d'art were expensive. "But it all looked like it was unused. Bridget was really embarrassed by an old family picture and she took it off the wall so I couldn't look at it, and replaced it when we left."

Dave had stayed in the living room/rec room while she gathered some of her clothes in her bedroom. She called him in to show it to him. "It looked like it hadn't been changed a bit since she left, almost like a museum to their 'ideal' child, like someone might save if their child died. I really don't know why they wouldn't let her come home. I think she really wanted to."

Dave looked through Bridget's albums and she was humiliated when he came across a few of the Doors' records. She thought them "teeny-bopper" stuff. Her favorite recording artists were the Seattle group Heart, and the B-52s. She explained that it was because they were strong women doing creative work.

"The Doors weren't really doing music." Bridget laughed. "They just thought they were."

Dave and Bridget bought Pink Floyd's new tape, *The Wall*, which was what they identified with in 1980. Their love for music was, perhaps, their strongest bond. Bridget told him that she wanted to be a singer, and Dave realized that she had a lovely voice as she sang songs like Heart's "Heart of Glass" and "Tugboat Annie," or from B-52 albums. She talked about writing songs, but she never sang any for him. He would realize many years later that they were both "victims of rock," with grand plans but no action to carry them out. It didn't matter in their fantasy world.

Dave would do almost anything to please Bridget. She once admired a plaster seagull anchored to an iron base behind a dentist's building. "I twisted that seagull for about forty minutes until it came loose. The next day, we walked by that same spot hand in hand, laughing because two guys were out there scratching their heads and arguing about where the bird went. They didn't even glance at us and we laughed openly about it and at them."

They often ran into teenagers that Bridget had known from Bellevue High School, and she told Dave afterward that she felt they looked down on her. She hadn't fit into the social life there, where many students came from wealthy homes. "They're just jerks," she said.

Dave had gone to Lake Sammamish High School, which was more laid-back, situated as it was near the newer, less posh neighborhoods. Later, his mother had sent him to private school—Icthus—on Mercer Island, one of the upper-class bastions among Seattle suburbs. But neither of them made him feel like an outcast as Bridget seemed to believe she was.

Dave sensed that he was the most intelligent boyfriend she had had, and her intelligence matched his, but they were both broke and there was no way they could make a home together. "I may have painted a darker portrait of us than I should have," he would say with the wisdom gained over two decades. "We were cynical and messed up, but our emphasis was on staying above it all. We were a bunch of people with great potential but low self-esteem. Bridget and I were perhaps the most extreme examples of that. We bonded."

Bridget worked that summer of 1980 as a maid at a Holiday Inn and then at a nursing home, making minimum wage. She had always been attracted to people who were down on their luck. Just as she had rescued stray animals when she was a girl, she now tried to save people in trouble. Toward the end of the summer, she got involved with a teen named Brian who had a huge hole in his leg because he'd fallen on a sprinkler while he was intoxicated. She looked after him and changed the bandages on his wound.

"The guy was seriously messed up," Dave said. "And I think she felt sorry for him. It lasted for about five days. . . . When I asked her about him afterward, she dismissed him with 'He's a dreamer. He'll never get anywhere—all he does is *talk*.' It hit a little close to home, and I knew what she was thinking. We were all dreamers."

Bridget was always too thin, and Dave fought gaining weight. She had either low blood sugar or diabetes—he can no longer remember which—but she loved candy and told him she had to eat it for health. "I remember isolated things about her," he said. "That Paul Simon's only movie, *One Trick Pony,* was her favorite movie, and blue was her favorite color."

As the summer waned, Bridget and Dave drifted apart. She snapped at him one day for being too negative about the future, and said she had no intention of hanging around in Bellevue for the "rest of her life."

"For once, I didn't have an answer," he said.

They weren't together any longer, but they kept in regular touch. Bridget dated other guys for a while, but not seriously. She lived for a time in a halfway house and told Dave she had a caseworker who couldn't seem to help her. "She thinks my problems are unsolvable," Bridget said. She found the halfway house "awful," and told him in a disbelieving voice that she had met actual prostitutes for the first time in her life.

"I just listened to her," Dave said. "We were still both so messed up that getting regular jobs didn't really occur to us. She felt there was no way she could do it anyway without having someplace to stay. She thought the hookers at the shelter were scary. She didn't like their lingo or their humor."

Bridget seemed to be growing more desperate. She told Dave that she had encountered a man at Seattle Center who followed her. He thought she was a prostitute and propositioned her, and she had blurted, "Twenty bucks," and he'd said "Okay." But then he bought her a hamburger and they talked and she got scared and didn't want to go through with it.

"He took pity on her, and didn't make her do anything, but I could see that she was at least getting acclimated to the idea. I made a sick joke that twenty bucks was too cheap and she should ask at least forty," Dave recalled with regret.

The chasm between them grew after Bridget came to his house one day when his new girlfriend was there. He knew he had mentioned the other young woman too many times. After the two girls actually met, he never saw Bridget again.

"I introduced them and Bridget was polite, but I could see it shook her up. And then she left. I guess that as long as she didn't actually meet this person, it was safer for us and our illusion of 'twoness' where there was just her and me against a backdrop of everything else."

Dave got heavier into drugs, and he was too involved with his own life and problems to keep very close track of Bridget. Sometimes a mutual friend would let him know what she was doing. He heard she was living in a motel on Aurora Avenue with someone named Ray. Before Dave knew it, almost two years had passed and he hadn't really seen her. He was with someone else, writing songs and working at minimum wages.

Although Bridget had told Dave that she wasn't welcome at her parents' house, that wasn't really the way it was. She had been living at the Bellevue house she grew up in for three months in late 1981.

Bridget was determined to get her GED and she, too, had gone to Renton's continuation school. There, she had met the man named Ray. They made an oddly matched couple; she was much taller than Ray, a very small man, whose father was something of an entrepreneur in restaurants and clubs. She was pregnant, again, and due to have the baby between Christmas and New Year's.

She and her mother discussed what she should do. The Meehans weren't impressed at all by Ray. He had punched Bridget while she was pregnant and broken her ribs. The couple often argued, split up, and went back together. His father was a nice man, but Ray was spoiled, unfaithful, and a drug user. Even so, Bridget said she didn't want to give her baby up for adoption. But she could not come up with a plan for keeping it and supporting it.

"What are you going to *do* with a baby?" her mother asked imploringly. "How can you take care if it?"

At seventeen, Bridget hadn't changed that much from the days when she hid cats in her room. "But I really want it," she would answer.

Dennis, who was home for Christmas vacation from college, remembered his sister then. It would be one of his final memories. For most of her pregnancy, she barely showed, but she was close to term in December and she was "very pregnant and awkward." She had always been so slender, strong, and agile that it seemed strange to see her that way. He agreed with his parents and siblings that she was in no position to try to raise a newborn. Ray couldn't be counted on.

In the end, Bridget probably made the right choice, the unselfish choice, for her baby. She knew she couldn't take care of herself, much less a baby. She decided she would give it up for adoption.

On Christmas day, Bridget, her mother, and her brother, Dennis, went to Providence Hospital. Her family was with her as she gave birth to a baby boy, whom she named Steven. Dennis took pictures of Steven, and they memorized his face. They all loved the infant, but they had no other choice.

Ray's father paid the hospital bill at Providence. For her own reasons, Bridget chose to tell her friends that her baby had died right after being born. On New Year's Eve, Dave received a phone call and he recognized Bridget's voice instantly, even though he heard only a bone-chilling wail that became a high-pitched shriek or maybe hysterical laughter. And then she hung up.

He would always believe that her call was a cry for help after her baby "died," but he didn't know where she was or how to reach her. Bridget was now at least two intermediaries removed from him, and he had heard she and the man she lived with were doing harder drugs.

In actual fact, Bridget didn't do drugs during her pregnancy, and it's possible that she never used again. But she felt so empty after Steven was given up for adoption, and said she was going to move back with Ray despite all the discussions she had with her mother. In an unusual reversal of stances, it was Bridget who said that she "needed a man in her life," and her mother, caught up in the new philosophy of Women's Lib, who argued that Bridget was smart and strong and didn't need to settle for any man who came along. She didn't need Ray or anyone else. She had earned her GED and she could go to college and be whoever she wanted to be.

But Bridget waffled, even though she stayed in her parents' home until the end of January 1982, and they hoped that maybe she would remain with them until she really got on her feet. Tragically, she moved back with Ray in early February, and they continued their migrating lifestyle—from motel to motel.

All of them missed the baby, even though they knew they had made the right decision. Dennis Meehan was reading a Seattle paper ten days after Steven was born and he came across an article about a foster family who had taken in dozens of children, even adopting children who were disabled. The mom held a baby in her lap, and he recognized Steven, who looked happy and healthy and safe.

Dennis called his mother over and showed her the article, saying, "Look, Steven's on his way—he's okay!"

Bridget conceived again within a month to six weeks. Again, it was Ray's baby, and, again, she was living a lifestyle where she couldn't care for a child. Still, she called home regularly.

Bridget and Ray moved to Chehalis, Washington—eighty-two miles south of Seattle—to stay with a friend of Ray's. Ray himself had no visible means of support.

In May 1982, Mary Bridget Meehan turned eighteen. She was legally an adult, but she was still lost, no matter how many hands were held out trying to rescue her, and she carried within her another life that would need love and care. She visited a clinic in Chehalis for a pregnancy test on June 8, 1982. According to the doctor there, her baby was due on November 27. She never returned to the clinic, although she did reach out to a battered women's shelter, where she complained that Ray was hitting her again.

The couple moved back to Seattle, and Ray's father, who owned a nightclub, paid for their lodging frequently. Once again Bridget was very pregnant and Ray's father worried about her. She and Ray stayed at a motel on the highway and then at the Economy Inn, and finally at the Western Six. In some ways, she was the same Mary Bridget that she'd been as a little girl. She smuggled three cats and a dog into their room, hoping the manager wouldn't find out.

And now, in September, she had disappeared. Ray would not admit to Port of Seattle detective Jerry Alexander that Bridget was working as a prostitute, but Alexander found others who said she was. Sometimes she took her dog with her, walking along the highway near Larry's Market, the gourmet supermarket. On the day she disappeared, Bridget had brought the dog back to the motel room she shared with Ray and left again. Ray said he had been working on the old car that belonged to Bridget, and he'd had his head in the engine compartment when she called "Good-bye" to him.

Where she had gone after she walked away from the Western Six Motel, nobody knew. When Ray reported Bridget missing, even he was confused about how pregnant she was; he thought it was either seven or eight months. The task force detectives doubted many of his answers. They learned from people who knew the couple that he often tried to persuade his friends to "get a girl to work the streets for you, too."

"Bridget seemed too sweet and too intelligent to get talked into that," one man told Jerry Alexander, "but I can't say for sure."

Her brother Dennis had difficulty believing that she would have been involved in prostitution so far into her pregnancy, but he could visualize her accepting a ride from a stranger. She liked to put on a tough veneer, but she still had her basic trust in the goodness of people.

It was herself that she didn't really like.

Those who loved Bridget searched for her, but they didn't find anyone who had seen her after that last day: September 15, 1982. Nor did the task force. Ray moved out of the motel, leaving Bridget's cats behind. Animal Control picked them up. Ray threw away Bridget's drawings and possessions, and stopped calling her parents. He found another girlfriend.

WHEN DAVE, Bridget's long-ago soul mate, was forty, he had a dream about her, an intense dream. In the dream, he and Alison, who had been with him for years, were living in a nice little farmhouse somewhere and Bridget and a guy who seemed "okay" came to visit at the farm and they had a nine-year-old boy and a dog with them.

"We all visited and it was very pleasant, and then they had to leave. I walked them out a long drive, but something went wrong between me and her friend and we started yelling at each other. At the end of the dream, she had gotten the child out of there, and it was just me and him. I was going to go back in the house and get a gun—very strange because I've never owned one. I was very upset when the dream ended."

Awake, he had the unshakable impression that the woman in the dream really was Bridget and he was being visited by the part of her that still lived. She looked as she would have looked twenty years later.

"I found myself thinking that I really needed to call her and ask how she'd been . . . and then I remembered."

Dave still felt Bridget's presence and wondered how to tap into that. He turned on his computer and typed "Bridget Meehan Green River" into the search engine.

There were, of course, several articles that popped up. He had never known exactly when Bridget vanished or when she had died— if, indeed, she had. He looked absently at the date and realized that this early morning was *exactly* twenty years since Bridget walked down the highway into some dark oblivion.

"I actually got scared. I knew I wanted to talk to somebody about Bridget. I don't think I'll ever get over it."

7

THE KING COUNTY public's reaction to a yet unknown number of murdered "prostitutes" reflected views that ranged from disapproval and distaste to sympathy and sorrow. Rigidly judgmental editorials popped up in a number of small-town papers in the south end of the county. Essentially, the writers blamed the victims for being out on the street and taking such foolish chances. Beyond that, they accused lawmakers of being lax in controlling sex for sale. Interestingly, nobody blamed the johns who patronized the young women in short skirts, high heels, and, now that the weather was cooling, little rabbit-fur jackets. It seemed somehow more politically correct to condemn the dead girls themselves.

I LIVED in Des Moines, a little town where the victims were both disappearing and being found, and I passed too many young women who stood on the fog lines along the Pacific Highway. "Fog line" is a literal term; by late September in the Northwest, there is a great need for reflective strips along the side of the road because the wet black asphalt disappears into the thick mist that falls after sunset.

Sometimes over the years ahead, I would pull over and attempt to talk with the very young girls, trying to warn them of the danger all around the Strip. A couple of girls nodded and said, "We know, but we're being careful. We use the buddy system and we take down license numbers." Others said they didn't care, that only dumb amateurs got caught. One or two stared at me coldly as if to say "Mind your own business."

I had known any number of working girls in my life. I met dozens of them when I was a student intern at Hillcrest. There were absolutely beautiful girls as well as sad, homely girls there. A few years after that summer I spent "in reform school," I ran into one of my Hillcrest girls in the bus station in Portland. She hugged me as if we were sorority sisters, and told me she had gone back to "the life." Irene was still gorgeous and assured me she was doing well and making a lot of money. She had an older "boyfriend" who had set her up in an apartment.

Another Hillcrest alumna was a resident in the Seattle city jail while I was a policewoman, and she shouted my name as I booked in another prisoner. Janice asked me how much I was making, and I told her "Four hundred a month." She grinned and said, "You could make more than four hundred a week if you did what I do."

"But you're in jail," I said, "and I'm free."

She shrugged and smiled wider.

It wasn't just being free, and we both knew it. They were all living through bad times, no matter how much they protested. I think the saddest was the girl I had to arrest because a senior policewoman spotted her going into a hotel with a sailor and ordered me to follow her. I didn't want to, because it didn't seem fair; why should we arrest her and not him, too? The young woman limped badly and she was very pregnant. By the time we reached the room and the manager slipped his key in the lock, the sexual act, whatever it had been, was over. The "scarlet woman" was sitting in bed, eating a hamburger. She had sold herself because she was hungry. But she had broken the law, and while tears ran down her face, I took her down to be booked into jail.

I have never forgotten her.

On the opposite end of the spectrum was a woman in her late thirties who used the name "Jolly K." Jolly K. had transcended a decade or more of prostitution to establish a nationwide support group for parents who battered their children. A striking woman with auburn hair and impeccable grooming, she had become highly respected when I interviewed her for a magazine article in the seventies.

"Weren't you ever afraid to be alone with men that you didn't know?" I asked her, after she explained that she usually met her johns in the cocktail lounges of hotels.

She shook her head, "No, I could tell if they were safe after talking to them for five minutes or so. I was only beaten up twice . . ."

Only twice.

DICK KRASKE's detectives expanded their efforts and covered more and more ground as they followed up both tips and witnesses' statements. Each missing girl had family, friends, and associates, and even if talking to them led nowhere, there was always the chance that it might.

Dick Kraske noted that there was a positive side to the investigation, as frustrating as it was. Police and those involved in prostitution are not really natural enemies, but they view each other warily. "Usually, our people are out there trying to arrest them," Kraske commented. "The women have their own communication system, and that's where a lot of our information is coming from. We have been getting more help—quite a bit more—from the prostitutes than from the pimps. Some of them are very credible, and they're very concerned.

"They talk to each other. 'That guy is kinky. That one is weird. I saw a gun in the pocket of the guy's car. Stay away from him.' They know and recognize the weirdos."

Now the prostitutes were running scared, and as widely diverse as their mutual goals were, the frightened women and the frustrated cops were cooperating with one another.

There *were* a lot of weirdos out there. Some of the earliest theories speculated that it might be significant that the SeaTac International Airport was right in the middle of the "kill zone." Could the killer be someone who flew in and out of Seattle? Perhaps a businessman—or even a pilot. Exploring that premise, Kraske said that his task force had issued bulletins asking for information about prostitutes who might have been murdered near other major airports in the country. If a frequent flyer was killing girls in Seattle, wouldn't it make sense that he was doing the same thing near other airports?

It was a good idea, but Kraske said, "We didn't get anything back on that at all. So we still feel it is probably someone in this state."

Officially, there were still only six victims.

As SEPTEMBER turned into October, there was an obvious decline in the number of young women strolling the Pacific Highway. A lot of them were frightened, particularly when their network said that there were more missing girls than the police were talking about. It wasn't just the Green River, which seemed distant from the SeaTac Strip to many of the girls; Giselle Lovvorn had been found murdered only a block or so off the Strip.

 AND THEN acquaintances of two more teenagers realized that they hadn't seen the girls in their usual haunts for quite a while. One was sixteen-year-old, five-feet-seven, 125-pound Terry Rene Milligan. She had been living with her boyfriend in a motel on Pacific Highway near S. 144th Street. He reported her missing and then promptly disappeared before detectives could ask him questions. The motel manager where Terry lived said the last time she'd seen her she was arguing with another girl, allegedly over a pimp, but the witness couldn't describe the man or the other girl. Four of the dead and missing women were white, and four, including Terry, were black.

Terry shouldn't have been out on the highway; she'd had so much going for her. She had been a brilliant student, and had dreams of going to Yale and studying computer science. She'd been active in her church, too, but when she became pregnant while she was still in middle school, her dreams got sidetracked. She adored her baby boy, but she dropped out of school and never went back.

Pierce Brooks had listed characteristics he deduced about serial killers as he urged police all over America to recognize the danger. One of his findings was that serial killers murdered intraracially— that is, whites killed whites, and blacks killed blacks. There weren't enough Asian or Indian serial killers to gather statistics. Oddly, the Green River Killer didn't seem to have any preference about the race of his victims. No one knew yet what race he was, but his preferred victims so far were young, vulnerable women he apparently encountered on the highway. He hadn't broken into homes to rape or murder women in the SeaTac area.

But he had been more active in a shorter time in taking victims than any killer in the Northwest to date, including Bundy. The investigators learned that another girl had vanished only one day before Terry Milligan went missing. Kase Ann Lee, who happened to be white, was gone. She was sixteen, too, but the only picture available of her made her look thirty-five. Kase had once lived in the same motel as Terry Milligan, but that might be only a tenuous connection. Certain hotels and motels clustered around the airport were temporary homes to many young prostitutes.

Kase's husband told police she was gone from the $300-a-month apartment they shared at S. 30th and 208th South. Both Terry's and Kase's addresses were right in the circle where the Green River Killer prowled.

KASE LEE was a pretty little thing, although her eyes looked old and tired in the photograph the task force had. She had strawberry blond hair and blue eyes, and weighed only 105 pounds. Even as defenseless as she was, somebody had been mistreating her. Members of her loosely knit circle of friends told detectives that she often had cuts and bruises on her face as if she had been badly beaten. She wouldn't tell them who had done this to her.

Two weeks earlier, police had been called to the motel where she lived in response to a fight, which did not involve Kase, and that alarmed many of the residents, most of whom avoided direct contact with law enforcement whenever possible. The task force detectives got all the information they could in their first contact, knowing that most of the witnesses would have moved on when they came back. They were right; strangers occupied the motel rooms when they returned.

Both Kase's husband and Terry's boyfriend were quickly eliminated as viable suspects. It could have been *anyone* the teenagers had met along the SeaTac Strip, some faceless wraith who killed them and then disappeared into the fog.

Since Mary Bridget Meehan, Terry Milligan, and Kase Lee hadn't been found, they were not officially listed as Green River victims. There was always the chance they were alive and well in some other city.

Their families could only hope that was true.

8

THE OFFICIAL GREEN RIVER toll remained at six, as investigators Dave Reichert and Bob LaMoria continued to seek out witnesses or suspects. One suspect, however, planted himself firmly in the focus of their attention. Far from avoiding detectives, an unemployed cabdriver named Melvyn Wayne Foster was anxious for the media to know that he was central to the Green River investigation. Foster, forty-three, had a rather bland face with a high-domed forehead, and he wore metal-rimmed glasses. He looked more like an accountant or a law clerk out of the thirties than a cabdriver. But he liked to present himself as a tough guy who wasn't afraid of a fight.

And he knew the SeaTac Strip very well, just as Dick Kraske knew Foster very well. "I was a brand-new cop back in the early sixties," Kraske remembered. "I worked in the I.D. Bureau in the old jail, and as 'the new guy,' I was assigned to fingerprint all the new prisoners at the mug location on C Deck. Mel was on the list that day, en route to the State Reformatory at Monroe for auto theft."

Kraske forgot all about Mel Foster until September 9, 1982, when Foster strolled into the Criminal Investigation Division with an offer to provide information on some of the Green River victims.

"I assigned Reichert and LaMoria to talk with him while I checked Records to search for Mel's name," Kraske said. "I pulled up his fingerprint card, taken when he was nineteen years old, and my signature was on it."

Melvyn Foster appeared to be consumed with interest in the missing and murdered girls. He even offered the detectives his psychological theories on what the killer might be thinking. When he was asked where he got his experience as a psychologist, he said he'd "taken a couple of courses in prison."

Foster's prison records indicated that he had tested above average in intelligence while he was incarcerated, but he certainly wasn't a trained psychologist. Still, he claimed to have assisted other law enforcement agencies as an "unpaid intelligence operative." He gave Dave Reichert and Bob LaMoria the names of two cabdrivers *he* considered likely suspects.

The young detectives looked at Foster with interest, although their faces didn't betray what they were thinking. Any astute detective knows that killers often like to be part of the probe into the murders they have committed, just as arsonists are drawn to the crowds that gather at the fires they have started.

IN HIS CAREFULLY DRAWN OVERVIEW of similarities in the characteristics of serial killers, Pierce Brooks had already noted that many of them tend to be "police groupies," and his supposition would be validated over the years: Wayne Williams, the Atlanta Child Murderer; the Hillside Stranglers in Los Angeles in 1978—Kenneth Bianchi and his adopted cousin Angelo Buono—who killed both prostitutes and schoolgirls to feed their own sadistic fantasies; Edmund Kemper in San Jose, who murdered his grandparents, his mother, her best friend, *and* coeds; and Ted Bundy all enjoyed their games with the police, perhaps as much as their killing games. Some had gone so far as to apply for jobs in law enforcement. Apparently jousting with detectives was a way of extending their pride over killing and evading detection.

Serial killers, once imprisoned, often correspond with one another, comparing tolls of human misery and competing for an awful kind of championship. Was Melvyn Foster aiming for a spot on the hierarchy of serial murder?

He had no hope of becoming a detective, except in his own mind. He had two convictions related to auto theft and he'd served almost nine years in prison. However, he seemed to harbor no animosity toward police, and glowed with pride as he said he had come forward to assist the task force with his knowledge. He told them he was quite sure he had known five of the victims.

"How is that?" they asked.

"I like to hang around with street kids," he said. "They're out there on their own with nobody much to help them."

Foster painted himself as a kind of unofficial social worker who came to the aid of runaways and teenagers when they were in trouble. He laughed when he told reporters later that he had gotten acquainted with prostitutes because "I took my coffee breaks in the wrong restaurant."

Melvyn Foster's interest in the young women who had gravitated to the highway wasn't entirely altruistic. He admitted that he had also received sexual favors from some of the girls "as a way of settling the books" when they couldn't pay their cab fares, but he stressed that he was basically a benevolent influence in their lives.

Not surprisingly, Foster fit neatly within the parameters of the kind of killer the task force was seeking. Reichert, who was ten years younger than Foster, wasn't nearly as streetwise as the experienced con man, and tended to see him as a prime suspect rather than as a man who craved notoriety.

Reichert and Bob LaMoria questioned Foster extensively, and he did, indeed, become more and more interesting. First, he'd mentioned knowing some of the victims, and then he denied it, saying they must have misunderstood. When he submitted to a polygraph test on September 20, 1982, he flunked. Now he waffled, saying that he *might* have known them, but that he sometimes had trouble putting names and faces together.

The two cabdrivers whose names Foster had given to the detectives also took lie detector tests. They passed. Foster backpedaled, trying to explain why his answers appeared deceptive: "I believe I have a nervous problem that causes me to flunk lie detector tests."

After the disappointment when Debra Bonner's and Giselle Lovvorn's boyfriends were cleared, it seemed that the investigators might have found the right man. Foster looked good. He knew the SeaTac Strip, had known at least some of the victims, flunked his polygraph, and was a little too fascinated with the investigation— all indicators that kept the task force detectives' eyes on him.

IN THE EARLY FALL, the task force had only one other viable suspect: John Norris Hanks, thirty-five, who had been convicted of murdering his first wife's older sister, stabbing her sixteen times. But that was only the beginning. He had served his time in Soledad Prison and was presently in jail in California on assault charges. San Francisco detectives said he was the prime suspect in six of their unsolved murders from the midseventies—all women who had been strangled.

Hanks, a computer technician, had come to the forefront of the Green River investigation when he was arrested in East Palo Alto on a warrant charging him with assaulting his wife in Seattle. They had been married less than a month when, on September 9, she reported him to Seattle police officers after he had bound her ankles together and then choked her unconscious in their downtown Seattle apartment.

He was smart and he'd been a perfect prisoner, but something in Hanks hated women and he had attacked both relatives and strangers. "Wherever he is," a San Francisco police inspector commented, "women seem to end up getting killed."

And John Norris Hanks had been in Seattle in early July 1982— about the time the first Green River victims disappeared. On July 8, he'd rented a car at the SeaTac Airport, charging it to the company he worked for. He never returned it; the 1982 silver Camaro was found abandoned in the airport parking lot on September 23.

King County detectives could not ignore a suspect who seemed to have a fetish for strangling women and had been in the SeaTac

Airport area in the time frame of the Green River body discoveries. They traveled to San Francisco to question him, but he appeared to have a sound alibi—at least for the Seattle-area murders. People had seen him in San Francisco during the vital time period. Gradually, Hanks faded as a workable suspect in Washington State. He was sentenced to four years in prison for the assault on his bride.

THAT LEFT MELVYN FOSTER in the top spot, although he apparently didn't realize that could be dangerous to him. Still confident, Foster gave task force detectives his verbal permission to search the house in Lacey, Washington, where he lived with his father. The small, shake-sided house was fifty miles south of the SeaTac Strip. It had several sheds and outbuildings. All of the rooms were filled with furniture or tools or "stuff" of one kind or another, the possessions of an old man who had lived there for many years, along with all of Melvyn Foster's belongings.

It made a very long day for the searchers looking for something that might link Foster to the murdered girls. It was probably an even longer day for the man who had drawn their attention to himself. Melvyn Foster became annoyed as the hours passed and he watched the detectives and deputies poking through his father's house. He had apparently expected them to take a cursory look and go away.

Foster went public on October 5, 1982, announcing that he was a suspect. He invited reporters to watch the sheriff's deputies and detectives who were watching him. "All they found were some swinging singles magazines I received *unsolicited* in the mail, and a bra one of my ex-wives left behind in a closet," he told reporters afterward, with a tinge of outrage in his voice. That didn't make him a killer.

Speaking almost daily with television reporters, Foster was a shoo-in for a spot on the nightly news. But now he offered reasons as to why he couldn't possibly be the Green River Killer. He pointed out that his car wasn't drivable in mid-July and he wasn't currently strong enough to strangle a young girl who was struggling, much less pick her body up and throw her over a riverbank; he'd been limping since March because of torn cartilage in his knee.

With reporters jotting down his words, Foster became more garrulous and confidential. He explained how he suffered from a rare kind of "nervous autonomic tic" that always showed up on lie detector tests even when he was telling the truth.

Foster said he had not been lucky romantically. He'd been married and divorced five times, but he said he hadn't given up on finding love. He was thirty when he married for the first time, but it lasted only 121 days because his bride "just couldn't stand domesticity and she just up and quietly disappeared." He married the next year and that one lasted long enough for them to have two sons. Four years later, he divorced his second wife when she became clinically depressed and was admitted to a mental hospital. After moving back in with Melvyn and their sons, she subsequently died of an overdose of lithium.

"We had a very special thing going for seven years," he commented. "I miss her every day."

His third wife was a rebound affair and lasted less than six months. He said he'd divorced her when she slapped his two-year-old son. "That one ended on the spot," he said firmly.

The fourth union was even shorter—only six weeks, another rebound. Foster had taken his boys to California by then, and he said he had his paramedic's license. He met his fifth wife in Anaheim, and she was already pregnant when he met her.

His last wife had divorced him because she claimed he'd hurt her five-week-old baby deliberately. Foster explained what really happened. The baby had suddenly stopped breathing, and "being a trained medic, I picked her up to resuscitate her. When I grabbed her, my right hand was a little stronger than it should have been, and it inflicted six in-line fractures on her rib cage."

Foster said that the pediatrician at a dependency hearing had testified in his favor, but the infant was taken away from both his wife and him. (The doctor, when contacted, disagreed, saying, "She was taken away because of some injuries that shouldn't have happened to a baby that young. The injuries were never fully explained, and the whole situation at home was not good.")

Between that loss and Foster's work as a cabbie and friend to street people in Seattle, his last marriage had collapsed, too. The divorce was final in June 1982, but by that time he was already engaged to Kelly, a seventeen-year-old runaway from Port Angeles, Washington.

His cabdriver friends acknowledged that Foster liked young girls, and said the girls had used him. "They called him a 'Sugar Daddy,'" one man said, "and he'd buy them meals or clothes or give them back rubs." Kelly, now his ex-fiancée, explained that she broke up with Foster because he'd become obsessed with a fourteen-year-old girl. "He worshipped the ground she walked on."

Foster admitted that his sex drive finally overcame his reservations with Kelly, but swore he had not touched any other teenagers. And he denied that he would ever hit or hurt a woman, although he didn't back away from a fight with a man. "For many years, I have only harmed men in defending the helpless, or, with no reasonable alternative, myself, and with the aggressor on the ground, I would end the incident by walking away; murder is not in me to commit."

Ending his press conference on a positive note, Melvyn Foster said he was corresponding with a pretty twenty-three-year-old bartender in West Virginia who was interested in moving to Washington State to marry him if they could raise the money for travel and a place of their own. "You get those daughters of a coal miner's family and you've got somebody who will stick it out with you, so I think I'm going to go for it," he said with a grin.

Despite his obvious enjoyment at being newsworthy, Melvyn Foster's efforts to join the investigation had brought him a lot more attention than he expected, and it wasn't positive attention. It would be a safe bet to believe he regretted ever coming forward to "help" in the first place.

He complained to the cameras that the task force members had made a terrible "mess" when they searched his house. "That was interesting to watch on TV," Dick Kraske remembered, "because I personally instructed the crime scene specialists and everyone else there to put things back in order before we left. We even washed all of the coffee cups we had dusted—with negative results—and hung them back on the rack in the kitchen."

As incensed as he claimed to be, Melvyn Foster always seemed to be there, a presence at the edge of the Green River probe, as if he couldn't stay away. Green River detectives now placed him under surveillance for at least three weeks, monitoring all his movements twenty-four hours a day.

The officers who kept track of him noted that he met with another prominent figure in the investigation most evenings at the Ebb Tide restaurant in Kent, just a few hundred feet from the Green River, to share confidences and cocktails.

Barbara Kubik-Patten was a middle-aged housewife, mother, and self-styled psychic/private detective. She had inserted herself into the investigation even before Foster. Indeed, on the Sunday in August when investigators pulled three bodies from the Green River, Dick Kraske had looked up to see two Kent detectives approaching on either side of a woman. The woman, Kubik-Patten, had somehow heard of the body retrieval. She had prevailed upon the Kent investigators to take her to the river.

Convinced that she had had visions of murder that had come true, she would continue to insist that she could be vitally important to the Green River Task Force. Kubik-Patten would not have been particularly memorable except for the fact that she and Foster spent a lot of time together, and she kept appearing on both the SeaTac Strip and on the banks of the Green River.

Although she was not known in psychic circles in the Seattle area, Kubik-Patten insisted that she "saw" and "heard" things that ordinary people didn't. She told Dave Reichert that she was quite sure she had picked up Opal Mills sometime during the summer while the teenager was hitchhiking.

Later, on July 14, something had drawn Kubik-Patten to the Green River. She said she had seen a small pale-colored car there, and heard screams. The name "Opal" or "Opel" had vibrated over and over in her head. Sometimes, Kubik-Patten said, she had chased after the mysterious car, and sometimes she recalled only that it had been parked near the river and then sped away, distancing itself from her so that she couldn't catch up. She now believed devoutly that she must have been present when Opal Mills was being murdered.

It is a rare detective who gives much credence to psychic visions. All of their training teaches them to look for what can be proven and demonstrated in a court of law, something that can be seen, felt, touched, even smelled. Psychics tend to "see" landmarks like "mountains" and "trees" and "water," and Washington State is rife with all three.

Barbara Kubik-Patten's precognition seemed to be more precise, but her timing was questionable. Was she simply "remembering" something that was now fairly common knowledge after a media blitz on the Green River cases? Or had she actually been at the location where the bodies of Opal Mills, Cynthia Hinds, and Marcia Chapman had been found?

Kubik-Patten called Dave Reichert and Detective Fae Brooks every few days with new insights and predictions, making herself a constant thorn in their sides and actually hampering them from doing their work. She herself became supremely frustrated when she felt they weren't taking her seriously, which, in all truth, they weren't. She was a nervous, intrusive presence when they needed every minute they had to follow up real tips and possible witnesses.

Worse, she was probably contaminating possible witnesses' memories as she planted herself on the Strip and began to play detective herself.

Kubik-Patten was particularly interested in solving Opal's murder, feeling that she had a psychic connection to Opal. She was a frequent visitor at the Mills home, and conferred often with Robert Mills. Garrett Mills remembered her visits.

"She used to tape Melvyn, trying to trap him into saying something that would incriminate him. Then she would bring the tapes over and play them for my father. There were some awful things on those tapes, and I sometimes think that she forgot that she was playing them for a victim's father. Finally, my father got mad at her and threw her out."

Kubik-Patten told detectives she had learned that Opal had spent a few nights at the Economy Inn on S. 192nd and 28th Avenue South, a motel within walking distance of Angle Lake Park, where Opal had placed her last phone call—a collect call—to her mother on August 12.

When they followed up on that, the investigators found that Opal had never been registered there, although Cynthia "Cookie" Hinds had. Probably Opal had stayed overnight with her on occasion.

Like Melvyn Foster, Kubik-Patten appeared to crave attention, and she had an uncanny sense of when reporters might be visiting a site. Whenever something brought the media to the Green River's banks, she was always there—watching and searching—and she was not averse to approaching and interrupting their coverage.

How Foster and Kubik-Patten met is a mystery, but they soon joined forces, making a curious couple who were rendezvousing not for romance but to discuss how they could solve the Green River murders.

Kubik-Patten became familiar to the media and thrived on that. One day in the fall of 1982, at the request of a writer-editor from a national magazine, I was at the Green River shoreline near where Wendy Coffield's body had been discovered. Barbara Kubik-Patten appeared as if she had levitated from the thick reeds along the bank. She told the writer about her astounding knowledge that came from another level of consciousness, and was disappointed when he didn't ask her to pose for the photographer who accompanied us.

Some time later, Barbara phoned and invited me to join her and

Foster at the Ebb Tide for cocktail hour, curiously assuring me, "Melvyn won't hurt you as long as I'm there." I demurred.

Whether Foster was pumping Kubik-Patten for information, or she felt *she* was interrogating him while they sipped cocktails, they were a constant couple in the smoky lounge near the first body sites.

But by late fall 1982, Foster had had enough police attention. He announced that he no longer wanted to be involved in the Green River cases. He called reporters to issue more statements.

"I feel like I've got absolutely nothing to hide because I haven't done anything," he said angrily. "I think they are reacting to some substantial pressure on the cost of [my] surveillance. There have been no murders connected with the Green River mess in the last two and a half months, so why do they want to pull a second search of my house, outbuildings, and property? It's beyond me."

After their surveillance teams reported that Melvyn Foster was spending a great deal of time near the Green River, detectives *had* decided to undertake a more widespread search of his father's house and property. With a search warrant, they removed several more items, including letters from Foster's former wife and his new girl-friend in West Virginia, along with some nude photographs of two young Seattle women, neither of whom matched known Green River victims.

"Some guy who drives a hack mailed those to me last week," Foster complained. "He was trying to frame me."

The calendar on Melvyn Foster's living room wall noted dates in July when he'd taken his car in for repairs, and detectives took that, too, along with some hair samples. Explorer Search and Rescue scouts and dogs searched the Fosters' house and property in a wide range around it. They didn't find anything that seemed to have evidentiary value, and they certainly didn't turn up any bodies.

Still, Foster seemed hesitant to give up his status as a suspect, and the cachet that went with it, as he told reporters he had no knowledge of the slayings or the killer. "I would like to get my hands on the man who did [it]," he added, vehemently.

He hinted that he was thinking about hiring a lawyer because his civil rights had been violated by being watched constantly. He told reporters that he had prepared a six-page protest that he was sending to the F.B.I.

As Thanksgiving approached, with their two top suspects fading on them, there were only two detectives assigned to work full time on the Foster aspect of the Green River case. Six uniformed officers worked in teams around the clock, keeping track of Melvyn Foster's comings and goings. But Dick Kraske admitted, "We can't watch him for the rest of his life."

Officially, Melvyn Foster's visibility in the Green River investigation diminished until he was yesterday's news, but Barbara Kubik-Patten was still convinced that she had the power to find the Green River Killer.

Dave Reichert, however, couldn't let go of Foster as a suspect—too many things matched. He spent his own off-duty time checking on what Foster was up to, and often took the long drive to Olympia, which enraged the now-out-of-work cabdriver. Foster singled Reichert out as the detective he hated the most.

9

MELVYN FOSTER was right in focusing on Dave Reichert as an enemy. Although he had been in the Major Crimes Unit for less than two years in 1982, the young detective was relentless in his determination to catch the Green River Killer. Reichert tracked Foster, often taking time away from his wife and three small children to do so. In 1982, they were all under ten, and family meant a lot to Reichert.

Dave Reichert was the oldest of seven brothers. He was born in Minnesota, although his devoutly religious parents moved to Renton, Washington, a year later. His maternal grandfather was a Lutheran minister, and his father's dad was a town marshal. Two of his brothers would grow up to be state troopers. The young detective attended Concordia Lutheran College in Portland, Oregon, on a small football scholarship. He met his wife, Julie, there and they eventually had three children: Angela, Tabitha, and Daniel. Reichert coached a grade school football team even before he and Julie had children. He and his family were familiar faces in their church.

Reichert had come close to losing his own life while on duty. Answering a call about a man holed up in a house, he had underestimated his dangerousness. The suspect sliced Reichert's throat with a razor-sharp knife, barely missing the carotid artery on one side. If he had cut just a little deeper, Reichert could have bled to death.

Dave Reichert loved his job and he was full of energy at thirty-one. He believed devoutly that one day he would catch the Green River Killer. So did many other detectives and officers in the King County Sheriff's Office.

It didn't seem possible that one man, or even two men working together, could kill a half-dozen women and get away with it for long. Surely mistakes and missteps would be made, and they would have him.

As THE CHANCE of connecting Melvyn Foster absolutely to the victims grew dimmer, any number of suspects bubbled to the surface of the investigators' awareness that fall of 1982.

Kent had a disturbing case that began on October 5, a disappearance that had both similarities to and differences from the Green River victims. Geri Slough, twenty, left her Kent apartment early that morning to go to a job interview. Along with fifty other women, she had answered an ad that appeared in several south-end papers seeking a receptionist for a company called Comp Tec. Geri had circled the ad that listed a phone number and an address.

She was heading toward that address on 30th Avenue South to meet the company owner: "Carl Johnson." He had sounded like a nice man on the phone, and had been encouraging about her chances of being hired.

But Geri Slough never returned to her apartment, and she didn't call her friends to report on her interview. Her car turned up the next day in the Park-and-Ride lot just a block off the south end of the SeaTac Strip in Des Moines. Her purse and some of her bloody clothing were discovered in South Pierce County—almost on the Thurston County line. This location was some forty miles from where her car was abandoned, but in an almost straight line down the Pacific Highway.

Three days later, on October 14, a fisherman found Geri Slough's body floating in Alder Lake. She had been shot in the head. Geri Slough had absolutely no connection to prostitution, and the manner of her murder was different from the strangled Green River victims, but her age matched and the location of her disappearance matched.

Kent detectives tracked down the address in the "Help Wanted" ad and found the Realtor who had rented the office space to the Comp Tec owner. Carl Johnson *had* leased this tiny office, but the phone he used was in a nearby phone booth. In the office, the investigators discovered a large section of carpet that was saturated with dried blood. The crime lab tested it and found it was Type A. Geri Slough had Type A blood.

That was all they could prove at the time. DNA identification lay in the future, and Type A is one of the most common blood types.

But the man who claimed to be "Carl Johnson" had come to the attention of police in another jurisdiction even before Geri Slough's body surfaced. In reality, he was Charles Raymond Schickler, thirty-nine. A few days after Geri Slough disappeared, he was arrested by Kitsap County deputies in connection with an auto theft and break-in.

The car, a 1979 Grand Prix, was being checked by Washington State Patrol troopers after he appeared to know a great deal about the disappearance of Geri Slough.

It had apparently all been an elaborate plot to lure young women to Schickler. There was no Comp Tec. Although Schickler had no history of violence, he had been arrested for mail fraud. A dozen years earlier, he had used another alias to place an ad in a coin collectors' magazine offering rare coins for sale. According to court records, he collected $6,000 but never delivered any coins.

Charles Schickler had long suffered from manic-depression, soaring from ebullient plans to bleak depression. Once, when he was in the manic phase of his disease, he had leased a huge space and installed fourteen phones for a business that was only in his head.

But Schickler, a former mental patient, would never answer questions about Geri Slough or anything else. Using a sheet, he hung himself in his cell in the county jail, without ever explaining what had happened after Geri Slough arrived at his "office."

Geri Slough's murder and the Green River murders shared headlines on western Washington newspapers for a few weeks, and then the Slough case disappeared.

But the Green River headlines continued.

Any time a murder is still unsolved within forty-eight hours of its discovery, the chances that it *will* be solved diminish in direct proportion to the time that passes. Now, the term *serial murder* was being used to refer to the Green River Killer, whoever he was.

With the press clamoring for more details, Dick Kraske gave them something—information that was already a rumor on the street. He said publicly that all six known "river" victims had died of "asphyxiation," although he would not say whether it was by strangulation or suffocation, and turned away more questions by being somewhat inscrutable, "There are different ways of strangling people," he said.

How many victims were there, really? There was no way of telling. If disappearances weren't reported, no one would know to look for them. And almost all the girls who worked on the street had several names. They had a real name, and sometimes more than one real last name because a lot of them had come from broken homes with a series of stepfathers, and then they had more exotic-sounding street names.

In retrospect, there were far more missing women than anyone knew. Despite the reasons they chose not to *live* at home, many young working girls kept in close touch with their mothers or their sisters, calling at least once a week to allay their relatives' fear, and as a kind of lifeline for themselves. But others flew free, far away from home and family.

With the holidays ahead, some families were bound to realize that a daughter hadn't come home or even called. The detectives wondered if the killer was enjoying Thanksgiving and Christmas with friends or family, sitting down to turkey dinners and opening presents with a clear-eyed smile hiding what lay beneath his mask. *Was* he a wealthy businessman or an airline pilot who lived far away from the darkened, rain-puddled streets of the Pacific Highway? Was he even, as the predominant rumor among the lay public now said, a police officer himself?

I heard that rumor a hundred times. The killer was a rogue cop, someone the women knew—and either trusted or feared.

10

ALONG WITH FELLOW F.B.I. special agents Robert Ressler and Roy Hazelwood assigned to the Behavioral Science Unit, John Douglas was among the first to agree with Pierce Brooks that there was, indeed, a category of murderers who fit into a serial pattern. Someone taking victims one after another after another after another. There had to be a differentiation between mass murderers, spree killers, and serial killers. The early 1980s brought together the Green River Killer saga and the forensic psychology experts who understood the inner workings of aberrant and destructive personalities.

The B.S.U. had received accolades for its agents' ability to formulate profiles of killers. They were no more blessed with psychic ability than most working detectives, but they had had the opportunity to interview any number of killers, evaluate their answers, compare them to known truths, and study the affect of their subjects. From there, they connected the psychological dots.

Their profiles were most useful in cases where police agencies around the United States needed second opinions. If they were already weighing the likelihood that one suspect among two or more was the guilty one, profiling often worked. The B.S.U. agents could say, "We think it's *this* one." It was more difficult for them to describe phantom killers from scratch; tests with multiple choice answers are easier than open-ended tests. And the Green River Killer was still a phantom.

In the first six months of the Green River Task Force, there were a number of suspects: Melvyn Foster, Max Tackley, John Norris Hanks, and possibly even Charles Schickler. John Douglas now used his experience and the information supplied to him by the Green River Task Force investigators to draw a profile.

Douglas began with his take on the victimology of the six known dead women. He deduced that all of them were either prostitutes or "street people." Their ages and race hadn't seemed to matter to the killer. It had been Douglas's experience that even the savviest street people could be tricked or fooled.

He felt the lay public's belief that the killer was a cop or someone impersonating a cop could be on target. Douglas said this was a common device used to reassure or intimidate potential victims. A badge or fake uniform could help someone accomplish his first goal—control over the girls on the street, whose lifestyle made them vulnerable. Calling them "victims of opportunity," he said they were easy to approach; they often initiated conversation with potential johns.

The F.B.I. profiler sensed that one man was responsible for the death of all the victims, a man who wasn't worried about being discovered at either the abduction or the body sites.

"Crime scene analysis," Douglas continued, "reflects that your offender is comfortable at the crime scene location."

Douglas believed that the killer felt no remorse over his crimes, and that he probably felt that the girls deserved to die. "He probably even feels he is providing a service to mankind."

"The crime scene further reflects that your offender at this point in your investigation is not seeking power, recognition, or publicity. He is not displaying the victims after he kills them. He does not want his victims to be found, and if they are eventually found, he has the mental faculties to understand that items of evidentiary value will be more difficult to develop . . . if he disposes of victims in a body of water."

Next came a more detailed description of a man with no name and no face—*yet*. It seemed to John Douglas that the man now referred to as the "GRK" had either worked, lived, hunted, or fished near the Green River area. Like most serial killers, he would be highly mobile, although he would be most likely to choose a conservative vehicle at least three years old. It was probably an ill-cared-for van or a four-door car.

"Your offender has, in all probability, prior criminal or psychological history," Douglas wrote. "He comes from a family background that included marital discourse [*sic*] between his mother and father. In all probability, he was raised by a single parent. His mother attempted to fill the role of both parents by inflicting severe physical as well as mental pain on [him]. She constantly nagged her son, particularly when he rebelled against all authority figures. He had difficulty in school, which caused him to probably drop out during his junior or senior year. He has average to slightly above average intelligence."

The killer was probably attracted to women, but felt "burned" by them because they had spurned him or lied to him. "He believes he was fooled one too many times. In his way of thinking, women are no good and cannot be trusted. He feels women will prostitute themselves for whatever reason and when he sees women 'openly' prostituting themselves, it makes his blood boil."

John Douglas believed the killer was drawn to the SeaTac Strip and its open prostitution because he had suffered a recent failure in a significant relationship with a woman in his life. It could well be that he had been dumped for another man.

"He seeks prostitutes because he is not the type of individual who can hustle women in a bar. He does not have any fancy 'line' as he is basically shy and has very strong personal feelings of his inadequacies. Having sex with these victims may be the initial aim for your subject, but when the conversation turns to 'play for pay,' this

Although the Green River Killer had operated in his "comfort area," Douglas felt that he was now having difficulty sleeping and was experiencing periods of anxiety, scanning newspaper accounts to see how thorough the investigators were. "He fears being detected."

To ease that fear, the GRK might turn to alcohol, or even to religion.

In the Behavioral Science Unit's experience, media coverage could have a profound effect on an unknown murderer. If the press stressed that the case had dead-ended and nothing was happening, the killer might feel he was "off the hook" and be able to cope very well with memories of his crimes.

Douglas suggested possible ways the media could help in flushing out the Green River Killer. If they mentioned how advances in forensic science and new techniques were helping to track him, he might well interject himself into the probe hoping to throw the detectives off.

A somewhat grisly suggestion from the profiler was to have the media give the location of cemeteries where the victims were buried. On a night when the Green River Killer couldn't find a new victim, he might desecrate their graves.

Another ploy that sometimes worked was to create a "Super Cop Image." The media could glorify one detective as an ultimate investigator assigned to the case. That man could give TV and newspaper reporters derisive quotes about the "demon" killer, while he painted the victims as angelic. This had worked in the past to draw a killer out of the shadows and into a dialogue with the top man.

There was another, opposite, possibility to consider. A psychologist or a well-liked reporter could give statements that the killer was the *real* victim, not the women of the streets. There would have to be a means for the killer to contact this sympathetic person who he felt would understand him.

What would entice one multiple murderer wouldn't necessarily be effective with another. But there was a chance one of the schemes would work. The man the task force wanted to find might risk being identified and arrested, or he might be glorying in his success at duping the detectives who hadn't caught him yet.

When—and if—the investigators had enough probable cause to execute another search warrant, John Douglas suggested that they take special care to take away scrapbooks, pornography, and any personal diaries they might find. Some killers papered their walls with newspaper clips about the murders they had committed, or kept macabre souvenirs and photographs, clothing, jewelry, even locks of hair. These things would be pure gold in a murder trial.

Historically, taking advice from the F.B.I. has often been difficult for local and state detectives, but communication got a lot better with the demise of J. Edgar Hoover. Special agents were no longer encouraged to appear above the crowd, and the exchange of information—once one-sided, with little being offered by "The Bureau"—was flowing more freely.

Even so, there remained a certain enmity. Sharp, old-fashioned cops with long experience at hitting the bricks and canvassing for information still came up with their own profiles, honed by their seat-of-the-pants instincts. But the F.B.I. and the Green River Task Force were engaged in a war with an unknown killing machine. Anything that would help stop him and trap him was more important than personal egos.

With the wisdom that comes with hindsight, Douglas's first profile would prove to be very accurate in some areas and totally off the mark in others.

THERE WERE, indeed, more working girls missing in King County than anyone yet realized. Although their names hadn't yet appeared on an official "missing" list, something truly frightening was occurring.

 DEBRA LORRAINE ESTES disappeared on September 20, 1982. She had just passed her fifteenth birthday. The last time her family saw her, she had dark hair permed in a Jheri curl close to her head, and wore little makeup. Debra had run away from home many times, and her mother, Carol, worried herself sick over her while her father went out looking for her. She was a wild child who was impossible to rein in. One of her relatives, who sometimes let Debra stay a few days when she was upset with her parents, tried to explain. "Life was a game to Debra."

Although her parents didn't know it, Debra had gotten a prescription for birth control pills at Planned Parenthood when she was only ten. She routinely added four years to her age, and there was no law requiring that parents be notified when teenagers asked for birth control advice.

The last time Debra's parents had reported her as a runaway was in July 1982. They were never really sure where she was or whom she was with, although that wasn't for lack of trying on their part. That July, she had come home with a friend who was a few years older than she was, Rebecca "Becky" Marrero. Debra asked if Becky could move in with the Estes for a while, but Carol Estes had to say no, that wasn't possible. That angered Debra and the two girls left.

Becky found an apartment in the Rainier Vista housing project, and Debra moved in with her. Through Becky, Debra met a number of men in their twenties. Some were even older, including her boyfriend in the summer and fall of 1982. Actually, "boyfriend" was a euphemism. Sammy White* was a pimp. He and Debra stayed at most of the familiar motels along Pac HiWay: the Moonrise, Ben Carol, Western Six, and the Lin Villa in the south end of Seattle. Whether Sammy knew she was only fifteen isn't known.

The Esteses had had three children, but they'd lost their son, Luther, in an automobile accident. And now Debra was missing. Their other daughter, Virginia, worried with them.

As young as Debra was, she had nevertheless been booked at least twice into the King County Jail, and her mug shots looked like two different people. The most recent one showed a girl with golden blond hair, wearing very heavy eye makeup and bright red lipstick. Even her own mother would have had trouble recognizing her. Blond or brunette, Debra was extremely pretty and very petite, but her young life was troubled.

She went to a King County deputy some time in September 1982, telling him that she had been hitchhiking on the highway when a man in a white pickup truck opened his door and agreed to take her to the SeaTac Mall on S. 320th Street. Instead, he had driven to a lonely road and forced her to perform oral sex and then he raped her. He had stolen what money she had. But when Debra Estes reported the sexual assault, she used her street name: Betty Lorraine Jones. She told detectives Spence Nelson and Larry Gross that the rapist was about forty-five, five feet eight inches tall, and had thinning brown hair and a small mustache.

When the two detectives located witnesses who had seen the truck going in and out of the wooded area Debra described near 32nd Avenue South and S. 349th Street, she agreed to file charges. It was about September 20 when Larry Gross picked her up at the Stevenson Motel in Federal Way and took her to the sheriff's office to view "lay-downs" of mug shots of suspects. Spence Nelson drove her back to the motel. Neither detective knew Debra by her real name. She was "Betty Jones" in the pending case, a witness who had suddenly bailed on them.

Sammy White was in the motel when she got back. They were a couple now, but it was the usual setup where Debra made the money and he "protected" her. She dressed that night to go to work. White would recall that she wore dark slacks, a dark gray or black V-necked sweater shot with glittering gold or silver threads, and a dark pink thong. She told him she hoped to make enough to pay for a larger unit with a kitchenette so she could cook supper for them.

Debra's hair was newly dyed jet black, and she wore earrings but he couldn't describe them. When Debra didn't come back, Sammy waited around the Stevenson Motel for two or three days and then moved out. The owner cleaned the room, put Debra's clothes into a plastic garbage bag, and moved them to a storeroom until she could come to pick them up.

As the months passed with no word at all from Debra, her father prowled the seamy streets near the airport. Tom Estes even tried to infiltrate the world that had snatched his daughter away, desperate to find someone who might have seen her. He was alternately angry with the police and despairing, afraid he would never see her again.

Fae Brooks and Dave Reichert would eventually contact more than a hundred people who knew Debra Lorraine Estes/Betty Lorraine Jones. They learned she had been in way over her head, spending her days and nights in some of Seattle's highest crime areas, appearing to be eighteen or twenty when, in reality, she was only fifteen. They managed to list some possible witness names, but more often the two detectives were given the runaround by people who wanted nothing to do with the police.

Sammy White was the shiftiest. He was living here, there, and everywhere. They finally caught up with him while he was living with his sister. Like most of the pimps they had questioned, Sammy put on a sanctimonious face as he bragged that he'd managed to get Debra off Ritalin (speed). "I warned her that being out on the streets was dangerous," he said.

The big question was: Was Debra Estes really missing? Or had she simply decided to move on to California or some other place? She was young and capricious; if, as her aunt said, she saw life as a big game, then new adventures might have seemed exciting. Still,

Debra had Sammy White's initials tattooed where they would always show. She must have cared about him to get that permanent mark. Would she have left him without saying good-bye?

Fae Brooks sometimes felt that Debra was still in the area, especially when new information came in on sightings. Someone registered at the Western Six Motel in her name as late as December 2, 1982. She was apparently with her friend Rebecca Marrero at that time.

LINDA RULE turned up missing six days after Debra Estes. But she had been living in the far north end of Seattle, near the Northgate Shopping Mall, more than thirty miles from where Debra was last seen.

LINDA JANE was sixteen years old when her family virtually disintegrated. Her father, Robert, and her mother, also named Linda, divorced and Linda turned to life on the streets. Her younger sister, Colleen, who idolized Linda, stayed with their mother. The girls looked nothing alike; Colleen was tall and hearty-looking with pink cheeks— like their father. Linda was a petite, fragile girl who resembled their mother, except that she was a little taller and she bleached her hair a very light blond.

Sometime between two and four in the afternoon on Sunday, September 26, Linda left the room she shared with her boyfriend at a small brick Aurora Avenue motel. She wore pin-striped blue jeans and a black nylon jacket. She walked north, headed for the Kmart, where she planned to shop for clothes. Linda's street name was "Ziggy," after the cigarette papers used to make marijuana joints. It never seemed to fit her; she was softer and more feminine than that.

Linda's boyfriend wasn't particularly upset when she didn't come home that night. "I assumed she'd been arrested," he told Seattle police detective Bob Holter. "It was daytime, and she wouldn't have been 'working' on Aurora in the afternoon."

Linda had a lamentably familiar background. She'd dropped out of junior high school, and she was a moderate drug user—marijuana and Ritalin—but she was happy the day she left the motel. She and her boyfriend, Bobby, twenty-four, were planning to get married and she hoped they could have a regular, "normal" life.

Bobby looked for Linda in all the places he figured she might be. She wasn't in jail—she hadn't been arrested for prostitution or for anything else—and none of her friends had seen her. He kept careful notes on his search for her, and made a missing persons report.

 DENISE DARCEL BUSH, twenty-three, was from Portland originally, and she sometimes traveled to Seattle to work for a few weeks. Portland is 180 miles south of Seattle, less than a three-hour drive. Young prostitutes were a little frightened in Oregon, but they figured that the killer was striking only in Seattle.

In Portland, the street girls called their work area "The Camp." They worked downtown between 3rd and 4th to the east and west, and Taylor and Yamhill to the north and south. Now that vagrants had taken over much of Burnside Street, most of the women rented motel-apartments by the week up on Broadway.

"All they had to their names," a onetime prostitute recalled, "was a pack of cigarettes, the motel key, and some change. Their pimps would wait for them down in the Lotus Bar, and they got the real money. *They* had Jheri curls and Adidas outfits and real leather coats. A lot of the girls wanted to go to Seattle because they heard the money was better up there.

"I was older so I usually worked the hotel lounges. When a girl was gone for a while, I didn't pay attention—because I figured they'd gone to Seattle or Alaska. Funny how we assumed they just went on with their lives when, in reality, they were missing or dead. . . ."

Denise Darcel Bush *had* gone to Seattle in the fall of 1982. She had a "boyfriend," but she was alone the last time anyone saw her on October 8. She was crossing the road on Pacific Highway South and S. 144th, a corner that was proving to be the epicenter of the ballooning number of cases. Like so many of the girls who were disappearing, Denise left in the middle of life. She was going on a short errand to a convenience store to buy cigarettes. In the past, Denise had suffered bouts of epileptic seizures, but they were controlled with medication. At some point, she'd had a medical procedure involving her brain and her skull had a small hole in the bony process there, but she rarely thought about it. Only people close to her knew about it.

Denise was seen on one side of the highway, but she never made it across, or, if she did, no one who knew her ever saw her after that.

So many young women were disappearing, yet it was impossible to verify that they were gone against their will.

 SHAWNDA LEEA SUMMERS, eighteen, went missing on October 7 or October 8 from the very same intersection—either the same night as Denise or the next day. The date was fuzzy since no one reported Shawnda missing for almost a month. Alarms were not really sounded yet because it was so difficult to tell the missing from those who had taken to the road to find better turf.

And then Shirley Marie Sherrill seemed to have evaporated from her usual haunts, too. She was nineteen, a lovely looking girl with light brown hair and hazel eyes, who was five feet nine and weighed 140 pounds. Shirley sometimes worked The Camp in Portland, Oregon, but her home city was Seattle. And that was where one of her close friends and co-workers saw her just before she disappeared on October 18. They had lunch before they set out to work—Chinese food in Seattle's International District. But they weren't secretaries or lawyers, and their "work" was out on the street.

 "THE LAST TIME I saw Shirley," her friend remembered, "was in Chinatown. She was talking to two men in a car. She looked really nice that day, and I assumed that she was going to go with them, but then I got picked up. And I never saw her after that."

On Christmas Eve, 1982, a young woman named Trina Hunter went missing from Portland. Trina's cousin would recall that she never wanted to be on the streets, but older male step-relatives had forced her into it. "They kept her locked up in the attic—one of those where you had to put a ladder up to get out of," the cousin said. "They beat her, and only let her down to go to work. She tried to go to the police but nobody ever believed her."

The landslide of human loss was accelerating, but it continued to be sub rosa. The people the lost girls associated with didn't particularly like or trust police and were reluctant to approach them with missing reports.

■

 BACK IN KING COUNTY, Washington, dark-eyed Becky Marrero, twenty—Debra Estes's good friend—had been gone from White Center, a district west of the SeaTac Strip, since December 2. Becky often left her year-old baby, Shaunté, with her mother, and she sometimes said that it would be better for the baby if her mother adopted Shaunté. On the day Becky left she turned back to her mother and said somewhat inscrutably, "I'm going to be gone for a long time, and where I'm going, I can't take a baby."

Her mother thought she was joking or lying, and besides, Becky didn't pack a suitcase, but took only a small blue carry-on-type bag with an extra pair of slacks, a blouse, and her makeup. She asked her father for twenty dollars to pay for a room for one night, and he gave it to her.

Becky Marrero was planning on taking a bus, her usual mode of transportation. Her mother believed that she had gone out to make some money for Christmas, but she never came back. Detective Fae Brooks established that Becky had registered at the Western Six Motel through December 1, 1982. And, of course, someone had signed Debra Estes's name in the guest log as being in the same room with Becky.

Even though there were reported sightings of Becky Marrero after that, none of them could be validated.

 IT IS LIKELY that the last Washington State disappearance of 1982 occurred on December 28, when Colleen Renee Brockman vanished. Colleen was only fifteen, a rather plump and plain girl whose photographs show her in jumpers and turtleneck tops. In one, she is wearing braces and holding a stuffed doll.

Colleen lived with her father and brother near the Lake Washington Ship Canal in the north end of Seattle. She had run away a couple of times before, only to come back within a few days. This time, there was no question that she meant to go. No one was absolutely sure why she had left; she had a crush on some boy, and she may have wanted to be with him.

Colleen took a lot of things with her, enough so that her father filed charges against her in the hope that it might bring her to the attention of law enforcement more quickly, and that she might get some juvenile court–required counseling. All of her clothes were gone, all of her Christmas gifts, and also her family's stereo and some money.

One of Colleen's friends, Bunny, had run away a few years earlier, when she was only thirteen. "*I* was abused," Bunny remembered a long time later. "I *had* to leave. I had no choice."

Colleen's father always felt that Bunny had somehow lured his daughter away. That wasn't true. Bunny had nothing at all to do with Colleen Brockman's leaving home. She hadn't even been in contact with her. But Bunny considered herself lucky; she never had to walk the streets, and always found a place to stay. "God was good to me," she said gratefully.

Bunny hadn't seen Colleen Brockman for about three years when she ran into her old friend. Colleen had told other friends that she was miserable at home, but she hadn't gone into specifics, or if she had, they were not forthcoming with detectives about her reasons for leaving. She didn't tell Bunny either, but she seemed thrilled to be out on her own. Bunny realized that Colleen was prostituting herself.

"I was about seventeen the last time I saw her," Bunny said. "She told me what she'd been doing and I was instantly terrified for her. She seemed very happy with her new life, though, and she said most of the guys were really nice to her—buying her presents and taking her to dinner. She was pretty naive. I think she thought that meant they loved her in some way. I told her she shouldn't do that because she might get hurt. She admitted to me that one guy raped her. He told her that if she did everything he told her to do, he wouldn't hurt her, so she did, and he let her go. She said it would never get worse than that."

But just before the dawning of the new year—1983—it looked as if something much worse had happened to Colleen Brockman. Despite her father's missing-person's report and his criminal complaint, she was not found immediately and she didn't come back home.

The other girls who were working the highway didn't really miss Colleen because they didn't know her very well. "She didn't fit in," one of the Strip regulars said. "The guy she was with wasn't really . . . ahh, he didn't know— They were just trying out the lifestyle, and it was a much bigger sacrifice than she was prepared for."

Christmas of 1982 was such a sad and anxious time for so many families. Some knew their daughters were dead; others had no idea where they were. Were they being held captive somewhere? Were they being tortured? Maybe they'd been sold into white slavery. In a sense, it was easier for the families who had held funerals and knew where their daughters, sisters, and cousins were buried. The ones who waited agonized, but occasionally they could still feel a small glimmer of hope.

There wasn't an extended "official list" yet because no one knew just how many names would be on it. And most of the girls who had escaped with their lives in late 1982 considered themselves just plain lucky, yet still nervous about making a police report.

Penny Bristow* had been working at a minimum-wage job near the SeaTac Airport in November. When she ended her shift, it was dark and looked like rain and she dreaded the walk to her apartment. She was in the early stages of pregnancy and didn't feel very well, anyway. She could have hailed a cab, but that would take more than half of what she'd made that day. So she stuck out her thumb.

A man in a pickup truck stopped to pick her up near S. 208th Street, and she could tell he was looking at her speculatively, wondering if she was a working girl. She knew that world, and she was trying to avoid it. But when he offered her $20 for oral sex, she agreed. She needed the money. Artlessly, she asked him if he was the Green River Killer, and, of course, he said he wasn't. He even showed her his wallet with money sticking out, and flashed various pieces of I.D., one from his job.

She agreed to go into a nearby woods with him.

Though it was November and chilly, he wore shorts instead of trousers. She knelt to perform oral sodomy, but he was apparently impotent and didn't become erect. That angered him, and he suddenly reached down and knocked her into the dirt and leaves with his fist, trying to push her face into the ground. She felt suffocated and fought back with everything she had, at the same time pleading with him to let her go. She wished mightily that she had walked home in the rain because now she feared she was going to die.

He was shouting at her that she had bitten him on the penis, which wasn't true. Somehow, he had gotten behind her and she felt his arm, surprisingly strong, around her neck in a choke hold. She kept struggling and begging him not to kill her.

For an instant, he loosened his grip to get an even stronger pressure against her neck arteries and Penny managed to duck and twist away from him. She ran faster than she had ever run before. He tried to follow her but his shorts, around his ankles, tripped him up. By the time he pulled them up, she had raced up to a mobile home and pounded on the door, screaming. She was hysterical and sobbing as the people let her inside.

When Penny finally did tell the Green River detectives about what happened to her, her memory was still very precise.

The man had been white, in his thirties, with brown hair and a mustache.

11

HE WAS A STRANGE LITTLE BOY who seemed half-formed, a newt in a world of stronger creatures. It wasn't that he was missing any features or limbs, but his face was like a bland pale puppet's with deep-set, painted-on eyes. His dark hair flopped lank across his forehead and there was already a faint vertical dent above his nose. He was a slow child who took a long time to commit most things to memory, his recall full of gaps.

He often felt that he didn't fit into his family because there wasn't anything special about him. His parents had other kids and they always had dogs and so many cats that he couldn't remember all their names. School was very, very difficult for him. He could not understand how anyone was supposed to read when all the letters were jumbled around. Other kids in his class saw words, but he didn't.

He was one of those students who sat either in the back of the class where he wouldn't bother the other kids, or in the front where the teacher could keep an eye on him.

Although he couldn't actually remember it himself, his father sometimes talked about the time he had almost drowned, or at least his parents *thought* he had drowned, and how scared and upset everyone was, and how grateful they were to find him alive and not drowned in the water at all. That made him feel somewhat better— that they must really care about him, although it didn't seem like it. His mother was very efficient and busy, and his father came home from work and sat in his easy chair and watched television.

The boy was a bed wetter and that was humiliating. It wasn't so bad when he was really little because other kids wet the bed, too.

Probably even his brothers did. But he couldn't seem to stop, even after he was out of grade school and into junior high.

After a while, his mother got annoyed with him and told him she couldn't understand why he made so much work for her. She didn't yell at him, but she set her mouth in a tight, annoyed grimace so he knew she was displeased. He helped her strip his bed, and then he had to go sit in a tub full of cold water while she washed his legs and bottom and his pee-pee.

He had allergies, too, and his nose was always running. If he wiped it on his sleeve, his parents told him that was filthy, but he didn't always have a tissue.

They usually lived in nice enough houses, but they moved so often that he always felt unsettled. He never really got to know the other kids in his class at the Catholic elementary school. Sometimes he had fun playing, but he always felt kind of sad or maybe angry because it seemed he had so many things wrong with him. He remembered that when he was seven or eight, he was always getting lost. That was mostly when they lived in Utah. He didn't know why but he couldn't seem to orient himself when he wandered too far away from home—and had trouble finding his way back.

One time, he had a "big, huge side ache," and he literally thought he was going to die. There was no one around where he was, and his side hurt so bad that he just had to lie down and rest for at least two hours. And when he was finally able to walk home, he was in trouble for being so late, and no one would listen to him when he tried to tell them that his belly hurt him so much he couldn't move.

He often thought that he was going to die of something before he was twenty-one. Everything he did turned out bad: his schoolwork, his bed-wetting. He didn't fit in anywhere, not even in his own family. He suspected that his parents had brought the wrong kid home from the hospital because he wasn't like his brothers. If he didn't come home at all, he figured nobody would miss him much.

Somewhere around this time they moved up to Pocatello, Idaho, but things weren't any better. He wasn't very big and bullies picked on him. There was one boy at his new school named Dennis who used to wait for him in an alley after school and beat him up. When he came home with his clothes torn, his nose bloodied, and his face scratched, his father got angry. Not at Dennis, at *him*.

"If you come home one more time beat up," his father warned, "*I'll* beat your ass myself."

Then his father softened a little and taught him how to fight. He showed him how to put his hands up and to jab and punch, so he didn't just have to stand there and let Dennis hit him.

"I got Dennis down on the ground once," he said, "and held his arms, and I could tell my dad was watching and he was smiling." He and Dennis were both crying by then, but his father seemed pleased as he walked back to his gas station a block away.

But, somehow, *he* was still angry. He would think about things he could do to other people to hurt them. He was a pretty good fighter now. He learned he could hold his opponents on the ground and keep them from moving if he put his feet or his knees on their shoulders.

Then he flunked school and was held back. That made him so mad that he pegged rocks at the school's windows and smashed a lot of them.

More and more, he fantasized about violence. It had been so satisfying to beat up Dennis and to hear the school windows shattering, *and* to get away with it.

He started setting fires when he was about eight—not houses, but garages and outbuildings. He found some newspapers stacked in a garage a few houses away from their house on Day Street, and he was playing with matches and set the fire. He heard the fire engines coming as he hid in his basement at home. He didn't come out for a long time, not until after dark. Nobody knew he did it.

When he was older, he was playing with matches in a dry field at Long Lake where his grandfather owned some property. He lit the grass, and then tried to stomp it out, but it quickly got away from him. He didn't mean to do it, but fire always fascinated him.

That boy grew up in the fifties, seeming to be such a nonentity that no one beyond his small circle would ever know his name. It would be decades before his entire story was told through interrogations and interviews and a full-scale investigation the like of which had never been seen before. His every secret thought would be exposed, studied; each facet turned and held up to the light of day so that the mundane became horrendous, the salacious channeled to the deep perversion that it was.

12

THREE DECADES LATER in Seattle, 1983 lay just ahead. Few were sad to see the old year end. It had been a terrible time for a lot of people, but an exceptionally newsworthy era. In January 1982, Wayne Williams had been convicted of killing two of twenty-eight murdered black children in Atlanta. Claus von Bülow was found guilty in March of the attempted murder of his wife, heiress Sunny von Bülow, who went into a permanent vegetative state after he allegedly injected her with an overdose of insulin. (His conviction was later overturned.) Comedian John Belushi died of a combination of speed and heroin that same month. In happier news, Princess Diana gave birth to her first son, William, in June. But Ingrid Bergman died of cancer in August, and Princess Grace of Monaco drove off a cliff in September, suffering fatal injuries. In October, Johnson & Johnson took Tylenol off the market after eight people were fatally poisoned by strychnine-laced capsules. Pierce Brooks had flown to Chicago to try to help in that investigation. The Excedrin poisoning case was still open in Kent, although it didn't get much national media play.

It got a lot more, however, than the Green River Killer cases, which were virtually unknown beyond Washington and Oregon. They had gripped Northwest residents and captivated the regional media, but nothing seemed to be happening in terms of an arrest or charges that would lead to a trial—or trials.

FRESH AIR, views of Elliott Bay, and even windows had never been perks for detectives in the King County Sheriff's Office. Their offices were located on the first floor of the King County Courthouse, an antique building with marble hallways and a foundation so shaky that structural engineers warned that a substantial earthquake could bring it tumbling down. Major Crime Unit investigators' desks filled one big room and the overflow was squeezed into small side rooms that held only three supervising officers. Command officers had offices, but they were tiny and had no windows either. Rooms where suspects were questioned were cramped.

Now, the Green River Task Force met in the same hidden space in the King County Courthouse where the "Ted" task force had worked back in the midseventies. Its narrow war room was across the hall from the Narcotics Unit, both half a floor up the back stairs at Floor 1-A. Two detectives could barely stand side by side with their arms outstretched without bumping into the walls. About the only thing 1-A had going for it was that it was private; no outsider could approach it without being stopped.

Maps and charts and victims' photographs were tacked on the walls. Stacks of paper piled up, waiting to be sorted. The phones rang constantly. It was a "boiler room" in every sense of the term.

Fae Brooks and Dave Reichert were fielding most of the calls that were coming in. Reichert still looked as if he were in his early twenties; he grew a small mustache that made him look only slightly older. Most people close to the sheriff's office still called him Davy, because it fit him.

Fae Brooks had made her bones in the sex crimes unit. She was a slender, classy black woman with a café au lait complexion. Intelligent and soft-spoken, she wore the big spectacles that were popular in the early eighties.

Some of the phone calls they answered were from anxious families or boyfriends of young women who hadn't been heard from. More were from tipsters who were sure their information was vital. There were dozens and dozens of calls, and trying to respond to them all and even hope to follow up was like putting one finger in a dike that threatened to burst at any moment.

A number of tips and referrals were impossible to say "yes" or "no" to in terms of their possible connection to the Green River Killer. In late January 1983, a man laying water pipes along a shallow ditch only a hundred yards from Northgate Hospital was removing some brush when he was horrified to see what appeared to be a human skeleton beneath the branches. The location was almost on the north Seattle boundary line, so it was handled by the Seattle Police Department.

The desiccated remains were of a small human. The King County Medical Examiner's office removed the bones carefully, but an autopsy failed to reveal any cause of death. The body had no soft tissue left; the young female could have died from any number of causes.

The teeth, however, matched Linda Jane Rule's, the blond girl who had been missing for four months after she left her motel room to walk to the Northgate Mall. Sergeant Bob Holter and Captain

Mike Slessman of the Seattle Homicide Unit were fully aware of the Green River murders, but they could find no absolute link between them and Linda Rule. Lifestyle? Yes. Location? Not really. Most of the missing women had last been seen in the south county area, not in the north end. "Technically," Holter said, "we're not calling this a murder—we don't have enough to go on for that—but the results are the same. She is dead, and we don't know why or how."

BY early March 1983, the dread that there was still someone out there on the highway grew. The women who fell into the endangered category counted the possible victims and had to fight back panic. Still, almost all the young women who worked the SeaTac Strip or along the dangerous blocks on Aurora Avenue North believed that they would be able to recognize the killer. He must surely be giving clues that the missing girls hadn't picked up on. Each working girl had a picture in her mind about who she would not go with. Many of them worked on the buddy system with other prostitutes, saying "Remember who I'm with" as they got into cars. Some would not accept car dates, others wouldn't go into a man's motel room, or his house.

 ALMA ANN SMITH was working the corner of S. 188th Street and the highway on March 3, 1983. The huge and expensive Red Lion Inn was located there, across the street from the airport. This was no "hot bed" motel; the Red Lion was one of the nicer places to stay in Seattle, with its richly carpeted corridors, hand carvings, and exterior elevators that echoed the Space Needle's. There was a pricey gourmet restaurant on the Red Lion's top floor. If the Green River Killer was scruffy-looking, he would be noticed immediately at the Red Lion and quickly hustled outside by hotel security.

Alma came from Walla Walla, Washington, a world away from Seattle. Brook Beiloh, her best friend in seventh grade, remembered her as an extremely generous girl who "didn't have a malicious bone in her body."

Brook recalled the childhood days they had shared. "Walla Walla was still untouched by crime twenty years ago. Kids played in the streets till dark. We rode our bikes to every corner of that small town without fear and without supervision. This was the place where a latchkey kid didn't need a key because who locked their doors? After seventh grade, I didn't see Alma very often. She would be in class one day, and then you wouldn't see her again for three to six months. When she came back from wherever she went—or maybe ran away to—she always made an effort to contact me. We would hang out for a day or two, and then she'd be gone. I don't know the story behind this behavior, although I asked her one time where she always took off to, and she simply replied, 'Seattle.' Alma was a couple of years older than me, but I still remember thinking how terrifying it would be to be alone in the *city!*"

Once, Alma sent Brook an eight-by-ten picture of herself, a studio shot, with a letter on the back. Alma's hair was blonder than when she was in the seventh grade, but she still had great eyes with arching brows. "I don't know where she got it, because Alma never had a lot, so this gesture touched me deeply," Brook recalls. "I saw her last in December 1982, just three months before she was murdered."

Alma had a lot of friends, and she and some of the other girls who plied their risky trade along the Strip agreed to try to protect each other. Alma and her roommate and best friend, Sheila,* were both looking for johns on March 3. Sheila left with a man first, returning to the bus stop about forty-five minutes later. Alma wasn't there, and Sheila figured she'd found a trick.

"Anyone know where Alma went?" she called to young women nearby.

"She left with some guy in a blue pickup truck."

"White or black?"

"White—just an average-looking guy. You know . . ."

Sheila grew concerned when an hour passed and Alma didn't come back. She had a "hinky" feeling, but she couldn't say why. She wished she had been there to get a license number or something. She waited nervously for Alma to come back.

Alma never did.

 DELORES WILLIAMS was another girl who found the bus stop in front of the sumptuous motel a good place to meet wealthy johns, and to take shelter from the rain, too. Delores had a lovely smile, and she was tall and slender. She was only seventeen. The storms of March whipped and keened around the towering wings of the Red

Lion, and the bus stop with its partial paneling was cold, but business was usually brisk.

Still, by March 8, Delores didn't wait there any longer. Her friends thought maybe she'd found a better location.

BOTH DAVE REICHERT and Fae Brooks still felt that Melvyn Foster was a good suspect. It was hard for them to write him off because he had, it turned out, known some of the first six victims, however briefly. And he did fit into the part of the John Douglas profile about suspects who liked to hang around the investigation and savor their memories. Foster continued to brag that he'd be glad to punch the killer out if he ever ran across him, and claimed that the police were wasting time concentrating on him when they should be out looking for the real killer.

Dick Kraske could see that two detectives couldn't possibly keep up with the overload, and he transferred four more investigators in to help: Elizabeth Druin, Ben Colwell, Pat Ferguson, and Larry Gross. Detective Rupe Lettich, who had been the head narcotics detective in King County for a long time, was right across the hall and he helped, too. But the twenty-five-person task force was no more. Morale was low and the public didn't seem to care all that much about young prostitutes out on the SeaTac Strip. They weren't *their* daughters.

But silently and stealthily, more of them were being trapped like rabbits in a snare.

Spring arrived with daffodils, tulips, cherry blossoms, and Scotch broom bursting as they always have from rain-sodden earth. Hopes, however, did not. The girls who had gone missing in the fall and winter apparently weren't in Portland or Yakima or Spokane or any other city on "the circuit."

SANDRA K. GABBERT was seventeen on April 17 when she strolled along the Strip near what appeared to be the most dangerous corner—Pac HiWay and S. 144th. The Church by the Side of the Road was three blocks away, the 7-Eleven was a block away, and the motels that catered to four-hour occupancy for only $13 and cheap weekly rates were clustered around that intersection. Although she'd been a star on the girls' basketball team, Sand-e had dropped out of school because she was bored, and now she was living with her teenage boyfriend. They were barely able to afford motel rooms and fast food. Her mother, Nancy McIntyre, knew that Sand-e was selling herself to make enough money for that, but she couldn't stop her. Sand-e's street name was "Smurf," and she had a kind of insouciant charm, as if she didn't take herself all that seriously.

Maybe Sand-e didn't remember where the other girls had vanished, or maybe she didn't care. She had the untested confidence common to the young; she was indestructible.

Nancy had been on her own with Sand-e since her divorce when her little girl was two. Only forty-one, Nancy had worked as a barmaid for years and life was tough. Now she made minimum wage as a maintenance worker for the Seattle Parks Department. She didn't even try to debate the moral issues of prostitution with Sand-e; she was worried about her daughter's survival. "I said, 'Sand-e, you could get yourself *killed* doing this,' and she said, 'Oh Mom, I'm not going to get killed.' She didn't want to hear about it or talk about it because she knew I was so scared. She could turn one trick, take half an hour, and make as much as she made when she worked for Kentucky Fried Chicken for two weeks. Now, you try to show someone the logic of getting a legitimate job," Nancy said with a sigh. "I realized if I tried to force her to stop, I'd have alienated her from me. And I'd go through anything before that—even prostitution."

The last time Nancy saw Sand-e, they ate at a Mexican restaurant, and Sand-e talked about her plans to go traveling to San Francisco and Hollywood. "I put my arms around her," Nancy recalled as tears coursed, unbidden, from her eyes. "I said, 'I love you, baby. Please be careful.' She said, 'I love you, too. I *am* careful.' I watched her walk along the front steps, and I knew I wasn't going to see her for a long, long time."

Four days later, Sand-e was gone.

WITHIN only a few hours, Kimi-Kai Pitsor, who was sixteen, got into an old green pickup truck on 4th and Blanchard in downtown Seattle. By taking the I-5 Freeway, it was possible to travel the fourteen miles between the two locations in under half an hour, unless someone tried to do it during rush hour when traffic backups were the norm.

Could the same man have taken both teenagers in one night?

Bundy had taken two victims on one Sunday afternoon eight years earlier. But those young women were sunbathing at the same park. Was it imaginable that this man was trying to break some dark record?

Kimi-Kai and Sand-e looked somewhat alike, youngish for their age, with dark hair and bangs. Sand-e had been alone just before she disappeared, although she and her boyfriend had walked together to the 7-Eleven only a few minutes before. She had left him behind as she crossed Pac HiWay. And Kimi-Kai was walking with her boyfriend/protector when she signaled a man in a truck to turn around the corner so she could get into his vehicle without being seen.

Kimi-Kai, whose street name was "Melinda" had tried working down in Portland for a short time, but the girls there pegged her as "very innocent and naive." With her boyfriend, she had headed for Seattle, along with several other young women who'd been in Portland, because the word was you could make more money there. But the word was wrong; Portland wasn't where it was happening. So they returned to Seattle.

For the second time, detectives had the description of a vehicle (beyond the small white car Barbara Kubik-Patten said she saw by the Green River). Again, it was a pickup truck. Kimi-Kai's boyfriend described an older green truck with a camper on the back and primer paint on the passenger door. He thought it was either a Ford or a Dodge.

Halfway into April 1983, and two more teenagers had failed to come back or to call anyone they knew. The trucks' descriptions were printed in Seattle papers, but the investigators weren't too hopeful that it would help. There were a lot of older trucks, some of them green, some blue, some brown and tan, and a whole lot of them with primer spots.

FOR SOME REASON murder victims and most serial killers are often referred to in the media by their first, middle, and last names. Is it, perhaps, to give the victims dignity? As for the killers, is it to distinguish them from other men with similar names? Or does it, unfortunately, imbue them with extra infamy? *Theodore Robert Bundy, Coral Eugene Watts, Jerome Henry Brudos, Harvey Louis Carignan, John Wayne Gacy.*

Hearing the full names of the hapless teenagers who encountered the Green River Killer could not help but evoke thoughts of how short a time had passed since they were tiny babies, whose parents lovingly picked out enchanting names, with carefully chosen middle names, in the hope that their daughters' lives would unfold like flowers. Even parents whose own lives had been bruised with disappointment hoped for a better future for their children.

Kimi-Kai Pitsor's mother, Joyce, loved her baby's name so much that she embroidered it on her sheets and blankets. In Hawaiian, it meant "golden sea at dawn."

Talking with veteran *Seattle Post-Intelligencer* reporter Mike Barber, Joyce Pitsor described Kimi-Kai as a petite girl who loved unicorns and anything purple. Like many girls her age, she hit a defiant streak almost at the very moment she entered puberty. She fell in love with a boy and wanted to be with him more than her mother thought prudent. Railing against curfews and rules, Kimi left home in February 1983 to move in with her boyfriend, but she called her mother every week.

"Kimi was very adventurous," Joyce remembered. "She wasn't afraid. She wanted to see how life worked and never took anyone's word for anything. She had to see for herself. I remember telling her, 'Be a little girl for a while. Enjoy yourself. You have all the time to be a grown-up with all those problems.' But she wanted to be an adult so bad."

And now, Kimi-Kai was gone. If anyone had ever viewed her as tough, her mom knew better. "She could put on the most bravado routine, especially if she was terrified. What it really was was bordering on hysteria." Joyce Pitsor had seen that when she rushed down to juvenile court to stand by Kimi-Kai when she was in trouble.

Now, waiting for word was torturous for her mother, who had already lost two of her children—one at birth and one as an infant. She was a woman who loved kids; she had adopted three biracial children because she did care so much. But she hadn't been able to convince her own daughter to wait just a few years before she plunged into the adult world.

And within only two months of "freedom," Kimi-Kai was gone, too.

THE NEW WEST MOTEL was on the Des Moines end of Pac HiWay across 216th to the north of the Three Bears, with a convenience store between them.

SOMETIME in the third week of April, Gail Lynn Mathews, twenty-four, registered at the New West. Gail was an exotic-looking woman with luxuriant black hair. Her most distinctive feature was her extremely full, lush mouth. She was living with a thirty-four-year-old man from Texas named Curt, whom she'd met at Trudy's Tavern near the airport in 1982. At that time, she'd had a little apartment across from Trudy's, but she lost it when she couldn't make the rent in February 1983. For weeks after that, Gail lived a week or two at a time with friends of friends of friends.

Except that she was older than most of the Green River victims, Gail Mathews's lifestyle was similar to theirs. She had been married, but she was either divorced or separated by the spring of 1983, and she was down on her luck.

Neither Gail nor Curt had much money or permanent jobs; they drifted while he gambled in card rooms and she nursed a beer in the bar, waiting to see if he'd win enough for a meal and motel. Curt's extensive vocabulary reflected his intelligence and education, but either drugs or alcohol had sidetracked him. His regular haunts were the White Shutters, Trudy's, and the Midway Tavern. Now and then, Gail contributed money to the kitty. She never told Curt where she got it, and he never asked. Their lives had become a day-to-day existence. They had no car and no permanent residence.

On the last night Curt saw Gail, things were normal—for them. They had stayed in the New West for a few days, but their rent was up and they were both broke. On the night of April 22, they were in the VIP Tavern a few blocks north of their motel. They shared a couple of beers while Curt played Pac Man. Gail watched him, not talking to anyone else in the tavern.

Finally, Curt decided to head to the Midway Tavern, which was across the Kent–Des Moines Road from the Texaco station and the Blockhouse Restaurant. He hoped they had a poker game going there, and he'd have a lucky night.

Gail told him she would try to find a way to keep their motel room for another night or two. He walked away from the VIP Tavern, leaving her there alone; she knew the woman bartender. It was more than a mile to the Midway, so Curt decided to catch a bus. He waited at the familiar intersection at 216th and the Pac HiWay. Idly, he watched traffic and noted a blue or possibly green Ford pickup passing. It wasn't new by any stretch of the imagination, but it was noticeable because it had so many sanded "circular" marks on it, as if it was primed for a paint job.

Curt was startled to see Gail sitting in the passenger seat beside a man with light hair who appeared to be in his early thirties. He was wearing a plaid shirt that made him look like an "outdoorsman."

Curt's arm was half lifted to wave at Gail when he was surprised by the way she looked. "She seemed dazed," he would tell F.B.I. agent "Duke" Dietrich later. "She was staring straight ahead. It was bizarre. She was looking right at me, but it was as if she didn't see me. I'm sure she could see me—it wasn't dark out yet."

He waved harder, but Gail didn't respond. If she was trying to signal him that she was in some kind of trouble, he couldn't decipher it. She was sitting far away from the driver, right next to the passenger door. He watched as the truck turned left and disappeared. "I don't know how to explain it," Curt said, "but I felt fear—fear for her because I sensed she was in danger. I ran across the road toward the truck and tried to catch up with it, but the driver made a left turn and sped up."

Curt had watched helplessly as the truck disappeared. The bus came by and he got on, telling himself that he was overreacting. He spent an hour at the Midway Tavern, but nobody wanted to play poker, so he trudged back to their motel room. He watched the highway for a long time, waiting for car lights to turn into the motel or the sound of Gail's footsteps scrunching the gravel. There were a few cars, but Gail didn't come back that night.

Curt called 911 to report her missing. He said later that he was told that he couldn't make an official missing person's report because he was not related to her.

Curt waited for Gail to come back or leave a message for him at the motel office, but there was nothing. He stopped at all the places along the highway where they'd gone together. No one remembered seeing Gail recently. He couldn't help it; his mind turned to thoughts about the Green River Killer. Both he and Gail were aware of the missing and murdered girls, but she had never been afraid. He'd warned her about hitchhiking, too, but she told him not to worry about that—she could take care of herself.

He wondered now why Gail had looked so strangely at him—or, rather, *through* him—when he waved at her. Somehow, the man behind the wheel must have been controlling her. Maybe he was holding a knife against her body so she didn't dare cry out. Maybe a gun. Why else would she have not even waved or smiled at him?

They'd been together for almost a year, and they'd become close. Curt didn't buy the idea that Gail would simply leave him with no explanation. It was true they hadn't had much money, and life was tough for them, but they had always believed that if they pulled together, they could get out of the hole they were in and build a better life. But drugs were important to Curt, too, and eventually he moved on, unsure of what had happened to Gail.

By the time an investigator knew what had become of Gail and tracked Curt down, he was an inmate in a Texas prison. When he was returned to Seattle to be interviewed by Dr. John Berberich, the Seattle Police Department's psychologist, Curt agreed readily to be hypnotized. Maybe there was something hidden in his subconscious that would help catch her killer. A license number or a more complete description of the truck and driver.

Despite their best efforts, Curt could recall nothing beyond the odd, frozen look on Gail's face the last time he saw her.

 EIGHT DAYS after Curt saw Gail Mathews in a stranger's truck, that same intersection was the scene of an apparent abduction. Marie Malvar was eighteen, a beautiful Filipina, the cherished daughter of a large family. They didn't know she was out there on the highway at S. 216th, near the Three Bears Motel, trusting that she was safe because her boyfriend, Richie,* was with her to note which cars she got into and to make sure she came back safely in a reasonable time.

The young couple watched as a dark truck approached the intersection from the south. As it pulled over, they could see a spot on the passenger door that glowed lighter than the rest of the truck, a coat of primer paint. Marie spoke to the driver, nodded, and then got in and the stranger's vehicle pulled onto the highway again.

As he usually did, Richie followed, keeping pace, and then pulling alongside. From her gestures, it appeared to him that Marie was upset. He couldn't hear what she was saying, but it looked as though she wanted to get out of the truck. The driver slowed down, but only to turn around in a motel parking lot and then accelerated as he headed south. Richie did the same, but he didn't make the light at S. 216th. It turned red and he had to stop. He watched as the pickup truck turned left and headed east—in the direction of the Green River. As soon as the light changed, Richie turned left, too.

Because he was less than a minute behind the pickup, Richie thought it was strange when he saw no taillights ahead, neither going down the Earthworks hill on 216th, nor headed north or south on Military Road, which ran parallel to the highway. Tossing a coin in his head, he drove south on Military, but there were no vehicles at all between the intersection and the Kent–Des Moines Road a few miles south. There didn't seem to be anyplace the truck could have turned off, because Military and the I-5 Freeway were so close together and there were no on-ramps along that section.

Richie didn't see the almost invisible street sign that led to a narrow cul-de-sac on the right side of Military Road. It was easy to miss, especially in the dark. Bewildered, he drove back to the parking lot to wait for the guy in the truck to bring Marie back.

But he never did.

Because he and Marie had been engaged in prostitution, Richie was hesitant to go to the police. He was just as nervous about telling her father, Jose, because he feared his wrath when he learned that Richie had let Marie take such chances. Still, when four days went by with no word from her, Richie went to the Des Moines Police Department. There, he talked to Detective Sergeant Bob Fox. Richie reported Marie as missing, but he didn't tell the whole truth about what he and Marie had been doing out on the highway. If he had, Fox, who had investigated many homicides in the city of Des Moines, and who was well aware of the Green River cases, would have reacted differently. Instead, Richie's evasiveness made Fox wonder if he hadn't harmed his girlfriend himself, or, more likely, Marie Malvar and Richie might have had a fight and she'd left him on her own.

Jose Malvar was very concerned. Marie wasn't a girl who stayed away from home for long, and she called frequently. Now there was only silence. Jose picked up Richie and said they were going to find her, demanding to know just where she and Richie had been when she disappeared.

Jose, Richie, and Marie's brother, James, started at the intersection where Richie had seen the pickup truck pull away. They inched east on 216th, down the long winding hill, and then back and forth along Military Road. They were looking for some sign of Marie, or the truck with the primer spot on the passenger door. They checked driveways and carports. There weren't many houses on the west side of Military Road going north—only a new motel sandwiched in a narrow slice of land just off an I-5 Freeway ramp. But when they headed south, there were many modestly priced homes on both sides of the road.

On May 3, the trees were all leafed out and dogwood, cherry, and apple trees were blooming. After making several passes, they finally spotted a street sign on the right side of the road: S. 220th Place. Turning in, they found an almost hidden residential street, a cul-de-sac with eight or ten little ranch houses. In the driveway of a house near the north end of the street, they all saw it: an old pickup truck. They got close enough to look at the passenger door. It had a primer splotch on it.

They immediately called the Des Moines Police Department, and Bob Fox responded. He and another detective knocked on the door while Marie's father, brother, and boyfriend watched. Fox was talking to someone, nodding, asking another question, and nodding again. Finally, the front door shut and the Des Moines detectives walked slowly down the walk.

"He says there's no woman in there," Fox told Jose Malvar. "Hasn't been a woman in there."

The man who said he was the owner had struck the police as straightforward enough, and he hadn't been nervous, just curious about why the police were knocking on his door. Fox didn't even know if his was the same truck Richie had seen, and he hadn't pushed his questioning very hard. There was no probable cause to search the small house whose rear yard backed up to the bank that sloped to the freeway. The guy who lived there was friendly but firm when he said he lived there alone, had just bought the house, in fact.

Her boyfriend and relatives who were searching for Marie Malvar watched the house for a while, frustrated and anxious. Was Marie in there? Had she ever been? They fought back the urge to go up and pound on the door themselves, but, finally, they drove away. Still, they came back at odd times to check. It was the closest they could be to Marie, or at least they thought so. Where else could they look?

DETECTIVES were inclined to believe that none of the men who had driven battered pickup trucks was likely to be the killer they sought. With both Kimi-Kai Pitsor's and Marie Malvar's last sightings, the girls' boyfriends were positive that the drivers had seen them watching. It didn't make sense that a killer would be brazen enough to take that kind of chance. It was more likely that Kimi-Kai and Marie had met someone else after they got out of the trucks.

One murdered girl, who was found near Pac HiWay and S. 216th almost a year before and who had seemed to fit into the Green River victim profile turned out to be an unrelated victim. The Green River Killer wasn't the only dangerous man trolling for victims in the Seattle area. Patricia Jo Crossman *was* working as a prostitute and, like the others, she was in her midteens when she died violently, her body tossed from a balcony into bushes. Thirty-year-old Thomas Armstrong III, who was arrested and prosecuted for that crime, tried to convince Judge Robert Dixon that Patty Jo's death was related to the Green River murders, even attempting to link his ex-wife, Opie, to the killings. The ex-wife's apartment house was burned down a month after Patty Jo's murder.

It took two trials to convict him, but prosecutor Linda Walton argued that detectives had found absolutely no connection to the Green River cases. There was, however, overwhelming evidence that Armstrong had killed Patty Jo on April 8, 1982.

On April 8, 1983, Armstrong was sentenced to life in prison.

And the real Green River Killer still roamed free, taking more victims, most of whom simply disappeared from the motels and streets where it was normal for them to be around for a time and then be gone. Their friends assumed that they had simply moved on.

13

WITH THE KNOWLEDGE that we have today, the so-called Green River Killer, whoever he was, seemed to be in a homicidal frenzy, proceeding along the path that serial killers so often take. For them, murder is addictive, and it takes more and more of the "substance" to satisfy them, or to make them feel, as two infamous serial murderers have said, "normal."

AS THE WEATHER grew warmer, his pace increased. Martina Theresa Authorlee, nineteen, was at the prize spot near the Red Lion on May 22, 1983, but not on May 23 or any day after. Born in West Germany where her father was in the army, Martina had moved back to the United States with her parents in 1968 to live on the sprawling Fort Lewis

Army Base south of Tacoma. Her ambition was to have a service career, too, and she had joined the National Guard and left for six weeks of basic training in 1982. But she was given a medical discharge and never completed her time in South Carolina. After that, she seemed to lose direction. Without explaining to her parents what had happened, she moved to Hillsboro, Oregon, that summer, but she still called home twice a month.

Martina came home for Mother's Day, 1983, and spent some time with her family. As far as they knew, she intended to go back to Oregon after her few days' visit. She told them she had a job, but they didn't know what she did. Nor did they know that she had been arrested for prostitution and served two days in jail in Seattle. They sensed she was troubled, but she was a girl who kept her thoughts to herself.

Assuming she was back in Oregon, they weren't unduly worried until they heard nothing more from her, not even at Christmas.

CHERYL LEE WIMS, eighteen, vanished on May 23 from the central district in Seattle. It was the night before her birthday. She was a softly pretty girl with a shy look about her. Should she be on the list? Or was she too far away from the Strip? She had had some problems with drug use, according to her mother, Ruth Wims, a nurse, but she could not picture Cheryl involved in prostitution, even though she had become somewhat secretive. The worst problem her mother ever had with Cheryl was that she was missing too much school.

The only job her family knew about was as a busgirl in a downtown restaurant. There, her boss described Cheryl to detectives as "quiet, conservative, and conscientious." Her name and Martina's were added to the Green River Killer's agenda.

Yvonne Antosh had come all the way from Vancouver, British Columbia, to the Pac HiWay Strip. She was nineteen, a most attractive young woman with very thick auburn hair that fell like scalloped curtains around her face. And she, too, disappeared from the highway. Someone recognized her on May 30, as she stood near S. 141st, but they never saw her after that.

There were so many of them that it seemed almost impossible that they hadn't been seen with whoever was taking them away. The girls on the street were edgy, looking twice into cars at men who leaned forward to ask them if they were "dating." They tried to look out for each other, too. They went off alone, but their friends attempted to remember the cars or something about the johns they left with.

A number of the suspected victims seemed to disappear in bunches, several of them within a very short time period from the same spots on the highway. It was almost as if he were a fisherman who discovered a well-stocked location and returned again and again until he had "fished" that part of the lake dry.

Now, in 1983, his favorite trolling areas were along the Pac HiWay, with emphasis on the cross streets of S. 144th, S. 188th, and S. 216th.

CONSTANCE ELIZABETH NAON, twenty, drove a fifteen-year-old Chevrolet Camaro that she often parked at the Red Lion at 188th when she was working the street. She was a lovely young woman with perfectly symmetrical features, and she did pretty well financially, but she had a drug problem that ate away at her money. She also had a straight job at a sausage factory, and on June 8, she planned to pick up her paycheck there. She called her boyfriend to say she was on her way to visit him and would be there in twenty minutes. She never arrived.

Police found her Camaro in the Red Lion lot late in June. It was dusty and cluttered with Connie's possessions, but there was nothing in it that could tell them where she was or what might have happened to her.

FOR A LONG TIME, it was difficult for her family and friends to know just when Carrie Ann Rois, sixteen, dropped out of sight. Carrie, who looked like the prettiest cheerleader in any high school, probably vanished in mid-July 1983. Originally, a close friend thought she'd gone missing in March, but, later, task force detective Mike Hatch talked to enough people to realize that Carrie had been seen on Memorial Day weekend, and for perhaps a month after that.

How could a family lose track of a daughter who was so young? It was hard for her mother, Judy DeLeone, to keep up with Carrie, even though she tried her best to rein in her emotionally fragile and headstrong daughter. They seemed to have everything working against them. Judy married twice after she was divorced from Carrie's father and their family seemed always to be in a state of flux.

Carrie was in the ninth grade in Nelson Middle School in Renton in November 1981 when Judy married for the third time. A few months later, in the spring of 1982, Carrie told social workers that her stepfather had molested her. She remained in the home until the second time she reported he was sexually abusing her. Carrie went to live with her natural father, but they didn't get along either. Carrie claimed that he'd hit her and left bumps on her head. She ran away and ended up at the Youth Service Center. When her father was notified, he said, "Send her home," but Carrie wouldn't go. She ran away again, walking out the front door of the detention center.

Carrie always had a lot of friends, and she usually had a girlfriend buddy who ran away with her, and other friends who gave them a room to live in for a while. At one point, Carrie and her fellow runaway lived in the laundry room of somebody's house.

Judy DeLeone would never live with Carrie again, but she worried about her constantly. She left the husband Carrie had reported for abuse, but her daughter still refused to come home. And then, on Christmas Eve, 1982, Carrie called her mother from a pay phone to tell her she missed her. Judy picked her up and they shared a wonderful Christmas Eve together, talking and catching up. Still, Carrie didn't want to move back home. Carrie had a court-appointed guardian and Judy couldn't force her to come home. Trying to keep their tenuous connection alive, Judy agreed to drive her to the house where she was staying with a girlfriend.

From time to time, Carrie was placed in group homes and she always got along well. One social worker recalled that Carrie idolized Brooke Shields, whom she felt she resembled, and wanted to be a model herself one day. But she was a jackrabbit, a runner who was always game for a walk on the wild side. And she was also a paradox. While she was attending Garfield High School in Seattle in the spring of 1983, she played the flute and wore her uniform proudly in the marching band. Her grandfather, Ken Rois, bought her the flute, hoping her interest in music would settle her down.

It did, for a while, but then somebody stole the flute from her school locker. Carrie loved parties and had experimented with marijuana, cocaine, and alcohol. Her best friend, and runaway buddy, Margaret, was placed in the Echo Glen juvenile facility, and when she was released, she found that Carrie was hanging out at a lot of places that could be dangerous, including "My Place," a topless tavern on the Strip. She had new friends, many of whom Margaret didn't know.

Margaret was convinced that Carrie had disappeared on March 24, 1983. "The last time I saw her," she told Mike Hatch, "Carrie was standing near the Safeway store on Rainier and Genessee Street. She was wearing blue jeans and a tan coat with high brown boots. She had on pink or purple nail polish."

But Carrie was still going to high school at that point, and records show she skipped school only a couple of times a week. She was a striking girl, five feet eight, with green eyes, and such exquisite features that anyone who saw her remembered her.

Neither her mother nor her father knew where she was, but there was every reason to believe she was alive in March, April, May, June, and at least some part of July in 1983. But she was working the streets, using the unlikely pseudonym of "Silver Champagne." She usually wore "a ton of makeup," according to a university student she dated for a while. "I told her she was so beautiful that she didn't need makeup," he said, "but she just laughed."

Task force detectives learned that Carrie and her new friend Lisa had been frequenting the Strip along the two block area of S. 142nd to S. 144th in the late spring of 1983. She had had many friends who kept track of her. Several of them recalled hearing her talk about a peculiar experience with a "trick." Although she didn't mention the man by name, she said he had taken her far away from the Strip, driving her up almost to the summit of Snoqualmie Pass, an area that was fifty miles from the airport, to "see the snow." Spring blizzards are not at all unusual in the high elevations of the pass, as drivers who head up to ski or to drive to eastern Washington know.

Carrie had come back from her unusual jaunt. Her friends had seen her get out of a pickup truck safely, albeit a little intoxicated. All they remembered about the driver was that he was a white male who wore a baseball cap. Carrie said that he was "kind of weird," but she didn't elaborate. They thought it was very strange for her to have agreed to go on such a long trip with a john.

What they recalled about the truck was that it was brown and tan, or brown and white, with a camper on it. It wasn't a new truck, but no one who saw Carrie get out of it could give the make or the year accurately.

And then, sometime in June or July of 1983, Carrie Rois simply vanished. Her grandfather moved back from Honolulu to help look for her. Judy DeLeone was plunged into guilt and remorse and terrible worry. She had always believed that one day Carrie was going to come home, older and wiser, and not so anxious to run away. But the months ground on and there was no word at all from her daughter.

Christmas Eve, 1983, came and Judy sat by the phone, hoping against hope that Carrie would come out of hiding and call as she had the year before. But the phone was silent.

At least one other teenager had disappeared from the airport strip in midsummer 1983, although her ties to home had stretched so thin that no one reported her missing. Her name was Tammy Liles and she was sixteen years old in June 1983.

I HAD LIVED in Des Moines since 1963, and the corner of Pac HiWay and S. 216th was as familiar to me as our main street was. There were many reasons to patronize the shopping area at the highway intersection. The Safeway was up on the southwest corner of the highway, along with Bartell's drugstore, a popular Seattle family's chain. There was a hot-tub store run by a family with kids in my kids' classes, and I bought one for the backyard of the first house I'd ever purchased on my own. I'd almost signed an earnest money agreement on a house a block away from the 216th intersection until I found out the whole area was about to be taken over by the Port Authority and the houses torn down. Most people in Des Moines went to Furney's nursery with its acres of roses, trees, rhododendrons, and bedding plants, and so did I, pulling one of their red wagons around to fill with plants. That was close to the northwest corner.

Locals didn't know that the Three Bears Motel was a hot bed motel; it looked cozy from the outside. So did the New West Motel, which was next door to a long-term care facility. In the early eighties, this section of the old highway wasn't considered sleazy. My family had eaten dinner at the Blockhouse Restaurant a few blocks south to celebrate birthdays, holidays, graduations, and sometimes after somber funerals and memorial services.

Even though I was a true-crime writer, I didn't think of this section of Pac HiWay as part of the Strip; the dangerous part was supposed to be several miles north, near the airport. Ironically, S. 216th was the intersection where I always felt safe after I'd driven up the dark, winding road from the Kent Valley floor and the Green River.

But I was misinformed. I had no idea how many of the missing girls lay dead within a few blocks of that intersection. Nor did anyone else.

ROSE JOHNSON* was, arguably, one of the more beautiful of the dozens of girls who vanished during the Green River Killer's peak killing swath from 1982 to 1984. In many ways, her life before she landed on the streets was similar to her sacrificed sisters; in some ways it was far worse.

Rose grew up in the south end, dropped out of school before graduating, and was allegedly the target of incest by several male members of her family. Her mother, a woman of strong opinions who was angry at life, angry at her, and angry at her own circumstances, blamed her daughter for the breakup of her marriage. Rather than taking Rose's side when she came to her and said her father was molesting her, her mother saw her, instead, as a rival. She accused the teenager of deliberately trying to seduce him, and sided with her husband.

Enraged, he made life hell for his daughter. She had no privacy; he took her bedroom door off the hinges. She had to dress in her closet or behind a blanket. She never knew when someone would come in. When her window was broken in the coldest part of the winter, her father refused to fix it, and she was freezing, despite the cardboard she wedged into the empty frame. He padlocked the cupboards and the refrigerator so she couldn't find anything to eat at home. It was up to Rose to survive any way she could.

The only thing she had to sell was herself. She bought an old beater of a car with some of the first money she made; if she couldn't make enough to pay for a motel room, she had the car to sleep in. It wasn't that bad in the summer months.

Rose was afraid of her mother, more because of the venom she seemed to exude than for any physical punishment the older woman administered. Even when her father finally moved out, Rose didn't go home. It was still dangerous for her there.

"The first time I met Rose's mom," one of her close friends recalled, "it was in the Fred Meyer store in Burien. She walked up behind Rose real quietly, and she scared her. They had a few words that weren't very nice. When the woman walked away, I asked Rose who in the world that woman was. She said it was her mom. I couldn't believe it. She was so mean to Rose. I could see that Rose didn't mean anything to her."

Rose sometimes parked her car in the lot at the Red Lion Motel at 188th and Pac HiWay, but more often she left it in a little weed-filled lot next to Don the Barber's at 142nd and the highway. Don recognized her because she was there often. As he cut hair, his window looked directly over to the lot, and he saw Rose meet johns there dozens of times. She would lock her car and leave with different men, and then come back later. Don recalled that he noticed her because she was very pretty and very young, and unlike most of the girls who strolled the Strip, he never saw her with a male protector.

"I don't know how long she'd been parking there," Don said, "but one day, she just wasn't there. Or the next. Or any day. She never came back. When I saw her picture in the paper later, I realized why she wasn't there any longer. She was dead. He got her, too."

What Don did not know was something that would shock him more than Rose's disappearance. The man who killed her had sat in his barber chair regularly for decades, chatting amiably and laughing at Don's jokes.

Like many of the Green River Killer's victims, Rose sniffed cocaine when she could afford it. It blurred the harsh edges of her life and gave her a false sense that things were looking up. Early on the day she vanished, she had called a friend and arranged to buy some cocaine.

"When she never showed up, I didn't think too much about it," her friend said. "'Cause that's how people like that are. But a few days later a friend of ours called and asked me if I'd seen Rose, and I told her I'd talked to her just a few days earlier. We spread the word and tried to find her, but none of us ever saw her again."

Her family didn't report her missing for a long time. When they did, they were vociferous about their anger with the task force.

14

THE BOY GREW OLDER but he was still behind in school and in social interaction. His parents had moved yet again—from Idaho to Seattle—and he had to start all over trying to make friends. He was about thirteen now and he still wet the bed most nights. His mother was out of patience. Now that he was on the verge of puberty, he was both angered and sexually excited when she washed urine from his genitals. She had so much control over him. She was tougher in her way than his father was. She kind of bossed his father around, too, and she was the one who got things done. He and his brothers called her "the warden."

She went off to her job dressed for success, wearing nice clothes and jewelry and with her face made up perfectly. She was very popular and competent in her job. When he was smaller, back in Idaho, she had been kind to him, and they worked on puzzles together. Even though she was gone all day working in their father's gas station, he sort of remembered that she had come home to cook. It didn't matter; they weren't hungry, and they had plenty of things to do. And she had tried to help him with reading. "I had a really hard time reading."

But his mother wanted things really clean and scrubbed away at his genitals after he wet the bed. Once aware that hands touching his penis felt good, he thought about sex quite a bit. It wasn't a subject that was mentioned or explained in his home and so he didn't ask questions about whether what he felt was normal or not. From something his mother had said, he did know that masturbation was one of the worst sins of all. Worse than raping someone.

Two girls about his age lived right next door to their Seattle house. They had a pool and he was able to watch them surreptitiously as they splashed around in their bathing suits. They didn't know he was watching, so he was often invited over to join them.

He became a window-peeper, or, rather, he tried to see through blinds. He had a crush on one of the neighbor girls, whom he termed "an older lady," although she was really only seventeen. He hung out with her younger brothers and was at her house a couple of times a week, watching television.

By this time, he often got erections, and he almost always did when he was in her living room. That summer, she watched the TV set from an easy chair, but he sat on the floor and managed to slyly pull aside his shorts so that she could see his erect penis if she happened to glance his way. He thought she'd be impressed and want to have sex with him, but she never gave any sign she'd seen him.

Although she didn't appear to notice that he was exposing himself, he fantasized about talking to her and asking her to have sex with him. He was fourteen, but he was still in the sixth grade, taller than almost everyone else in his class because he'd been held back.

He once looked into her bedroom window at night, hoping to catch a glimpse of her in her underwear, or maybe even with no clothes on at all. He found she had pulled down all the shades. He rapped softly on the window, thinking she might come out and join him, or maybe even ask him into her bed. But, suddenly, the lights went on and he heard the front door of her house open and the sound of heavy footsteps. Her father raced around the house and almost caught him. He managed to run home just in time.

Once, while he was alone with a younger girl cousin, he enticed her into the woods by giving her a nickel. There, he put his hand up her skirt and touched her between her legs. But she tattled and he was punished.

Sex occupied his thoughts, but he had no outlet. He became a frotteur, cleverly brushing himself against girls, or so he thought. His hands would drift across girls' and women's breasts as if accidentally. Sometimes, they stared hard at him as if they knew what he was up to. He had to be careful not to touch the same girls too many times and make them suspicious.

He was way behind his class, and now he even had trouble keeping up with kids who were younger. He was angry a lot of the time, but you couldn't tell it by looking at him. He didn't have any friends outside of school and he considered himself a "loner." Nobody even cared enough about what he was doing to punish him. He could pretty much do what he wanted, and nobody told him not to—because they didn't know.

He enjoyed hurting things, killing birds in the fruit trees in his backyard. But, then, so did his brothers. They shot at birds with their BB guns and laughed when they dropped to the ground. Sometimes they hit their targets and the birds flew away, but they flew crooked.

One day he was alone at home and he felt mad at everyone. One of their cats came up to him, wanting to be petted. But he was mad at the cat, too. He got an idea. His family camped out quite often and they had picnic coolers that shut down tight to keep the food inside cold as long as possible.

He grabbed the cat and forced it into the cooler, and then he shut the lid tightly. He made himself wait until the next day to look inside again. The cat was stiff, dead. It had clawed the inside of the cooler in its fight to get out, but someone would have to look closely at the hard white surface to see the scratches. He was pleased that it hadn't been able to escape suffocation.

His anger sated, at least for the moment, he got rid of the cat's body, although he claimed a long time later that he really couldn't remember what he did with it. They lived on a busy road and cats were always getting killed. Maybe he threw it out there and figured nobody would know the difference. Maybe he buried it someplace or put it under a bush where the lower branches would hide it. After he got over his anger by hurting or killing something, he was always scared and hurried to cover up what he'd done so no one would know.

He washed out the cooler and put it back where he'd found it. He didn't tell anyone about the cat, not even his brothers. He figured they had so many cats around that no one would ever notice.

He was thirteen or fourteen when he discovered that killing something made him feel strong and important. What more power could anyone have than deciding what was going to live and what was going to die? When people laughed at him, he had secrets now that they couldn't guess.

He had carried a knife with him everywhere he went ever since he was in the sixth grade. It was black and had four blades that folded out of it. He liked the feel of it in his pocket.

Did he plan what he did? No, he was sure he hadn't. He hadn't planned to break all those windows at his school; it "just happened" when he picked up the first rock. He sometimes wondered why he did "bad things."

Either the school or his mother made him see a psychologist after they found out that he'd broken so many windows again. He himself wasn't sure why he had done it. One minute he wasn't thinking about it, and the next minute he'd had a rock in his hand. And it felt good watching the glass shatter and fall to the ground. The psychologist tried to hypnotize him, but it didn't work. He had too much control over his mind for that. His parents had to pay for what he'd done, and they were angry.

He was sure he wasn't expecting to do anything to the little boy either. He was walking toward a dance at his junior high school that evening, and found himself in a lot where there were trees and bushes. When the six-year-old boy came by, he said he was surprised to find himself reaching out to pull him into the bushes. And then he had the knife out and open, or maybe he'd already had the blade exposed.

He stabbed the little boy just once, a quick jab that pierced the child's kidney. When he pulled the knife out, there were gushes of blood. He felt ashamed for just a moment, but he walked away as if everything was normal.

And then he ran and hid in the basement again. He wasn't afraid the boy was going to die; he was much more worried that he was going to live and be able to identify him. He stayed around his house for quite a while after that. He didn't want to draw attention to himself.

Sometimes he wondered which bad things were worse. It almost seemed that they were worse when he got caught. If he didn't get caught and wasn't punished, he could make them go away in his head more easily. The kids at school knew that he was the one who broke the windows, and he suspected that some of them admired him for doing it, that they might have wanted to do it themselves sometimes.

But it might be different if they knew he was the one who stabbed the little boy, because they could think that it was a cowardly thing to do. What would people think of him for hurting a little kid? He might even have to go to reform school if people knew it was him. In the end, he was kind of proud that he didn't get caught. But he was scared, too, of how much trouble he would be in if anyone found out. A teacher had found the little boy and carried him to a safe place where an ambulance and police were called. The boy lived but didn't tell who had stabbed him because the child didn't know. So no one found out and he didn't get punished.

Bad things happening to people excited him. A little boy drowned in the public swimming area at Angle Lake while he was swimming there, and he thought about that a lot. He was really fascinated when a woman who lived near them was murdered, and he worked the details of what might have happened to her over and over in his head. It was on a hot summer night and she went for a walk around the block with only her bathrobe on—just to cool off. Somebody strangled her with the cord of her bathrobe.

He talked about that mystery a lot with his father. He thought she got raped, too, and he kept going over different scenarios. Maybe she had a fight with her husband because she spent too much or she was cheating on him. Maybe it was a neighbor or the woman's secret lover or even two guys working together. There were many "maybes" to think about, and he was so clever at coming up with different motives and methods and suspects that he thought he would make a good detective.

15

THE PATTERN of abduction was moving south—down to S. 216th and Pac HiWay. Both Debra Bonner and Marie Malvar had vanished near the Three Bears, albeit months apart. And those of us who lived in Des Moines didn't feel nearly as distanced from criminal violence as we once had, perhaps smugly sheltered in our little town that curved around Puget Sound.

Keli Kay McGinness was a striking blonde, a buxom eighteen-year-old with a heart-shaped face and blue eyes with a thick fringe of dark lashes. She divided her time between the Camp in Portland and the Strip in Seattle, sometimes even traveling to southern California. In the early summer of 1983, she and her boyfriend had left Portland to see how things were going in Seattle, hometown to both of them.

 WHEN they worked Portland, Keli usually started on Union Avenue early in the evenings, and then moved to the downtown area around eleven PM. She was very self-assured and seemed older than she actually was. "She was at the top of the ladder of the girls on the street," a woman who had worked in the Camp in the eighties remembered. "Keli wore this white rabbit-hair coat and I could never tell if she wore a wig or whether her hair was just bleached and she used lots of hair spray. She was really friendly with a girl named Pammy Avent, whose street name was 'Annette.' Keli had a lot of street names."

My correspondent, who was a mature woman in a completely straight career when she contacted me, asked that her identity not be revealed as she looked back at the way the Camp was twenty years before. Of course, I assured her that it would not be.

"A lot of the girls were out there for the social aspect besides [being there] to make money—playing video games and visiting with each other at the Fun Center—but not Keli. She was focused on making money. She usually walked alone while the other girls walked in pairs. Keli had this strut and she stared into every car that passed her."

The last time anyone who knew her remembered seeing Keli McGinness was at seven thirty PM on June 28, 1983, at the now-familiar corner of the Pac HiWay and S. 216th. That night she was wearing a tan short-sleeved sweater, blue jeans, a long camel-hair coat, and very high heels. The Three Bears Motel was on that corner, and the desk clerk's register showed that she checked in at ten PM.

Keli's boyfriend reported her missing the next day, but Des Moines police detective sergeant Bob Fox wasn't convinced that she had met with foul play. He had seen too many adults and older teenagers leave of their own accord. He told a reporter, "There's no law against a person saying, 'I've had it. I'm leaving.' I just don't know, and I don't think we will know, until we hear from her one way or another."

Keli was so attractive that people who saw her remembered her, but like Marie and Gail and so many girls before her, nobody along the Strip saw her.

THERE WERE OTHER CASES that might or might not be connected to the series of disappearances in 1983, and the murdered victims in the last half of 1982, enough cases that it set investigators' teeth on edge, wondering just who might be out there, always alert to vulnerable females.

On July 9, 1983, King County patrol officers took a report from an eighteen-year-old secretary who had been violently raped. She was a classic victim: a little intoxicated, upset over an argument with her boyfriend, so upset that she stomped away from their table at Anthony's Homeport restaurant at the Des Moines marina. She'd been served alcohol because she carried fake I.D. Crying and angry, she was in a phone booth calling friends for a ride home when a stranger in a pickup truck pulled over and asked if she needed a ride.

She shook her head and tried to pull the folding door closed, but the man grabbed her and forced her into his truck before she could react.

"I'll take you anywhere you want," he said, now oddly polite.

She gave him her boyfriend's address in tony Three Tree Point, hoping against hope that she would spot him on his way home and he would save her. The driver followed her directions but he drove right by the address, ignoring her protests. He headed toward the small town of Burien, grabbing her hair in his fist and telling her he would kill her if she tried to escape. In Burien, he parked on the grounds of a boarded-up school and raped her. Fighting him, she was finally able to hit the door handle and tumble out of the truck. She ran, and a nearby resident responded to her frantic knocking.

Treated in a hospital's emergency room, the frightened girl could tell officers only that the man told her his name was "John."

"What did he look like?"

She shook her head. "I don't know. It was too dark."

There was no suggestion that this victim was working the streets. She had simply been in the wrong place at the very wrong time. Her description of the pickup truck was similar to the trucks seen on Pac HiWay.

Keli McGinness's last-known location was about two miles from the Des Moines marina. Two disturbing incidents nine days apart. Ironically, the articles about both eighteen-year-olds shared space on the front page of the *Des Moines News*.

ON MAY 8, 1983, King County detectives had quietly investigated the discovery of a woman's body in a location some distance from the Green River and the Strip. The circumstances surrounding this body site were so bizarrely ritualistic that they had first thought it had to be an entirely different killer. And the investigators were scrupulous about not releasing full information on what they found. Should they encounter either the actual murderer or a compulsive confessor, only they and the true killer would know these details.

Carol Ann Christensen, twenty-two, was the single mother of a five-year-old daughter, and she'd been excited on May 3 because she had finally landed a job after a long time of looking for work. Carol Ann lived near the Pac HiWay, and she shopped there, on foot because she had no car—but she was definitely not a prostitute. Her new job was as a waitress at the Barn Door Tavern at 148th and the highway. It was close to the White Shutters, the restaurant/bar that attracted singles, and only two or three blocks from the small mobile home park where Carol Ann lived, close enough that she could walk to work.

∎

CAROL ANN had worked only a day or two when she failed to come home one night. Her mother was frantic. Carol adored her little girl, Sarah, and would not have deliberately left her. If she could get home to Sarah, she would have.

The terrible answer to where Carol Ann had gone came within a few days. Carol Ann Christensen's body was discovered in an area known as Maple Valley, which is about twenty miles east of the airport Strip. Much of Maple Valley would be built up in the next twenty years, but it was heavily wooded when Carol Ann disappeared. A family searching for edible mushrooms had to go only a short distance off the road into a shady patch of salal, ferns, and fir trees to find the precious morels and chanterelles bursting from the woods' leafy floor.

They forgot all thoughts of mushroom-hunting when they came upon a grotesque tableau. A woman lay on her back in a half-sitting position, but they could not see her face. Someone had pulled a brown grocery bag over her head. Her hands were folded across her belly, and they were topped with ground sausage meat. Two dead trout, cleaned and gutted, lay vertically along her throat. A wine bottle that had once held Lambrusco had been placed across her lower abdomen.

This was a "staged scene," not uncommon to sexual psychopaths. It is a way to taunt detectives, silently saying "Catch me! Catch me!" And at the same time, announcing, "Look at how clever I am, and you don't even know who did this. You can't catch me!"

Carol Ann wasn't in the river, and she hadn't been left close to the Pacific Highway. She was not a prostitute. Still, like the first Green River victims, she had been strangled by ligature, in her case with a bright yellow, braided plastic rope, which her killer had left behind.

She was fully clothed in jeans; a Seattle Seahawk shirt; a white, zippered, polyester jacket; and blue-and-gray running shoes. The grocery bag said "Larry's Market" on it, the high-end supermarket located on the Strip.

Carol Ann Christensen's murder was originally investigated by the Major Crimes Unit of the sheriff's department, rather than the Green River Task Force, because both her lifestyle and the M.O. in her death were so different. Later, when her address and employment indicated she had lived and worked right in the kill zone, it was quite possible that she might well belong on the list with the other victims.

Although it is rare for serial killers—and by 1983, the Green River Killer *was* referred to that way—to murder someone they know personally, it is not unheard of. Carol Ann Christensen might have believed that she was going on a date, a picnic, with someone she knew and trusted. She was dressed for a picnic and the Maple Valley woods where she was found were pleasant in the spring. But even though her body was not that far from the road, the woods were dark and there weren't that many people around. If the man she was with took off his deceptively friendly mask and began to hurt her, her screams for help would not have been heard.

Eventually, Carol Ann's name went on the ever-growing list of possible victims of the Green River Killer.

It was fortunate that the King County investigators had followed their usual triangulation measurement routine in the Maple Valley woods. No one would recognize them now. They have become a sprawling neighborhood of modern homes called Patrick's Faire.

There would be no more bizarre staged body sites. Whatever point the killer had wanted to make had evidently been accomplished. As Pierce Brooks always did, the task force investigators kept trying to put themselves into the mind of the killer, to think as he thought, to walk where he walked, but it was very, very difficult.

He didn't think like anyone they could ever imagine. He wasn't crazy, of that they were sure. If he was insane, he would have made some misstep by now, flipped out and done something to make them notice him. Instead, he was still playing his bizarre, malignant games.

16

ALTHOUGH her boyfriend insisted that Keli Kay McGinness would have contacted him if she was okay, out of all the young women who had disappeared, the task force and her own girlfriends figured that Keli had made it out safely. She had sometimes hinted that she might just change her lifestyle and go for something more rarefied, and she had told her mother that if she ever really got out of Seattle, she wouldn't be back.

She had the looks and the brains to accomplish that. And, surprisingly, Keli had the background that would let her slip easily into an upper-class milieu. Her whole life had been a study in contrasts.

She'd grown up too fast, though, maybe because she had too many father figures, perhaps because she had gone from hard times to wealth and back again.

Keli's birth parents were attractive, personable, and doing well financially. Her father was a handsome and garrulous car salesman, well known in the south end of King County, who earned good money. Her mother was a beautiful singer with high hopes of becoming a star.

In 1984, Elizabeth Rhodes, a *Seattle Times* reporter, did a remarkable reconstruction of Keli's life. Rhodes, who is now the *Times*'s reigning expert on real estate, hasn't forgotten the young woman she wrote about two decades ago: "Keli isn't easy to forget," she told me. "You have to wonder where she is now."

Like my own daughter, Leslie, Keli was born in Virginia Mason Hospital in Seattle. Keli would use many street names and many birthdates, but her real birthday was April 17, 1965, and if she is alive, Keli would be in her late thirties now.

Her parents' union lasted until she was two and a half and her mother was twenty-seven. By accepting small gigs in local venues, Keli's mother was able to support the two of them, and they grew very close. Like the popular song by Helen Reddy, Keli was one among many of the missing girls who had bonded early with their mothers—"You and Me Against the World."

Two years later, Keli's mother married an entrepreneur whose fortunes were soaring. He was more than willing to share his wealth with his bride and new stepdaughter. They all lived on Queen Anne Hill in a virtual mansion, a home that would cost well over two million dollars today. Keli Kay had sixteen rooms to romp through, and she could sit on a padded window seat and gaze through bay windows at downtown Seattle and the ferry boats on Puget Sound.

The pretty little girl had her own horse and riding lessons, music lessons, weeks in exclusive summer camps where other rich girls went, and orthodonture that corrected her slight overbite. Her hair was brown then, and her grade school pictures show her smiling carefully so her braces wouldn't show.

As her stepfather's business acumen increased, both of Keli's parents worked long hours. She often spent more time with a babysitter and housekeeper than she did with her mother and stepfather, but she was a bright child and she got A's in school and won spelling bees. She was lonely a lot of the time, but she adored her mother and was especially happy when they were together.

"We were very, very close," her mother told Elizabeth Rhodes many years later. "I loved her as a daughter, but she was also fun to do things with. The best thing about Keli was her wonderful personality. She had a witty personality, quick and sharp."

The small family had lots of good times—trips to Hawaii and Mexico, cruising on their fifty-foot yacht from Elliott Bay to the San Juan Islands—and mother and daughter had all the wonderful clothes they wanted. It was a lifestyle few Seattleites enjoyed. It lasted only five years. Then her mother and stepfather divorced, and the life that Keli Kay had thrived in was over, a quick curtain dropping down on her world of privilege. She and her mother went back to an ordinary existence.

She was almost eleven then, a particularly disturbing time for young girls. More than the wealth and all that came with it, Keli Kay had to feel that her stepfather had divorced her, too. Her father had left her, and now another father figure walked away from her. To salve her own feelings, she blamed her mother for the divorce.

Quite soon, her mother married again. This stepfather wasn't rich and he wasn't very nice. Her mother came home from work early one day and caught him throwing a rocking chair at Keli. Her leg was already bruised from a beating with a wooden coat hanger. That was the end of that marriage; her mother would not allow anyone to hurt Keli.

Keli was thirteen, an age when even girls in stable families act out and become "different people." Any parent of a teenage daughter can attest to that. And Keli had lost too much, too rapidly. Her grades dropped and she began to run away from home—but only for a day or two. She, who had always been an obedient and fun child to be around, became sullen and defiant. She was still smart and still creative, but she saw the world through a dark cloud now. Life had betrayed her.

Keli had also suffered the worst experience any young teen can. She was babysitting when she answered the door without checking to see who was there. It was five teenage boys, drunk and rowdy. They pushed their way in and Keli went through a horrendous ordeal of sexual attack—a gang rape.

At three AM, her mother got a call to come to a Seattle hospital and found her thirteen-year-old daughter traumatized to the point that she couldn't speak. Keli had known some of the boys and was afraid of them, because they were leaders in the wilder crowd at a local high school. If she agreed to testify against them in court, she thought they would hurt her more. And besides, she was ashamed.

Keli wrote a poem a little while later, a poem her mother didn't find until she had run away from home for good. Elizabeth Rhodes quoted it in her article:

> "Looking back through the pages of yesterday,
>   All the childhood dreams that drifted away
> Even the box of crayons on the shelf
> Reflect bits and pieces of myself . . .

She was only fourteen when she wrote that, regretting that she "had to grow up." Her life as she knew it was over, and there were hints that growing up hadn't been the usual maturation that the years bring. She ended her poem:

> "But I know now in my heart and mind
> I had to leave it all behind
> And as a tear comes slowly to my eye,
> I stop and ask myself,
> Why?"
>   —Keli K. McGinness

And then Keli McGinness was on the streets, as if somehow the pain would lessen there. She bleached her hair and wore clothes that played up her D-cup bust. If you can call it that, she was a success, working the Sunset Strip in Hollywood, The Camp in Portland, and coming home to Seattle's Strip. She fell in love with an African American boy two years older than she, and she was pregnant at fifteen.

Keli Kay carried two babies to term before she was eighteen. Unlike Mary Bridget's, both of Keli Kay's babies survived.

Did Keli herself survive? Probably not; her status is still in limbo. Her first baby, a boy, was born in California. She brought him home to Seattle to show to his two grandmothers. His paternal grandmother offered to look after him, but Keli decided that he should be adopted, and he was.

But both teenage parents regretted that, and within six months, Keli was pregnant again. They had planned this baby as much as they were capable of planning in a lifestyle that involved constantly moving and living in cheap motels. Somehow they thought that keeping this second baby would make their love stronger and impress their families that they were mature.

It was a little girl, a lovely baby girl who combined the most attractive features of both her young parents. Again, the father's mother was willing to help raise her, but Keli's mother had never been able to accept her daughter's boyfriend. She blamed him for Keli's lifestyle, and she was opposed to a biracial union. Keli told her she was prejudiced, which she was, but only because of what she felt Keli's lover had done to her.

She had pleaded in vain with Keli to leave the streets. She didn't have to have a pimp/boyfriend. Her mother would help her. They were still friends as well as mother and daughter, although Keli was the worldly-wise one as her mother struggled to cope with what Keli had become. Still, they stayed in touch with each other, talking in the way people do whose experiences with life barely touched. They loved each other, but they couldn't help each other.

Keli tried to explain, "I'm a prostitute, Mom. How could I ever make the kind of money I am making now doing anything else?"

As her acquaintances from The Camp recalled, Keli did make top dollar. When it wasn't raining and cold out, the girls in Portland and Seattle could bring in more than $3,000 a week, although most of it was turned over to their pimps. Ironically, Keli's childhood, when she had moved easily among the wealthier members of Seattle society, gave her a polished image that attracted the richest johns.

But she couldn't do that and take care of her four-month-old baby girl, too. She was doing fine so far, and between Keli and her boyfriend, someone was always with her. But Keli knew she wasn't in a position to be a full-time mother. She took her baby to a religion-based child-care agency. No, she did not want to put her up for adoption. Keli asked that she be placed in a foster home, but just long enough for her to serve some jail time for an earlier prostitution arrest that was hanging over her head. She couldn't say exactly when she would be back to pick up the baby, but she insisted she was coming back. There was no longer someone in either her family or her boyfriend's family who was able to care for the infant, although they all said they loved her.

Keli McGinness showed up at the jail on May 25 and served her seven days, secure in her knowledge that her baby was already safe in a foster home.

Although both their parents disapproved—his mother was unable to even say the word *prostitution*—Keli's boyfriend picked her up from jail in his six-year-old Cadillac convertible and they drove to Portland, a regular pattern along "the circuit" for them. He waited in a restaurant lounge, as he always did, for Keli to come back with the money she had earned. As all the "boyfriends" of the missing women have said, he "really loved her" and worried about her, afraid she might meet some weirdo.

Keli herself felt fairly safe, even though she knew about the Green River Killer. She would not get into cars; she took tricks to motel rooms that she rented. She told people who loved her and cops who arrested her that "It won't happen to me."

Keli considered arrests part of the cost of doing business, and she was philosophical about fines and the jail time she occasionally had to serve. By adroitly changing her names, birth dates, and identification, she managed to skate free many times because the arresting officers couldn't find her current name in their records. But sometimes she got caught, and she would shrug her shoulders and accept the law's edicts, laughing as she said, "You got me!" She knew most of the vice detectives and she was polite with them, accepting the fact that sometimes it was their turn to win.

The vice cops did win in Portland on June 21, 1983, and Keli spent three days in jail in Oregon. Her legal schedule was crushing, though, and she had to be back in Seattle for a court appearance on June 28. She told her attorney that she would be back in time for that, but she didn't show up, and the judge ordered a bench warrant for her arrest. According to her boyfriend, they had come back to Seattle, but for some reason Keli didn't want to go to court. Instead, they spent that day together.

And then Keli checked into the Three Bears Motel. The desk clerk verified that. Her room cost about $22. A little after nine, she was on Pac HiWay, strolling down toward the Blockhouse Restaurant where the clientele, mostly Des Moines residents attracted by the prime rib, fried chicken, and the senior citizen discount, were having dessert, or sitting in the crowded bar as the live entertainment began. She wouldn't have found any johns there, but cars coming off the I-5 Freeway at the Kent–Des Moines exit would slow down at the sight of her.

Keli McGinness never returned to pick up her baby girl from the church agency. The baby's father said he didn't get any of the messages that the agency left for him. Their fourteen-month-old daughter was too young to know that her mother was gone, and there was no one else in the family who could take care of her. Keli's baby girl was adopted when no one came for her.

Keli's mother hadn't seen her since Mother's Day, 1981, when Keli drove to eastern Washington to see her. She hoped against hope that her daughter had decided to get lost somewhere far away. At least that would mean she was alive.

17

DURING the summer of 1983, the newspapers around Seattle ran a lot of stories about women who might or might not be missing, but they were seldom on the front page. And no two articles tabulated the same names. Some said a dozen were missing; other coverage wondered if it might be as many as nineteen. And they all vastly underrated the inherent danger of a deadly hunter who roved unchecked throughout King County. Somehow, he was still blending into the background, never drawing attention to himself.

Keli McGinness was the last to disappear in June, as far as the police knew. Coincidentally, the next girl on the list was also named Kelly, although she spelled it differently. She resembled all the other young women in that she was blessed with the freshness of youth, even those whose only photos were mug shots where they looked tired and sad.

Kelly Ware, twenty-three, smiled happily in the pictures her family had. She had long dark hair and huge brown eyes. She disappeared on July 18, 1983. Just like Cheryl Wims, Kelly was last seen in the central district in Seattle, an ethnically mixed neighborhood a few miles east of downtown, where streets crested and then plunged down a long hill toward the shores of Lake Washington.

■

IT HAD BEEN almost exactly a year since the first five bodies were found in the Green River, and yet the only other victim to be located who seemed to be linked to the GRK was Giselle Lovvorn, the self-confident blonde, who had a genius I.Q. and had been discovered in the deserted property area south of the airport. Surely, there were so many more lost girls out there somewhere, calling out silently to be found.

Now, slowly, as if the earth itself were aware of the dread anniversary, it began to give up the pathetic remains of more victims who had been left there.

On August 11, 1983, a couple, who had gone to pick apples from abandoned trees in the same overgrown yards where Giselle Lovvorn was left, stumbled across bones behind three empty houses. They hurried to call the sheriff's office.

What lay behind the shells of homes was merely a skeleton, still partially covered with brush and trash, much of it scattered by animals. But there was a skull, too. That could help immeasurably in identifying whose remains they were.

While anxious families watched and tensely waited, Dick Kraske spoke carefully to reporters. Yes, his office had some possibilities of matching the dental work of the deceased to known and suspected victims. The task force had compiled records from as many dentists' charts as possible.

The Green River victims, however, weren't the only missing persons near the airport. One long-unsolved mystery was the disappearance of Joyce Kennedy, a Pan American ticket agent, who had walked away from her counter after finishing her shift way back in 1976. She had never been found. Port of Seattle detectives had preserved her records for seven years.

Dick Kraske still didn't comment to reporters on a specific number of possible victims in the Green River cases because, quite frankly, he didn't know. He couldn't know. In August 1983, many who were gone had yet to be reported as missing. Kraske noted that, officially, there were seven young women missing—which, when added to the six girls who were known to be dead, made thirteen. But three of the missing hadn't been gone long enough to be in the state of complete decomposition that the apple tree victim was.

Dental charts showed matches to the skull that established the identity of Shawnda Leea Summers. Shawnda, who had once lived in Bellevue, had been missing since either October 7 or 8 in 1982. Her family had looked for her in vain for ten months, and it was likely that she had been here beneath the apple trees since her disappearance.

It was impossible to determine the cause of her death. There were no broken bones, no skull fractures, no bullet holes nicking the bones they'd found. Animals had scattered the tiny neck bones that might have indicated strangulation.

Two days after Shawnda was found beneath the airport flight path, another set of remains was found buried nearby. They were not easily identifiable, and the first victim to be known only as "Bones" was added as a possible to the Green River list.

Would he stop killing now that two more victims had been discovered? Would he find that the investigators were getting too close and feel as if he was in imminent danger of being caught? If he was true to serial killer form, the so-called Green River Killer might very well be spooked enough that his grim handiwork was being revealed to move on. It had to be only a matter of time before more of the missing women surfaced. And with every body discovery, the chance that he had unwittingly left something of himself behind, some tiny bit of damning evidence, would grow.

At least, the public was becoming more aware that there was someone truly menacing still roving free. The King County Sheriff's Office now had three hundred suspects, along with their names, descriptions, and witnesses' suspicions and accusations. Still, it was problematic whether the GRK was hidden somewhere in that roster of suspects.

I WAS HAVING a small taste of what the detectives were going through as they fielded waves of phone calls and messages. All during 1983, I received phone calls from strangers—at least one or two every night at first, and then about one a week. A lot of people had read my book *The Stranger Beside Me,* published two years before the Green River cases began. They wanted to compare their feelings with my own because I had known Ted Bundy well—or at least I thought I had. Many were hesitant to call the task force directly, or they were impatient because they hadn't had an immediate response. All the callers believed that they knew who the Green River Killer was. They didn't know how many other people felt the same way. I didn't mind being a conduit for frustrated tipsters, but I knew

I was getting only a minuscule number of tips compared to those the sheriff's detectives were juggling.

In the beginning, I found most of the callers believable. In fact, at the end of most calls, I'll admit I thought "This has got to be the right man," only to find the next tip, and the next, even more compelling.

Surprisingly—or perhaps not surprisingly—a lot of women were turning in their ex-husbands. Some even suspected the men they were still married to. I had once been a sex crimes detective in the Seattle Police Department for a year and a half. Combining that experience with the fourteen years I wrote about homicide and rape cases for fact-detective magazines, I thought I had heard everything. I was mistaken. My callers had been married to, or were still married to, some of the kinkiest men I'd ever heard of. And most of them lived in the south end of King County.

One woman said her husband invariably returned from sales trips with baggies full of various-colored pubic hair. Another's husband liked to cut up *Playboy* centerfolds and then play at rearranging the severed limbs and heads. And one ex-husband was apparently writing a book from the first-person viewpoint of a teenage streetwalker. His concerned ex-wife wondered if this was a bad enough sign for her to rethink reconciling with him. I didn't know, but I told her it certainly would have given me pause.

After hearing dozens of weird stories, I could see that the Green River cases were rapidly becoming the most difficult challenge any law enforcement group could encounter—not because the task force wasn't getting enough information from the public, but because it was getting too much.

It was fairly easy for me to discern when a tip was from a deranged informant. The woman who believed her son-in-law had killed a hundred people and hidden their bodies in the woods behind his house seemed suspect, especially when the number grew with every minute—and my watch indicated I'd been on the phone with her for more than an hour.

Psychics with "visions" called, but their information was never precise enough to be of any help. Barbara Kubik-Patten called me a lot, complaining that the task force detectives were not giving her the attention she deserved.

Still, many of my callers were quite rational people who were worried sick that someone they knew was the Green River Killer. I typed up the information that seemed to make an awful kind of sense and passed it on. Eventually, the task force detectives gave me a stack of their official tip sheets so I could streamline the process of sending them information on possible suspects. I didn't expect to hear back from them; they were too busy to report to me, or to anyone beyond the relatives of the missing girls.

18

HE DIDN'T STOP KILLING.

The fact that more bodies had been discovered seemed only to have added another dimension to the Green River Killer's game. He waited exactly one week after Shawnda Summers was found before he went out prowling again.

 APRIL DAWN BUTTRAM had just moved to Seattle from Spokane. She was almost eighteen, a pretty girl with blond hair and rosy cheeks, who would have looked in her element at a country church supper or a square dance. She was just a little over five feet tall, and she had sometimes weighed as much as 175, but she had slimmed down quite a bit. Hers was an all too familiar story. Overnight, April had changed from an obedient child to a teenager who quit school, tried drugs and alcohol, and wanted to party all the time.

She was eager to leave Spokane for the much more cosmopolitan city of Seattle, and she wouldn't listen to her mother's arguments against it. April was confident she could make it. When she reached her eighteenth birthday, she could collect a $10,000 trust fund a relative had set up for her. But in the middle of the summer of 1983, April planned to catch a ride to Seattle with two girlfriends, one of whom had permission to drive her mother's car on the trip. None of them had any notion of what dangers might be out there, or much common sense.

"One night," April's mother recalled, "I caught her crawling out of the window, carrying a suitcase. I gave up. I just told her, 'At least have the guts to go out the front door.' And she did. And she never came back."

The trio of Spokane girls had picked up three male hitchhikers on their way to Seattle, but they were lucky so far. The men didn't harm them—they were just grateful for the ride. A few days after they got to Seattle, April and her girlfriends split up.

The last accurate sighting of April Buttram was in the Rainier Valley in southeast Seattle around the middle of August 1983. She was still seventeen, but she was definitely planning to travel back to Spokane, three hundred miles away, to withdraw her trust fund money. She didn't make it. The money remained, untouched.

April was officially reported missing on March 24, 1984, after months of denial on her family's part. Her mother feared that she would get a phone call one day telling her that someone had found April's body, but there was only silence.

DEBORA MAY ABERNATHY was twenty-six, and she had come to Seattle along a circuitous route from Waco, Texas. She was a frail little woman who stood five feet tall and weighed only ninety pounds. She had very attractive features, but she sometimes put on horn-rimmed glasses and instantly looked like an old-time, stereotypical librarian, very prim and studious. She, her boyfriend, and her three-year-old son came to Seattle in late July of 1983 looking for a fresh start.

They were soon out of funds. A kindhearted couple met the down-and-out family in a store and invited them to stay in a room in their house until they could "get on their feet." Debora, wearing a burgundy jumpsuit, was headed toward downtown Seattle on September 5 the last time her little boy and boyfriend saw her.

TRACY ANN WINSTON was going to be twenty on September 29, 1983. Of all the young women one might expect to find in jail, Tracy seemed the least likely. She and her parents and two younger brothers all loved each other a lot. Any one of them would do anything to protect her. But Tracy had had her problems, too, almost from the moment she turned thirteen and plunged into puberty. It is, of course, an age when parents often wonder what has happened to their sweet daughters, and when daughters find their parents boring, old-fashioned, and uncaring. Tracy disappeared on September 12.

The investigators thought they had detected a pattern. If the

Green River Killer was responsible for these recent disappearances, he seemed to be taking victims a week apart at this point, almost exclusively on weeknights. Did the days of the week mean something important, or was it mere coincidence? But Tracy's vanishing broke the pattern. Counting back, they saw that she was last seen on a Sunday night/Monday morning between eleven PM and one AM. She had been in the King County Jail in downtown Seattle on a loitering charge.

Tracy bailed out of jail, and she was walking along Cherry Street, near the jail, when she was last seen by a cabdriver she knew who pulled up beside her. (It was not Melvyn Foster.) She needed a ride to the place where she was staying out in the north end of Seattle, but he told her he had a fare in the other direction out to the airport. Later, the driver told Green River investigators about their conversation.

"I'll be back in forty-five minutes," he'd promised Tracy. "Stay here and I'll see that you get where you need to go safely."

Tracy had called her father, Chuck Winston, from jail that night; she had been mortified at being locked up for the first and only time of her life. The experience had shocked her so much that she vowed she would never, ever do anything that might put her there again. She begged her father and her mother, Mertie, not to come down, saying, "I don't want you to see me in here, not like this. *Please* don't come down here."

And they had honored her wishes, fighting the urge to get in their car and hurry down to 9th and Cherry.

Mertie and Chuck Winston had been just about Tracy's age when she was born. "I was an older woman though," Mertie remembered. "In those days, a female was considered of age when she was eighteen, but a male had to be twenty-one, and I was a couple of months older than Chuck. His mother always looked upon me as a 'scarlet woman' who seduced her son."

Tracy was born in Tacoma, Washington, where her mother had been born. Mertie was working at the phone company and Chuck was getting ready to go into the air force, so Mertie lived with her maternal grandmother at the time of Tracy's birth. Their circumstances were such that Mertie couldn't take care of Tracy and work, too, but she fell in love with the baby who had deep dimples just like Chuck's. A Catholic Charities caseworker tried to help Mertie decide what would be best for Tracy.

At the time, it seemed that placing the baby in a foster home was the best plan. But Mertie's heart ached from missing her baby. She spent every extra penny she had to buy booties, blankets, and little dresses for Tracy and her caseworker saw to it that they were given to Tracy's temporary foster mother. "I found out later that the woman had a baby girl herself, and she was giving Tracy's things to *her* baby," Mertie recalled. "Finally, I couldn't stand it. Tracy was meant to be with me all the time, so I went and got her, and I was so happy."

Chuck Winston, whose talent and interests lay in military communications, was sent to an air base in Savannah, Georgia, and Mertie and Tracy went with him. They found a tiny apartment that had been carved out of an older home. Their landlady was very nice but the steamy, oppressive heat of Savannah was suffocating to anyone who had been raised in the Pacific Northwest. The worst, however, were the cockroaches.

"I'd never even seen one," Mertie said. "Our apartment had a huge kitchen—compared to the rest of the place—with a big old stove. It was pushed so close to the wall that I was afraid the electric cord might be wearing through, so I pushed and pulled it out into the room a little bit. Well! There was a large hole in the wall, and these cockroaches came flooding out all over the walls and floor. Tracy thought it was funny, but I freaked and was fending them off with a Downy fabric softener bottle. I grabbed Tracy and we went to a park until Chuck got home. I was holding Tracy and sobbing and I told Chuck, 'I have to go *home!*' He got very quiet and he said, 'Okay, I'll get you a bus ticket and send you back home.'

"That woke me up," Mertie said with a smile, "and I told him, 'No. I can take it.' We were there only six months. Chuck was slated to go to Vietnam . . . to be dropped into the backcountry ahead of troops and set up communications lines. Those men had a very high mortality rate, and the air force noted Chuck had a wife and a child, and they transferred him to Sacramento, California, instead. That's where our son Chip was born when Tracy was three and a half."

Chuck Winston considered a service career, and Mertie said she would go along with whatever he decided. But, in the end, he returned to the Boeing Airplane Company and they came home to Seattle. Their luck was teetering on the edge. By 1967, Boeing stock dropped and "They turned the lights off in Seattle." Chuck was laid off shortly thereafter, but he found a communications job with a Fresno company. Kevin, the youngest of their children was born in Fresno.

They were a typical family of the sixties and seventies, with a little house in Fresno that had a "swamp cooler" instead of air-conditioning and a blow-up wading pool in the backyard. "We used to drive up to see the sequoias with the kids to cool off," Mertie remembered. "The air smelled so clean up there, and it felt like home, but you could see the layers of heat coming up from the valley floor as we drove back to Fresno, and the kids would be cranky and tired by the time we got home."

Illness in their extended families led them to return to the Seattle area, and they settled in Burien, a few miles from the SeaTac Airport. Tracy had grown to be a tall, slender girl who had a special bond with her dad. Chuck taught her how to play baseball and she was one of only two girls allowed to join the boys' Little League team in District 7. "She could throw from center field to home plate without bouncing it once," her dad said proudly. At five feet nine, 150 pounds, Tracy played forward on the Glacier High School first-string girls' basketball team.

As close as Tracy was to her dad, she was a typical teenager with her mother, always taking the opposite stance from whatever Mertie suggested.

"It got so bad," Mertie Winston said with a wry smile, "that I couldn't even take her shopping. My mom would take her, and when Tracy brought home her clothes, I had to pretend to dislike the things I *did* like. Tracy would say, 'Do you like this?' and I'd kind of drag out my answer, ' . . . Yeah . . . ' And so she'd say, 'You don't like it. You hate it, but I'm going to wear it!' "

It was teenage stuff, and almost any mother would recognize it. "Tracy used to tell me, 'You're more concerned about what I wear than about who I am!' " Mertie said. "And all I could do was shake my head and say, 'You're changing so fast, I don't know who you are. . . . ' "

Things were still fairly normal for a family with a teenager. Mertie and Chuck went to all of Tracy's games and school activities. When there were concerts or other events that Tracy and her friends wanted to attend, a group of mothers arranged to drive them there and pick them up.

When Tracy was thirteen she became friends with a sixteen-year-old girl who was planning to run away. The girl coaxed Tracy, insisting that they should run away together—along with the other girl's eighteen-year-old boyfriend. Tracy was intrigued by the idea. The other girl's father called Chuck Winston and said, "We've got a problem."

And they did. Tracy always believed that she could help her friends with their problems. When the sixteen-year-old girl and her boyfriend actually made it to California, they called Tracy and urged her to steal money from her parents, take a bus, and meet them.

Reasoning with Tracy didn't do any good. "I told her that she was too young to deal with their problems, that she couldn't even handle her own problems yet," her mother said.

Chuck attempted to talk with Tracy and, thinking he would help her understand her mother, he told Tracy about how hard it was for Mertie when Tracy was just a baby, how she'd had to fight to get her back from Catholic Charities.

"It backfired," Mertie said. "She was shocked. Now, everything I did was not only wrong, it was wrong in triplicate. She said I didn't love her. I tried to explain that I was trying to protect her because I wanted her to be safe, not because I didn't love her. But she kept demanding that I prove I really loved her by letting her do what she wanted."

In vain, Mertie warned Tracy that she could not always judge others by how they looked or what they said, that she could not automatically trust people. "You can't just trust blindly."

"Mom," Tracy retorted, "I'm amazed that you have any friends at all."

One spring afternoon, as Tracy was trying to determine her own self-worth, she demanded that her mother prove to her that she was more important to Mertie than anyone else. They sat on the Winstons' front porch as Tracy spelled out what she needed in order to feel good about herself.

"I want you to love me more than you love Chip . . . or Kevin."

"Oh, Tracy," Mertie said, "I love you all differently. What do you want from me that you think I'm not giving you?"

"I want you to leave Dad and Chip and Kevin and just go away with me and we'll live by ourselves," Tracy said.

When Tracy Winston was little and could not yet count, she had told her mother, "I love you nine, and ten, and *twenty-one!*"—her little girl's idea of the most anyone could love somebody else. But now she was sixteen, and Mertie tried to explain what it was like, back in the days before Tracy could remember, how much she had always loved her oldest child, her only daughter, and how she had fought to keep her when she herself was not much older than Tracy. Most of all, Mertie told her that she did, indeed, love her "nine and ten and *twenty-one!*"

And Tracy, who rushed to trust everyone else, could not bring herself to trust her mother's love, even though it was her mother who stayed up late to pick her up from her job at a Dairy Queen in a borderline neighborhood. "I couldn't let two young kids close up the place all by themselves." Mertie sighed. "But she saw that as my controlling her—not that I was there because I loved her."

Tracy met a man who was nineteen, older than she was, a smooth and glib sociopath who was already on his way to prison. Her mother detested him, so, of course, Tracy adored him. Even his own sister warned Mertie and Chuck that they had to keep Tracy away from him if they could. "He's a con man," she said. "He's slick and he'll change her so you won't even recognize her."

His sister was right. Tracy fell totally in love with the man who had decided to groom her to be absolutely dedicated to what *he* wanted. "She would do anything he asked," her mother recalled. "And she was gone all the time—anywhere but home because we wouldn't let him call her. We tried tough love . . . and she left so she could see him. She thought he was a nice guy, and that we weren't giving him a chance.

"He controlled her," Mertie recalled, "and even when he was in prison at the Monroe Reformatory, he wrote her terrible letters: sexual letters, demanding letters, guilt-producing letters. They were clearly designed to appeal to her sense of fair play and concern for other people, and prove to her that he couldn't live without her. He said he loved her more than anyone else, and that she had to prove her love for him. Chuck wrote to the warden and asked him to stop this guy from writing to a teenage girl, and the warden said he couldn't do that; it would take away the prisoner's rights. And we weren't supposed to open his letters or throw them away because that was against the law."

When Tracy's lover was paroled from prison, her parents were beside themselves. "He called here once," Mertie said, "and I let him have it, using language I never use. I told him to stay away from Tracy. He never called again, but I think Tracy was seeing him. We got no help from anyone, and we didn't know what to do. I found out that Chuck was going out at night, looking for Tracy. He took an aluminum baseball bat with him because he had to go to really bad places. When the police said they couldn't do anything, Chuck finally walked into the Georgetown Precinct carrying his bat. He told them he was going to use it if he had to, and they said they'd have to arrest him if he did."

"So follow me then," Tracy's dad said.

Two uniformed officers did follow him as he went to a house where he thought the occupants were hiding Tracy. He banged on the door and demanded that they send Tracy out, but they said she wasn't there. Chuck Winston and the two cops looked through the house and found that indeed Tracy wasn't there, but she had been.

Tracy's parents seldom knew any longer where she was staying. She still came to see them—for Mother's Day and Father's Day, for Thanksgiving and Christmas. She wouldn't tell them where she was living, but she would come home for dinner.

"We always sent her away with care packages," Mertie said. "Mostly canned food, macaroni and cheese. For a while, she lived with a gay man who was a chef, and that seemed a little safer to us. Chuck would drive her home, but when he went back to see her, he'd find out that wasn't really where she lived."

The last time Mertie saw Tracy was on Mother's Day, 1983, and it was a good visit. They gave each other a big hug and Mertie said, "I love you!" and Tracy said, "I love you, too!"

Her parents had come to a place where they realized they couldn't follow Tracy everywhere. She was almost twenty now, and they had two other children to raise in a time when the job market was iffy. Mertie was working on commissions only, and her hours weren't predictable.

"I don't know if she was ever prostituting," Mertie said. "I can't imagine that it was a regular thing for her. I know she wasn't at all hardened. I talked to one of the jailers on that last weekend when Tracy was in there, and she told me, 'She has no business being here; she's like a frightened rabbit.'"

Tracy had been on the verge of changing her life that Sunday night when she told her dad not to come down and get her, not to see her in jail. "Oh, Daddy," she said, "you and Mom were so right. I'm going to get myself together, get my GED, go to school. I'm going to make you and Mom so proud of me."

As September passed, and then October and November, Mertie

Winston had an awful feeling. They hadn't heard a word from Tracy after her call from jail. She had said she was making a new start and they would be proud of her. Maybe she was taking steps in that direction and wanted to surprise them with a fait accompli, or at least with proof that she was on her way. But when Tracy didn't come home to take her brother Kevin trick or treating or to eat Thanksgiving dinner with the family, Mertie knew she had to do something.

"I thought that I would call up the police and report her as a missing person, and then they could check her social security number and tell us where she was working, or where she had been recently. And they took my report. I had to tell them that I just didn't know where she had lived last. 'I know my daughter,' " Mertie told police. " 'She *always* calls home, but now she hasn't.' Even after Tracy was out of the house, she always called at least once a week. When three or four weeks went by and she didn't call, I knew it was going to be bad. I wouldn't accept it in my heart, but I knew."

When the Winstons got a phone call from Randy Mullinax, who was very gentle as he told Chuck that he was one of the detectives working on the Green River Task Force, Mertie heard her husband say "Green River Killer?" and she felt an almost physical jolt. She knew what this call meant—that Tracy might be one of his victims, even though Mullinax assured them that there was nothing definite yet and his was just a follow-up call on the missing person's report.

Mertie took the phone and described how tall and slender Tracy was, how deep the dimples were on both sides of her mouth when she smiled, and how pretty she was. Mullinax had seen that when he looked at Tracy's mug shot from King County Jail. He had also seen how scared she looked, a doe caught in the headlights as the jail camera clicked away.

Now that they had to face the worst possibility of all—that the Green River Killer might have gotten hold of Tracy—the Winstons were terrified for her. When her name was added to the Green River list, Mertie was unable to escape the fear and anxiety that grew with each passing day. She could no longer rationalize and tell herself that Tracy was all right, that maybe she had gone to California as her friends tried to tell her.

"I was actually crawling on my bedroom floor, trying to get away from myself, but of course I couldn't," Mertie remembers some twenty years later. "I ended up crouched in a corner in a ball.

My friend, who loved Tracy as much as I did, begged me to try to sleep. She coaxed me to lie down and rubbed my back, until I finally fell asleep from sheer exhaustion.

"I had a dream. I was at Evergreen High School in the gym, and there must have been a dance going on. There was a stage, and the bleachers were pulled out and there were adults sitting on the bleachers. Those round, faceted mirror balls were twirling overhead and casting their lights on the crowd.

"Tracy was there in front of me, with that wonderful smile of hers. I could hear her talking although I couldn't see her mouth move. She kept smiling at me and I heard her say over and over, 'I'm okay, Mom. I'm okay now. Don't worry about me. Everything's okay.'

"I woke up with a jolt and I didn't know where I was. I believed—and I still do—that Tracy had been there with me in the room. It was the most peaceful I've felt in the last twenty-seven years." But Mertie sensed that Tracy was never coming home again, that she would never see her again.

The months alternately dragged and flew by. "We talked to anyone and everyone who might know Tracy's whereabouts, asking who she'd been seeing, where she might have been. Her best friends were twins and had a much wider network than we did. We got reports that she'd been seen in Vancouver, Canada, and California. We passed it all on to the Green River Task Force, no matter how insignificant it seemed to be, whether it was rumor or fact. They treated the information with priority and importance."

Tracy must have encountered someone who pulled her from her life into oblivion on September 12.

Mertie was more disturbed than reassured when Tracy's second cousin, Chris, who was nine months older than Tracy, told her about having met Tracy once with an older man. Chris was slim and blond and, like her cousin, a very pretty girl. She remembered the last time she'd seen Tracy and called Mertie and Chuck. It was either in the spring or fall of 1983, probably sometime in September. Chris had been waiting for a bus near the high school she'd once attended when a car drove by and somebody yelled and waved at her. She recognized Tracy, who was riding with a man Chris didn't know. The driver pulled over and Tracy told Chris to get in and they'd give her a ride to wherever she was going.

Chris got in the backseat. Tracy introduced the man as "Gary" and said that he was a friend of hers who was helping her look for a job. Then Tracy turned to the man and kidded, "Chris and I are the bad seeds in the family."

"Hi," the driver said flatly. He was quite a bit older than Tracy, a rather nondescript man. All Chris really remembered about him were his eyes. "He didn't really look at me when I got in," she recalled, "but he kept watching me in the rearview mirror. I'll never ever forget his eyes, and the way he kept watching me. He made me so nervous staring at me that I made up some excuse to get out of his car."

She couldn't remember the vehicle the man was driving, but Tracy had seemed to know him, and she certainly didn't appear to be at all afraid of him.

 MAUREEN FEENEY was as Irish as Mary Bridget Meehan, and she looked it. She could have been a nanny or a college student or a novitiate in a nunnery. Although she wasn't beautiful, she had a nice, open face with pretty blue eyes and she smiled often. She came from a large family, and at nineteen she was emotionally immature and naive, but she yearned for adventure and to be on her own. Maureen was thrilled to find a little mother-in-law apartment she could afford in January 1983. She moved to Eastgate, a neighborhood just south of the I-90 Freeway near Bellevue, and she worked for the Eastside Christian School, a benign place for a girl whose family was concerned about her.

Maureen had never dated in high school, and she still didn't have a boyfriend. Her best friend recalled that she talked to Maureen almost every day on the phone, and she'd been surprised that her shy friend was going out to clubs and had started drinking. That wasn't like Maureen, and she wasn't handling alcohol very well. Sometimes her words slurred a little on the phone.

Like so many teenagers, Maureen's self-image in high school had been very low; although she wasn't anorexic, she had occasionally cut herself with razor blades—thin, shallow slices—on her upper arms where it wouldn't show. She once told her best friend that she'd sat in her family's garage with the car motor running. Her mother had found her before anything bad happened.

Maureen loved her first tiny apartment, but she had to move out when the landlord told her a relative wanted to move in. She found another place in Seattle's Central District at 15th and E. Madison, an area with a much higher crime rate than Eastgate. She told her mother she had chosen her new neighborhood because she wanted to work with underprivileged children. She did get a job at a day-care facility and worked there in the late summer/early fall of 1983. Her friend Kathy visited her almost every day. Toward the end of August, Maureen told Kathy that she had a boyfriend, and she seemed excited about that. She'd met him at a bus stop near her apartment. She noted their meeting in her date book: "August 23— I met Eddie J.* today!"

Kathy was anxious to meet Eddie J. She knew he was of a different race from Maureen, but that didn't matter as long as he was nice to her friend. But he was never there when Kathy came to Maureen's apartment. There was always some excuse why he had to be out and about.

Although Maureen usually spent her weekends at her family's house or at their vacation home, they still felt uneasy about her living in the Central District. Her brother Brian sent her a check for quite a bit of money so she could afford to move back home, but she evidently didn't want to. She told Kathy that she and Eddie J. were going to go to California.

"How are you going to afford that?" Kathy asked.

"Oh, Eddie J. has lots of ways to make money," Maureen answered. "We'll be fine."

But she never got to California—at least as far as detectives could determine. Exactly one week before Maureen's twentieth birthday, she left her apartment forever. It was September 28, 1983. Three years later, Eddie J., a reluctant witness, told task force detective Kevin O'Keefe, who was on loan from the Seattle Police Department, that Maureen left sometime between five and six PM that day. "She told me she was going to the Seven-Eleven. I fell asleep after she left and I didn't wake up until about eleven that night. She never came back."

Eddie J. thought she might have gone looking for a job. He had found a newspaper with an ad circled on Maureen's dresser. It read "Exotic Dancers Wanted: 'Sugar's.' " The name "Bob" was written in the margin beside the ad.

The thought of sweet Maureen Feeney performing as an exotic dancer seemed ridiculous to her best friend and her family. Eddie J. claimed to be completely baffled about where she might be and said he had no idea about her activities outside of her day-care job.

Her employer, however, said that she had seen "a notable personality change" over the two months before she vanished. Only a few days before September 28, Maureen had come to her and said she wouldn't be needing a job for very long because she was "coming into money."

She told her mother that she planned to quit her day-care job because she couldn't get enough time off when she needed it. Another resident in the apartment house where Maureen lived told O'Keefe that he had heard her having an argument with Eddie J. in the hallway the night she disappeared.

Maureen's brother Brian and her brother-in-law searched for her for a long time, putting up posters with her picture anywhere they thought people might recognize her, asking for someone, *anyone,* who might have a clue to where she was to come forward.

But it seemed if she had walked into the twilight and been swallowed up by the night.

19

PERHAPS the most frightening thing about the Green River murders was the bleak interweaving of the disappearances and the discoveries of bodies. How the puppeteer must be enjoying his string-pulling. One thing the task force detectives were sure of—was that he was out there someplace, watching. If he didn't actually live in the south end of King County, Washington, he was most certainly flying or driving in and out to kill again and again. He must be having a ball watching television and reading newspapers.

Whether *he* was the person who sent helpful advice to the Green River investigators may never be proven absolutely. But a "helpful" directive came into their headquarters. It was written in shaky handwriting, and was rife with spelling mistakes. The writer, anonymous, titled his work: "Going About Catching the GRK."

He explained that he was the GRK, and that he had been doing many things to throw the detectives' investigation off track. For instance, he bragged about dating between twenty and forty "prostetutes [*sic*] whom he hadn't killed. I needed them out there alive in case I got caught—to say I didn't hurt them.

"All custumers dont want photos taken of them with prostetutes All police cars should cary a small camera (instamatic) Take pictures of custumers with ladys. Out of car & in. If the lady died he would be the last one seen with her."

The writer admonished the police to have better relations with the women on the street, and to ask them about their customers.

They were already doing that.

"All crime sites take vedio of people watching (That wouldn't have cought me though)."

It was September 1983 now. And there had been three more disappearances in one month. It had been fourteen months since the first body was discovered in the Green River.

TEN MILES SOUTH of the Strip, a winding road leads down toward the once-verdant Green River Valley from Pac HiWay at about S. 272nd Street. Close to the bottom of the hill is a narrow road: Star Lake Road. In the mid-1980s, both sides of the road were thickly wooded, even though new homes and an elementary school were only a few blocks away. On the downhill side of the road, twenty-five or so feet beyond the shoulder, a deep gorge dropped away, ending in a narrow creek.

On September 18, 1983, what would become known as the "Star Lake Road site" began to be unveiled. Although it seemed impossible—and still does—a passerby found skeletonized remains near a tree just where the bank started its plunge downward. It was so close to the road, how could it be that no one had smelled the unforgettably horrible stench of a human corpse, unburied, disintegrating? How could a body have lain there undiscovered for so long? Was it possible that someone had carried the bones there after the person had died?

More likely, the body had "self-buried." Many so-called shallow graves are not graves at all, but the natural result of the coming and going of seasons. Along Star Lake Road, as this body had decomposed, it literally returned to earth, sinking into the damp browning maple leaves beneath it. Wind storms brought more leaves down on top of it. With rain, snow, and wind, it would sink deeper with every season.

On the shoulder of Star Lake Road some fifteen feet from the body, which would not be identified for a long time, someone had dumped a load of garbage with a battered pair of work boots on top of it. But in the springtime, there would be silent benedictions there, too, a half-dozen white trilliums, a wildflower so rare that it is illegal to pick it in some areas, sprouted from the leaf carpet.

■

Yvonne Shelly Antosh, who had come to Seattle from British Columbia, had been staying at a motel on the Strip with a girl she'd known since they were both children. In the almost five months since she disappeared on the highway, she hadn't gotten in touch with her friend or with anyone else who knew her.

She couldn't have, because Yvonne's body had been left far away at S. 316th and the Auburn/Black Diamond Road. Long since skeletonized, her remains were discovered on October 15, 1983.

Connie Naon, whose car was found abandoned in the Red Lion parking lot, was dead, too. Gone on June 8, 1983, from S. 188th and the highway, Connie was found on October 27 very close by—at S. 191st and 25th Avenue South, almost directly under the flight path of planes taking off to the south. She had been left in the weeds near some big-leafed maple trees on empty land behind Alaska Airlines' headquarters and the Sandstone Motel and Restaurant.

Two days later, in the same area, detectives located the remains of Kelly Ware. She had last been seen alive downtown on Madison Street on July 18, and she was found on October 29 at S. 190th and 24th Avenue South.

20

While Kelly, Connie, and Yvonne were being found, more young women were disappearing.

Mary Sue Bello, twenty-five, was older than most of the missing girls and considered herself streetwise. She vanished on October 11, five weeks before her birthday. Almost everyone she met liked Mary, and her family treasured her, but she had taken chaotic chances with her life from the moment she entered puberty. Her mother, Suzanne, had cried millions of tears over Mary, and begged her to choose a different lifestyle.

But Mary had only laughed. Nothing was going to happen to *her*. She was too savvy to be conned by someone like the Green River Killer.

■

ANY EFFORT to understand Mary Sue has to begin years before her birth, because few of us come into this world without either suffering or benefiting from what has gone on before.

Despite years of searching, Mary's mother, Suzanne Draper Villamin, had been able to glean only a few facts about her own life. Until she was ten, she believed that the parents she lived with in a comfortable home in Seattle's Magnolia area were hers by birth. She was born in 1942, in an era when adoptive parents often chose not to tell children about the real circumstances of their birth. The Drapers decided to let Suzanne believe she was theirs. But she was in for a terrible shock.

"I was in the fifth grade—in Mrs. Graves's class," she remembered. "One of the kids in my class overheard my mother telling Mrs. Graves that I wasn't really hers, that I was adopted. My classmate couldn't wait to tell me, and it had a awful effect on me. I went home and told my mother what I'd heard and asked her if it was true. She had a terrible fit, but she would only admit that I was adopted. She wouldn't tell me where I'd come from, and she discouraged my trying to find out."

All Suzanne knew was that her birthday was April 9, 1942, and that she'd been born in Seattle. Later, she found out that her birth name was Beverly K. Gillam or Gilliam. When she was a little older, she found out more. Her parents had been married, and she was her mother's fourth child and possibly her father's, too. She wasn't sure. She'd had twin sisters five years older than she. They had blond hair and blue eyes.

"There was a boy, too," Sue said. "My mother drank heavily—I learned that. One time, she left the three older kids alone while she went out. There was a fire and they were able to save my twin sisters, but my brother died. And my parents broke up because of that."

At some point in 1942, Sue's mother headed for Alaska, but she left Sue, only a few months old, alone in a rooming house. It was three days before anyone discovered her and called the police.

"I was taken to the Medina Children's Home," she said. "And the Drapers adopted me when I was six months old, and since I wasn't old enough to remember anything, they just let me grow up believing I'd been born to them."

Her adoptive father was a strong, handsome man who was a

foreman in a warehouse for a company located in Magnolia, one of Seattle's most desirable neighborhoods, and the woman she would always call "mother" was a housewife. Her life with them was comfortable and happy. She grew up an only child, doted on by her parents and her maternal grandmother. But, from the time she was ten, she'd always wondered about her birth family.

"I've tried so many times to find my sisters," she said. "But the Medina Children's Home told me they'd had a fire and their records burned. I looked through the old newspapers, too, but I never found anything."

Sue Draper became pregnant and gave birth to a baby girl, Mary Sue, when she was only fifteen. "Oh, I made my share of mistakes, too," she admitted. "My folks made me marry Mary Sue's father. It was 1957 and women didn't raise babies when they were single then."

The Drapers had always been kind to Sue and they stood by her, even though they had insisted that she marry her boyfriend, who was nineteen. The marriage didn't last; her husband went off to prison before Mary Sue was six months old.

"He wasn't a very good robber," Sue recalled. "He tried to hold up a Savings and Loan, thinking it was a bank. And then he broke into a cash register and got only a screwdriver and a penny. He tried to open the safe with the screwdriver."

Sue and baby Mary moved in with her parents. And the deceptions began again. Mary Bello grew up believing her grandparents were her parents and that Sue was her older sister. It was the same situation in which Ted Bundy grew up—a subterfuge that backfired for both Mary Bello and Ted Bundy, leaving them full of distrust and rebellion. For that matter, Sue had been in the same boat herself.

Mary Bello found her baby book when she was ten—the same age her mother had been when she discovered *her* true parentage. But she was more aggressive and demanding than Sue had been. "She wanted to know why we hadn't told her the truth," Sue recalled. "I didn't know what to tell her. She didn't understand how rough it was for me to try to raise a baby alone when I was only fifteen. But Mary was never the same after she found out the truth."

When Mary was about twelve, Sue bought a little house across the street from her parents, hoping to make a home for her daughter. But it was too late. Mary wouldn't mind anyone. She ran away repeatedly, quickly got into drugs, and learned that she could make older men do things for her because she was pretty. Mary Bello wasn't thirteen yet when she was committed to Grand Mound, the Washington State Training School for adolescent girls.

"That was about the only education she ever had, even though she was very intelligent," Sue remembered. "By the time she got home two years later, she was lost to us. She would come home off and on, and then she'd get mad and leave. If she was mad at me, she could go to my folks' house. My mom would baby Mary and let her get away with things, just like she did when Mary was a baby. For many years, Mary never faced up to anything. She would go from me to my mom's, to her friends, and then back again to me. She always had someplace to go when she got angry at whoever she was staying with."

Mary Bello was emancipated when she was fifteen years old. She wasn't really employable in a straight job. She worked for a while at a Burger King, but lost her job because her friends kept coming in and causing a commotion. She was a lovely girl with pale skin, and dark eyes and hair. She was five feet seven and willowy, and she found it easier to use her looks to make money than to work at minimum wage jobs that were meant for kids.

When she was nineteen, Mary followed her mother to Arizona, stayed for a little while, and then went on to Texas by herself. She worked as an exotic dancer in Tucson and got a discreet tattoo; it was a tiny lobster etched low on one buttock. Her favorite record to dance to was "Summer Nights" by Glen Campbell.

Although she seemed satisfied with her life, Mary had always wondered what her real father was like. She'd met him only briefly once when she was about sixteen. At that time, he'd told her he had "found religion." He was preaching on street corners and collecting money "for the poor." Sue found out he kept the money for himself, to buy liquor. She tried to keep that information away from Mary, feeling that it would be better if she didn't know her father was a con man.

At nineteen, Mary was still determined to know her father. Reluctantly, Sue Villamin told her where to find him in Arizona, but she went along and parked nearby because she didn't know what he would do.

"He tried to rape her," Sue said. "He locked her in his place and wouldn't let her out. I had this big German shepherd with me and I pounded on the door until her father finally let her go. But Mary had to accept that she really didn't have a father. Never did have."

Remembering her only child, Sue's eyes misted. "Mary went through so much pain. She was waiting in a man's car once when he went into a fish restaurant to get a take-out dinner. But he'd really gone in to rob the place. She didn't know he was going to do that, but she was arrested for robbery, too, and she was convicted and had to serve time at the women's prison in Purdy. She said it wasn't too bad; she got to stay in these separate little 'apartments' up on the hill."

Headstrong and willful, teenage Mary Bello blamed her mother for the bad things in her life, and she grew addicted to drugs—heroin and cocaine—turning to prostitution to pay for her habit. She took chances all the time, sure that she had a protective shield around her. Even though Sue Villamin couldn't understand why Mary chose the life she had, they began to grow closer when Mary was in her early twenties. They were friends now, and that made sense because they were only fifteen years apart in age.

Mary was a rebel but she was kindness personified. She would help anyone in need, often giving her last dollar to beggars on the street. And she had a wild sense of humor. "I'd get so mad at her," her mother said, "and then she had this funny little smile. I couldn't stay mad."

Mary was a good cook, and she loved holidays, never missing Thanksgiving or Christmas with her family. On the last Christmas of her life, she showed up with her arms full of presents, none of them wrapped. In 1982, she had "overbought" for everyone, but she looked delighted as her mother and grandparents enjoyed their gifts.

Mary Bello was afraid to trust men enough to love one, although she may have loved a man named "Jimmy." He wasn't a pimp, and he cared for her. Following the pattern she'd set all of her life, she would live with him for a while and then move out. But, in her twenties, she always came back to him.

Sue Villamin begged Mary to stop prostituting herself, and Mary looked at her as if she were speaking another language. "She'd been robbed and beaten by johns, and she still wouldn't quit," Sue remembered. "She wanted me to know what her life was like. And I didn't want to hear. It seemed like the more I shut my ears, the more she told me. She said she didn't like it, but it supported her habit, and it gave her a certain kind of 'power' over men. I don't know, maybe because of the way her father treated her."

Sue pleaded with her to find another way to live.

"No," Mary replied. "This is the way I have to make my money."

They talked quite a bit about the Green River Killer and Mary pooh-poohed her mother's concern. "Don't worry about it. I can avoid him. Mother, he'll never get *me*—I'll be all right. I don't want to hear about him!"

And then she laughed because it was so ridiculous for anyone to be concerned about her.

One thing her mother never knew was that Mary was very aware of the threat the so-called Green River Killer posed—not so much for herself, but for the vulnerable kids who had just come to the Strip. On September 12, 1983, her concern had led her to call a detective she knew on the task force with a tip.

"Look," she said, "I want you to know that I had a date with a really weird john. I'm okay, but he has a lot of knives in his car and at his house, too."

The guy was older, and he drove a recent model blue sedan. She didn't know the make of the car or the license plate number, but she recalled that his house was at 218th and Military Road. Mary Bello's report was checked, and it became part of the huge permanent file on the unsolved Green River cases.

Finally, Mary and her mother reached a kind of détente. Mary lived in one or another of the motels on the Pac HiWay, and Sue lived in a mobile home about ten miles south on the same highway. All that summer of 1983, Mary was trying hard to overcome her heroin habit, which necessitated her going to Tacoma—a fifteen-mile trip—every day to get methadone to ease her withdrawal symptoms.

"She would take the bus down to my trailer," Sue said. "And I would drive her on down to Tacoma, wait for her, and bring her back to my trailer, and she'd catch the bus again."

Sue had a fleeting feeling of doom on that beautiful October day, like a tattered gray curtain brushing by the yellow maple leaves. She watched Mary's back as she walked away from her trailer toward the bus stop.

"I love you!" Sue called out.

"Mary looked back and she smiled at me. That was the last time I ever saw her. I think I *knew* it was, too, and there was nothing I could do to stop it."

■

MARY BELLO always called home every two days, no matter where she was. Now, her birthday passed, and Thanksgiving, and Christmas. Her grandmother was diagnosed with terminal cancer and they all hoped she would call. They needed her. "She's just gone off someplace," her grandmother said. She had always avoided letting harsh truths surface. "She'll show up. You watch, she'll show up."

It would be a long time before any of them knew where Mary was. Sue Villamin kept a quote close to her that helped her deal with losing Mary: "Times Change; Love Doesn't." She also had a thought of her own that others might heed: "The punishment for prostitution should not be death."

But she didn't know if Mary was dead or alive.

21

THE CRIME SCENE searches multiplied in the fall of 1983. The overburdened and underfunded Green River Task Force not only had new disappearances to investigate, but the detectives were retrieving the pathetic remains that had begun to surface. Each body site had to be carefully raked and sifted, the tiniest speck of what might be evidence preserved and labeled: fibers, hairs, rocks, paint chips, twigs, loose finger- and toenails, bits of bone, rotted pieces of cloth, fragments of cheap jewelry, tiny slips of paper, a cigarette, photos and moulages of tire tracks, a condom. The detectives badly wanted to find something that would turn out to be absolute physical evidence that they could link to the man they'd looked for for the last fifteen months.

Young women who had been on the verge of life months or a year before had been reduced to scattered bones, many with missing limbs. Except for Carol Christensen, none of them was fully clothed, and the question about whether Carol even *was* a Green River victim remained unanswered. Her body site had obviously been staged, while the latest bodies found appeared to have been merely thrown away. If their killer was so careless with his victims, detectives still hoped he might have been slipshod about leaving something of himself behind.

They might not have had the physical evidence they needed, but there was a definite pattern to what some news reports were crassly calling "dump sites," an unfortunate way to describe where human beings had been left.

If the SeaTac Strip between S. 144th and S. 288th was to be seen as the center of a giant circle, it had quickly become obvious that the Green River Killer was leaving several of his victims together in three general areas, north and south and east. He couldn't go very far west without coming to the shores of Puget Sound. But he could expand almost exponentially in the other three directions.

The south and north end of the Port Authority's property (SeaTac Airport) had aspects that would have tempted someone who wanted to hide what he had done: empty houses and foundations, overgrown weeds and shrubbery, long stretches of deserted fields, and, always, the high-pitched roar of jet planes overhead. And, of course, all of this acreage was barely more than a stone's throw from the Pac HiWay Strip.

Whoever he was, the Green River Killer seemed to have operated on the "cluster" theory—leaving more than one dead girl in each location. Sometimes there were two together. Sometimes three. And, in some areas, there would eventually be six or seven, although that was a grim possibility that no one working on the case could yet even imagine.

Maybe he had some crazy sense that his victims shouldn't be alone, and so he'd left them with "friends." Not likely. Someone who could kill so many teenagers and young women wouldn't care about that; his plan to dispose of the bodies of his victims had to be a convenience for himself or an obscure symbol that meant something to him. And pragmatically, he would have needed to be rid of them as soon as possible so he wouldn't be caught with a body in his vehicle, or his house or hotel room. That was only common sense.

 HE DISPOSED of the dead girls, but he kept replacing them. Pammy "Annette" Avent, who sometimes worked The Camp in Portland, was back in Seattle on October 26, but apparently not for long. Later, her friends realized they'd last seen her in the Rainier Valley area.

■

ON OCTOBER 28, Patricia Anne Osborn, nineteen, was in the other end of Seattle, almost at the city limits on Aurora Avenue North. The "trick stops" on Aurora were the intersections of the 1100 block, the 8500 block, and the 10500 block. Patricia had been arrested three times for prostitution in 1983, and she was walking along Aurora when she was last seen. Her parents lived in Oregon and didn't realize that she was gone. When she didn't contact them over the holidays, they reported her missing. But she had really been missing for three months.

Pammy was black and Patricia was white—the Green River Killer seemed to have no racial preference. Instead, he chose the most vulnerable—and the prettiest—of the girls who risked their lives every time they got into a car with a stranger.

If all of the women were his victims, it seemed that the GRK was driving up and down the I-5 Freeway, slipping off on exit ramps the whole length of the city. It also looked as if he was picking up his pace. For serial killers addicted to murder, it takes more and more murders for them to maintain the modicum of normalcy they show to the outside world.

IT WAS SUNDAY, October 30, 1983. At about three that afternoon, Delise Louise Plager, twenty-two, was expected at the home of a good woman friend. A mutual male acquaintance, who had allowed her to keep a few of her belongings in his storage unit, waited on their friend's front porch. Delise wanted to retrieve some items, including a Halloween costume she had promised to bring home for her friend's child. She was supposed to be taking the bus to the house near 15th Avenue and Columbian Way, an area slightly northwest of the Rainier Valley section of Seattle.

Delise, who had been called "Missy" since she was a little girl, was living temporarily with a friend. She had two children of her own, but she was having a rough time supporting them. She had had a rough time for as far back as she could remember. She had blue eyes and blond hair and a perfectly proportioned face, faintly sprinkled with freckles, but her eyes looked as if they had seen it all and found it bitterly disappointing.

Given the circumstances of her life, that wasn't surprising.

Missy Plager was bitter and as fragile as a butterfly, and yet her last day on earth was spent trying to make a child happy. Life is rarely fair, and for some especially vulnerable children, life is one sad experience after another. For Missy, about the only thing life gave her was a pretty name and a few people who really cared for her, even though they weren't able to protect her for as long as they had hoped they could. By the time her life got really rocky, she had many names. Sometimes she was "Misty," and sometimes she was "Roxanne Dunlap" or "Carrie Bailey." Her real birth name was completely different from any of those. Her parents had named her Lisa Veronica. Some said her true last name was Sansisan.

Before Missy and her twin brother, Jon, were five, their birth mother was found to be unfit. The reasons were cloudy but it's probable that her excessive drinking was the deciding factor. Missy was born "dead," but the attending nurse was able to resuscitate her. The babies went home to a tenuous situation. Their birth father left when they were about six months old, and their mother already had a little girl a few years older, the result of an earlier liaison with another man. Missy's parents, Dennis and Patricia, were divorced later that year—in 1960.

Missy and Jon were removed from their first family, and taken to the Catholic Children's Organization facility. Missy was an appealing child and she was soon adopted, but her new parents found her difficult to deal with. Perhaps because of her failure to breathe at birth, she was hyperactive and needed patience and special medications.

In reality, Missy may have suffered the most from grief and separation. She had lost the twin brother she loved. They had bonded together before birth, but were placed separately for adoption. She was formally adopted in July 1968. Through the years ahead, she kept looking for Jon, but the family who adopted him wanted to cut all cords to the past, and Missy was not allowed to see him or contact him. They had always been together, the only comfort either of them had. Missy remembered her brother vividly, and she worried about him. A kind social worker found where he had been placed, and although she couldn't tell Missy where he was, she was able to tell the little girl that she had seen him and spoken to him, and he was doing okay.

Tragically, Missy would not find him again for many, many years, and she cried inconsolably for her lost brother. She was a very pretty little blond child, and her adoptive parents, who lived on a ranch, hadn't expected the personality problems that soon became apparent. They had older sons and their experience with parenting had been normal and fairly serene, but Missy was excitable and too loud and nervous, and she had a great deal of trouble concentrating.

In desperation, when Missy was ten or eleven, her adoptive parents placed her in the Antonian School for Special Children in Cheney in eastern Washington. It was a Catholic institution whose director was Sister M. Antonia Stare, O.P. The nun's family owned the land where the school stood.

Missy's houseparents at the school did their best for the thin, little girl who seemed to bear the weight of the world on her shoulders. She had lost her birth mother, her half sister, and her twin brother. Although she was unaware of it, her mother and father had married and remarried other partners. She had another half sister, her birth father's daughter by a different woman, but she didn't know that. In a sense, being at the school, Missy had also lost a real home with her adoptive parents who had tried valiantly but just couldn't cope with her hyperactivity and mood swings.

Missy did go home on weekends, and she was medicated for ADHD (attention deficit hyperactivity disorder) only on those Saturdays and Sundays when she desperately needed it all the time. But Sister Antonia did not believe that hyperactive children should be treated with pharmacological solutions such as Ritalin, particularly not when they were in school, and so when Missy came back on Sunday night or Monday morning, she literally went through chemical withdrawal, week after week.

One time she came back from a home visit and her housemother found that Missy's buttocks were slightly bruised. It wasn't difficult to leave marks on Missy—her fair skin was thin and delicate. She sobbed as Sister Antonia took photos of the bruises. She wasn't crying because of the pain but because she was afraid she was going to get someone in her family or their friends in trouble.

Missy was pubescent and had begun to develop tiny breasts. She whispered to her housemother, Barbara, at the dinner table that some older boys she encountered had pinched her and teased her about them. "All I could do was tell her that I was sorry," Barbara recalled, "and that I knew that must have hurt her feelings, and that they shouldn't have done that to her."

It may not, however, have been all one-sided. Because she had been so robbed of nurturing up until the age of five, Missy craved physical contact. For most of her life, she was unable to say "no" to boys and men who hugged her and kissed her. She had missed out completely on the normal cuddling all babies need.

One of the saddest nights the housemother could remember was when the school put on a little show. "I don't think Missy had any hope that her family was going to come, but her adoptive mother did come. Missy was so glad to see her that she was overwhelmed and she started to cry immediately. Poor Missy kept sobbing all through the performance. Later, she was so proud to introduce her mother to the staff. It was obvious that she loved her mother, who was trying hard to deal with the problems that had begun in Missy's earliest years."

Despite everything Missy had been through in her short life, she still cared deeply and loved deeply. She was not a hardened little soul unable to bond or form attachments. A volunteer at the school, Thelma "Woody" Johnson, worked one-on-one with Missy, calmly helping her to slow down and speak more quietly.

"Woody was wonderful with Missy," the little girl's housemother recalled. "My husband always remembers her as a child with 'sparkle.' There was still so much hope and promise there."

As the months passed, Missy's emotional problems became more evident, and it was decided that she should be moved to a residential facility where she would be allowed fewer home visits. It was agonizing for Barbara and her husband to see Missy pack up to go and not be able to stop the transfer. She thought that Missy, of all people, needed a place where she felt she had some roots. "After she left, I was allowed to talk to Missy once on the phone," Barbara said. "I told her I missed her—and I did."

Years went by without any word from Missy, and then Barbara learned that she had been placed in Echo Glen, a facility near North Bend, Washington, for teenagers who had been in trouble with the law or who needed to be locked away from the world. "We could only imagine what had brought her to that point," Barbara remembered.

A lot had happened to Missy, and not much of it was good. Besides being hyperactive, she had a learning disorder that made school very difficult for her. She had been in Echo Glen for treatment, and she had also spent some time in the Maple Lane School for Girls. All through her teen years, she kept the dream alive that one day she would find her real mother and father and her brother, and that they would reunite and be a happy family.

Missy grew tougher, at least on the surface, but those who knew her recognized her vulnerability. She had a lot of "substitute" sisters and mothers who gave her somewhere to stay and tried to imbue her with a sense of self-worth. But she was a challenging guest or tenant. A terrible housekeeper, she didn't clean at all unless she had to find something she needed under a pile of clothes or dirty dishes.

There were too many times when it seemed Missy was fated to die young. She was in a devastating car crash in 1977. Her hip and jaw were broken, and her skull fractured. She had to have a tracheotomy to breathe, but, once again, she survived.

Out of school and more or less on her own, Missy got several tattoos, marks that might have made her identifiable if anything fatal happened to her. She had "Love" on the back of one hand, "Frank" inside one of her arms, a good luck symbol on one of her fingers, and a butterfly on her knee. They were amateur tattoos, either etched there by a friend or by herself. But she had a commercially created tattoo on her right shoulder, a dragon.

Looking for someone she could love, Missy had two children out of wedlock—a little girl, Nicole, in 1976 or 1977, and a boy, Darrell, in 1979. She was not seriously involved with either of the men who fathered her babies, but she loved her children. Even so, she was not emotionally equipped to take care of them. She'd missed out on those desperately important first five years when little girls learn how to be mothers by emulating their own mothers.

Sometimes the children were with her, but, more often, the friends she had cultivated as family took care of Nicole and Darrell. Missy was, after all, only sixteen when she gave birth to her older child, and eighteen when she had Darrell.

If her life had been a television movie, there would have been a happy ending for Missy in 1982. A girl she met on Seattle's Capitol Hill stared at her and remarked, "You know, you look enough like my boyfriend to be his twin!"

And she was. Missy had found the twin brother she'd lost seventeen years before. He lived in Tacoma and he knew where their father was. His name was Dennis and he was living in Texas. Missy called her father, and he put her in touch with her mother, who had remarried several times and now lived in Reno, Nevada.

When Missy called Patricia, her mother invited her to come down for Christmas. Both of them had high expectations of a sentimental reunion. Instead, it was a disaster. Patricia, who had not taken care of Missy and her twin brother, was raising her boyfriend/husband's children. Her alcoholism had progressed, and she really wasn't ready to take on the daughter who'd been out of her life for so many years and now had two children of her own.

As Missy tried to tell her mother about how tough her life had been and how she had missed having her own family, Patricia felt both guilty and repelled. Missy's being in group homes and girls' training schools bothered her. She had somehow expected a grown-up daughter who had turned out well.

Patricia, who worked for a film-processing company in a kiosk in a strip mall, didn't have the funds to help Missy move close to her and her current male companion. Besides, Missy was her usual self as a house guest and left everything a mess. Patricia was close to her older daughter; Missy was more of a burden. And after too many drinks, Patricia said a terrible thing. "You've got so many problems," she told Missy, "maybe it would have been better if they hadn't resuscitated you when you were born."

It was like a knife in Missy's heart. She had spent her whole life counting on her dream, and now she realized that her mother didn't even care if she was alive or dead. Worse, her mother seemed to wish she had never lived.

Missy called her father and told him that things hadn't gone well in Reno. She was going back to the Seattle-Tacoma area. Her mother had bought her a one-way ticket as a Christmas present. "When she left," her mother recalled later, "I gave her a turquoise-and-silver ring. It wasn't expensive, but she told me she'd never take it off."

It was almost 1983, and after that, Missy just seemed to drift. She missed appointments with social workers and counselors to talk about her children and what would be best for them. She lived here and there. Her half sister (her father's daughter by another woman) found Missy and told her she'd been searching for her for twenty years. She had traced their father's genealogy and found Missy. Joanie* came up to Washington State and they tried living together for about two weeks, but it was too late to establish a sister/sister relationship. Joanie's life had been better than Missy's and she had a solid career and different values.

Around that time, Missy tried suicide, leaving long vertical scars on her wrists. Some of her friends found her in time, but she didn't believe in anything anymore. By 1983, she hated men. It seemed as though every man she'd ever known had either ignored her or mistreated her. Her twin was down in Texas with their father—both of them on parole after serving time for some kind of scam—working in a restaurant together. There was a good chance her daughter was going to be adopted, and her son was living with her friend Maia, who was the closest thing to a mother Missy had, but she was scared to death that the Washington Department of Social and Health Services was going to take Darrell away from her, too.

In early 1983, Missy lived for a few weeks or a month at a time with men she thought were friends—they weren't. She confided in Maia that she realized one older man was trying to groom her to be a prostitute by getting her hooked on drugs, so she left him.

But Missy did get hooked on drugs. She bought some at a building that was once a church but was anything but that in the summer of 1983. It had become a teenage "rave" club called The Monastery. The Seattle Police Department and the King County Prosecutor's Office were investigating the seamy dark club and would close it down within two years, but it was an easy place for underage kids to score drugs in 1983. Missy was in the process that summer of getting a grotesque tattoo—a werewolf that extended from just beneath her chin to her lower abdomen. It wasn't filled in yet; just the ugly outline was traced.

Finally, she gave in to the pressure to work the streets. In April 1983, she'd been living in a tiny basement apartment, where she could just about afford the cheap rent. A few months later, she called a female attorney who had helped her before. "She was strung out on drugs and terrified that she would lose her kids," the woman recalled. "I hadn't talked to her for a while and I don't know what happened . . . she'd been enthusiastic about going back to school to get her GED, but now she was going downhill fast. She had always been looking for approval, and failing in most categories. I know she lied to her mother when she left Reno, telling her that she had a boyfriend waiting for her to come home. But she didn't. She had no one."

Missy's intimate friends knew that she would not allow johns to have actual intercourse with her. She would perform only oral sex, telling those women closest to her, "Anything else would be a violation of my inner body." "She would do car dates or go to motels," a friend who was like a sister said. "She would never go to a john's house."

And still, Missy hoped to get enough money and a good enough apartment to bring her children home. In the early fall of 1983, she was attending parenting classes, praying that she would need them.

But she was a paradox. Only weeks later, Missy and the friend who was like a sister, who had also turned to prostitution, traveled to Olympia, Washington, to earn "big money" by participating in a threesome. The john didn't pay them, laughing at them instead. From there, on a whim, they either took a bus or hitchhiked to Virginia or North Carolina where the other girl had relatives. There, they had a disagreement and split up.

Somehow Missy scraped up the money to get back to Seattle. She made it home and moved in with another friend, only to disappear at Halloween. Maia reported her missing when she never showed up to go to the storage unit to pick up the Halloween costume. She described Missy's petite figure, her blond hair, her tattoos, the little turquoise ring, the "trache" scar, and the gap she had between her upper middle front teeth. "Her teeth are pretty nice, but she does have that space there."

Just before Christmas, 1983, Missy's father, Dennis, received a strange phone call at his home in Texas. It was a woman who cried, "Dad! I'll be home for Christmas!" And then the line went dead. He could not say whose voice it was.

Barbara, Missy's long-ago housemother, recalled hearing that Missy was believed to be a victim of the Green River Killer. "Then, of course, came the horrifying day when we heard her name on the news, and saw her sad face in a picture in the newspaper," Barbara said. "She did not deserve that fate. She was a sweet child who had so much working against her. And the sadness continued when we read that she was a mother herself and that her children had been taken from her. We never learned any of the details, but it was not surprising that the cycle would be repeating itself, as is so often the case. It is important that someone, somewhere, be on record that she was a child who really cared, that she mattered, and that she had suffered so much heartache and loss in her short life. And she didn't deserve to die such a horrific death."

NONE OF THEM DID.

Pammy Avent, Patricia Osborn, and Missy Plager were all slender and small-boned. Kim Nelson, twenty, also known as Tina Lee Tomson, was almost six feet tall, and a strong young woman. She had a sullen sexiness, short yellow-blond hair, and D-cup breasts that made her especially attractive to the men who drove along streets and highways looking for "dates." For some reason, it was always the tall police officer decoys who attracted the most johns along the Strip. Maybe it was because the tall girls were unusual and stood out from the average.

BORN in Michigan, Tina grew up as Kimberly Nelson. She had dropped out of Ann Arbor's Pioneer High School in the eleventh grade and somehow made her way to Seattle, with many stops along the way. Back home, she had her mother, Greta; her stepfather, Ed Turner; and sisters who worried about her. Her father, Howard Nelson, lived in Florida. But Tina had stretched the cord leading home too far to go back. She'd phoned her sister to say she wouldn't be coming home for Christmas 1983, because she couldn't afford the trip. Her mother sent her money, but Kim never showed up.

By the time Tina was living in the Northwest, she was the sole support of a pimp, a man who was distraught when she was sentenced to the King County Jail for prostitution in early October 1983. He had whined that he didn't know how he would survive without the money she provided by turning tricks. She was three or four months pregnant, but that didn't matter to him. Her pregnancy may have been the reason why she didn't go home to Ann Arbor for Christmas, but more likely, she couldn't go home ever again.

After the holidays, Kim's boyfriend called her family to ask if she was with them. They told him they hadn't talked to her since long before Christmas.

Kim/Tina had so many street names that sometimes even she had trouble remembering "who" she was at any given moment. She and her girlfriend Paige Miley didn't know each other all that well. Paige knew Tina as "Star," and that was all. Their pimps were friends, and they moved the young women who kept them from having to find honest jobs from place to place, wherever the men felt there was the most money to be made.

When Kim/Tina/Star got out of jail just before Halloween, she and Paige were driven from Aurora Avenue in north Seattle to the SeaTac Strip, and they moved into the Ben Carol Motel. They worked two nights at the Evergreen Truck Stop in Federal Way, but Paige got arrested by Scott Wales, an undercover King County detective, warned, and released.

Afterward, Paige was never absolutely positive of the date when she last saw Tina. It was either the day of Halloween or November 1. She did remember it was raining hard at eleven in the morning, and it was cold out. Detectives Randy Mullinax and Matt Haney's records showed that Paige had reported Tina missing on October 31. Of course, she reported her as "Star" Tomson aka Tina Tomson. The fact that most of the missing and murdered girls had so many aliases was one more burden the Green River Task Force had to juggle as investigators patiently worked their way through a morass of information.

If Tina disappeared on Halloween morning, that would have been only twenty hours after Missy Plager vanished. Tina and Paige had stood talking just before noon at 141st and the Pac HiWay, as the rainy wind ruffled their hair. They weren't familiar with the Strip and probably didn't realize they were right at ground zero in the south end. They were aware of someone called the Green River Killer, but Tina wasn't afraid of him. "Star wasn't afraid of anyone," Paige said. "She would get in a car with anyone—she was so confident she could take care of herself."

Tina said she was only going to work long enough to "earn the rent money." The rent was only about $25 a night; the two girls were also trying to save money by cooking their own meals in their room.

Paige picked up a trick first and left with him for a car date. When she got back fifteen or twenty minutes later, Tina wasn't standing by the highway, so Paige figured she either had a date or she'd gone back to their motel. It was so cold that she decided to return to the Ben Carol. But Tina wasn't there, and she didn't come back—ever.

Two days later, as Paige looked up and down the rain-soaked highway, a dark red pickup with a white canopy stopped and the driver signaled to her. "Didn't you hang around with a tall blond girl?" he asked.

That made the hairs stand up on the back of her neck. She shook her head slightly. He offered her money to turn a trick with him, but there was something about him that Paige didn't like. He refused to go to her room; he wanted a car date. She didn't go with him.

The case of the tall blond girl whose name was either "Star" or Tina Tomson or Kris Nelson or Kimberly Nelson was assigned to Mullinax and Haney. Paige had described the man in the red pickup as white, in good shape, about five feet ten, wearing a plaid shirt and possibly a baseball cap. Probably around thirty-five years old.

According to Paige, "Star" had been wearing black, pin-striped slacks, a pink blouse, a long black leather coat, and blue Nike shoes the last time she had seen her. Nothing else was missing from their motel room. Detective Cherisse "Cheri" Luxa took possession of Star/Tina's things—a few clothes, hair rollers, toothbrush, makeup—and put them into evidence.

ONLY A SMALL PERCENTAGE of the missing girls' remains had been found. The killer had somehow managed to hide most of them, a fact that brought horrible images to the minds of the public and the task force detectives. He had left most of the bodies thus far discovered unburied, hastily covered with tree branches or debris. He didn't appear to care anything about them, just threw them away like broken dolls.

Still, the task force detectives found that he had gone to the trouble of burying the dead girl someone found on November 13, 1983, in a wooded area only a few hundred yards west of Pac HiWay and about four blocks from the Red Lion. Actually, there were two victims—a young woman whose womb still cradled her almost full-term fetus. The baby had died with her. The pregnant girl lay faceup with her knees slightly bent to the left. She and her baby weren't buried more than two or three feet deep, but the killer had scooped out enough dirt to cover this victim's body. What had been different? Was it because this girl had been pregnant and that had made his violence more shameful? Did he, perhaps, have some feeling for his victims?

This grave had held Mary Bridget Meehan, who had lost her first two babies through miscarriage and been persuaded to give her third up for adoption. Now she had been robbed of giving birth to this infant, or to any baby ever again.

How many more victims were there? Were they searching for some brilliant maniac who could take on experienced investigators and thumb his nose at them?

It seemed so.

22

SCHOOLWORK never got any easier for him, although he took some satisfaction in his ability to have secrets from all the students who thought they knew everything.

As much as he fantasized about having sex with various girls and women, he hadn't had much luck actually accomplishing it. There was a girl who was a couple of years older than he who lived over in Kitsap County. They'd hooked up once and that was the first time he'd actually had sexual intercourse. She was a lot more experienced than he was, and he knew she was a little scornful of his performance.

"For some reason," he said later, "we never did it again. I don't know why. Just didn't."

He wasn't a reader or good at math, but he was pretty good at fixing things, and his dad taught him about cars, even though, like everything else, it took him a lot longer to learn the steps than it would most people. He liked hiking and fishing and being in the woods. He liked being alone and watching people who didn't know he was watching them.

He worked as a busboy at the Hyatt Hotel near the airport in 1965 and 1966, and then he got a job at the Gov-Mart Bazaar, a store that sold mostly bargain items bought from closeouts at other companies. He finally had a few girlfriends in high school, but they wouldn't have sex with him. Eventually, he did meet a girl who would agree to go steady with him. He bought a hamburger from the fast-food place where she worked, and when he took a bite, he found she'd slipped in a piece of paper with her name and phone number on it. On a date, he attempted to have sex with her at a drive-in movie, but he ejaculated prematurely before he even entered her. After that, they had intercourse regularly.

HE HAD HAD so much difficulty with reading and academic subjects that getting through school seemed an endless process. He was twenty when he graduated, and he hadn't given much thought to what he was going to do in life. He considered joining the service and learning a trade there.

The war in Vietnam still raged and he stood a good chance of being drafted, so he joined the navy. Before he was sent to his duty station in San Diego, he got married to his steady girlfriend, Heather. They had a "military wedding," as he described it, at Fort Lawton in Seattle.

She was a year younger than he was. They were married by a military chaplain in August 1970, and she moved with him to San Diego. They seemed to get along all right for the months he was in training in California, although he was on a ship for several days each week. When he was in port, they had sex a few times a day. Other than that, they didn't do much that was very exciting, but she seemed happy enough to him.

And then he shipped out to sea for several months. She was alone in a strange city in a strange state. Neither of them was very mature, and they began to accuse each other of infidelity. Since writing was difficult for him, his letters weren't particularly tactful.

Actually, they were both cheating. He didn't feel that visiting prostitutes when he was away from home should count, as he had a very strong sex drive. He formed fleeting relationships with a half-dozen Filipina prostitutes. She was bored and lonely, and moved in with another young woman—a girl who was married to a marine. And she began to date, too.

He checked into sick bay because it hurt to pee, and was told that he had a venereal disease. He was very angry about that because he had already had gonorrhea once. Maybe he thought it was like the measles or mumps and he wouldn't get it again, but he was really steamed this time. Apparently the cautionary films shown by the navy failed to make an impression on him. He had rarely worn condoms, but a long time later he insisted he didn't blame the Filipina prostitutes. They had always treated him well and introduced him to more exotic sexual practices than the missionary position.

He had been an angry boy and his rage grew when he became an adult, although he kept a very tight lid on it. He was still drifting and apparently had no insight at all into his own motivations for doing things.

His bride recalled that when he returned from sea duty, she confessed to him that she had been so lonely that she had dated other men. He would steadfastly deny that he ever knew for sure whether she had been unfaithful and assert that he didn't question her at all when he was transferred to Washington and she suggested he drive back to Seattle on his own.

He left his young wife in San Diego. It was a fatal blow to their marriage. He prevailed upon her to come back to Seattle, and she did, but she stayed only a week, telling him "This marriage isn't working" as she left for the airport.

Inside, he had never been that sure of himself, and being cuckolded hit him harder than it would most men. He branded his wife a "whore" and they were divorced less than a year after their marriage.

He wasn't soured on marriage, however. He was anxious to

meet another woman, one he could trust. He quickly began frequenting places where he could meet women, and he dated three or four of them in rapid succession, although none of his relationships lasted more than a few months.

And once he had discovered prostitutes, he patronized them, too.

23

IT TOOK A WHILE for Jerry Alexander to track down Bridget Meehan's old boyfriend Ray. The Port of Seattle detective was still assigned to her case since her body was found within his department's jurisdiction. Ray was pretty foggy at first about his life with Bridget, but his memory grew clearer with every contact. Finally, he admitted that Bridget had been working the Strip. Asked if he remembered any particular johns, he recalled her talking about one who drove a blue sports car with a vanity plate.

Alexander ran the vanity plates through the Department of Motor Vehicles in Olympia and got a hit on the second one that seemed right. It was for a blue Karmann Ghia whose registered owner lived within two miles of the Strip.

The man was in his thirties and seemed normal enough, almost meek in demeanor. He admitted readily that he occasionally paid for sex, and that he'd been with Bridget. "I'm attracted to girls with big breasts, and I saw her walking her dog near Larry's," he said. "She had a lonely look about her."

He didn't seem a likely suspect; his answers were forthright, and the task force detectives had questioned hundreds of men who had either been turned in by tipsters or arrested by undercover officers posing as "prostitutes." Many of them seemed far more sinister than this guy.

Alexander ran the man through records and got somewhat shocking results. He had a record as a mental case. Another detective had contacted him on a report totally unconnected to the Green River murders. "He's 219-5/16th," the other officer said. (In Washington State, mental cases are referred to as "220s" because police officers back in the very early days received a bonus of $2.20 for arresting such potentially dangerous subjects.) "He thinks he's a spy, he's suicidal, and sometimes he carries a nine millimeter."

But he probably hadn't killed Bridget Meehan; he had a solid alibi for the time period when she disappeared.

As 1983 DREW TO A CLOSE, Sheriff Vern Thomas pleaded with King County politicos for funding that would allow the investigation to be expanded, and while some listened with concern, at least one voiced his doubt that the county's image would be much improved by spending taxpayers' money on investigating the murders of "hookers."

It was an appalling comment, but it reflected the opinions of some citizens. It was an odd November. While some people were angry at the girls who were forced to work the streets even though they were frightened, there was another contingent accusing the task force of failing to care about the victims just because they were prostitutes.

The solid citizens marched, carrying signs that said "Clean up our community!" and "No more prostitution!" Little League moms walked beside their uniformed sons, and mothers pushed their babies in strollers with balloons tied to them. They carried signs in their parade that demanded action. One woman said she was terrified that the Green River Killer might start abducting "nice" girls and killing them.

Seventy-five people crowded into the South Central School District boardroom and demanded that the sheriff's office do more about keeping prostitution away from their children.

"We'll never stop prostitution," the businessman who had organized the meeting announced, "but get them out of our community!" The self-righteous businessman backed down only a little, allowing that probably the dead girls were somebody's daughters and their parents must be grieving.

Lieutenant Dan Nolan, a seasoned and dedicated investigator, who had been working the Green River cases for months, suggested a whole new concept to many of those outraged citizens. Perhaps they might exert a little pressure on the johns, rather than condemning the girls they paid to have sex with.

To the people who had gathered there, it seemed a very backward way of approaching the problem. They nodded as someone said that everybody knew that it was the prostitutes themselves who were the cause of the problem. Scarlet women with no respect for themselves. Trollops. Promiscuous women who chose the lazy way to make a living. They had seen hookers in movies and knew what they were really like.

And they were so wrong. Offering sex for money is not a profession that glorifies women; it is a profession born of desperation, poverty, alienation, and loneliness. But one of the men who had sponsored the citizens' protest dismissed prostitutes easily, saying, "They do it because they really like sex."

To the detectives who had virtually abandoned their own families in their desperate search for the killer, the criticism coming their way was like pouring salt into an open wound. On the more positive side, a reward was suggested for information leading to the arrest of the Green River Killer. It began with a $500 donation, and by November 25, 1983, grew to $7,600.

It was easy to pick apart what the investigators had done—or had not done—in some critics' eyes. Experts were brought in to look at the Green River probe thus far and recommendations were made. Dick Kraske, Dave Reichert, Fae Brooks, and Randy Mullinax tried to take the evaluations with an open mind, but it was difficult for them. Unless someone had been in the trenches of a ghastly series of homicide cases, how could they know what it was like?

Some of the advisers who were asked to look at the way the cases had been handled did know, because they had been there. Bob Keppel, once a King County detective, had been a lead detective on the Bundy case and was now assigned to the Criminal Division of the Washington State Attorney General's Office. In his new position, Keppel had taken a second look at a number of cases that had stalled in the cumbersome wheels of justice and brought some of them to trial with resulting convictions. He was also visualizing a computer program called HITS that would "collect, collate, and analyze the salient characteristics of all murders and predatory sexual offenses in Washington."

Keppel had used an almost "stone age" computer to try to winnow down all the suspects turned in during the search for "Ted." Bob Keppel was a very intelligent and organized investigator who was making a name for himself with his emphasis on cross-referencing reports, suspects, dates, times, places. Even though computers were not really a large part of homicide probes in the early 1980s, they were not unknown, and Keppel was ahead of the game in that department. He would stay with the Green River Task Force far longer than he expected to.

Despite a temporary lull, both Keppel and Dave Reichert believed the homicides were still going on. They were the yin and yang of the task force, with Reichert's tendency to seek action and Keppel's analytical approach. Occasionally, they would frustrate and even anger each other, but they were both dedicated to tracking down the same quarry, so they worked it out. If there was one thing Bob Keppel had learned, it was that no detective should become overly possessive of his case to the detriment of the real goal. And no department should get involved in a "turf war" over a high-profile investigation.

F.B.I. special agent John Douglas, whose forte was profiling, flew into Seattle in late 1983 to take a close-up look at what was happening in King County. Douglas, for reasons entirely separate from the Green River cases, would be lucky to leave this investigation alive.

In early December, he collapsed in his hotel room with tachycardia and a fever nearing 106 degrees. His brain was seizing and he was near death when fellow F.B.I. agents checked his room because they hadn't heard from him. John Douglas was diagnosed with viral encephalitis and would not be able to work on the Green River cases, or any others, for six months. As it was, his recovery from paralysis and threatened brain damage was remarkable. In the years since, Douglas has been involved in any number of high-profile cases, including the JonBenet Ramsey murder, and has gone on to write several best-selling books.

Before he became ill, however, Douglas had suggested a technique that might be successful if the task force should ever be sitting across a table from a viable suspect. To allay feelings of deep embarrassment and shame and to elicit admissions that were ugly and shocking, Douglas said the questioners could separate the person in front of them into two categories: "the good Sam" and "the bad Sam." That would allow him to disconnect from what the "bad Sam" had done.

It was a great idea—if they ever got that close. But as Christmas, 1983, approached, morale was down in the Green River Task Force. The few detectives working the cases complained of the same things the "Ted" Task Force had hated: sitting in a stuffy, cramped office; sorting though mountains of paper, tips, and notes; trying to find the common denominators that might lead them to a suspect they could interrogate.

The detectives who tracked the wraithlike killer had worked overtime for more than a year, but received virtually no support from the public because they hadn't arrested anyone and seen the case through to a satisfactory trial and a conviction.

Dick Kraske was transferred from the Criminal Investigation Division in late 1983, trading jobs with Terry Allman who had been commanding the North Precinct. Frank Adamson would be taking over the Green River Task Force.

Kraske had had a lot of bucks stop at his desk in the Bundy investigation, and it had continued during the Green River murder cases. In many ways, Kraske had the toughest job in the toughest serial murder case in America. "The first year of the investigation was anything but the model for interagency and interdepartment cooperation," he recalled. "A lot of it could be attributed to the anxiety surrounding the leadership and what the commitment would be to the investigation. One of the many problems with the Bundy case had been the 'buffer zone' between the leadership and the 'person in charge of the investigation.' "

For Kraske, who had been deeply involved in both the Bundy and the Green River cases within the space of seven years, that meant that the sheriff himself should have been ready to step up and be responsible for whatever happened in the Green River cases, as well as help get the funding the investigation desperately needed. But there were three sheriffs during the late seventies to 1983, and Kraske felt he had no support from any of them, not until Vern Thomas became the head man.

The 1982–83 Green River budget was a little under $10,000. One day, far in the future, the task force tab would be estimated at $30 million, and even that wasn't enough. But in 1983 that would have sounded like an impossible brave new world of forensic science and its attendant costs.

"That is not to say I am abdicating from any mistakes that were made during my involvement," Kraske said. "It's just that it would have made things a little less difficult if you had known that you had the support these investigations demanded."

Kraske saluted Sheriff Vern Thomas, and executives Randy Revelle and Paul Barden because they were committed to helping the task force as it metamorphosed over the years.

Years later, Dick Kraske would comment wryly that a lot of people probably believed that he had retired in 1984 when he left the Green River Task Force. But that wasn't true at all. He would serve the King County Sheriff's Office for another six years, some of his best years on the department, although he almost died from internal bleeding in 1985. Doctors could find no cause and he recovered. Anyone who ever worked on a serial murder task force could probably identify the cause easily enough. Ulcers, migraines, heart attacks, bad backs, accidents, and even cancer seem to stalk them.

Over the years, this endless investigation would prove to be, quite literally, a man-killer.

In November 1983, when Vern Thomas became the new sheriff, he brought in all those in command positions to discuss a battle plan for a second task force. Everyone agreed that they needed more money and more personnel. The transition wasn't easy. Dick Kraske would have liked to stay with the hunt. An intense man, a stickler for details, Kraske had done a good job, but he and his detectives had not been able to catch the Green River Killer.

In many ways, Kraske had been working at a disadvantage. The terrible scope of the murders was hidden at first, so in the first years, the Green River Task Force was inadequately staffed. The original task force had only five detectives, with three more detectives working other unsolved homicides in the sheriff's office. The eight of them shared five cars. Their early-day Apple computer wasn't backed up by a surge protector. It was 1982 and 1983. Most people didn't know what a computer was, and were even less prepared for power surges.

"We were told that absent a surge protector, the data that had been entered had been eliminated by a power surge most likely originating in the building's elevator system," Kraske recalled. "We were never able to catch up to organizing all the information we were receiving in a retrieval system that could have saved a lot of valuable time."

More than anything, it was the agony that everyone on every task force felt or would feel because they were failing to stop the man who kept killing and killing and killing. If he knew that the King County Sheriff's Office was gearing up its efforts to catch him, the Green River Killer wasn't in the least dissuaded from his grisly avocation. So far, he had walked away free. Even as Christmas lights twinkled on the huge fir tree outside the Southcenter Mall, he was prowling along the nearby streets that paralleled the I-5 Freeway.

∎

 LISA LORRAINE YATES vanished two days before Christmas 1983. She was a very attractive nineteen-year-old with dark eyes, thick blond, wavy hair, and, despite her troubles, very much loved by her family. Her niece, Veronica, ten years younger than Lisa, thought her aunt was as lovely as a princess.

"She was young and beautiful," Veronica remembered, "gifted, loving, and funny. I thought she was so cool. She was killed when I was nine. And she was supposed to come pick me up right before she was murdered. She had promised me a winter picnic in the park and I was looking forward to that for such a long time."

Lisa had been shuttled around from home to home for much of her young life. She lived for a long time with her sister's family, and Veronica thought of Lisa more as an older sister than an aunt.

After that, Lisa lived by her wits.

24

FRANK ADAMSON was shocked to learn he would be the next commander of the Green River Task Force. Sheriff Vern Thomas told him that he would be reporting directly to him. That was fine with Adamson, and it would have made Kraske's job a lot easier if he'd had the same direct line of communication.

With seventeen years on the department, Adamson had worked in almost every unit in the King County Sheriff's Office, although he had such a quiet mien that a lot of his fellow officers didn't realize it. When Adamson became the lieutenant in charge of Special Investigations in Major Crimes, Lieutenant Frank Chase was in charge of Homicide in the unit. Chase had a remarkable memory for names and faces, and he was amazed when he realized how long Adamson had been on the department. "How come I've never seen you before?" he demanded.

Adamson only grinned. He looked a little like Bob Newhart, only with much darker hair, and he had a similar sense of humor and low-key approach to problems. His outward appearance was always relaxed, no matter what might be churning beneath the surface. He was one of the smartest cops in the department and one of the best liked, managing even to head the Internal Investigations Unit without making enemies. In that position, Adamson knew a lot of in-house secrets about various officers, and was fully aware of the rumors that said the Green River Killer was a police officer.

It was from Internal Investigations that he was summoned to the new task force. Adamson was, however, a contradiction—a cop who was an intellectual and whose wife, Jo, was a playwright. Adamson loved the poems of Dylan Thomas and Theodore Roethke; he was a policeman who had once intended to be an attorney. Although he often walked away from crime scenes depressed by man's inhumanity to man and the blind unfairness of tragedy, only Jo knew it. Adamson maintained a calm and capable facade.

While most wives might moan at the thought of their husbands stepping into the powder keg that was the Green River investigation, Jo Adamson was pleased. She believed in her husband, and she herself was seething at the injustice dealt out to the victims. "I'm a feminist," she told reporter Mike Barber of the *Post-Intelligencer,* "not a radical, but I get so angry at these women being killed. What it says about our culture—a man out there killing for his own perverted purpose."

The Adamsons lived in Maple Valley in a deep woods, and that helped smooth the edges of death and disaster that are cops' frequent companions. They had a good marriage and they admired each other's talents. Jo had had her plays produced and Frank was very proud of her. She was impressed with the honesty that was at his core. They had a teenage son, a number of big and fluffy cats, and collectors' eyes for chiming clocks and wonderful sculpture. Like Kraske, Adamson, who was forty-one in 1983, had once been a marine.

As the guard changed and an enthusiastic Adamson stepped in to run the task force, success seemed possible within months. He had forty detectives now, eight times what the first task force had, and they moved out of the dingy space between floors in the King County Courthouse to more spacious quarters in the Burien Precinct area, closer to the crime scene sites.

This new task force also had a lot more money. Captain Mike Nault, who now oversaw the Major Crimes Unit, had given a figure to the new sheriff and the command force of how much money he thought the Green River investigation merited, and the powers that be doubled it. They now seemed to be in a win-win situation.

Adamson accepted that his team had to begin by playing catch-up, reevaluating the information gleaned in the first eighteen months and moving forward. And as in any battle, the commander and the troops who now came to the front were fresh and confident. Those who were pulled back were battle weary. Dave Reichert, Bob LaMoria, Ben Colwell, Rupe Lettich, and Fae Brooks stayed with the fight. Adamson knew all too well that he, too, would have to deal with the media. The headlines were growing larger and the coverage of the Green River murders more frequent as the list of possible victims expanded.

"I honestly thought," Adamson remembered, "that because I had good people, we would have this thing solved within six months. In hindsight, I think we probably should have."

The second Green River Task Force had one senior deputy prosecutor assigned to work on the cases with them. Al Matthews joined the investigation in early 1984. He would remain with them until 1987.

WHEN ADAMSON moved into his new job during the holiday season of 1983, Shawnda Summers, Yvonne Antosh, Connie Naon, Kelly Ware, Mary Bridget Meehan, and an unidentified body had been found. Many, many more women were missing, some of them victims who had yet to be reported.

Five days before Christmas, 1983, Kimi-Kai Pitsor's mother learned where her daughter was. And Frank Adamson had to deal with the first body found on his watch. It wasn't really a body; it was only a skull.

"We had a list of twelve women who were victims—*known* victims—and not all of them would turn out to be Green River victims," Adamson recalled. "Then there was a list of missing women sent to us from the Seattle Police Department with twenty-two possibles on it. Most of them would be found and were, indeed, Green River cases. I was in Major Crimes only fifteen days when Kimi-Kai Pitsor's skull was found in Mountain View Cemetery. She was one of those twenty-two, and she was one of the youngest of all. She was barely sixteen. That was shocking to me."

The small skull in the cemetery was found about eighteen miles southeast of the airport. It might well have been from the cemetery, a body unearthed by grave robbers and scattered. Vandals in cemeteries had struck often in the south county. The site was almost on the boundary line of the small town of Auburn. But it wasn't a skull ripped from a grave. It was Kimi-Kai, found thirty miles from where she was last seen in downtown Seattle. It was out in the open, not in an overgrown wooded area where the other victims had been found.

"We thought this killer was playing with us," Adamson recalled, "when he put the skull right there. Some of the investigators thought that maybe it had been hidden and a coyote had carried it to where it was found."

He called in Search and Rescue volunteers to help look for more remains. "We went a hundred yards down an extremely steep grade, searching for more bones or clothing. It was so steep that we had to use fire truck ladders so Search and Rescue could maneuver on the hill. I was worried about the people searching—some of them were kids. Once, someone dislodged a rock and it almost hit one of the kids in the head.

"But we found nothing at all. It was my choice not to go any farther down because it was just too dangerous. The hill went all the way down to Highway Eighteen."

Although they found no more of Kimi-Kai's remains, a forensic dentist was able to match the teeth in the skull to her dental charts. Her mother heard the news without shock. She had accepted a long time before that Kimi was gone. With great sadness, she whispered, "She's not hurting now. She's not cold. She's not hungry. She's no longer in any kind of pain. That's been tormenting me for the last nine months."

As ADAMSON'S TASK FORCE moved forward, the investigators acknowledged that there were probably a lot more than a dozen victims of the Green River Killer. Adamson himself believed that. Had the killer's favorite disposal site not been located with the finding of three bodies in the Green River in August of 1982, the man they sought probably would have left all of his victims there.

But the new commander had prior experience with bodies left in water; gases formed by decomposition are so strong that he'd seen a body in an earlier case pop to the surface even though it was weighted down with a concrete block connected to chains.

Adamson felt that both Wendy Coffield and Debra Bonner had originally been left in the secluded spot farther north up the Green River where the other three women were discovered. "But once we found them," Adamson said, "he couldn't go back there anymore, so he had to find new places to leave the bodies."

∎

IN EARLY 1984, the first order of business was to be sure that all the information the new task force had and all that continued to come in was organized. "You're overwhelmed with information," Adamson recalled, "and it's not very well organized. We redesigned the case file books so we could find things easily. We got the physical evidence together. We had one room with case binders listing the Missing, the Homicides, and the Physical Evidence."

In the early eighties, it was much more difficult to gather absolute physical evidence that will identify a murderer than it is now. Twenty-two years have made a tremendous difference. DNA matching was not a standard forensic tool then. Nor was the computerized Automatic Fingerprint Identification System (AFIS) in general use. The F.B.I.'s old fingerprint system had grown archaic, depending mainly on time-consuming manual methods to match suspect ridges and loops and whorls to the fingerprints in its vast files.

Before AFIS, it took two months for police departments to get reports back on prints submitted for matching in a normal request. Funds to complete the bureau's goal of automation—thirteen years in the making—were not included in the national budget. The F.B.I. still needed $40 million to completely computerize its system, and Washington State was not yet set up to hook into it.

In the beginning, the Green River Task Force used the Alaska fingerprint identification system. Tests on blood or other body fluids were pre-DNA. All criminalists could accomplish *absolutely* was to differentiate samples submitted as being from humans or from animal species. They could tell if the specimen had come from a secretor or a nonsecretor (meaning that a small percentage of humans do not "leak" their blood types in their body fluids). For subjects who *were* secretors, criminalists could determine their blood types. That seemed like a lot two decades ago.

The one thing that was certain, and that had been certain since Dr. Edmond Locard of Lyon, France, directed the very first crime lab in the world, was his Exchange Principle. Formulated in the early years of the twentieth century, Locard's theory became the basis for any investigation of any crime scene: Each criminal leaves something of himself at a crime scene, no matter how minute, and takes something of the crime scene away with him, even if it is infinitesimal. Every new generation of detectives—and television shows like *CSI*—works on Locard's principle. But each decade brings with it more sophisticated tools to help the detectives find the minutiae that solves crimes.

As the Green River investigation moved through the eighties, there would be many advances in forensic science. The earliest, however, required a good portion of each substance to be tested— hair, blood, semen, chemicals, paint, and so on—because the various lab processes would destroy the samples submitted.

Even so, the second Green River Task Force was extremely optimistic in early 1984. Deluged with tips from the public, from prostitutes and street people, and from psychics, they investigated and cataloged all of them. However, they had to have a system to establish priority.

"We had 'A,' 'B,' and 'C' categories," Adamson explained. "A's had to be looked at as soon as possible, and they had to be eliminated conclusively before we moved on. B's were people who might be good suspects, and we certainly needed to look at them, but we could take more time to get to them. C's might possibly be suspects, but, with them, we didn't have a lot to go on and we felt it wasn't really important to get to them in the near future."

One of the problems Adamson tried to monitor was the natural tendency of detectives to fixate on one suspect, and one suspect only. Homicide detectives are human like anyone else and they aren't infallible, although their job requires that they produce irrefutable evidence that a prosecutor can present to a jury.

"I kept telling my staff that we had to remember not to get myopic," Adamson said. "When a detective became too focused on a single suspect, I reminded him—or her—that all of us got 'obsessed' with certain people. One of us might be right, but all of us couldn't be right."

Dave Reichert was still convinced that Melvyn Foster was the Green River Killer. Another detective was positive the killer was a Kent attorney whose clientele included a disproportionate number of women in the "vice trade." The lawyer lived very close to where the first five bodies had been left in the river, and this suspect had once spent time in a California town where there were several unsolved murders of women.

"I'd see that attorney, who was in his forties, occasionally," Adamson said. "He was always immaculately dressed—not a hair out of place. I thought to myself, 'No way is this guy gonna get in any river, get wet and dirty, and then show up in court.' I'd been down to the river in my dress shoes, and a month later, you could still see the grime on them, and *I* didn't get into the water. The real killer would have had to wade in there in the silt and mud."

The suspicious-acting attorney was later murdered by a disgruntled tenant in one of the shabby apartment houses he owned.

All of the investigators felt deeply, and it was tough for them to let go of their beliefs. There were just too many truly bizarre people who came to their attention. Even Adamson would soon have his own "favorite" suspect, just as they all did. Rather, he would have *three* preferred suspects. Some of the public didn't care who the Green River Killer was. They demanded only an early arrest.

Most of the time, all majors and above in the sheriff's office were too busy with administrative duties to actually go out in the field, but each was required to perform "Command Duty" every few months. "I'd go out and check in with various precincts, respond to what was going on out in the county. And I used these times to drive by three guys' places," Adamson said. He wasn't sure what he might see, and he really didn't think he was going to be lucky enough to find them doing something incriminating just as he drove by, but he felt compelled to check on them.

One of Adamson's prime suspects was an older man a young prostitute had reported as a very peculiar "client." She had agreed to meet the man at a motel on the highway, and he was quite a bit older than the usual johns. He'd seemed nice enough at first. He'd even taken her to the House of Values and told her she could buy whatever clothes she wanted. Then he took her to his house, which was close to the Green River. He owned a good-size property with many acres of land and a barn.

But once the man—Ingmar Rasmussen*—took the girl into his house, he refused to take her back to the highway. He kept her there for a week, showing her a special police badge. She didn't know whether to believe him or not. He proudly showed her his barn. With a sinking feeling, she saw that one area of the walls was plastered with pictures of women. He took pictures of her, too. She wondered if they were going to end up on the wall. Worse, she wondered where she might end up.

Rasmussen obviously was well off, and he didn't really hurt her, but she felt trapped because she was his prisoner. Finally, he took her back to the motel where she had met him. When she told detectives about the rich man with the barn full of female photographs, it sounded as if she had only an overactive imagination. However, she was able to lead the detectives back to Rasmussen's spread of land and point out the big house and barn set in the Green River valley.

In a ruse to take a look inside, Captain Bob Evans once drove alone to Rasmussen's place in an unmarked white Cadillac. He knocked on the door and when Rasmussen opened it, Evans said his car had broken down. The wealthy farmer was arrested on charges of suspicion of unlawful confinement and a search warrant was obtained for his property.

The task force investigators saw that there was a round door in the barn ceiling, held in place with big spikes. They swarmed over the barn, wondering what arcane discoveries they might make. But they were to be disappointed. "We didn't find any pictures there," Adamson said, "although we did find one of Rasmussen's cameras, and when the film was developed, our informant's pictures were there."

If this had been a horror movie, Ingmar Rasmussen's isolated barn would have been the ideal place for a serial killer to hide his victims. But this was the real world, and he, like so many others, was removed from the suspect list.

He was a little kinky, all right, and he had taken young prostitutes to his barn for photo sessions. A private investigator a worried Rasmussen had hired told Adamson that the pictures had been in the barn all along, even during their search, but the old man had taken them down from the barn wall and put them in a drawer.

"We'd gotten very good at outdoor crime scenes," Adamson said wryly, "but we were rusty on working indoor scenes, and we'd missed the photos."

25

WHILE THE CONSERVATIVE CITIZENS of south King County tended to blame the business of prostitution and vice for the shadow over their lives, they didn't really care to become involved. Responding to their complaints, King County executive Randy Revelle called a meeting in the Tukwila City Hall. Ironically, although Revelle, Sheriff Vern Thomas, and Captain Frank Adamson showed up to answer questions and listen to concerns, only four townspeople attended. The leaders of the probe and a gaggle of reporters were present, but nobody else seemed to care.

One person asked if the sheriff's office thought the killer would strike again, and Frank Adamson answered an unequivocal "Yes."

The Green River Killer had no reason to stop killing. As far as the detectives knew, he hadn't even come close to being caught, and he must, indeed, be enjoying his "success." Historically, serial killers don't stop—they accelerate. Unless such murderers are arrested and incarcerated for other crimes or they become physically unable to stalk victims or they die, they keep going. In the rare case, a radical life change—marriage or divorce or severe illness—can call a halt to their obsession to destroy lives.

So, of course, the man they were looking for was going to kill again. And they were afraid it was going to be soon. They were right.

 MARY EXZETTA WEST vanished from the Rainier Valley neighborhood on February 6, 1984. She had a sweet face and a shy smile. She lived with her aunt and she was always thoughtful about coming home on time. She had left her aunt's house at midmorning that Monday. In exactly a month, Mary would have turned seventeen, but she didn't make it that far. In six months, she would have given birth to a baby, but very few people knew that she was pregnant. She didn't know what she was going to do when she began to show.

It was odd that so many of the GRK's victims were killed so close to their birthdays. He couldn't have known when they were born, not if he was picking them up as they happened to cross his path when he was in his killing mode. It had to be only grim coincidence.

IT HAD BEEN twenty months and the victim toll kept rising. Many people were anxious and restless, including the man himself, although the men and women who were looking for him didn't know that. Women's Libbers were stridently blaming the Green River Task Force and law enforcement in general for failing to really try to protect them by not catching the Green River Killer.

The GRK was not strident at all; he merely wanted to up the ante a little and make the tournament of terror more interesting.

On February 20, *Post-Intelligencer* reporter Mike Barber, who had written extensively about the Green River cases, had a letter routed to him from the City Desk. It had arrived in a small, plain white envelope with a Seattle postmark.

The typewritten address was incorrect:

Seattle postintelligencer
fairview n john
PO Box 70
Seattle WA 98111

Actually, the street address belonged to the *Seattle Times,* but somehow the letter got to the *P.I.* The sender had added "very inportent" to the envelope.

Barber read the message inside, which had no spaces at all between the words, and at first, it seemed incomprehensible. He looked at it several times to see what the "code" might be, if, indeed, there was a code. And it still made little sense.

Gradually, he began to draw diagonal lines between what might be words and the information became clearer, although the writer was either uneducated or striving to appear so.

> whatyou eedtonoaboutthegreenriverman
>   dontthrowway
> I first onebokenordislocatarmwhy
> 2oneblackinriverhadastoneinthevaginawhy
>   3whysomeinriversomeabovegroundsomeunderground
>   4insurancewhogotit
>   5whosetogainbytheredeaths
>   6truckdisoutofstatefatherhadpaintedorinriver
>   7somehadfingeralscutoff
>   8hehadsexaftertheydeadhesmokes
>   9hechewsgum
>   i0chancefirstoneblackmaledhim
>   iiyouworkmeornobody
>   i2thinkchangedhismo
> bussnessmanorsellman
>   i3carandmotelreservation
>   i4manseenbiglugageoutofmotelwasheavyneededhelp
>   keysidcardatroadi8whos
>   i5wheresolosesomeringandmisc
>   i6outofstatecop
>   i7don'tkillinnoonarealookinoutside
>   i8onehadoldscarse
>   i9momaplehadredwinelombroscsomefishanddumpedthere

20anydurgsorselling
2iheadfoundwhofountitwhereisrest
22whendietheydiedayornight
23whatourntheremouthsoreisitatrick
24whytakesomeclothesandleavereast
25thekillerwheresatleastonering
26realestmanisoneman
27longhaultruckdriverlastseenwithone
28somehadropemarksonneckar.dhands
29oneblackinriverhaddoraononly
30alstrangledbutwithdefermetheds
3ioneblackinriverhadworkedformetro
32mosthadpimpsbettingthem
33escortmodelingforcedthemofffearofdeth
34maybepimphatergetbackatthem
34whofindstheboneswhatareththerefor
35manwhithgunorknife
36someonepaidtokilloneothersarethideit
37killwhotheyareorisitwhattheyare
38anydeaddiferthenrestt
39itcouldamanportladsomeworkedthere
40ehatkindofmanisthis

therewasabookliftatdenneysignotthisotof
    itbilongstocop

The letter was signed: "callmefred."

"Call me Fred." Well, that was clear enough, although it was unlikely that the tipster was really named Fred. The letter had probably been written by someone who wanted to play detective. He was offering motives that anyone might think of, but he was also giving a lot of information that wasn't generally known. After Barber finished trying to separate the words into some kind of sense, he turned the letter over to Dave Reichert.

At the request of Bruce Kalin, a task force evidence specialist, Tonya Yzaguerre, a latent print examiner for the sheriff's office, examined it for fingerprints. Using the Ninhydrin process—which uses chemicals and heat and can bring up prints left even decades before—Yzaguerre found one that would be saved in the hope that someday they would glean prints from a Green River crime scene or body site. And then she sent the letter on to the F.B.I., both for John

Douglas to evaluate for its content and in the hope that the type-writer used might be identified.

The F.B.I. lab felt that the typewriter was probably an Olympia style with a horizontal spacing of 2.60mm per character, and it had a fabric ribbon.

Despite the fact that the letter writer had referred to heretofore unpublished information like "One black in river had a stone in the vagina. Why?" and "Mom maple had red wine lombrosco some fish and dumped there," John Douglas wrote to Bruce Kalin that he didn't feel the real Green River Killer had written the letter.

"It is my opinion that the author of the written communiqué has no connection with the Green River Homicides. The commu-niqué reflects a subject who is average in intelligence and one who is making a feeble and amateurish attempt to gain some personal im-portance by manipulating the investigation. If this subject has made statements relative to the investigation which were not already re-leased to the press, he would have to have *access* to this information [via] Task Force."

As for calls that had come in telling the task force where bodies might be found, Douglas was also skeptical. "Your caller is not specific enough to establish himself as the 'Green River Murderer.' However, he does have the capacity to imitate and be a 'copycat' killer."

Douglas said that the Behavioral Science Unit of the F.B.I. had found that very few serial killers of this type had communicated with the media or an investigative team. When true serial killers had called, they gave very specific details to establish their credibility. "That is part of their personal need," he pointed out. "Having feel-ings of inadequacies and lacking self-worth, they must feel powerful and important."

Douglas advised the task force detectives to demand that the man who called them give more precise directions to any alleged body site. Then they were to deliberately stay away from that loca-tion. "This will anger him and demonstrate that you are stupid and ignorant and cannot follow simple instructions. [He] will be com-pelled to telephonically admonish you and/or oversee your investi-gation at the 'wrong' crime scene location."

Douglas still doubted that either the letter writer or the phone tip-ster were the real GRK. But there was the threat of a deadly copycat.

That was all the Adamson task force needed. Another serial killer. The real question was how many people not on the task force itself knew about the triangular stones placed in the vaginas of some of the first victims, and also about the wine bottle—indeed, Lambrusco—and the fish left on Carol Christensen's body? *I* knew, but I never told anyone what someone on the task force had told me. Some *Seattle Times* reporters found out, too, but they did not publish it. These pieces of information were definitely not generally known, and they hadn't been mentioned in newspapers or on television.

It was almost impossible to tell if the letter Mike Barber received was the real thing. In retrospect, I believe it was. But there were so many tips coming in—to the Green River Task Force, to well-recognized journalists, and, yes, to me.

In 2003, as I went through the huge stacks of material I'd saved for twenty-two years, I came across an envelope virtually identical to the one Barber got. It is addressed to

> Mrs Ann RULE
> c/o POST-Intelligencer
> 6th & Wall
> Seattle, Wasjington
> 98121

With a Seattle postmark of April 24, 1984, it had been sent two months after the first letter. This address for the *P.I.* was correct. The mistake in the spelling of Wasjington had been corrected with a pen. On the back flap, it said,

> "Andy Stack"
> GREEN RIVER

and in ink:

> G-R (209)

Someone at the *P.I.* had scribbled my box number on it and forwarded it. There is nothing inside the envelope now, and I cannot say for sure that there ever was by the time I got it. I don't know who wrote "Andy Stack" on the back of the envelope, but that was the pen name that I used for almost fifteen years when I wrote for *True Detective* and her four sister true-crime magazines. Very few people knew that at the time. The "209"? I have no idea who wrote that or what it meant. Was it the 209th tip the *P.I.* had received? Or did it mean something to the person who mailed it?

The mystery envelope was sent at a time when I was receiving so much information from readers and people interested in the Green River cases that I could barely keep up with it. As always, I passed on the most likely sounding information to the task force.

One thing I had not known was that there was someone who kept track of my public appearances, someone who often stood eight or ten feet away from me, watching. Over the years, I gave scores of lectures in the Seattle area, and people always asked about the Green River Killer. I often commented about my feeling that I must have sat in the next restaurant booth from him, or stood behind him in line at the supermarket. But that was only logical, deductive reasoning. Most of his victims had been abducted within a mile or so of where I lived, and many of their bodies had been found that close, too. All of us who lived in the south King County area had an eerie sense that we might know him, or, at least, that we must have seen him without realizing who he was.

In the mideighties, I was as confident as Frank Adamson and Dave Reichert were that it was merely a question of how many months it would take to make an arrest, and I often made predictions off the top of my head, assuring the audience that I believed he would be caught by Easter or Thanksgiving . . . or surely by the next Christmas.

And I believed it myself, never really thinking that the man who was so elusive might be sitting in a darkened auditorium, listening.

26

WHEN THE LETTER sent to Mike Barber was revealed, I took a crack at being a cryptographer. There is no question in my own mind that it was written by the real Green River Killer, obviously a man who knew many secret things but who had extremely limited grammar or spelling ability:

Translated by author:
What you need to know about the Green River man

Don't throw away.

1. First one broken or dislocated arm. Why?
2. One black in river had a stone in the vagina. Why?
3. Why some in river? Some aboveground? Some underground?
4. Insurance. Who got it?
5. Who set [stood] to [gain] by their deaths?
6. Truck is out of state. Father had painted [it] or [it's] in [the] river.
7. Some had fingernails cut off.
8. He had sex after they [were] dead. He smokes.
9. He chews gum.
10. [There is a] chance the first one blackmailed him.
11. You work [for] me or nobody.
12. [I] think he changed his M.O.
    Businessman or salesman.
13. Car and motel reservation.
14. Man seen [carrying] big luggage out of motel. [It] was heavy [and he] needed help. Keys [and] I.D. card [are at] Road 18.
15. Where so close some ring and miscellaneous?
16. Out of state cop.
17. [I] don't kill in no one area. Look in [and] outside.
18. One had old scars.
19. Mom [or one] Maple [Valley] had red wine Lombrosco, some fish dumped there.
20. Any drugs or selling?
21. Head found. Who found it? Where is the rest?
22. When did [they] die? Day or night?
23. What tore their mouths, or is it a trick?
24. Why take some clothes and leave [the] rest?
25. The Killer wears at least one ring.
26. Real estate man is one man.
27. Long haul truck driver last seen with one.
28. Some had rope marks on neck and hands.
29. One black in river had odor on only.
30. All strangled but with different methods.
31. One black in river had worked for Metro.
32. Most had pimps betting them.
33. Escort modeling forced them off fear of death.
34. Maybe pimp had—or got—back at them.

34. (sic) Who finds the bones? What are they there for?
35. Man with gun or knife.
36. Someone paid to kill one. The others are [to] hide it.
37. Killed [because of] who they are. Or is it [because of] what they are?
38. Any dead different than [the] rest?
39. It could [be] a man [from] Portland. [Or] someone [who] worked there.
40. What kind of man is this?

There was a book left at Denney's sign. Not this. Out of [doors.] It belongs to [a] cop.

Maybe the GRK wasn't out there in my audiences very often. Maybe he actually resided a long way away. Although those of us in the south King County area still tended to believe that we lived in safe small towns—Des Moines, Riverton, Tukwila, Federal Way, Burien—our world had changed. In 1984, the SeaTac International Airport was known as the Jackson International Airport in honor of Senator Henry Jackson, and in the course of a year ten million people flew in and out of it. A quarter of a million people drove friends, families, and business associates to their flights or picked them up. If the Highline School District, which encompassed my children's schools, were to incorporate as one city, it would be the fourth largest in the state of Washington.

Schuyler Ingle, a reporter for the *Seattle Weekly* with superior researching skills, looked at those figures and realized that 150,000 people passed through the Strip area in a month. Transients, yes, but from every class of society, both very rich and very poor and everything in between. They stayed in 4,500 motel rooms or slept wherever they could.

Lieutenant Jackson Beard headed the Pro-Active Team for the new task force. There were plainclothes officers on the Strip most nights. Female police officers dressed and made-up to look like prostitutes strolled beside the road at least one night a week. Male officers tried to keep an eye on them, waiting for the signal that a john had taken the bait. The Strip had become an uncomfortable place for both the real prostitutes and their customers, who would have to figure out a way to tell their wives and/or girlfriends why they'd been arrested.

Sooner or later, the task force detectives were sure they would catch the Green River Killer in their net. If he was still out there, he was going to approach the wrong woman. The Pro-Active Team's decoys were concentrating far more on arresting and questioning the johns than the girls who made a meager living on the street.

But if they stopped the right john, how would they know it was him? They didn't know that yet—unless he gave enough of himself away for them to get a search warrant for his house or his car. Unless he'd kept souvenirs of his victims, or photographs. Unless the science of DNA progressed to a point far beyond where it was in 1984.

He was out there. But as far as they knew, he wasn't one of the dozens of men they arrested for propositioning the disguised police officers.

In mid-March 1984, he probably watched with some satisfaction as a group of women who called themselves the Women's Coalition to Stop the Green River Murders mobilized. They planned to march to "take back the night," and to point up their perception of the inadequacy of the Green River Task Force. They were joined by a San Francisco group called U.S. Prostitutes Collective.

"We are calling on all women to end the farce of the Green River murder investigation," Melissa Adams of the coalition said in a news conference. "It is the responsibility of all of us to take action, and we must do it now—because women are dying."

Men would not be allowed to march in the downtown Seattle parade that would begin at the Pike Place Market, proceed along First Avenue to University, up Third Avenue, and end at Prefontaine Square next to the King County Courthouse. However, they would be encouraged to watch and show support. The local chapter of the National Organization for Women and various domestic abuse and child abuse groups were supporting the coalition.

Two actual prostitutes were to be imported for the rally, one from San Francisco and one from London, women who would stand in for local working girls who were too frightened or embarrassed to be singled out for the crowd. It was two decades ago, and a different era. Women's Libbers were often strident because they felt there was no other way. "The issue is the killing of women," Adams said. "But we are showing unity with prostitutes who are the victims of this killer—and victims of a sexist society.

"Violence against women is an All-American sport."

Perhaps it was. Certainly, even though the millennium has arrived, far too many women are still being sacrificed to domestic violence. But the coalition had chosen the wrong target, and it wasn't the Green River Task Force, whose members yearned to catch the man who was killing young women far more, if possible, than the women who marched with banners that disparaged them. To have their overtime efforts and their near-pulverizing frustration called "a farce" was a bitter pill, although they had grown used to being undermined.

Dave Reichert, who had been with the task force continually for the longest time—almost two full years—probably felt the brunt of their derision the most. It was difficult to keep going when so many leads evaporated into nothing, where sure bets as suspects were cleared of any connection to the Green River cases and walked away.

"What we are finding out," Reichert said, "is that police departments aren't organized to handle a case like this. It's not dealt with that often."

That was true enough. But Seattle now had two almost back-to-back serial killing sieges. First, Ted Bundy—and now the Green River Killer. Frank Adamson's task force reorganized, giving specific detectives responsibility for certain victims: Dave Reichert would be in charge of the investigations in the deaths of Wendy Coffield, Debra Bonner, Marcia Chapman, Cynthia Hinds, Opal Mills, and Leann Wilcox. Jim Doyon and Ben Colwell would work the cases of Carol Christensen, Kimi-Kai Pitsor, Yvonne Antosh, and the woman known only as Bones #2. Rich Battle and Paul Smith handled the murders of Giselle Lovvorn, Shawnda Summers, and Bones #8. Jerry Alexander and Ty Hughes traced the movements and people connected to Mary Bridget Meehan, Connie Naon, and Bones #6.

Those, of course, were only the victims whose remains had been found. Sergeant Bob Andrews, called "Grizzly" by his fellow detectives, would work missing persons with Randy Mullinax, Matt Haney, and Tom Jensen. Rupe Lettich would do follow-up on all homicide cases, but there was still a huge job left—the outpouring of tips and suspect names coming in willy-nilly from the public. Cheri Luxa, Rob Bardsley, Mike Hatch, and Bob LaMoria would try to field those and pass them on to the most likely investigators.

Until the day when, hopefully, a suspect would be identified, arrested, and convicted, the public would have no idea of how desperately hard they all worked, pounding pavements, making tens of thousands of phone calls, talking to people who told the truth, those who shaded the truth to suit themselves, and others who outright lied to them. It was akin to crocheting an elaborate tapestry as big as a football field, inserting each tiny stitch as new information began to match old intelligence.

All the while never knowing what centerpiece—whose face—was going to emerge in the middle of the tapestry.

THEY DID IT ALL without complaining and seemingly without letting their critics get under their skins. But sometimes the jeers got to be too much. Women shouting that the new Green River Task Force wasn't even trying annoyed Lieutenant Danny Nolan because, if anyone knew how hard they were trying, it was Nolan. He had a poker face and a wry sense of humor.

But he didn't find the Women's Coalition humorous. Their sit-ins and marches interrupted the order of business for the task force, which already had enough problems. Cookie Hunt, a short, heavyset woman who was blind in one eye, was one of the most stubborn critics. She organized an all-night sit-in outside task force headquarters, then housed in what had once been an elementary school. Cookie was so earnest in her crusade and so guileless that it was easier to feel sorry for her than to take offense. But she, too, was fighting the wrong target.

Nobody thought Cookie was a prostitute; she was just trying to help them. I used to offer her rides when I spotted her standing in the rain on the highway. She would grudgingly accept only because she knew I was friendly with the detectives and wrote positive things about them.

Frank Adamson worried about Cookie, too. He took criticism more philosophically than his crew did. On one windy, stormy, pounding-rain night, he couldn't stand to watch the picketers walking in the cold rain. So he invited them in and told them they could demonstrate inside, and sleep in the hallway. They accepted. Some of the other task force detectives wondered how Danny Nolan was going to react to the sight of the "libbers" when he came to work in the morning.

"I'll tell you how," Adamson said with a grin. "He'll walk in, take one look, and he won't say a word. Watch."

He knew his lieutenant. Nolan spotted the hallway full of sleeping demonstrators, marched past the first office in line, which was

Adamson's, into his own office next door, and slammed the door. A few minutes later, he came back to Adamson, fuming, and said, "What the hell do you think you're doing?"

The detectives watching doubled over with laughter. They had to when they could; there was little to laugh at.

Five days after the coalition's march, Reichert's and Keppel's prediction came to pass; the homicides were continuing, and the Green River Killer took another victim. Cindy Smith was seventeen, but she looked younger. If Keli McGinness had resembled Lana Turner, Cindy Smith looked more like Punky Brewster. All the missing girls were individuals, all attractive, but such different types. And all so young.

 CINDY SMITH had left home and was living in California, much to the concern of her mother, Joan Mackie. Joan was relieved when Cindy called in the middle of March 1984 to say that she was coming home. She was engaged and she was happy and wanted to come back to her family. Joan sent her money for transportation and was delighted to see Cindy. "She didn't even unpack her suitcase," her mother recalled. "She was in such a hurry to go see her brother."

It was the first day of spring, March 21, when Cindy disappeared. She had been heading for her brother's job, and the last time anyone saw her, she was at the corner of Pacific HiWay South and S. 200th Street. Ironically, she had come all the way from California to meet her killer on her first day back home.

Cindy was white. As far as the task force investigators could tell, there were twenty white girls missing and fourteen black girls. By April 20, 1984, they had discovered a total of four sets of unidentifiable bones, and, without a full skull and jaw, they couldn't be sure whether those were the final remains of Caucasian or African-American victims. They didn't even know if they had found all of the Green River victims. There were a number of names on the Green River Victim/Missing Person List that had an asterisk next to them, signifying "Not on Official List." Quite likely, there were names that should have been reported and never were.

Every expert on this "new" kind of murderer said that they don't stop killing of their own accord. Serial killers don't quit. But something must have changed in the GRK's life, making him less hungry for murder or causing his rituals to become more difficult.

Maybe he had less privacy. Maybe he was happy, which seemed unlikely.

In truth, he might have been running a little scared. Although the investigators didn't yet realize it, he had already walked into one of the snares they'd set on Pac HiWay, and been questioned by Detective Randy Mullinax, who had worked this daunting serial murder investigation almost from the beginning. Mullinax had noticed how often he was on the highway and the way his eyes followed the girls on the street. He took his information, wrote out a field investigation report (F.I.R.), and let him go. He was only one face among so many and he hadn't appeared to be a viable suspect. The man admitted he liked paying for sex, but he had a solid work record, a local address, and he hardly seemed the type.

The quiet man wasn't really that concerned about being stopped. He figured the cop wouldn't remember him. Actually, he was wrong. Mullinax's antennae had gone up and he recalled that stop well, although he couldn't really say why. Just a longtime cop's "hinky" feeling.

Indeed, the confident man would be stopped again, admitting this time to Detective Larry Gross that he patronized prostitutes, but he seemed to be a totally nonthreatening type, just another guy in a plaid flannel shirt and a baseball cap, a blue-collar working stiff, single.

27

AFTER HIS FIRST WIFE left him and returned to San Diego, he'd begun to look for female companionship. He was in his early twenties then as he cruised "the loop" in Renton, a Boeing town about seven miles east of Burien and Tukwila where he grew up. On weekend nights, the loop was filled with cars that circled past the high school and the theaters again and again, cruising with windows down and music blasting. The crowd was mostly made up of students, but some of the drivers were a little older. It was a casual place to meet someone.

He met a woman named Dana Brown* when he saw her and pulled close to her car on the Renton Loop. They exchanged names and phone numbers. She was quite different from his ex-wife. Dana was short and very, very heavy. She had a sweet face, but she'd never really dated when she went to Mount Tahoma High School in Maple Valley because the boys all wanted cheerleader types. She was very nice to him, and thrilled that he was so interested in her.

She found him fun and funny, and he liked her because she acted as if he were wonderful. She didn't seem to notice that he wasn't particularly intelligent. Once he was out of school and out of the service, most people seemed to accept him as a regular person, and not someone to be left behind. His ego needed the attention he got from Dana after what had happened in his marriage. It wasn't very long before they had moved in together in his tiny house in Maple Valley Heights. It was isolated and power lines zinged over the backyard, making a lot of people veer away from it, especially when the television news said that scientists warned that living too close to power lines could cause cancer.

Since he was old enough, he'd always had a job, and he had begun to work at the Kenworth Truck Company. He wasn't making much money, but he was learning a lot about painting the mammoth rigs that could sell for hundreds of thousands of dollars. His ten-mile commute over country roads from Maple Valley was easy in the early seventies; it was long before builders began to carve wide swaths out of the evergreen forests surrounding Seattle to accommodate housing developments with names like Firwood Heights and Cedar Mist Estates.

Maryann Hepburn* hadn't seen Dana for years, although she remembered her from high school. Maryann's last name was Carlson then and she was a senior at Tahoma, two years older than Dana. "You know how younger girls will kind of attach themselves to you in high school?" she asks. "Well, I was Girls' Club president, and I was overweight. These two sophomores—Dana and Carol—were fat, too, and every time I turned around, there they were, my chubby sophomore groupies. I guess I was proving to them that you could be chubby and popular at the same time. So I got to know them, and was friendly with them, but there's a big difference between sophomores and seniors in high school."

Dana and her family had moved to Washington State from one of the southern states where they had a little farm. Maryann went home with Dana once in a while and she could see that the Browns were totally into country-western music. "Her dad, who was a lot older than her mother, played the fiddle and Dana played the guitar. They belonged to some group called Country Fiddlers or something like that, and they used to play songs on the radio sometimes, and go to hoedowns, or whatever, where the fiddlers competed."

After she graduated from Mount Tahoma, Maryann Hepburn went to business school in downtown Seattle, and lost touch with Dana. "I met my husband on a blind date, and he was from Miami, so we moved there for a while," she said. "I hated everything about it. It was flat and hot and humid. I was so glad to get back to Washington. It was a little after that when Dana called me."

Dana said she was married now and was calling to tell Maryann that she had just had a baby boy: Chad.* "He was way, way premature," Dana said, "and I had to have an emergency C-section because he wasn't breathing right or his heart was too slow, or something like that."

Chad was in Children's Orthopedic Hospital in Seattle in an incubator, and Dana said she had no transportation to visit him. Her husband was working nights, and they had only one car. Maryann, who had had a baby girl herself six months earlier, felt sorry for Dana and volunteered to drive her.

As Dana led her toward the neonatal intensive care unit (NICU) nursery, she warned her friend, "He's a little small."

"He was so small," Maryann remembered, "I don't think he weighed even two pounds. I'd never seen a baby so tiny. It was a miracle that he lived at all."

But Chad did live, and he finally weighed enough so that his parents could take him home. Maryann and Dana, reunited, found they had a lot more in common than they had in high school. Their husbands worked for companies that were practically next door to each other, and they were outdoor guys who liked to cut wood together or fish while the wives visited.

Maryann was never sure just when Dana married her husband, but she knew that she was his second wife. She had the impression that they got married after Dana became pregnant, but it didn't matter because they seemed happy together. "I liked him," Maryann said. "His eyes twinkled and he had a great smile. What is the word? Charismatic. He was charismatic. He really wanted people to like him—so much so that he went out of his way to charm them. He was the kind of guy who would stop and help if your car broke down beside the road, always anxious to lend a hand. Dana was the same way, wanting friends."

It seemed to Maryann that Dana's husband made jokes about things most people wanted to hide. He turned his defeats into funny stories. She always remembered standing next to him in his back-yard in Maple Valley Heights when he laughed and said, "Well, I married a thin blonde and that didn't work out, so this time I married a fat brunette to change my luck."

The two couples often got together on weekends for potluck dinners. None of them had much money, so they ate a lot of spaghetti and hamburger casseroles. They didn't drink much either, but they sometimes had a glass of cheap wine. The women would laugh and say they got along so well because they were both over-weight and had such skinny husbands. What had hurt so much in high school didn't seem to matter anymore.

The two couples went to church together, too. There was a minister who was trying to start a new Southern Baptist congregation, and he was a dynamic speaker and ambitious proselytizer, knocking on doors to bring new worshippers into his church. There was no actual church building yet, so they held their Sunday and Wednesday services in the Aqua Barn, a compound in Maple Valley that featured both a swimming pool and a stable that rented horses.

Dana's husband often stood to read the scriptures aloud to the congregation. "He was so skinny," Maryann Hepburn recalled. "He had his hair combed down over his forehead and he looked like a boy wearing a man's suit, but he was very serious in church."

Their pastor's views were truly archaic in a world where women's rights were beginning to emerge. He preached that wives and daughters would be barred from Heaven if they didn't obey their husbands. They were not allowed to wear the color red, or to cut their long hair. "Women were nothing in his eyes," Maryann said. "We were not allowed to teach Sunday school or be choir directors or do any job where we had any authority. Dana's husband believed everything that Pastor said, but my husband took issue with it. When Pastor told us that we were 'Sunday Morning Christians' because we didn't go to every function they offered, that was pretty much the end for us."

Dana's husband, however, followed the minister's edicts absolutely, and she didn't seem to mind. She did what he said. He and Dana had moved to a little house in Burien, and they were fixing it up. Dana chose a pretty shade of blue to paint the bathroom, but he forbade it. "It's going to be white," he said firmly. "Everything in here has to be white."

And it was.

Dana's mother-in-law was almost her exact opposite. Mary was a salesperson in the Men's Department at the JCPenney store in Renton. She was a brunette in her late forties and always impeccably dressed with perfect accessories. Friends described her as "very well put together." She took great pride in her managerial position in the JCPenney hierarchy.

Dana's mother-in-law bought all of her husband's clothes, just as she did for her sons. She always knew ahead of time about Penney's sales and also used her employee discount. Although it rankled Dana, it only made sense for Mary to buy her husband's clothing.

Mary didn't approve of Dana, either. Her housekeeping wasn't up to Mary's standards, and she felt her daughter-in-law didn't take very good care of Chad. He was a frail boy with reddish blond hair who always seemed to have a runny nose. He had inherited his father's allergies and had to take medication for that, and he was so full of energy that he never put on any fat.

Dana wanted to have another baby, but her husband didn't. As much as he loved Chad, he didn't think they could afford to raise two children. He wanted Dana to have her tubes tied.

As the years passed Dana gained even more weight and she was miserable about that. Her husband didn't complain much, but she knew he would like her to be slimmer. Finally, she broached the subject of having gastric bypass surgery. In the late seventies, it was a new procedure, almost experimental. But Dana wanted it, and finally he encouraged her to go ahead with the operation.

The gastric surgery worked spectacularly well—maybe too well. Within months, Dana went from plus sizes to a size 7. She had never worn clothes that small. She suddenly became a very attractive woman and men did double takes when they saw her. It made her husband a little nervous. He had never worried that she would leave him, but now she had a lot of men noticing her. "Guys started to come on to Dana," Maryann said, "and she'd never had that happen before.

"Dana was working in Penney's, too. Her mother-in-law got her the job. Even though they had their issues, Dana and her husband were always over there, visiting, and her mother-in-law babysat for Chad a lot."

By this time Dana and her family had moved again. They had lived in three or four houses in the south end of King County, while the Hepburns stayed put. Their new place was on Star Lake Road. Like the Maple Valley Heights house, it was in a very secluded area, down at the dead end of a road.

During one of their shared meals—at the house on Star Lake Road—their hosts disappeared after dinner, leaving Maryann and her husband, Gil, in the house with the children. Their guests cleared the table and waited. It was quite a while before Dana walked in with a funny grin on her face. She pulled Maryann inside and whispered, "Bet you can't guess what we just did?"

When her friend looked mystified, Dana laughed and told her that she and her husband had gone outside and made love—he liked it that way. Maryann thought privately that it wasn't a very polite thing for the host and hostess to do, but she let it go. Dana was so happy with her new figure that she seemed years younger than she was, almost like she was having a delayed teenage time.

Both couples enjoyed country-western music and liked to go to a spot called The Beanery on the East Valley Highway near Kent. When Dana's husband had to work nights, Gil Hepburn would drive Maryann, Dana, and a mutual friend, Diane, to the country-western bar.

"That's when things started to go downhill in Dana's marriage," Maryann said. "Gil would dance with all three of us, and we had a good time at first. But then Dana started slipping out the back with some guy. She always told her husband that she was staying overnight at Diane's house because it was too late to come home alone while he was working."

It blew up when Dana's husband called Diane's house one night, asking for his wife. Told she wasn't there—that she had never spent the night at Diane's house—he was stunned. His comfortable, overweight wife who had done what Pastor ordained and wanted only to keep house and be a mother had turned into a femme fatale. When her baffled husband questioned her, Dana said that Diane was lying, that it was Gil who was cheating on Maryann, and they were all trying to cover it up. Dana also spent time at the Eagles' Lodge, often coming home well after 2 AM, worrying her husband more.

By this time, Dana's gastric bypass was working more than it was meant to. She wasn't getting enough nutrients to survive and her weight plummeted. She had no choice but to have her alimentary canal reconnected. If she didn't, she would die. Now her husband insisted that she have her tubes tied while she was under the anesthesia and she agreed. One child was enough.

But the marriage was destroyed. The man who had never fit in anywhere now had two wives who had betrayed him, and he couldn't forgive either one of them. By the spring of 1981, their divorce was final. He would pay Dana child support, and have custody of Chad on weekends and some vacations. He resented giving Dana his hard-earned money. It made him furious.

He had come up in the world in his jobs and in buying more and more expensive houses, but he kept striking out with women. Prostitutes were easier than trying to pick up women and ask them for dates.

28

FROM THE BEGINNING of his stint as the Green River Task Force commander, Captain Frank Adamson acknowledged that he wasn't a veteran homicide investigator. If there were people who could enhance the task force's effectiveness with their expertise, he wanted to invite them on board. Bob Keppel was borrowed back from the Washington State Attorney General's Office. Keppel, with his "Ted" Task Force experience and his ability to organize diverse information, could be both an important expediter and a somewhat cold critic. So be it.

The F.B.I. sent Gerald "Duke" Dietrich, who was a humorous and deceptively easygoing special agent in the San Francisco office of the Bureau. Dietrich was an expert on child abductions and homicide. He had once actually wired a tombstone with a tape recorder to trap the sexual ravings of a necrophile. He and his former partner, Special Agent Mary Ellen O'Toole, had an enviable record of crime solving in California.

Adamson also contacted Chuck Wright, a Washington State Probation and Parole supervisor. Wright taught courses at Seattle University on violent offenders and sexual deviancy. Adamson was looking for someone inside the probation system who would be able to quickly evaluate suspects—who were now euphemistically called, "persons of interest." Many of the men the task force was looking at had prior records. Wright's background would be of tremendous help in searching the system for sexual offenders, and he could work with Adamson and Dr. Chris Harris, a forensic psychiatrist, as one more mind to try to understand the killer they were looking for.

Sheriff Vern Thomas asked Amos Reed, then head of the Department of Corrections, if the task force could "borrow" Chuck Wright to act as a liaison. Reed said, "Of course."

"The first thing I saw on Frank Adamson's bookshelf was the American Psychiatric Association's *Diagnostic and Statistical Manual of Mental Disorders,*" Wright remembered. "I had never seen a police officer who had that 'cookbook' to use as a tool—and not only did Adamson have it, he'd read it. We were both readers and we hit it off right away."

Wright was allowed into the back room of the task force headquarters where the "body map" was kept, covered with a tarp so that no reporter might accidentally see it. "The map was punctured with an overwhelming number of colored pins. Each pin represented a body, and these seemingly endless colored beads took me aback. How could there be so many bodies and we normal citizens not even know this?"

Every body site had been videotaped. At first there had been sound on the tapes, but the officers who had to deal with the horrors they found often swore or used four-letter words to defuse their own feelings. Wright suggested, "We have to think there may be a jury one day who will see these tapes, and listen to your profanity, and that won't help the prosecution.

"The sound was turned off," he recalled.

Chuck Wright saw how difficult it was to know what was evidence and what had simply been thrown away in trash piles: women's underwear, cigarette butts, beer cans. To be safe, they took it all.

Despite the things he had seen during his many years as a probation officer, Wright had a number of unique experiences as he worked with the task force. As a winter sun set one night, he accompanied two plainclothes investigators into woods that grew darker with every step as the trees closed behind them. There had been a report that two bodies were hidden there. "It was pitch-black," he recalled, "and I asked, 'Aren't you guys scared?' and they whispered, 'No,' but when I turned around with my flashlight, I saw they both had their guns drawn—just in case."

They walked a little farther into the "black hole." "I took one more step and felt my foot go through some soft material, and my ankle and lower leg got wet with some warm liquid," Wright said. "My heart stopped and my mind raced. I swore, too, 'Oh shit! I just sank my foot into a body.' But it was only a rotten log."

One thing that impressed Wright was how concerned the King County officers were for the women on the street. "We parked on the SeaTac Strip, and we noticed a van pulling up ahead of us. The driver motioned to a young woman, and she walked over to the driver's window so they could talk. In no time at all, she walked around and got into the passenger side, but before she did, she looked back and smiled at us. I was surprised, but the officer I was with just smiled back at her. When the van started up, so did our undercover car. We followed the van, staying well back, and stopped when it stopped. The deputy with me explained that they tried to watch johns and their dates to be sure the women were safe.

"After they finished, we followed the van back to the highway. When the girl got out, she looked back at us and we could tell by her body language that she was okay. At least for that moment in time, that girl was safe."

The Pro-Active Team was developing rapport with the working girls as well as protecting them, and when they needed information about one of the men who picked them up, the women gave it. While the missing girls were very young and inexperienced for the most part, some prostitutes *were* streetwise and had learned to deal with the kinky demands of certain customers, including bondage and discipline, "water sports," and necrophilia.

One aspect of necrophilia astonished Chuck Wright, who thought he had covered almost every perversion in the class he taught on sexual deviancy. Since they were investigating murders, the task force detectives talked to prostitutes who were willing to fulfill the truly grotesque fantasies of men who wanted to have sex with dead women. One "specialist" said she provided a room with a coffin, flickering candles, and mournful organ music. She powdered herself until she was as pale as milk, and actually inserted ice cubes into her vagina so she would seem to be a truly *cold* woman, the opposite of what most men might want. She said she made $500 for such a specialized performance.

Seattle police raided an escort service and arrested two men for promoting prostitution. In the evidence seized, they found index cards with the names, addresses, business connections, and personal preferences of their clients. Although most of that information would never be released, the list was culled for clients marked "dangerous," and those with violent preferences were turned over to the Green River Task Force.

Such johns were added to the "persons of interest" list, and a few so-called respected citizens were shocked to be contacted by the detectives about their deepest secrets. But none of them could be linked to the Green River murders.

The women who made top dollar were the exception, of course. Wright remembered interviews with some of the families of the girls who had disappeared, many of them memorable because of the complete apathy he saw. "I was with two deputies who were trying to verify if a young teenage girl was 'just' missing or if she really was a Green River Killer victim," he said. "When her father answered our knock, we walked into a house that was so messy that none of us sat down. The place was littered with beer cans, and cigarette smoke filled the room to the point that my eyes started to water. When one of the deputies asked him about his missing daughter, the man was very nonchalant. He said he had no idea where she was. When the deputy noted that she had been gone for over two months according to the report, the guy said he was surprised by the news. But he didn't really seem surprised. Apparently, he was used to her not being around; he said he usually didn't know where she was. She had 'run off' so often that he had just stopped being concerned about her whereabouts or welfare.

"When we got back in the squad car, we could only shake our heads. How could any father not know or even care about his daughter? Her case just had sadness built into it. We found out later that she was working the streets somewhere in California. At least she was alive and maybe in a better place than if she'd been in her dad's household."

Wright got to know the members of the task force well. He could see that some were "sprinters" who wanted to catch an infamous serial killer and do it *now*. "Others were highly trained long-distance runners—and that's what Adamson needed, because it was clear it would be a long haul."

No one could have known just how long.

Probably the most distinguished adviser to come on board the task force was Pierce Brooks. He was, of course, *the* investigative genius in America on serial murder. Although he already had his hands full launching VICAP, the Violent Criminal Apprehension Program, working with the F.B.I. in Quantico, and he was officially retired from law enforcement, Brooks had yet to slow down. He was in his early sixties and his health wasn't the best; he had undergone delicate arterial surgery, and he would have dearly loved to spend his time with his wife, Joyce, in his home on the MacKenzie

River east of Eugene, Oregon. Instead, he was constantly flying between Eugene; Quantico; Huntsville, Texas; and Seattle.

Brooks and I worked together on the VICAP task force, and, along with John Walsh, we had testified on the threat of serial murder in America at a U.S. Senate judiciary subcommittee hearing in early 1983. Senators Arlen Spector and Ted Kennedy were two members of the committee who seemed to agree with what we had to say.

Now Brooks came to Seattle to evaluate the ongoing Green River investigation. He spent two weeks perusing the staggering amount of information gathered thus far by the first two task forces. His recommendation was that the investigation must continue, with as large a team as possible. If catching this killer meant doubling the manpower, then it should be done. Every public record, F.I.R., tip, clue, or possible bit of information had to be gathered and fed into the computer system they had.

Going back to the first serial killer he himself ever hunted, albeit in a time when even he didn't use the term, Brooks thought of Harvey Glatman, the so-called Lonely Hearts Killer. Glatman was a homely man with big ears who lived in a cheap apartment in Los Angeles. He didn't appeal to the women he met through a Lonely Hearts club, and he'd killed one who rejected his advance and only wanted to go home. After that, he had lured victims in Los Angeles by pretending to be a professional photographer. He took photos of his naive victims, some where they were tied up and gagged, telling them he was shooting covers for fact-detective magazines. But then he drove the helpless young women to the desert where he strangled them, lingering afterward to shoot more pictures.

Glatman had taught Pierce Brooks a lot about murderers like the Green River Killer. "I don't believe this killer selected the body disposal sites at random," Brooks told Vern Thomas, Frank Adamson, and Bob Keppel. "If he did, he is the luckiest serial murderer of all time. He knows pretty well, or even exactly, where he will dispose of the victims before the murders occur.

"Just for the moment, let's focus on four of the most prominent cluster sites: airport north, airport south, Star Lake, and the Green River. They are heavily wooded, somewhat concealed, and you think at first that this is an ideal location where someone would take anything to hide it—a body in this particular case—anything valuable. In this case, it was the body that was valuable."

Brooks knew what he was talking about. He explained that the bodies of the victims, and the killer's relationship to them, was what gave him power. He needed the secrecy and the knowledge that only he knew where the poor dead girls waited for him.

"It is a very high risk situation," he continued, "to go into an unknown area that is heavily wooded without knowing something about the location. I just do not believe that the killer went there with his victim the first time he had ever been there. I try to put myself in his position. Here I am a stranger in the area. If I want to dispose of a body and I'm driving down a nice, little winding hill and I have this body I want to get rid of, that would probably be the *last* place I would stop."

A stranger wouldn't know what was at the bottom of the hill, who might be approaching, or, in the case of an illegal trash dumping spot, if someone might drive up and catch him. No, he would have to be very familiar with where he went with a body. The Green River site—the first site—would have been especially iffy for someone unfamiliar with it. There were the fishermen along its banks, and local residents taking a shortcut home.

Brooks was positive that the killer either lived or worked nearby. He knew that stretch of river like he knew the back of his hand. He urged the task force detectives to learn who lived there, worked near there on a permanent basis, had worked there on a temporary project. Since the Green River victims had disappeared at various times of day and night, he suggested they check unions for work schedules, cab companies for their drivers' locations and shifts, military records from the many bases around Seattle and Tacoma.

"I have always felt this person might either be in the military or have been in the military," Brooks said. More than any psychic, and most detectives and F.B.I. special agents, Brooks could draw a picture in his mind, a profile of the serial killer they all hunted. He was quite sure that it was only *one* killer, working alone.

"The odds are that it would be a Caucasian—good chance that he is military, or had a military connection, is an outdoors type, is somewhat of a loner but is certainly not a total introvert. I can't believe that a person that picks up prostitutes on the street is the kind of person who walks into some kind of singles bar and tries to make it with some of the girls. I think this fella's a little bit backward that way, does not come on strong—that's why he goes for prostitutes, which, in my thinking, are the easiest victims."

Brooks speculated that the GRK might be a trained killer, taught that arcane skill in the service. "In other words, he could be a trained survivalist, knows how to kill and kill quickly. He is not a mutilator, has no interest in that. His sexual gratification is just with the kill."

Two men working together? Brooks said it was possible. It had happened before. Two men would explain how heavy bodies could have been carried so far up and down hills and into deep woods.

Even in the most organized investigation, Brooks pointed out that most of the serial killers captured were caught on a fluke. They had been stopped because of a traffic violation or because their cars had some defective equipment, and only then had patrol officers done Wants and Warrants checks and realized they had hooked a very big fish.

Frank Adamson and his team didn't care how they caught the GRK, just so long as they did.

29

IN THE SPRING OF 1984, the reports of missing women slowed to a trickle and then seemed to stop completely. There was the cautious sense that perhaps the Green River Killer's torrent of murder was over. Now, the thrust of the probe changed. It was as if he had divided his contest with detectives into two parts: the murder phase and the body recovery phase. Up until mid-March, the task force had found only fourteen of the missing.

In February and March, a new cluster site surfaced, and an earlier disposal area yielded another body fragment. On February 19, a partial human jawbone was discovered in the Mountain View Cemetery in Auburn, near where Kimi-Kai Pitsor's skull was found. It was not immediately tied to the identity of any of the victims.

On March 31, 1984, a man and his son were hiking when they came across the skeletal remains of a female in an entirely new location, far from the airport and Star Lake. This site was on Highway 410, twelve miles east of the town of Enumclaw and about thirty miles southeast of the SeaTac Strip. The topography and vegetation along 410, however, were typical of lightly populated areas in western Washington: fir forests, thick underbrush, isolated. Ironically, the White River coursed nearby.

The connection to the Green River investigation seemed remote to Frank Adamson. It was so far from the places where other victims had been left, and animals had dragged away most of the bones. There weren't even enough to make a positive identification. Every body found in Washington's forests couldn't be a GRK victim. Still, the bones were saved, and Explorer Search and Rescue scouts would be brought in to sweep the area for additional evidence.

More surprising were the discoveries east of Seattle. The newest site was located on the way to Snoqualmie Pass, the mountain summit where fifteen-year-old Carrie Rois had been taken by the stranger in the truck. But Carrie, missing now, had come back safely from that trip. On Valentine's Day, an army private who was part of a convoy to the Yakima Firing Range was using a rest stop in a heavily treed area when he came across a skeleton. It rested below a cliff at the base of Mount Washington. The site was close to Change Creek, a few miles east of the hamlet of North Bend off Exit 38 on the I-90 Freeway. I-90 connected Seattle and the coast to eastern Washington. Sheriff's personnel and Explorer Search and Rescue scouts combed the area, also known as Homestead Valley Road, for anything that might help identify the female skeleton.

Bill Haglund, chief investigator for the King County Medical Examiner's Office, tried to match the Valentine's Day victim's distinctive teeth, which had a wide gap between two upper front teeth, to the dental charts the M.E.'s office had on file without success.

She was to be known simply as Bones #8. Medical examiner Dr. Don Reay determined that the woman, who had brown hair, was Caucasian, and in her late twenties or early thirties. Her arms and her lower leg bones were missing, probably dragged off by animals. Reay estimated that she had been of medium height. She had been dead for three to six months.

That was all the information Reay released. He was trying, as everyone on the task force was, to hold back as much information as possible to eliminate compulsive confessors. The less specific information the general public knew, the better, although they also had to be warned of the danger. It was a double-edged sword.

A month later, on March 13, 1984, another skeleton surfaced three hundred yards away, her hands and part of one arm missing. A man looking for moss to sell to florists stumbled upon it. Again, searchers swarmed over the area, combing the underbrush in a one-mile section on either side of a now little-used stretch of old I-90. They found a pair of women's panties in the general region, but they couldn't be sure they were connected to the skeleton, which had lain there for from two to four months.

Bill Haglund was able to identify this second woman. It was Lisa Lorraine Yates—Lisa, who had promised her niece she would come to take her on a picnic soon. She had been one of the last girls to vanish—two days before Christmas, three months before her remains were found.

This site in the foothills of the Cascade Mountains was quite a way away from both the SeaTac Strip and Aurora Avenue North. Mount Si (also known as "Twin Peaks" after the popular television series) rose like a behemoth with fir forests climbing to glistening white snowbanks at the peaks' very tops. Nearby, the new freeway buzzed with traffic, much of it made up of huge trucks, rigs from all over the United States. Most drivers pulled off at Exit 34 for a hearty meal at Ken's Truck Stop, where they could take a shower, check into a motel, or even doze in the sleeper sections of their cabs. Ken's was a trucker's paradise, and the food was so good that most regular travelers stopped there, too. Camp Waskowitz, where fifth and sixth grade students from Highline public schools camped, was also close by.

What if the Green River Killer was a long-haul trucker? He wouldn't be the first serial killer who was, an ideal job for a man who wanted to avoid detection by ridding himself of his victims in isolated areas. That was one of the suggestions the anonymous letter writer had sent to Mike Barber of the *P.I.*

The new cluster opened up more possibilities. Frank Adamson ordered a thorough and tedious search between the South Fork of the Snoqualmie River and the very steep ridge that lay to the south. The searchers gleaned nothing of interest.

There were two easy ways to reach the North Bend site. One was by going east on I-90 from Seattle, across the first Floating Bridge, and the other was by traveling northeasterly along Highway 18, a much more isolated stretch of road that formed the hypotenuse of a triangle of roads from just north of Tacoma to Auburn, Kent, and Maple Valley, ending a few miles west of North Bend. It was mostly a two-lane road with some passing lanes and turnouts, and forests creeping almost up to the road itself. The two newly discovered bodies were at the eastern terminus of Highway

18. Was there a geographical "plan" in a stealthy killer's mind? Would there be more body cluster sites that might hook up to form a pattern? Only time would tell.

SEVERAL BODIES had been found south of the SeaTac Airport, and also just north of the runways. The next discoveries were also north of the airport, and closer to the ground zero corner of the Pac HiWay and S. 144th.

It was the first day of spring, March 21, 1984. Cindy Smith had just gone missing in Seattle, although her disappearance hadn't been reported yet. Bob Van Dyke, the caretaker of three baseball fields at 16th Avenue South and S. 146th, was clearing brush in preparation for the upcoming season when his Labrador retriever came running up to him with a bone in his mouth.

"I knew what it was, but I hoped that it wasn't," Van Dyke said.

It was a human hip bone. Van Dyke called the Port of Seattle Police because the baseball fields were in their jurisdiction, and they called the Green River Task Force. Lieutenant Jackson Beard was at the scene as soon as he could gather detectives and Explorer scouts. A necrosearch dog led them first to a copse of pine trees one hundred feet beyond one field's fence. There was a human skeleton there. It was that of a young female, and she was destined to be Bones #10.

The search that followed was the largest so far in the Green River investigation; sixty Explorer scouts walked shoulder to shoulder over several square blocks. Lieutenant Danny Nolan joined Beard to coordinate the searchers' efforts.

The next day, Chris Clifford, a dog handler, and his bloodhound—appropriately named Sorrow—located another body in the same area. Sorrow was an enthusiastic search dog who was more skilled at necrosearch than at finding living people. Dogs trained to find people seem to be good at either live searches or dead searches but not both—a trait that can be easily determined when they are only puppies. Discovering a corpse wasn't a victory for either Clifford or Sorrow, however.

"These hunts are real depressing," Clifford said. "And not very rewarding. Sorrow had this funny reaction, too. Like 'Hey, this isn't fun.' When he finds something that's dead, he gets real tentative. He just stops. I came around the corner and saw him just standing there, frozen."

Sorrow had found Cheryl Lee Wims, eighteen, missing from downtown Seattle for exactly ten months to the day.

As SAD AS the body discoveries were, Captain Frank Adamson's task force felt they were closing in on the man who had destroyed lives so heedlessly. Surely, with the recovery of eighteen victims' remains, something was going to break. As the investigators searched the area slightly west of the airport, they felt they were only hours from finding some piece of physical evidence that would lead them to him.

And yet, as I write this, it is exactly twenty years later. *Twenty years,* and I never write a book until a case, or a series of cases, has been adjudicated. Never has there been a homicidal mystery that had so many dead ends and mazes.

The headlines in the newspaper clippings I have saved about the discoveries of March 1984 are ironic, given the precipitous plunge of Howard Dean as a Democratic shoo-in in March 2004. It was an election year two decades ago, too, and the political commentators were just as anxious to jump to conclusions about the coming election, even though they knew that much in life can change so rapidly: "No Doubt Now: Hart is the Man to Beat—Gary Hart is the obvious leader for the 1984 Democratic presidential nomination!" (United Press International).

Despite their high hopes, Howard Dean's and Gary Hart's nominations were not to be, and neither was the imminent capture of the Green River Killer.

30

THE TASK FORCE had now looked at, and cleared, thousands of suspects: all of the A's, B's, and many of the C's. They had concluded that there was no shortage of dangerous, or peculiar, men in south King County in 1984.

A Kent motel manager named Douglas Jeffrey had a criminal record stemming from a rape conviction thirteen years earlier that his employers didn't even know about. A good-looking man with a wife and child, he had a great smile and a winning manner. It was the philosophy of the seventies and early eighties that sex offenders could be treated at Western State Hospital, rehabilitated, and released into society without using drastic measures like chemical or surgical castration.

Jeffrey, with his apparently stable family life, seemed to be a natural for rehab. He had been declared a treatable sexual psychopath and sent to the mental hospital rather than to prison. He participated in the approved treatment in the sexual offenders program: group therapy.

However, when Jeffrey was released and deemed a responsible citizen, he set about proving that group therapy had done little, if anything, to change his deeply ingrained patterns. It had only whetted his appetite. For more than two years, he entered apartments and houses in the East Hill section of Kent. Women woke up in the wee hours of the morning to find a man looming over their beds with a nylon stocking pulled over his face, making a grotesque mask that hid his real features. Some estimates placed his toll at over one hundred rapes. He used a knife to threaten the already terrified women into submission, and afterward he asked for their money and jewelry.

Sometimes he carried a camera with a time-release shutter so he could take pictures of himself and his victims during his sexual attacks. He also had a beeper to alert him when he was needed back at the motel where he worked.

Finally captured, Jeffrey pleaded guilty to seventeen counts of rape, burglary, and kidnapping in King County Superior Court. Becky Roe, long head of the Prosecuting Attorney's Sexual Assault Unit, recommended that he receive two consecutive life sentences. "I don't think violent sex offenders are treatable," she said succinctly.

Douglas Jeffrey had prowled in the town where the first Green River victims were found. He had the kind of benign look about him that would have made young women trust him. Could he be a killer as well as a relentless rapist? Possibly, but he was eventually dropped as a Green River suspect.

In the summer of 1983, a nineteen-year-old man, enlisted a friend, twenty, to help him kill his own mother. The woman, thirty-nine, was choked to death in the back of the battered van they lived in. Her son later admitted to detectives that they had also killed four women in the south part of King County, and he even described areas where they had left their bodies. He said he hated women, beginning with his mother. But then he recanted his confessions about murdering teenage girls. Both men were sentenced to long prison terms, and subsequently removed from the Green River possibles.

It was very difficult not to be enthusiastic about suspects who seemed a perfect fit. I fell into that trap myself any number of times. A few years into the Green River investigation, I received several letters from a man who lived in Washington, D.C. He was an attorney there. I verified that. He hinted that he had the answers to what had happened to all the murdered women, and he said he would send me tapes that would convince me.

But then he told me that he had played a large part in the Watergate scandal and that Carl Bernstein and Bob Woodward depended upon him for information. Upon hearing that, I began to doubt his veracity, if not his sanity. It was too pat.

When the tapes arrived, they consisted of hour after hour of my tipster's personal witnessing of an arcane cult that he said abducted women from the trick sites so they could be sacrificed. He had hidden in the shadows, he said, as he watched hooded people strangling young women in the light of a huge bonfire. The area he described was similar to the woods where many of the victims' remains had been found, but woods and forests could be found in any direction beyond the Seattle city limits. My "expert" knew many of the victims' names, and their physical descriptions were correct, but that information had been in the newspapers. He was so obsessed that I felt he had gone from his "Watergate" fantasy to a "Green River" fantasy.

And then I bought a copy of All the President's Men, and, sure enough, my correspondent had been a key player in the authors' contacts with Deep Throat. The man's name was unusual, and I was able to validate that he was who he said he was, that he lived where he said he did—in a Washington suburb—and that he currently held a position of some responsibility. I supposed he might be telling the truth about both newsworthy investigations, but I was more inclined to think that Watergate had unhinged him.

Just to be sure I wasn't looking away from truly important information, I took the "cult sacrifice tapes" to Dave Reichert and told him what I knew about the man who sent them. I let the informant know that his revelations were now in the proper hands, which he approved. And then I moved on. If the information was good, Reichert would deal with it. I never heard back from him. If he didn't have time to listen to hours and hours of someone rambling on about cults and human sacrifice, I can't say I blamed him.

One of my more insistent callers was a woman who lived in the south county area. She was certain that her estranged husband was the Green River Killer. I had heard from scores of women who were under the same impression about their ex-husbands, but this woman was relentless. Although it wasn't generally known, Marie Malvar's driver's license had been found at the SeaTac Airport weeks after she disappeared. Either she had lost it there herself, her purse had been stolen, or her abductor had wanted to make it look as though she had willingly flown away from her boyfriend and family.

The woman who called, named Sonya,* was fixated on the Green River cases, just as she was convinced that a major American retail corporation was spying on her. The latter seemed to me to be a paranoid delusion. In the Green River cases, she was particularly focused on Marie Malvar. That, too, could be part of a fantasy world. She was so frightened that she moved constantly, leaving me a different phone number every time she called.

"I went with my husband to the airport to see his mother and father off at the B gates," Sonya said breathlessly. "My husband pulled some cards out of what I thought was my wallet. I grabbed what I thought was my driver's license, but when I looked at it, it wasn't mine. There was a picture of a girl in her twenties with long dark hair. It had four names on it, but all I could see was the last name that started out 'Mal' before he snatched it back. He gave it to our baby to play with, but after his folks left, he reached for it and realized that the baby had dropped it. He was frantic looking for it on the floor, but they told us we had to leave the terminal because they were locking the doors."

Marie's license *had* been found near Gate B-4 at the airport by Michael Meadows, a maintenance worker for American Building Maintenance (ABM) while he was vacuuming on May 27, 1983, and he turned it in to Lost and Found, who then gave it to the Green River Task Force. But Sonya insisted that the airport had lost it and the task force didn't know about it. Eventually, she went on the Internet and hooked up with a self-styled female private eye in Texas who had also logged on to a chat room where the Green River murders were discussed constantly.

It was the kind of case that attracted wannabe detectives. Everyone in Seattle seemed to have a theory, but the prevailing rumor was still the one that said the Green River Killer was a cop. Four of the names people gave me as "absolutely, surely, the GRK" were detectives I had known for years. After a while, if I thought about it enough, I could almost begin to wonder if I had ever *really* known them.

They had ex-wives, too, and two different women called about two different cops they'd been married to once. One even said coyly, "Ann, you know him. You've had lunch with him."

That was a little creepy, but I'd had lunch with hundreds of detectives over the years. I hated the guessing games, and I was grateful when the officers' names were cleared.

No forensic technique was considered too strange to try in the search to identify either the victims or the killer himself. Some of the detectives were open to listening to psychics. Dowsers (who seek water in the ground with a forked stick) were encouraged to try to locate bodies, and a number of informants had been hypnotized to see if their unconscious minds would bring forth more specific information.

Betty Pat Gatliff was a forensic sculptor in Oklahoma. Along with a handful of forensic anthropologists and artists, Betty Pat's forte was to put faces on skulls where there was no flesh left. It sounds like a grisly kind of artistry, and it wasn't something I ever thought I could watch, much less do. I'd met Betty Pat once at a forensic science conference where I was presenting a seminar on Ted Bundy, and she called me when she came to Seattle. She invited me to join her at Dr. Don Reay's medical examiner's headquarters, which was then at Harborview, our county hospital facility. A little reluctantly, I accepted. At the M.E.'s office, I looked at the four boxes that held the numbered bones of the unknown victims as she selected a skull. I reminded myself that these bones had once been young women who deserved to have their identity known and to have funeral services and a decent burial or cremation.

Betty Pat began with the skull from the remains found in September 1983, beside the Star Lake Road. It had been steam cleaned and sterilized. Trying to see it through Betty Pat's eyes, I realized that all skulls don't look alike. There were many individual characteristics. The high cheekbones on this one suggested an American Indian heritage.

Betty Pat showed me how she attached erasers from ordinary pencils to the face portion. She'd found that thickness matched the skin and underlying tissue of most subjects. Then she began to add claylike "flesh" to bring out the features. Of course, if the person had been very fat or very thin, this method might not be accurate, but there was no way to tell because we didn't know whose face we were trying to bring back.

Carefully patting on clay, Betty Pat filled in the space between the erasers, and someone's face *did* emerge. When she was satisfied, she added dark brown glass eyes, eyebrows, and a dark wig.

We stood back, wondering. *Who are you?*

But this was not an infallible means of identification. It's impossible to know how much soft tissue—lips or the tip of a nose—was once there. Gender and racial characteristics can usually be determined by jaws and foreheads and teeth, so it's easier to know what color hair and eyes to add, but not always.

Had this woman plucked her eyebrows? What about makeup and the length of her hair? Was it straight or curly? Forensic artist Frank Bender of Philadelphia says he "talks" to the skulls he works on and gets a remarkable sense of who they were and what they looked like. Betty Pat Gatliff relied more on bone structure.

Although we didn't know it then, we were working on Gail Mathews—whose lover had seen her riding in the old truck with a stranger, and she looked right through him. She must have been very frightened not to call for help. Her clay face was calm now, and inscrutable.

When I looked at a photograph of Gail later, I saw that she had inordinately large lips, as if she had overdone collagen injections. But they didn't use collagen cosmetically in 1983; hers were naturally lush, so full that there would have been no way for us to recreate her real face.

Gail had not been the only victim left near the Star Lake Road. On March 31, 1984, six months after her remains were discovered there, a mushroom hunter moved through the shadowy trees along the ravine and came upon a human skull on the east side of the road. He backed out of the woods and called the King County Sheriff. Within a short time, Frank Adamson had gathered his crew of detectives and Explorer scouts. This was another very, very difficult region to search. The man who had left so many bodies seemed to prefer steep inclines, and this was one of the steepest. Maybe it was easier for him to roll his victims down the hill, away from prying eyes. If he was, indeed, the guy seen in several different trucks, he might even have had some kind of winch or step that helped him lower the victims from the back of his pickup. But his plan wasn't perfect. The trees had caught the dead girls and kept them from plunging all the way down.

It was to be an endlessly weary day for Adamson, hampered as he was by reporters who kept trying to go into the woods and look for evidence or even more bodies. The last thing he needed was a bunch of media types messing up any evidence at this site.

It didn't take long to find the remainder of the skeleton that went with the skull. But as the search progressed, the task force investigators discovered two more skeletons farther down the slope. And then more. Trees nearest each body site were sprayed with orange paint so that they had some kind of center point for triangulation measurements. Detectives marked the trees nearest to the remains: 1, 2, 3, 4, 5.

This would turn out to be one of the killer's favorite places to rid himself of the women he no longer wanted. As the crow flies, it was less than a mile from the Green River, where the first five of his victims had been found.

The woods themselves, usually silent except for the distant rushing sound of Mill Creek at the bottom of the ravine, seemed quite remote. But the site was close to Pac HiWay, although 272nd was considerably south of where the Strip ended. To the east, Smith Brothers' Dairy had dozens of milk trucks coming and going, and young families were building houses along 55th South and Star Lake Road. It would have been difficult for the killer to bring a body here in the daytime. After dark, it was possible that no one had ever seen him.

All weekend long, reporters lit on Adamson like mosquitos. At the time, he had no media spokesman to deflect questions, and everywhere he turned he stumbled over another reporter. He was a man who was seldom impatient or moody, but this was a bad two days. By the time he got back to task force headquarters, Cookie Hunt was waiting for him, having dogged his steps at Star Lake Road. "Cookie was so pushy," Adamson said. "When I went back to my office, I had 128 phone calls and messages, and I had had it. I found her very antagonizing that day."

He was exhausted. They all were. Officially, they now had twenty bodies. Adamson suspected that this was only the tip of the iceberg. When Dr. Don Reay and Bill Haglund let him know the identities of the latest victims located, it was clear that the killer was working with a kind of maniacal organization. As Pierce Brooks had suspected, the GRK obviously had his private dumping sites waiting before he went out to kill.

First, he'd used the Green River, and then the deserted blocks around the airport, then Highway 410 near Enumclaw and the mountain foothills off Highway 18, and finally Star Lake. There might be even more cluster sites.

The Star Lake Road victims were identified as Terry Rene Milligan, gone from the Strip on August 28, 1982—found on April 1, 1984; Delores Williams, missing from the Strip on March 8, 1983— found on March 31, 1984; Sandra Kay Gabbert, missing from the Strip on April 17, 1983—found on April 1, 1984.

(And when they finally identified Gail Mathews, they would realize that she was taken from Pac HiWay only five days after Sand-e Gabbert disappeared. Perhaps something had spooked the killer, and he had to drop Gail's body too close to the road. That would explain why she was found first. But no one knew it was Gail until she was positively identified in February 1985, almost two years later.)

The fourth body found off Star Lake Road was identified in the third week of April by Bill Haglund in the medical examiner's office, using dental records. She was Alma Ann Smith, the quiet, lonely girl who once went to seventh grade in Walla Walla. She had gone off to Seattle so many times because her father lived near there, bouncing from one parent to the other.

They did not find Marie Malvar or Keli Kay McGinness who had also disappeared in the spring of 1983.

THE GREEN RIVER MURDERER was becoming almost legendary, a fictional character not unlike Freddy Krueger in *A Nightmare on Elm Street* or Jason in the *Friday the 13th* series, current movies that teenagers flocked to watch as a cast of young actors fell victim to a stealthy killer who cuts them away from the crowd one by one and then murders them. But what was deliciously scary on the movie screen was bleak and ugly in real life.

If the killer was reading the newspapers and watching television—and the task force was almost positive he was—he was probably smiling; he was now being compared to John Gacy, Wayne Williams, and Ted Bundy in terms of body counts. And he was leading the pack.

Indeed, there were so many girls missing now, and so many who had been found, that I caught myself referring to them by their num-

ber in terms of the sequence of their disappearances. I was horrified
when that dawned on me. I never wanted to do that again, so I
stayed up all night with a large piece of construction paper, newspapers,
scissors, and cellophane tape. I attached their pictures to the
chart, and then wrote their names, descriptions, the date they went
missing, and the date they had been found. Too many of them still
had a blank space in the last category. But I had memorized their
names and faces, and they would be forever imprinted on my mind
as real human beings, not just numbers.

FRANK ADAMSON, the reader of poetry, knew T. S. Eliot's work well,
and he realized that April 1984 was, indeed, "the cruelest month,"
at least in terms of the number of women's bodies that were being
discovered.

Barbara Kubik-Patten, who truly felt that she was getting messages
from the dead girls telling her where fellow victims could be
found, sensed that Mary Bridget, Kimi-Kai, Opal, and a blond girl
she couldn't identify were talking to her, and she was extremely
frustrated that the task force detectives wouldn't pay attention to
her. The only investigator who had the patience to listen to her was
Jim Doyon, whom Frank Adamson termed "a sweet guy."

On April 15, 1984, Kubik-Patten tracked me down where I was
having Sunday dinner at a friend's house. I'd left the phone number
on my answering machine in case my kids needed me. Like most of
the task force detectives, I was growing weary of her insistence that
she had psychic visions but that nobody would listen to her.

Impatient that she had interrupted my rare dinner out, I finally
said, "You know, Barbara, your visions are too vague. I think you're
going to have to actually find a body yourself in order to convince
them. Most detectives aren't that impressed with psychics."

I knew that she had been showing up at body sites and getting in
the way of the investigative teams that were trying to gather evidence
while they staved off the press and curious bystanders. On
one occasion, Kubik-Patten and a woman friend had bulldozed
their way into the woods near a body site search. They found the remains
of an animal, which they believed was human, and poked at
it. Unfortunately, they aroused a nest of yellow jackets. Her friend,
who was allergic to bees, was stung and they had to flee in disarray.

The Wednesday after Kubik-Patten called me, a shovel operator
on a crew of loggers found human bones in a deep woods owned by
the Weyerhaeuser Company. They were scattered in a fifty-square-

foot area off the north end of Highway 18, near North Bend, and in an area where two victims had been located two months earlier.

Dental records and the discovery of a mandible (lower jaw) brought quick identification. The bones were those of Amina Agisheff, thirty-seven, who had been waiting for a bus in downtown Seattle and was the first woman on the missing list. It was a surprising answer to the many questions about her disappearance. She had been the devoted mother of three children, someone *never* involved in prostitution.

Even though Amina's remains were found close to earlier skeletons, her relatives could not believe that she fit the Green River victim profile, and neither did the detectives. She was too old, for one thing, and she had never been anything but a loving and responsible mother to her children. Her ethnic background was Russian, and she was part of an extended family who were always in touch with one another. Born in New York, schooled in Paris, she was a Montessori teacher and a waitress at the Old World Delicatessen in Ballard, the Scandinavian bastion in Seattle, far, far away from the SeaTac Strip. The thought that she might have been involved with prostitution was unfathomable to anyone who knew her. Whoever killed Amina may well have climbed on board the Green River Killer's bandwagon deliberately.

Barbara Kubik-Patten, accompanied by her two youngest children, hurried to the area near North Bend the next noon. Barred by the yellow tape that marked off Wednesday's search site, she entered the woods at a very similar spot a third of a mile away—also a gravel turnout from Highway 18—and began to search. She would say later that it was the voice of Kimi-Kai Pitsor that had told her to go there.

And she found a body.

Kubik-Patten rushed to where detectives were still processing the site where Amina Agisheff's scattered skeleton had been found. She approached Rupe Lettich, one of the investigators who did not believe in her otherworldly messages, and tugged on his sleeve. He shooed her away, telling her she wasn't supposed to wander onto the area being searched. She kept trying to get his attention, but Lettich had heard her cry wolf too many times. It wasn't until Frank Adamson drove up that she found someone who would listen. He knew that she had searched for an entry into the woods that would match the Agisheff site. "She had to go quite a ways into a copse of alder trees from the pullout to find the body," Adamson remembered. "The remains were covered with a green plastic garbage bag, and there were other bones of animals there. It was rather remarkable that she *did* find it."

With Kubik-Patten's discovery of this unknown victim on April 19, 1984, a strange coincidence, the investigation became even more inscrutable. The skeleton under the green garbage bag was not easily identified, and she became known, pathetically, as Bones #14. It was a long time before she would be identified as twenty-two-year-old Tina Marie Thompson. She was more streetwise than many of the girls who had been abducted, had brown hair and brown eyes, and looked a great deal like comedienne Carol Burnett. She had been tall and very slim.

BUT THERE WERE *two* Tinas. This Tina was not Tina Tomson aka Kim Nelson aka Star, the blond girl missing from the SeaTac Strip since the previous Halloween. *She* was still missing. Tina Marie *Thompson* had disappeared on July 26, 1983, and hadn't been reported missing for some time.

Could the killer possibly have known that he had killed two young women whose names were so much alike? Probably not.

But still . . .

I had to admit to being chagrined that Kubik-Patten had actually found a body four days after I'd told her that that was what it was going to take to give her credibility with the Green River Task Force, never dreaming she would actually find one. It almost made me wonder if she had any guilty knowledge of the murders. The investigators must have felt the same way. They gave her a polygraph test, and she passed. They also reasoned that it wasn't *that* amazing that she had stumbled across a victim. She had gone to the very next turnout where someone could pull off the road, and these turnouts were convenient for the killer; he had used them a lot. It might very well have been that deductive reasoning rather than ghostly voices had led her to pick a spot to search.

For several days, Barbara Kubik-Patten made headlines in Seattle papers, something she appeared to want for the previous two years. She explained to Mike Barber of the *Post-Intelligencer* that she had seen the Green River Killer *twice*.

Her first encounter had been, of course, at the Green River itself, where she saw the white car racing away. Now, almost two years later, she was able to give Barber a more precise description. She said she had heard a scream near the river and she and a male friend, whom she did not name, had seen the tall killer, but only in profile, as he walked across a clearing and got into a car. "He's white," she said firmly, "has brown hair, thin legs, and I'm not sure of his age, but he walks with a long stride—with long, slow-swinging arms."

She even had a sketch artist draw a picture of how she pictured the killer in her mind. She recalled that his car was "souped-up." She said she'd reached speeds of sixty miles an hour herself as she tried to catch his car, but he'd taken the curves like a professional driver. Where this driving feat took place is the question. Anyone driving that fast on Frager Road would surely have ended up in the river itself. The roads leading up the hill had such tight curves that nobody could go that fast without crashing.

Barbara Kubik-Patten announced that the Green River Killer was an "absolute genius" at getting rid of bodies, and she felt he had had some kind of special training that allowed him to outsmart the police crime lab. She also felt that the skeleton she found and that of Amina Agisheff held physical evidence that would allow the detectives to catch him.

Kubik-Patten believed she had vindicated herself, and she continued to show up at crime scenes and scan newspaper pictures of the victims so she could keep "in touch" with them more tightly.

This had been a compelling series of murders in terms of sheer numbers, and it was rapidly becoming more weird.

31

HE WAS ENJOYING the media coverage. He loved the attention, having been underrated all his life by most people, including his parents.

By the early eighties, he had been cuckolded by two wives—both "the skinny blonde and the fat brunette," even though he had joked about changing his luck by choosing different types of women to court. He had learned about prostitutes when he was in the service, but they had also betrayed him by giving him a venereal disease. As one acquaintance described him later, "He didn't seem like the sharpest knife in the drawer," but he had learned a lot about social interaction. And he still had a robust sex drive, which required female partners. He'd been taught that masturbation was shameful.

He found a gold mine in an organization for divorced people with children, and he mined it skillfully. He dated a dozen or more women he met there. Darla Bryse* initially believed that meeting her new boyfriend at Parents Without Partners was serendipitous. In many ways, her life experiences were quite similar to the Green River Killer's victims, just as they were much like those of his other girlfriends in PWP. She had suffered abuse and betrayal, but something in her still wanted to trust.

Born in Santa Rosa, California, to a housewife and a gas station owner–cum–construction worker, she remembered her childhood as being both loveless and frightening. "I was the oldest, and I knew I had two sisters," she said, "but one went away. That's about the only thing I remember before I was in first grade. My parents adopted my younger sister out to distant relatives."

Although one of her grandmothers lived with them, Darla did most of the cooking and housework. Her parents had an active social life, belonging to lodges and clubs. They drank a good deal and had little time for parenting. "A man who was married to one of my mother's friends abused me physically—sexually—and emotionally when I was very young," Darla said. "I think my mother knew about it, but she never did anything."

Darla never felt that she had much control over her life, although she acted out by being tough and starting a teenage gang. "I actually put razor blades in my hair," she admitted. "But I was really just looking for someplace to belong, I think."

Her first child was a boy, born out of wedlock. He was given to relatives. Darla wasn't yet twenty when she married her first husband, Jimmy.* She was very much in love with him, and was thrilled when they married in January. She got pregnant right away and gave birth to a girl in October. She had another son within the following year. "I didn't want to get pregnant again so soon," she said. "I had two little kids under two and I had this compulsion about keeping my house absolutely clean, but Jimmy got drunk on Christmas Eve and even though I begged him not to, he just about raped me. And I knew right away that I'd be pregnant. I was."

Darla couldn't cope with three babies. When her baby son started screaming relentlessly one evening, she fought back a compulsion to throw him at the fireplace. "It was just luck that Jimmy came home early from work. I felt like I was out of my mind."

She was suffering from postpartum depression, but it wasn't an emotional disorder easily recognized in the sixties. Jimmy had her locked up in a state hospital for three months and quietly filed for divorce. "I was so naive and so dumb," Darla recalled. "I didn't want a divorce—I loved him—and I didn't even know enough to get a lawyer. We were still going out once in a while and I thought we would be getting back together. And then my dad came to me and showed me a legal paper. Jimmy had been to court, and I didn't even know that the divorce had gone that far. Jimmy got the house, the kids, everything. . . ."

Jimmy began to date another woman and Darla couldn't bear seeing them together. She left Santa Rosa and moved to Seattle with her sister. She was a very good-looking young woman and she got a job easily—as a dancer in a lesbian bar in the basement of the Smith Tower in Seattle's Pioneer Square area. At that point in her life, she didn't care about much of anything. "I learned about 'Christmas trees'—dexadrine and blackberry flips," she said of her introduction to drugs. "There was a gal who worked in the bar who got a crush on me, but I told her I wasn't into that."

Darla still missed Jimmy, and she went back to Santa Rosa as often as she could to visit her children, hoping that they could get back together. He seemed glad to see her and offered to rent an apartment for her. She visited her children, and sat by the phone in her apartment, waiting for Jimmy to come by. They were intimate again, and she believed that he still loved her. "I got pregnant *again*," she remembered, shaking her head sadly. "I thought he'd be happy when I told him, but he said, 'It's not mine.' And it *was* his. I hadn't been with anyone but him."

All of her life, Darla had been looking for love. Her ex-husband's cruel response to what she thought would be joyful news threw her into the worst despair she had ever known. "I took Seconal and everything I could find that I'd bought over-the-counter, and I passed out, unconscious. I should have died, but my mother ran in unexpectedly. She was going to Mass and women had to cover their heads back then. She came to borrow a scarf from me, and she found me. And so my life was saved, and I was still pregnant. I thank God for that, now, because that baby girl is so important to me in my life."

Because she had attempted suicide, Darla was once more committed to a state hospital. When she was finally released, she moved in with women friends, avoiding men for almost eight years. She had decided to put her baby girl up for adoption, feeling that she wasn't an adequate mother. "But my best friend talked me out of it," she said. "And we raised her together. I'm so grateful that I didn't let Libby* go—she means the world to me."

Darla moved back to Washington State and worked for the state and for public utility companies. She was an employment counselor for a while, and then an Avon Lady.

On her own again in her early thirties, Darla opted to have a tubal ligation. She had given birth to five children, and all but one were being raised by someone else. She wanted to date men again and she feared more pregnancies. Her sterilization gave her freedom she'd never had, and she went through a period of promiscuity. "I was drinking too much then, and I think I wanted to prove that I could satisfy a man, and I found that I could, even though I never had an orgasm myself. For the first time in my life, I was in charge in my relationships. It gave me a kind of power over men. I looked good, and they would just melt around me."

Her flings with men lasted only six months, and she vowed to be a better mother to Libby. Her lifestyle changed dramatically from her days dancing in a lesbian bar and picking up men. Wanting a wholesome activity she could share with Libby, Darla joined Parents Without Partners in the late 1970s. She lived in West Seattle, and she attended group activities designed to help single mothers and fathers cope with parenthood and still maintain some kind of social life. Most of the group members lived in the south part of King County.

"We met in people's homes for discussions, had potluck dinners, or went to dances at the Kent Commons," Darla recalled. "Libby and I went on a lot of hikes and campouts with PWP. I was still drinking then, but we made a lot of friends and it was healthy for both of us to be exercising in the outdoors and up on the mountain trails. They were a good bunch of people.

"That's where I met him—at Parents Without Partners."

Darla had noticed the twice-divorced single father at other PWP functions and found him attractive, but he was living with another woman in the group. He had his son, seven-year-old Chad, on weekends and brought the boy to most of the picnics and hikes. He was obviously very proud of the little boy, who lived with his mother, Dana, during the week. He and Darla often signed up for the same activities where children were welcome so they could include Chad and twelve-year-old Libby.

One weekend, the group was hiking on trails in the Snoqualmie Pass foothills near Issaquah, and Darla found herself studying him. She thought he was quite good-looking, and muscular. He was about thirty, younger than she was by five years. "We found ourselves alone on the trail and we started talking. I found him very personable, and he was funny in a quiet way because he was pretty reserved. We both realized that we sort of hit it off, but he was still living with someone else so it wasn't going to go anywhere."

One evening that changed. "I started flirting with him, and he responded to me," Darla remembered. "I came right out and let him know that I was interested in him. It wasn't long before he broke up with the other gal. He moved out of her house, and moved right in with me. Just like that. That was in May 1981."

He paid his share of the household expenses, and although he didn't help her clean house, he did do yard work. Darla found him to be a very gentle man, although he wasn't particularly sentimental. "I can't remember that he ever brought me gifts, but I think he bought me a couple of cards."

They didn't have a lot in common. He never read books, and Darla was a reader, especially fascinated by true-crime books. She had read *True Detective* magazine from the time she was in junior high school. As far as she knew, he didn't read them. He wasn't interested in movies, but they watched television together in the evenings. Outside of PWP, he had very few friends, although he was close to one of his brothers. He often took Darla to visit his parents who lived a few blocks from Pac HiWay.

Although he had few interests, Darla found him to be an exceptional sexual partner. "I'd say his hobby was sex," she recalled. "He wanted to make love at least three times a day."

She didn't object to that, although she was a bit embarrassed at first by his desire to have sex out of doors, in his car, or in places where they could easily be discovered. At the time, he was driving a burgundy truck with a white canopy, and he always kept a blanket in the cab in case they came upon an interesting trysting spot.

"I got so it didn't bother me to have sex outside," Darla said with a laugh. "One time we were camping near the Yakima River and we were making out on the bank and a canoe full of people came paddling by and saw us. They laughed and waved at us, and we waved back. By then, I felt so comfortable and so uninhibited with him that it didn't faze me."

Darla sometimes took his lunch to him where he worked. They often slipped into one of the huge semi trucks parked there to have sex in the cab's sleeping area behind the driver's seat. Nobody ever caught them.

He kept pushing the parameters of danger. He liked the Southcenter Mall area. Darla didn't mind having sex in his truck in the Levitz Furniture Store parking lot, but she was very nervous when he told her he'd found a new spot. "There was this place where men were loading trucks at Southcenter," she remembered. "There was a cement barrier, some kind of fence about ten feet long and fairly close to the ground. He insisted that we have sex on the grass right on the other side of that fence and I could hear the men working only a few feet away. They could have looked over and seen us, but he wasn't worried about that."

He *was* a passionate outdoorsman and he loved to camp and fish, although Darla couldn't recall that he ever brought home any fish. Between them, they had collected all kinds of camping gear— tents, cooking grills, sleeping bags, and anything else they needed. Often, they camped for a week in the wilderness. Wearing nothing but a thin towel because he liked her naked, Darla cooked their meals on the outside stove.

Besides fishing, he liked to dig for old bottles alongside deserted railroad tracks. He drank very little and didn't smoke. He seemed to her to be a perfect mate. "He was neat and clean and considerate. He was very, very muscular—very strong."

They were completely open with each other in their discussions about sex, admitting fantasies they had. Both of them were experienced with any number of partners, although, as far as Darla knew, he was faithful to her while they lived together.

Once, when they were camping without their children in the Cle Elum wilderness in the Wenatchee National Forest, they agreed to try some bondage sex. Darla didn't object to being tied to a tree or even to being "staked out" on the ground with her wrists and ankles bound, "as long as it was safe."

He was excited about that, and even embroidered upon the basic concept by placing grapes and other fruit inside her vagina while she was helpless. They both found the innovative intercourse exciting, and he kept his promise not to hurt her. Theirs was certainly not an average relationship, but they were adults and it was nobody else's business.

There were, however, aspects of this man that troubled Darla. He never told her he loved her in so many words. She would have liked that, but if she had to ask him to say it, it wouldn't mean anything. More troubling for her, he wanted to go back to court and gain full-time custody of his son, Chad. "Chad was a good kid," Darla said, "but he was hyperactive, and I didn't think I could take having him around all the time."

As her lover became more enthusiastic about getting custody of his son, Darla came to a decision. "I remember when I told him that I had to break up with him. It was close to Christmas in 1981. We were in our bedroom and I was sitting on the floor while he sat on the end of the bed. I told him that I could not emotionally handle raising Chad full time. I had four of my own children who weren't with me, and I just couldn't take on Chad."

His head lifted and he stared at her, surprised. "And you never tell me you love me," she added.

His eyes filled with tears. "But I do love you," he said.

"I told him it was just too late to tell me at that point. He felt bad, I know, but he wasn't angry. He moved out of my house and we broke up, but we were still friends."

After he left, Darla's daughter Libby told her that there was something about him that gave her "the willies." She denied that he had ever molested her or said anything improper, but he had once come to her room to talk with her, and she just felt as if something was wrong. Darla was baffled; she had never known him to be anything but considerate and easy to get along with. She knew that Libby would have told her if he had made any untoward moves on her.

Early in 1982, he called Darla to say he'd bought himself a house in Des Moines, close to Pac HiWay. It was a small rambler. He was very proud of it, and he invited Darla and one of her girlfriends to a big housewarming party he was having. He'd also asked people he worked with and other PWP members.

"When we got there," Darla said, "he had refreshments laid out and his house was all cleaned up. But no one else came to his party. I felt sorry for him, and we stayed and tried to pretend that nothing was wrong, but I could see he was hurt. He showed us through his house and his backyard. I remember there were two big fir trees out in his backyard. Every time I drove on I-5 after that, I could spot his house by looking up at those trees." She recalled his backyard ended in a bank that dropped to the shoulder of I-5, the interstate freeway. The roar of the constant traffic on the freeway sounded like an ocean in a storm.

The only time Darla ever saw him show any anger was after their breakup. When his housewarming celebration was such a debacle, he invited her and Libby to dinner. She asked if Libby could bring a girlfriend, and he said that was okay. "Libby was just in her teens and you know how silly girls can be at that age," Darla recalled. "For some reason she and her girlfriend got the giggles at the dinner table. I told them to settle down because he had gone to a lot of trouble to fix dinner for us, but they just had to look at each other and they giggled harder.

"Well, he got furious. He really lost it. I'd never seen him even get a little angry before. I don't know if he thought they were laughing at him or what, but he shouted at them. He scared Libby. And we never went back to his house after that."

It wasn't long after that unfortunate dinner that Darla's ex started dating another woman from PWP—Trish Long.* Darla heard a rumor about six months later that he had contracted the herpes virus and she considered herself lucky to have avoided that. Even so, she remembered him as a nice guy and wished him well. She had made some mistakes in her life, but she didn't consider him to be one of them. Within five years, Darla met a man she would marry. She didn't expect that she would hear much about her old boyfriend after 1981. They had begun to move in different worlds.

32

IN MID-MAY 1984, there was a respite for the task force, and for the women who strolled the highway, always looking over their shoulders, always asking johns, "Are you sure you're not the Green River Killer?" And those who asked should have known he wouldn't tell them the truth, if he was.

At least, no new disappearances had been reported, but that didn't mean much. Frank Adamson had feared that the Green River

Killer might continue his pattern of numerous abductions and murders in April through October, and the task force detectives girded up for more trouble, even as they kept the Pro-Active Team on the highway with decoys and vigilance. The silence made all of them nervous. Where was their "warm weather killer"?

Parents who had waited for some word of their missing daughters lived anxious day by anxious day, tensing every time their phones rang. Almost a year had gone by since Judy DeLeone's co-worker was absolutely sure that he had seen her daughter, Carrie Rois, alive and well at Seward Park in Seattle. She had even come up to him and said, "Remember me? I'm Carrie—and you work with my mom."

Judy sank so deeply into depression that Randy Mullinax and Linda Barker, president of Friends and Families of Victims of Violent Crime, a support group active in the Seattle area for more than a decade, called Mertie Winston, whose daughter Tracy had been missing since the previous September. They suggested that the two women talk. Linda was afraid that Judy was suicidal.

"I didn't know what I could do," Mertie remembered, "but I agreed to call her. I began by saying 'I don't know what to say to you.' We ended up talking for three straight hours. I'd been baking cookies when Linda called and asked me to call Judy. I ended up burning at least three batches of cookies because Judy and I got so involved in talking. We were among the few people who could understand what all the parents were going through. Judy and I began to bolster each other up. We came to a place where we believed our daughters were together, that whatever had become of one had happened to the other. You search for ways to be optimistic, and we told ourselves that both Carrie and Tracy were alive and that they were okay and they would be coming home again."

On May 7, 1984, the Green River Task Force investigated the murder of a thirty-eight-year-old woman named Kathy Arita whose body was found near Lake Fenwick. The location was right—she was only a half mile or so from the Green River—but nothing else matched. She was a Boeing employee, missing for three days, and the mother of a seventeen-year-old son. Her body was fully clothed when she was found. She was quickly eliminated as a Green River Killer victim. There would be a number of other women killed in the same general area over the years ahead, each to be investigated as a possible GRK case. However, they proved to be unconnected, part of a predictable homicide rate in Seattle and King County—normal. No, no one can call *any* murder normal.

While the violence against the SeaTac Strip teenagers seemed to be, at the very least, on hiatus, there were serial rapists and killers active in other areas, and task force investigators from King County traveled all over the United States to confer with detectives in other jurisdictions: Anchorage, Alaska (where baker Robert Hansen admitted to killing seventeen women over the previous decade, hunting some of them with his bow and arrow. Human beings were only "game" to him); in Los Angeles, a freelance television cameraman, once a suspect in four rapes in Seattle, was charged with three California slayings.

Every time a spate of serial murders of women erupted—and they seemed to be increasing in the U.S.—the Green River detectives wondered if it might be their man who had moved on. If he had, he had left much tragedy behind to be discovered. On May 9, the M.E.'s head investigator, Bill Haglund, confirmed that the bones found near Enumclaw off Highway 410 were those of Debora May Abernathy, the transplant from Waco, Texas, who would never have willingly left her little boy behind.

Oddly, a man walking near the intersection of Highway 18 and State Route 167, many miles away from where Debora's body was left, found her Texas driver's license about ten feet off the shoulder of the road. Detectives who searched the area three months later discovered her son's birth certificate. Her killer had either accidentally or deliberately flung her documents from his vehicle. It was more likely that he did it on purpose to rid himself of any connection to the corpse he had hidden in the wilderness.

When her mother was notified that Debora was dead, she commented sadly, "She used to be a real nice girl."

I REMEMBER being interviewed about the Green River Killer and serial murderers in general by a reporter from the *San Francisco Chronicle* that May of 1984. I wasn't in Seattle; I was in Eugene, Oregon, attending Diane Downs's trial for the murder of one of her children and attempted murders of two others. I saved the resultant article by Susan Sward and Edward Iwata because it included coverage of the Green River murders—the first time, really, that anyone in the media outside Seattle acknowledged that they were occurring. That newspaper is yellowed and crackling dry now, its edges crumbling as I fold it out.

It seems strange to read my own comments to Iwata as I gave my thoughts on who the Green River Killer might be and what drove him: "[He] either possesses superior intelligence, or he's so streetwise or con-wise that he makes up for whatever [lack of] intelligence he might have. . . . The antisocial personality always sounds sincere. The facade is absolutely perfect."

In the same article, F.B.I. special agent Bob Ressler commented, "Most of these people are very, very human. The majority are normal in appearance and conversation, and certainly not insane or bizarre. They're not strapped in chains or straitjackets, and that's what makes them so dangerous."

The media coverage was accelerating, not just in western Washington and Portland, Oregon, but spreading into other states. Finally, on May 23, 1984, Frank Adamson and the rest of the task force got a much-needed right arm, a smart and gracious media spokesperson: Fae Brooks. Fae knew the Green River cases as well as anyone. She and Dave Reichert had worked on them in the very beginning. As the media liaison, she could tactfully stonewall the press without ever ruffling reporters' feathers.

Fae Brooks had joined the King County Sheriff's Office in 1978 as a patrol officer, the realization of a longtime ambition. She had once been a legal secretary, but her uncle was assistant chief of police in Washington, D.C., and she wanted to be a cop, too. She began on patrol out of the Burien Precinct, which now housed the Green River Task Force, and quickly moved up to be a detective in the Sexual Assault Unit. Brooks had been a recruiter for the department, too. She dismissed any thought that it was difficult for a woman, an African American at that, to go up through the ranks. "As long as you are a competent officer, it doesn't make any difference who you are."

She would prove that—and then some—over the years, moving up through the ranks.

ON MAY 26, reporters would clamor again for information. More bones had been found, this time near Jovita Boulevard, not in King County, but five blocks into Pierce County. The skull still had metal orthodontic braces on its teeth. Colleen Brockman, fifteen, who had believed that the men who picked her up on the SeaTac HiWay and sometimes took her out to dinner really cared for her, had lain for a year and a half undiscovered. The fate that her friend "Bunny" had feared had caught up with Colleen.

By June 16, 1984, the official toll of Green River victims was twenty-six. Eighteen of them identified; the rest only bones.

Tracy Winston was still missing, along with Kase Ann Lee, Debra Lorraine Estes, Denise Darcel Bush, Tina "Star" Tomson/ Kim Nelson, Shirley Sherrill, Becky Marrero, Mary Bello, Carrie Rois, Patricia Osborn, Marie Malvar, April Buttram, Pammy Avent, Mary Exzetta West, Keli Kay McGinness, Martina Authorlee, and Cindy Ann Smith. Maybe some of the unidentified bones would prove to be those of the missing. Perhaps not.

And, almost certainly, there were young women missing who had never been reported, girls who either had no close relatives and associates or who were believed to be living somewhere else or traveling.

There were new tips coming in, and some unresolved suspicions about prior suspects. In July 1984, Melvyn Foster told reporters that investigators had given him a "ride" to Seattle from his Lacey home, bought him lunch, and spent several hours showing him pictures of dozens of women and asking him questions. "It was all quite civilized," he commented with aplomb. He had been happy to share his experience and knowledge with them. He appeared to be somewhat pleased that the task force detectives had failed to arrest a viable suspect.

Foster bragged to Barbara Kubik-Patten that he and Dave Reichert were now "good buddies," and that Reichert was going to show him all the dump sites. He still had a kind of love/hate relationship with the police. Foster wanted very much to be part of law enforcement, and continued to offer his services as a "consultant" to any department that would listen to him. His father's home was in Thurston County, so he went to Neil McClanahan and Mark Curtis, high-ranking detectives in the sheriff's office, and offered to help them "clean up prostitution" in Olympia, Washington's state capital. One place he suggested they investigate was the "Roman Bath," where he said he himself had had sex with women. Curtis and McClanahan checked with King County on Foster's status and were told to go ahead and listen to Foster if they wanted to.

He would soon be cleared by the Green River Task Force of any guilty knowledge in their cases, finally omitted from the suspect roster during Frank Adamson's command.

"We bought Mel's car for $1,200 and processed it to the nth degree—even using the F.B.I.'s criminalists," Adamson recalled, "but we found nothing. There was a handprint on the trunk of his car, a small print, and we wondered if it was from a small female or a child. It was from his daughter. We cleared him because we were so thorough in searching his vehicle."

Every so often, Foster would get into trouble with the law, usually a scuffle of some sort. Once, he pulled a knife on a driver who cut him off in traffic. Still, he faded rapidly from the headlines, no longer "a person of interest."

Wendy Coffield's parents sued the State of Washington for negligence in not keeping careful enough track of her. They had hoped that she would be incarcerated for several years so that she might have a safer environment, and they were angry that she had been released to a facility without bars and locked doors. In the end, their suit went nowhere.

ON SATURDAY, July 31, 1984, I received a phone call from a man named Randy who said he lived in San Francisco with his grandmother. He said he'd read *The Stranger Beside Me* and decided to call me about two men he'd met in jail: Richard Carbone and Robert Matthias. Randy said he was quite sure they had killed at least some of the Green River victims, and they had also told him they had robbed a bank in Seattle. He gave me very detailed descriptions of Matthias and Carbone, right down to their prison tattoos. He was frustrated because he said he had called the task force and left a message for Bob Gebo, a Seattle police homicide detective on loan to the Green River investigation, and he hadn't yet heard back. I explained how many leads the task force investigators had to follow and that I was sure Gebo would get back to him when he could.

Three days later, I heard from Matthias himself. He said Randy had given him my number. He claimed to be afraid that his life would be in danger on any trip back to Seattle with detectives. I told him not to worry; I'd relayed his message and been told that Detective Paul Smith of the task force would be coming to San Francisco to talk to him.

Matthias called me several times, telling me about his dysfunctional childhood, and then he confessed to killing some of the Green River victims. But he broke into tears when I tried to pin him down about dates, seasons, and locations around Seattle. I'll admit I almost bought his story at first, because he was very, very, convincing. "Tell me something," I said, "because I'm curious. If you are involved in the situation up here, you would have either had to be very good-looking, drive a really nice car, or have a great gift of gab, because the girls were so frightened they wouldn't get in a car with just anyone."

"Two out of three," he said. "I don't like to brag, but I'm good-looking. I appear to be very, very nice. I can get people to trust me and feel comfortable with me in the first five minutes I talk to them. It's mainly the way I talk. I sound very naive when I want to. My tattoos throw them off sometimes, though, and I have to talk faster."

I didn't really trust Matthias, but he knew enough about the Green River cases for me to keep up a dialogue with him. Still, it was becoming obvious to me that he wanted to learn more from me than he wanted to tell me the truth. I deliberately avoided giving him any locations or information about the victims. Matthias thought they had all been pretty brunettes, and I let him think that. He was wrong about the manner of death, too. He mentioned using a gun, and said they had been beaten and cut, as well as strangled.

A half hour later, Richard Carbone called, or he said he was Carbone. His voice sounded remarkably like Matthias's. Either only one of the two prisoners was making the calls, or their voices and "confessions" had been rehearsed. Carbone, however, claimed that he and Matthias had killed women in three states—Minnesota, Oregon, and Washington. "We put the girls in the trunk of whatever car we'd stolen last, and then we left them."

Like Matthias, he was worried about the trip back to Seattle if they were extradited from California, and he wanted me to assure him they would be safe. Would I come along as an extra witness? He voiced his concerns that they would be deluged by the press and "fans when we're brought to Seattle and it hits the papers. There are a lot of sick people out there," he pointed out piously, "who get off on associating with people like us."

As I look at the eighteen, single-spaced, pages I typed out on Matthias's and Carbone's calls and then sent to Detective Bob Gebo, I realize I must have bought their stories enough to listen to them that long. But, as Matthias said, he had "a great gift of gab."

Paul Smith, Ed Streidinger (also on loan from the Seattle homicide unit), and Randy Mullinax flew to San Francisco to question Carbone and Matthias. They questioned them separately, of course. One said he'd killed eleven, and the other thought they must have killed sixteen. They were clearly blowing smoke.

Mullinax had counseled many victims' families and seen their grief and terror. His was a solid shoulder they could count on, and he told a lot of mothers that they could call on him whenever they needed to ask questions or just to talk. Now, he looked with loathing at the man who sat across from him because he knew he was lying; Matthias had his facts wrong. The usually taciturn detective reached across the table and grabbed the glib prisoner by the collar. "Listen, you S.O.B.," Mullinax said. "There are families out there *dying*, waiting to hear about their daughters. Don't you dare play with their hopes and emotions."

Both men admitted that they had lied about the whole thing. They figured it would be a good way to escape, expecting that they would be extradited to Seattle, guarded by only one detective apiece. Their plan called for one of them to create a distraction while the other stole the handcuff keys.

When Randy Mullinax told Mertie Winston about it later, he laughed that the pair was so dumb, they didn't realize they would each have had three or more guards, and they had never considered that they would have been in leg irons, too.

Mertie could tell that Mullinax would almost have welcomed the jerks making a move to escape. She bought Randy a plaque that said "Make My Day" and he quickly hung it over his desk at task force headquarters.

The investigation had been going on for a long time, and most of the families knew how hard the detectives were working, how emotionally invested they were. But there were a few parents who complained. They tended to be the ones who hadn't really looked after their daughters in the first place.

Mertie Winston and Randy Mullinax had grown up in the same general neighborhood in the south end, although they'd never met. She knew about his family, and he always asked about her boys. She knew that he would call her if there was any news at all about Tracy. Dave Reichert, too, seemed to care a lot about the families who waited, their agony almost more than they could bear. Some of the task force investigators admitted that they had to stay detached emotionally. There was just too much cumulative pain among the families and they felt they couldn't do their jobs if they allowed themselves to be caught in it.

"I used to take chocolate chip cookies down to the task force when they were headquartered in the old junior high school," Mertie said. "But it was difficult for me because that was the same school Tracy had gone to when things were so different. I had to pass close to her homeroom, and I heard the same bells ringing when classes changed. I couldn't stay very long. I wasn't comfortable in that school. It brought back too many memories."

Citizens and politicos grew restive with the expense of keeping a task force intact when it hadn't yet arrested a suspect. It wasn't turning out the way it did on television shows.

There was talk that the task force might be cut back in both personnel and funds. Thus far, the King County budget had had almost $2 million sliced out of it to fund the Green River investigation, and some felt that wasn't politically correct, not when there hadn't been any positive results in more than two years. Sheriff Vern Thomas explained that it was too early in the game to evaluate what the forty-person team had accomplished.

The plain fact was that there had never been a series of murders as difficult to solve as the Green River killings. The King County Sheriff's Department wasn't equipped to do it in the beginning, nor would any other department in the United States have been. Yes, King County had worked the Ted Bundy murders, but only three of Bundy's victims were found within its jurisdiction, three were Seattle police cases, one was a Thurston County case, and one girl had disappeared in Corvallis, Oregon. Subsequent Bundy victims were abducted from Utah, Colorado, and Florida. In the end, Bundy was never charged in Washington State, and he was convicted, of course, in Florida and executed there.

The Green River Killer was mainly striking in Seattle and King County, and seeming to do it with impunity. Those who hunted for him knew he was no superman, but his apparently stranger-to-stranger homicides, with so many names and identities, were the hardest of all to solve.

They needed time. Time for the computer to be programmed. Time to follow up the ten thousand leads that had by now poured into the task force. In October of 1984, their $200,000 computer went on line, a tremendous help for the task force in keeping track of things, such as how many times a certain name might pop up on an F.I.R. Cross-referencing leads and even nonthreatening johns could very well pop up a name that would be vital.

A lot of things were happening through the summer and fall of 1984, and the jabs at the task force became sharper as the months passed. It was hard to take. It would always be hard to take.

Frank Adamson had good reasons for not revealing any number of facts uncovered by the task force, and he and his detectives absorbed complaints from the public that nothing was happening.

They all knew that they cared about the victims and their families; taking the abuse thrown at them was just part of the job.

But something else was *not* happening, something hopeful. The disappearances had stopped.

33

DAVE REICHERT, the detective who had caught the first King County case, the murder of Debra Bonner, was now responsible for solving several of the more recent killings, and he chafed at the bit. He had worked day and night for years, a familiar sight in almost every photograph of body search scenes. His full head of chestnut-colored hair, shot here and there with gray strands now, fell over his eyes as he dug and sifted dirt in one wilderness or another. As they all were, he was looking for something the killer had left behind. Just one magic irrefutable connection to the wraithlike killer. And still it eluded him.

They were moving into their third year and the killing machine was still out there, even if he seemed to have slowed down. That didn't alleviate Reichert's feeling that there must have been something that he could have done, should have done, early in the game. More than most of the investigators, Reichert went over everything that had been done to find their quarry, looking for some link that had been overlooked. When he walked where he knew the killer had tread, he followed Pierce Brooks's edict to put himself into the killer's mind, to think the way he thought.

It wasn't an easy approach for a devout churchgoer, a family man who was used to setting positive goals and meeting them. Every detective had his or her own personality.

Bob Keppel was analytical, able to step back and see how the investigation should be organized. It wasn't that he didn't feel the pain of the dead girls and their families; it was more that he was able to set it aside for the moment and tap into his own experience in dealing with serial killers. If he was sometimes blunt with his critiques, it was more important to him to solve obvious problems with communication, record-keeping, and matching up information that might be vital than it was to hold anyone's hand.

Frank Adamson was very smart, very kind, and adept at handling his detectives. He didn't have a trace of the ego that mars many command officers' ability to accept help or advice. Whatever might work, Adamson welcomed it.

Randy Mullinax appeared to be the best at comforting families, a quality that he sometimes must have wished he didn't possess, and he was an indefatigable investigator.

They all worked hard, side by side with the young people from Explorer Search and Rescue (ESAR). The spring and summer searches were the easiest because it seldom rained. Even so, fir trees, alders, and a few big-leafed maples shut out the sun as they moved into the shaded woods, but the days were longer and there was no fog. The sound of their footsteps was muffled by the thick carpet of decaying leaves and needles beneath their feet.

In the fall of 1984, Frank Adamson had asked those citizens who were heading into the wilderness to keep a sharp eye out for some sign of the at least fifteen young women who were still missing. Long-abandoned bodies, left in the woods or other isolated places, are often discovered by hikers, mushroom seekers, or hunters. Leaves fall and their branches are bare and stark against a leaden sky, making visibility easier. Snowfalls collapse blackberry vines. Men in heavy boots break through underbrush and saplings as they look for pheasant, deer, and elk.

What had been hidden would eventually be found. If there was any emotion that still seeped from the quiet forests, it was the loneliness of someone shut away from home, family, love, and sunshine forever. The girls left near the SeaTac Airport lay in a prettier location beneath maple trees turned golden in October. That was, of course, small comfort to their families.

ONE NAME had been removed from the list—that of Mary Bello— and her mother, Sue Villamin, lived with the renewed hope that Mary was alive and well and had simply walked away from her life in Seattle. Maybe she hadn't been able to fight her heroin habit after all. It was better to think that Mary was still hooked than to know for sure that she was dead.

Mary's little lobster tattoo was unusual, and a policeman in Odessa, Texas, was sure that he had seen Mary dancing at a club in Odessa a few months or so after she was reported missing. She sometimes used the alias Roxanne Dunlap, and that was the name the Odessa officer recognized.

Still, Mary hadn't called home for a year, and a second Christmas without her was only two months away. Sue Villamin knew in her heart that, no matter what, Mary would have found some way to check on her and on her grandparents, even if she didn't want to be found.

On Friday, October 12, 1984, a man hunting for chanterelle and morel mushrooms off Highway 410 eight miles east of Enumclaw, an area already known as one of the Green River Killer's body sites, came across a skull and widely scattered bones. Some were animal bones, but many were human. The task force and the "brush monkeys," the young people of the Explorer Search and Rescue team who worked so many volunteer hours at every body location, moved in to gather evidence and find even the smallest bone. Sadly, they had all become adept at it, as they walked shoulder to shoulder across a very wide search area. When anything was found, it would be bagged and taped with the initials of the evidence officer, the date, time, and place. Dirt was shaken through screens to find minuscule bits and pieces of something the killer might have left behind, something belonging to the victim or to himself. They had learned to check the holes and tunnels of big and little animals, and found hair, small bones, shiny objects. By now, there wasn't a search team in the country that could work an outdoor body site any better than the Green River Task Force, thankless though the job was so far.

In his coveralls and boots, Bill Haglund, the chief investigator for the Medical Examiner's Office, was recognizable instantly to anyone who watched the news. So were Frank Adamson, Dave Reichert, Jackson Beard, Randy Mullinax, Dan Nolan, Rupe Lettich, Cheri Luxa, Matt Haney, Sue Peters, Mike Hatch, Jon Mattsen, Matt Haney, and Fae Brooks.

It was usually Haglund, however, who was able to give the final word on who the newest set of remains belonged to. After consulting the dental charts on file, he realized that Mary Bello should never have been removed from the list of possible victims. The Odessa, Texas, sighting must have been of someone else. She had been found almost a year to the day after she vanished. Gone October 11, 1983—found October 12, 1984.

Two police officers, a man and a woman, knocked on the door of Sue Villamin's trailer and told her that her daughter was dead. She was too distraught to remember their names.

"I sort of went to hell in a handbasket for a year," Sue says. "My mother didn't live a month after she found out. I know I wasn't the kind of mother I wanted to be with Mary. And so I thought she would settle down some day and have children, and I would do better with them as their grandmother. But I never had a chance to do that.

"I took some of Mary's ashes home with me. And I liked having them there, but they made me sad, too. One of my friends told me that it was too hard on me. I went to the Green River and I said a prayer and gently put her ashes in there.

"She didn't have a funeral service. My parents were afraid their friends would know what she'd been doing. Her street name wasn't 'Draper,' though, so nobody ever figured it out."

Widowed, with her adoptive parents and her daughter gone, without ever finding her birth family, Sue was living alone, by 2004, except for her dog Chico, in an apartment in downtown Seattle. She had become close to her father's widow, who was in her nineties.

It wouldn't be long before another body was found. Martina Authorlee probably never returned to Oregon in May 1983. She was up there off Highway 410, along with Mary Bello and Debbie Abernathy, close to the White River. A hunter found Martina's body on November 14, 1984.

On the shoulder of the highway, detectives found the sodden pages of a collection of pornography—magazines catering to sado-masochists and a paperback novel penned by a writer with little talent but a grotesque grasp of his readers' tastes. Was it a coincidence that the scurrilous material was there close to the remains? Or had the Green River Killer tossed it there to tease those who were a year behind him on a cold trail?

Dave Reichert and Bob Keppel weren't in King County in mid-November 1984 when Martina Authorlee's remains were identified. They were far away in Starke, Florida, on a mission that sounded like something out of *Silence of the Lambs*.

Ted Bundy would never deign to talk with Bob Keppel back in the years when Keppel was a young King County detective working on the murders of women in the Northwest, those murders that came to be known as "The Ted Murders." Ted was smart enough to know that the less he said to Keppel and his partner, Roger Dunn, the better, and he took some delight in avoiding them when he was out on bail during the holiday season in 1975.

By 1984, however, Ted was on Death Row in Raiford Prison, the Florida state penitentiary, awaiting execution for the murder of twelve-year-old Kimberly Leach. He was, in essence, silenced—no longer able to joust with detectives or to take advantage of photo ops with reporters. He considered himself *the* expert on serial murder, and he would tell me patronizingly in letters that I "didn't really understand serial killers," and I was "all wrong" in my conclusions about their motivation and psychological profiles. He liked to hint at things he could tell me, and then draw back, enjoying the tease.

I didn't know that Ted had already found an audience more to his liking, where he could expound upon his theories: Keppel and Reichert. The Green River Killer was threatening to break Ted's record, both in the number of victims and the years he had evaded arrest. Knowing Ted, that would have alarmed and frustrated him. The Green River Killer had probably killed more women than Ted, and he had remained free to kill more. Added to his edginess at losing his "throne," Bundy needed once more to pontificate, to chide, to advise, and to point out his superior grasp of the criminal mind. Who would be better than the top-ranked detectives from King County?

He also believed that as long as he remained useful to law and order, he could avoid the electric chair. He had nothing much to lose, and neither did Keppel and Reichert. Maybe Bundy did understand the way the Green River Killer's mind worked more than a normal man could. Maybe he would even shed some light on the Ted Murders that would give some answers to the parents of his own victims.

Ted sent a letter to Bob Keppel in the autumn of 1984, and Ted's former attorney, John Henry Browne, followed that up with a message from Ted to Frank Adamson and Keppel. Ted wanted to help in the Green River investigation. "He wanted to give his opinion," Adamson recalled. "I sent Keppel and Reichert to Starke to interview Bundy. I thought he might give something to Keppel that would allow us to charge Bundy here in Washington. I didn't think he could help on our cases. Clifford Olson [the Canadian serial murderer of children] had also contacted Adamson and Danny Nolan to offer his thoughts."

Characteristically, Adamson told Keppel and Reichert to go for it, to see what Bundy might have to say. He probably had at least as much to offer as the psychics who still described "water and trees and mountains."

And so on November 16 and 17, 1984, with no fanfare at all, Bob Keppel and Dave Reichert met with Ted Bundy somewhere in the bowels of Florida's most dreaded prison. Some of what Bundy opined would prove accurate, some would be off the mark, and some would be the boasting of a massive, but trapped, ego.

At the request of Captain Gary Terry of the Hillsborough County Sheriff's Office in Tampa, Florida, Reichert and Keppel also asked Ted questions about a Tampa man who had been arrested only that week as a prime suspect in the serial killer murders of nine young women who worked the streets of Tampa and St. Petersburg. Bobby Joe Long, a technician in the medical field, later admitted to multiple rapes and murders in a forty-five-page statement. His downfall had come when he kidnapped a teenager who worked in a doughnut shop, held her captive for days as he sexually assaulted her, and then let her go. He had believed her promises that she wouldn't tell anyone.

As odd as it may sound, the world of serial murder is quite small; investigators and experts eventually come to know each other, just as serial killers often correspond with one another. Bob Keppel would maintain a correspondence with Bundy and interview him again before Bundy had his final date with the electric chair. In the end, Bundy offered only theories that might one day be validated, but he couldn't lead Keppel or Reichert to the Green River Killer's front door.

THERE were still so many young women missing, and 1984 would end without any more bodies being discovered. And, seemingly, with no further disappearances. A third Christmas passed with only emptiness for the families who waited.

34

AND THEN IT WAS 1985 and, in America, the new year started off quietly. Because January 20 fell on the same Sunday as the biggest football contest of the year, Ronald Reagan's ceremonial inauguration for his second term in office was preempted for a day in deference to Super Bowl XIX. Reagan was sworn in legally, but quietly, as the San Francisco 49ers overwhelmed the Miami Dolphins. He graciously agreed to wait until January 21 for the public festivities.

Nineteen eighty-five was not a big year for news of violent

crime, and virtually no layperson outside the Northwest had heard of the Green River Killer. VICAP was not yet off the ground, so the problem of viable connections among and between law enforcement agencies across the country continued. It was quite possible that the Green River Killer *had* moved to another area, as serial killers are characteristically peripatetic. Or he was dead. He might well be in prison. He might even have had a sea change in his life, something so profound that it overrode his compulsion to kill—if only for a time.

A serial killer is, quite literally, "addicted" to murder. I have heard some of them phrase it just that way. Both Bobby Joe Long and Ted Bundy did. Their "fix" is killing, and the more entrenched their addiction, the more victims they require to feed their habit. Frank Adamson and the members of his task force could only hope that, if he was still alive, the Green River Killer would surely slip up before he killed any more young women.

In January 1985, Dr. Don Reay's office released a few more details about the four sets of unknown bones that no one had claimed. The first Star Lake victim's pelvis bore indications that it had once been fractured and one arm was dislocated. That could have happened as she fought her killer, but Gail Mathews's sister-in-law read this new information nervously as she remembered that Gail had broken her pelvis in a boating accident in 1980. She was right to worry. Bill Haglund announced that forensic experts had obtained Gail's X-rays from a Seattle hospital, and they were able to match them absolutely with the skeletal pelvis. Also in evidence was a small shred of skin from which criminalists had been able to raise a partial fingerprint—enough to compare to a known print. Gail's own finger had left its mark on her flesh. Bones #2 belonged to the darkly beautiful woman who had once aspired to be an artist. "She was really good at art," her estranged husband said about the woman who had originally come to Seattle from Crescent City, California. "She was just a nice young lady, down to earth."

Ken Mathews had custody of their young daughter, and Gail had often visited her child. The last time she had visited was in late March 1983. They had split up without rancor. "She just kind of got all mixed up," he said. "She had no real home and not many girlfriends. She was kind of lonely."

Gail had no record for prostitution, although she had lived on Pac HiWay South. Her extended family hadn't officially reported

The Robert Mills family, 1972 (REAR: Robert and Kathy; FRONT: Garrett and Opal). Opal and Garrett suffered from racial prejudice in school and stuck together fiercely. Garrett always felt responsible for his little sister's safety and his ultimate failure to protect her haunts him still.

5

6

Because Garrett Mills had survived delicate heart surgery at age five, he and Opal collected money to give to the Childrens' Orthopedic Hospital. Opal, whom her brother called "The Little Peanut," was still safe then.

One of the last photographs of Opal Charmaine Mills, at 14 or 15, 1981. As a teenager, Opal lived a rich fantasy life, fancying herself in love with boys and men she hardly knew. Gullible and vulnerable, she, too, was left at the Green River.

7

8

A brown truck with a camper shell didn't stand out as suspicious on the Pac HiWay "Strip" in the early eighties. Later, witnesses would remember this pickup, along with similar vehicles that patrolled the highway.

9

The Strip where prostitution proliferated from 1982 to 1985, the busy Pac HiWay that runs past Seattle's SeaTac Airport. It became the prime hunting ground for a serial killer who targeted teenage girls.

Sheriff's Lt. Dick Kraske confers with
his detectives at the North Bend body-
cluster site where several Green River
Killer victims were found.

10

Lt. Dick Kraske after his retirement. He was
at the center of both the "Ted" (Bundy)
murders in the midseventies and the Green
River probe seven years later.

11

12

In 1983, the first Green River Task Force posed for a photograph
in the cramped office between floors in the King County Courthouse. FROM LEFT: Elizabeth Druin, Pat Ferguson, Sgt. Bob
"Grizzly" Andrews, Ben Colwell, Dave Reichert. SEATED IN
FRONT: Lt. Dan Nolan. Despite questioning hundreds of people
about the murders, there were no easy answers.

Giselle Lovvorn, 17, traveled America following The Grateful Dead, but the freckled blond teenager with a genius I.Q. had decided to go home to her California family when she vanished from the Strip in July 1982. Her body was found in late September, the first victim of the GRK to be left away from the river.

13

Melvyn Foster, a taxi driver, knew the Strip and its habitués well. When he came forward to offer his advice to the task force, he instead became a "person of interest" as he revealed startling knowledge of the young prostitutes along the highway.

14

Detective Dave Reichert (LEFT) and Detective Mick Stewart during an extensive search of Melvyn Foster's father's home near Olympia, Washington, in September 1982.

15

1

Ann Rule, standing beneath the Peck Bridge on the edge of the Green River in Kent, Washington, at the exact spot where Wendy Lee Coffield's body was found in July 1982. No one could imagine then that Wendy was only the first of more than fifty victims.

Debra Lynn Bonner, 22, was found in the Green River a month after Wendy Lee Coffield. Although she rarely had a permanent address, Debra was deeply loyal to her family and always carried their photos and mementos.

2

A King County police diver holds
Debra Lynn Bonner's dress, found
in the Green River near her body
in August 1982.

3

4

An aerial photograph of the Green River as it winds through a fertile
valley in southeast King County, Washington. After the summer of
1982, the name *Green River* triggered thoughts of deadly violence
instead of serenity. The bodies of five young women floated there,
hidden by the tall grass.

Mary Bridget Meehan, 18, was a bright Irish adventuress, much loved by her family. She was a rebel who longed for a safe harbor, babies, and music, but she wandered too far to come home again.

16

17

Mary Bridget and her longtime boyfriend Ray. She was 8½ months pregnant with Ray's baby when she disappeared from the Strip on September 15, 1982.

Detectives and medical examiners remove the remains of Mary Bridget Meehan and her unborn child from a shallow grave only a few blocks off the Strip in November 1983. She was one of the few victims who had been buried rather than just dumped.

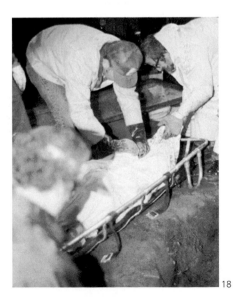

18

Constance Elizabeth "Connie" Naon lived in her car, worked at a minimum-wage job, and occasionally on the streets, trying to make it on her own.

19

20

Green River Task Force detectives look for physical evidence at the site where Connie Naon's, Mary Bridget Meehan's, and Kelly Marie Ware's bodies were found near SeaTac Airport.

Shawnda Leea Summers at the beach in a happier time. Missing for a long time, her remains were finally identified as those found in an apple orchard south of the SeaTac Airport, not far from those of Giselle Lovvorn's.

21

Frank Adamson led the Green River Task Force longer than any other command officer. He had high hopes of closing the cases, but after seven years the killer was still elusive.

22

Sandra Kay "Sand-e" Gabbert, 17, was a free spirit full of life. She told her mother that she could make more in one night on the Strip than she could in two weeks at a fast-food restaurant. In the spring of 1983, Sand-e promised her, "I'll be careful," and walked away into the night . . . forever.

23

25

Carrie Ann Rois, 16, wanted to be a model and actress but she met the wrong man. Once, he let her go, and she trusted him. In the spring of 1983, he didn't.

Carrie, age five, opens her Christmas presents. Her happy childhood days evaporated as she entered her teens and became a truant and runaway.

24

26

Carrie Ann Rois ended up in a dank ravine at this Star Lake body-cluster site. A dirt biker thought her skull was a football before realizing what it really was. Six victims were found here, and Carrie was the last to be discovered.

27

1985. Ann Rule stands at the Star Lake Road site next to a tree still emblazoned with a bright red "1" to mark where the first body was found. It was Gail Lynn Mathews, whose boyfriend had seen her last riding with a stranger in a pickup truck on the Pac HiWay.

28

These composites depict men seen with Green River victims before their disappearance. Police would like to interview them.

30

Kimi-Kai Pitsor, 16, vanished within a day of Sand-e Gabbert, but her remains were found far away in a different cluster—at Auburn's Mountain View Cemetery. This stolen Lincoln Town Car, pushed over a ravine, was unconnected to the four murder victims, but led searchers to the remains found nearby. Kimi-Kai was the only one identified.

Four witness drawings—individuals' memories varied greatly. Were any of them the Green River Killer?

29

Randy Mullinax spent many years on the Green River Task Force. A young detective here, he would become both a shrewd investigator and a tremendous comfort to grieving families.

Mary Sue Bello, 25, tried to help the Green River Task Force stop the roving killer when she reported a suspicious John.

31

32

While Mary Sue Bello had her wild side, she was also a loving daughter and granddaughter who was turning her life around when she disappeared. This is her mother's favorite picture of her.

The small house on 32nd Street South looked much like others. Friends, neighbors, and the owner's girlfriends who were invited inside had no idea what horrors took place here.

33

34

The Green River Killer's fortunes rose steadily as he moved to a better house and neighborhood during the two decades he eluded detectives.

The Green River Killer took his unsuspecting prey to his master bedroom in his first house to have sex, knowing what would happen afterward. Ironically, he chose a wall mural that resembled the lonely woods where he planned to leave their bodies.

35

Ann Rule helped Forensic Artist Betty Pat Gatliff rebuild a face on the skull of an unknown Green River victim found at the Star Lake cluster. It took X-rays of Gail Lynn Mathews's broken bones from a boating accident to confirm her identity.

36

Matt Haney joined the Green River Task Force in the mideighties, and partnered first with Randy Mullinax. Haney honed in on one suspect, but it would take almost fifteen years to prove he was right.

37

Delise Louise "Missy" Plager in one of her rare happy moments. A twin, she had to be resuscitated at birth and survived despite great odds. The space between her front teeth helped to identify her skeletonized remains.

38

Randy Mullinax (LEFT) and Fae Brooks (RIGHT) dig and sift dirt near where Missy Plager's remains were found in the forest near Highway 18 and I-90.

Tracy, age 7, grew up in a happy suburban family. She was only ten years past her childhood days when she vanished in September 1983.

Tracy Ann Winston trusted everyone and tried to help them. Sadly, her perception of evil was flawed, and she mistook a killer for a friend.

Tracy always loved baseball and, due to her powerful throwing arm, was one of the first girls ever allowed to play on a *boys'* Little League team. Here she hugs her mom, Mertie Winston, with whom she had a special bond.

In March 1986, Green River Task Force members and Explorer Search and Rescue Scouts prepare to search Cottonwood Park on the bank of the Green River. Lt. Jackson Beard, fourth from left in green jumpsuit, directed this search as he had many others. It would be thirteen years before they identified the remains as Tracy Winston.

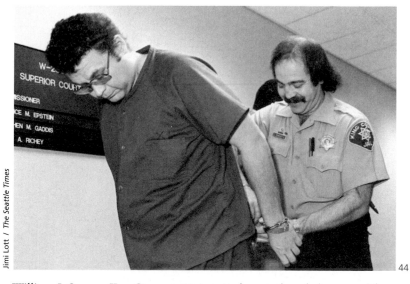

Jimi Lott / *The Seattle Times*

William J. Stevens II, a Gonzaga University law student, led a secret life for many years. His collections of police paraphernalia and pornography and his hatred of prostitutes triggered the Green River Task Force's suspicion. Entering a King County courtroom in 1989, he was now the prime suspect.

Gary Ridgway, who grew up near the Strip, was a familiar commuter as he drove the highway to the job he held for more than thirty years. Here he poses with his second wife, Dana,* with whom he had a son, but they divorced in 1981.

45

Gary's first two wives had issues with his mother, Mary, who continued to dominate her grown son's life.

46

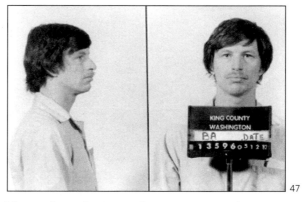

47

The newly single Gary Ridgway was arrested in 1982 for soliciting a prostitute, a minor charge.

48

Sue Peters and Randy Mullinax, Green River Task Force veterans, stand next to evidence folders. Along with Tom Jensen and Jon Mattsen, Peters and Mullinax were the detectives who questioned the prime suspect almost daily throughout the summer of 2003.

49

One prime suspect, a truck painter at Kenworth Trucks, denied that he had any connection to the victims. Even so, Green River Task Force detectives searched the rafters in the Kenworth plant for possible mementos—photos or jewelry—taken from the dead young women.

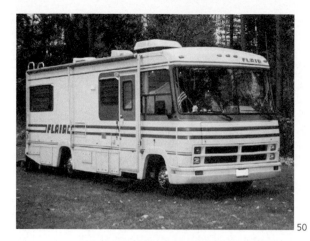

During their many years together, Gary Ridgway and his third wife, Judith, had gone from a camper "with a coffee can for a bathroom" to a sumptuous motorhome.

50

51

Judith laughingly called Gary and herself "pack rats," because they spent their weekends at garage sales, swap meets, and even dumps.

Gary Ridgway, 52, under surveillance, looks around nervously as he approaches his pickup truck on November 30, 2001.

52

Gary Ridgway after his arrest on November 30, 2001. He was stunned to find Detectives Jim Doyon and Randy Mullinax waiting for him when he left work on that stormy Friday.

53

When Ridgway was arrested, he wore jeans and a plaid shirt, the clothes described by abduction witnesses—but also the clothes worn by half the men in south King County.

54

Gary Ridgway wears coveralls after task force detectives bagged and labeled all his clothing, so it could be searched for trace evidence on November 30, 2001.

55

56

Dave Reichert, now the sheriff of King County, called
a news conference with Prosecutor Norm Maleng on
November 30, 2001, to announce the arrest of Gary
Ridgway. Now a grandfather, Reichert was a detective
for only a few months in August 1982, when he was
assigned as lead detective in the murders of Debra
Lynn Bonner, Cynthia Jean Hinds, Marcia Faye Chapman, and Opal Charmaine Mills.

57

King County Task Force investigators in the backyard of the Ridgways'
property in early December 2001. With a suspect in custody, they finally
had good reason to smile. LEFT TO RIGHT: John Urquhart, Tom Jensen,
and Steve Davis.

58

Task force investigators dug up the yard behind the house in Auburn, looking for the remains of victims still missing. After excavating the land around three of Ridgway's houses, they replaced the dirt and plants, having found nothing at all.

Washington State Patrol crime scene investigators processed the interior of Judith and Gary Ridgway's present and former houses. They wore booties and latex gloves to avoid cross-contamination with evidence, but found nothing of evidentiary value.

60

Patricia "Trish" Yellow Robe, a beautiful member of the Chippewa Cree tribe, was found dead in 1999. An autopsy found her death to be accidental—the result of an overdose—but, shockingly, the killer admitted to her murder. He had not stopped killing in 1985 as he previously claimed.

61

There are dozens of young women still missing in Washington and Oregon, including Keli Kay McGinness, who disappeared in the spring of 1983. Detective Sue Peters is still actively seeking Keli. The Green River Task Force continues and probably will for many years.

her missing until a year after her boyfriend knew she was gone because there were several erroneous "sightings" that made them feel she was all right. In truth, she had been dead for months when they started to worry in April 1984. The Star Lake site had begun to give up some terrible secrets, but Gail's skull hadn't been identifiable because her dental charts were not on file with the Medical Examiner's Office.

A month later, on March 10, a man riding a three-wheeler stopped on a sharp curve just east of the old Star Lake gravel pit. He climbed off his bike and walked back into the woods toward a steep ravine, looking for a new area where he could ride. As his eyes scanned the slope leading down to where the creek had made the dirt sour and boggy, something caught his eye, but his mind unconsciously tried to avoid the obvious. He stared at a roundish object, partially covered with moss. Was it a football helmet?

He knew it wasn't. But he didn't want to slide down into the ravine alone to check. He contacted a friend who was riding nearby and the two men went back to stare at the perfectly round *thing* that lay half-mired in the swamp. Together, they sidestepped down the hill, holding on to trees to keep from falling. It was what they had feared: a human skull.

It was too dark for a full-scale search, but the Green River Task Force was there the next day shortly after sunrise. They met at seven thirty and discussed their plan. The killer they had followed for so long had chosen such an optimum site that they were sure this must be yet another of his victims.

But who was it? It could be the last earthly remains of more than a dozen young women. KIRO-TV was already there, and the other channels were arriving, their reporters with mikes in hand, shivering against the trucks with transmittal satellites. The detectives tried not to notice them; as always, they were an intrusive presence in the disconsolate ambience of another body retrieval.

Water from springtime rains trickled steadily down the hill and added to the mire at the bottom of the ravine. The conditions were perfect for skunk cabbage, a native flower with huge, creamy yellow blooms and large leaves. Beautiful from a distance, it emitted a rank, sickly sweet odor when it was picked by unwary hikers, an odor that clung to them for days.

Dave Reichert and Mike Hatch searched for another way into the swamp while other detectives looked at the skull that wasn't very far from where Sand-e Gabbert and a dog's skeleton had been buried nose-to-nose. The bones had been scattered by animals and they found rib bones—twenty-three in all—an arm bone, a femur (thigh bone), and two clavicles. They put their hands into animal dens and found little bones there. The skull had six teeth missing from the upper jaw, and eight from the lower mandible. And then they located scattered teeth.

Randy Mullinax helped Bill Haglund package the remains. Eight hours after they began their search in the bog near Star Lake, Haglund announced that he had a positive I.D. At three twenty-two PM, they knew that fifteen-year-old Carrie Rois was at the Star Lake site, her body trapped in the muddy creek at the bottom of the ravine. "Silver Champagne," who had, indeed, looked so much like Brooke Shields, had been dead for a very long time.

But the media, eager to learn whom they had found, would have to wait. Randy Mullinax and Mike Hatch notified victims' advocate Linda Barker and arranged to meet her. Together, they would go to the U.P.S. offices where Judy DeLeone was at work. She mustn't hear the news on the radio or see it on television. She had waited almost two years, hoping that Carrie was safe someplace and would be coming home.

But, at some point, Judy had to know. When she looked up and saw the two detectives and Linda Barker walk into her office, her face paled. She knew without their saying a word.

Mullinax made sure that Steve Rois, Carrie's father, was notified as quickly as possible, too. For this victim at least, they could be sure that neither of her parents heard about it on the news. They tried valiantly to do it for all the parents, but sometimes zealous reporters got there first.

When Mullinax called Mertie Winston to tell her that Carrie had been found, she was near collapse, too. She and Judy DeLeone had succeeded in convincing themselves that their girls were together and were being treated the same by fate. When Mertie heard that Carrie had been found dead, it was the same as being told it was Tracy. She knew in her heart that Tracy was also gone. She just didn't know where Tracy's killer had hidden her.

35

HE *would* have some dramatic lifestyle changes in 1985, and that may have made a difference in the scope of his activities on the Pac HiWay and Aurora Avenue North. His solo travels would be curtailed certainly. His son, Chad, was getting older and more aware of what went on around him, and the man with so many secrets had become increasingly social. He felt at ease because he had bested them all for such a long time. He began to feel invincible.

Since he'd discovered Parents Without Partners, he had never lacked for feminine companionship; there were group activities in West Seattle and the south end every night of the week, as well as on the weekend. He dated a dozen or more of the women he met there. He met women at work, too, but they weren't as responsive to him. One woman recalled that he overstepped personal space boundaries.

"I'd just started working there—sometime in the mideighties—and he came up behind me and started massaging my shoulders," she said. "I wasn't at all comfortable with that. I tried not to be alone with him. It was just a gut feeling, but it was real.

"We worked in the rework area together. He talked about gardening, swap meets, garage sales. He would tell me about his marriages briefly, [saying] he was on his third. He was always touching the women at work and once he was reprimanded for sexual harassment. He was upset, asking me, 'Can you *believe* this?' "

She could indeed, but she didn't tell him that.

He always spoke to women who lived in his neighborhood and he seemed friendly. Most of them were married, though, and knew him only as a neighbor. One woman, Nancy, who lived a block away, worked at the VIP Tavern on the highway. He didn't drink much, usually a Budweiser or whatever was on draft in taverns, but he often stopped in at the Midway or the VIP taverns. "He was always fairly quiet, but also pleasant," Nancy recalled, "and a few times he gave me a lift home. Since he never drank much, I felt safe getting a lift home from him . . . until one night."

Instead of driving her straight home, he asked if she would mind stopping by his house for a few minutes. She saw no harm in that and vividly recalled sitting on his couch, drinking a beer. They were just having general conversation, and then he changed the subject to the Green River Killer.

"At the time, it was a popular subject," she remembered. "He became very serious, to the point of being physically tense. He asked me what I thought about the killer and what he was doing. I told him that if I were a prostitute, I'd find a different way to make money. He asked what I thought about prostitutes. 'Don't you think we're better off without them?'

"At that point, red flags went up left and right. I felt it was in my best interest to say: 'Yup. We sure are. At least the streets are getting cleaned up.' "

He seemed very intense as he explained that the police hadn't been doing their jobs, and she heard odd stress in his voice, a *thrum* beneath his regular voice: "We're much better off without them [the prostitutes] littering the streets."

Nancy was alert now; he had changed so much and fairly vibrated with tension. "He also knew that I knew quite a few psychics. He asked me if any of the psychics knew who the Green River Killer was. I told him that a lot of psychics had thoughts about it, but no one was talking."

"Why?" he persisted.

She told him that, "for one thing, the police wouldn't believe them. For another, they don't want to die."

He asked her what she meant.

Nancy studied him, choosing her words carefully. "The psychics are afraid that if they tell anyone who the Green River Killer is, they'll be killed before the police would take any action, so they're not saying anything—and they never will."

Nancy kept her voice soft as she casually told him that she was tired and really needed to go home. Would he mind? "He seemed to relax a little bit and said we could go any time. I told him I needed to go right away. I stood up to leave, but he stayed seated."

"Would you ever be a prostitute?" he asked her, his eyes boring into hers.

"No way!"

"That's good," he said, finally smiling and seeming to unwind a little. "I didn't think you would. Have you ever?"

"Of course not," she countered. "Have you?"

"That's stupid," he said.

"Just as stupid as your asking me."

Now he stood up and said "Let's go," and headed for the door. But as they drove the few blocks to her house, he brought up the subject of the Green River Killer again, and she tensed inwardly. He stressed that whoever was killing the girls was doing the city a favor.

"I brought up their families, saying how sad it was that some of them had small children who would grow up without their mothers," Nancy remembered. "He said this was something the prostitutes should think about before hitting the streets and he asked me if I'd changed my mind and 'agreed' with the prostitutes.

"Of course not! I just think it's sad when you think about the families. Mothers and fathers who'll never see their daughters again. Kids who won't get to know their mothers. I just feel sorry for them."

"They're better off without them," he told her flatly.

Nancy took a chance. "Do you really think that?"

He stared at her intently as they pulled up in her driveway and then said, "No! Of course not. Nobody deserves to die. Right?"

But he kept returning to one subject, as Nancy edged toward the passenger door. "Wanna hear something funny?" he asked.

"Sure."

"I've been picked up by the F.B.I. and questioned for *eight* hours about the Green River Killer."

"I was shocked and said, '*What?*' But he seemed to be kind of proud about that, and just laughed and said, 'Yeah. Can you believe that?' "

He explained that the police had found one of the missing girls' phone number in his phone book, but he only happened to have it because he was a friend of her sister's. He was quite calm at this point, and acted as if it was funny that he'd been a suspect.

He said he'd called his mother to come and pick him up at the sheriff's office. "At the time, I didn't connect the dots," Nancy said. "He was always nice to me, always well mannered, opened doors for me, and never took a step out of line. When I first saw his picture on the news [years later], I couldn't believe it."

Long after she sold her house and moved to Hawaii, she would be grateful that she'd given him the right answers on the last night he drove her home.

PART TWO

36

AFTER HE MOVED out of Darla's West Seattle home in December 1981, he apparently had only a few lonely weeks. It was Christmas Eve when he appeared at a Parents Without Partners party at the White Shutters Inn on Pac HiWay and joined a woman named Sally Cavetto.* He seemed somewhat emotional and upset, a rarity for him. Sally would recall that he muttered several times that he had "just nearly killed a woman." She assumed at the time that he meant he had almost hit a pedestrian.

Sally wasn't concerned about it because nothing really bad had happened. She dated him until May or June of 1982, until another woman in PWP told her that she had caught herpes from him, and suspected that he was frequenting prostitutes. Sally broke up with him.

Hardly deterred, he continued to select dates from the endless source of single women in PWP. He became engaged to another woman and they actually set a wedding date—for June 1984. But once again he was dumped. Many of his girlfriends soon realized that he was seeing several women during the same time period. Moreover, he was apparently picking up prostitutes.

His stamina for sexual encounters was well known. All of his girlfriends knew he wanted sex several times a day, and he preferred to do it outdoors in an exhibitionistic way. Indeed, the fact that he demanded intercourse so often had led each woman to believe he *was* being faithful, at least at first. And then they realized he had a seemingly infinite capacity to perform sexually. But emotionally, he seemed shallow, unwilling or unable to show any real affection.

And then he met a woman named Judith in early 1985. They shared a common history of failed relationships. After nineteen years, her first marriage had turned out to be a shocking disappointment. She had finally accepted that her first husband, whom she divorced in 1984, was bisexual and leaning heavily toward being totally gay. She couldn't live with his suggestions that he bring men home to share their marital bed. She was forty, and wasn't that sure of her attractiveness to begin with. Having a husband who preferred men damaged her ego even more. Her family seemed to be disintegrating around her. She wasn't sure what her older daughter was doing for money, and she was afraid to ask. She didn't want to know the answer.

Judith was living in an apartment close to the Pac HiWay with a woman friend and her younger daughter, who was eighteen. All she had ever wanted to be was someone's wife, a good mother, and keep a nice house. She hoped to remarry one day and she joined a group called Seattle Singles, but she didn't meet anyone there who seemed to be a likely prospect. There were always more single women than single men. Besides, the men gravitated toward the younger, slimmer women in the group.

Judith's roommate convinced her to attend one of the PWP country-western nights at the White Shutters, and she finally agreed to go even though she was shy and figured nobody would talk to her or ask her to dance. It was February 1985. She would always remember the date because she met a man that night who would change her life radically. It was his birthday and he told her the company he worked for had given him a couple of days off to celebrate it.

She was impressed by his job stability when he said he'd worked at the same place since he got out of high school—fifteen years. He mentioned that he was single, owned his own home, and even though he was driving an older brownish pickup truck with some rust spots on it, it was clean and had a camper on the back. He seemed pleasant enough, and he was definitely interested in her. They both liked country-western music, and when she left the White Shutters that night, she felt happier than she had in a long time.

He was four or five years younger than she was, but that didn't seem to bother him. Judith had met his ex-wife, Dana, even before she met him and there appeared to be no bad feelings between them. That was a good sign, she thought. He persuaded her to join Parents Without Partners, and Judith was soon enjoying an active social life.

She had never worked and her skills were as "a homemaker." When she met him, she was taking care of a woman and her two children, and also cleaning houses to make ends meet. She hadn't planned on facing life alone at forty, and it wasn't easy for her financially. She missed having her own house to take care of. Maybe her older daughter wouldn't be running wild if she had a place to come home to.

This man's kindness and his masculinity impressed Judith. She found him attractive, although she didn't consider looks the most important attribute in a man. He was quiet, but he was fun, too. At first, she only saw him once a week at the PWP meetings, but then he started calling and asking her to go out with him. He was working the swing shift in the spring of 1985, so their dates were mostly for dinner in the late afternoon.

"We used to go down to McDonald's on the highway," Judith would recall later to Detectives Sue Peters and Matt Haney. "I'd be coming home [from work] and he'd be going to work. We'd sit and hold hands, have a hamburger. Then I'd either go home to my apartment or to his house. That was after. I didn't go to his house till after a couple of months. Not right away."

Judith wasn't the kind of woman to jump into bed with a man until she really got to know him, so she didn't spend the night at his house for the first two or three months they dated. Beyond that, she was still hurt and unsure of herself from the times her ex-husband brought men home.

"He treated me just so gentle and perfect. I'm remembering now one time when we were out camping on one of the mountains or in the parks or trees or someplace. Greenwater, I guess that's what it was, out where you can just see the stars and everything. We were sitting in the back of the truck and talking and, you know, I let him know that I wasn't used to a man wanting me. And, you know, personal things. And he was gentle. He didn't rush or push. He wasn't forward or anything. Any sexual relations we had [were], you know, slow and comfortable."

Greenwater was a beautiful forested area, up Highway 410 east of Enumclaw, along the White River.

As time went by, Judith began to trust him and was relieved that his attention was focused only on her, and that he certainly wasn't the least bit gay. He didn't drink more than a beer or two, and she never saw him drunk. Once in a while, he would buy wine— Franzia, the kind that came in a box with a little spigot on the side.

They had similar interests—country-western music, of course— and they often went to garage and rummage sales. They both liked to go to the weekend swap meets at the Midway Drive-In Theater at Pac HiWay and S. 240th Street. She knew he liked the outdoors and going camping, and Judith looked forward to that.

Chad, his little boy, had his own room in his father's house for when he stayed there on his weekend visitations. Unlike Darla,

Judith didn't shy away from the possibility that if she was with him, his son would be a big part of his life, even though his ex-wife had primary custody. He, on the other hand, didn't object to her fondness for cats. His mother had always had cats. Judith felt as though the two of them just seemed to fit together.

He was "the best man" she'd known for a long time. "Nice, sweet, gentle," Judith said. He took her to meet his parents, and they were nice to her and so were his brothers. "They were the 'best' family."

He didn't have any particular hobbies or any interest in sports, although he occasionally went fishing and there was always camping out. But he did that with her. He had neither close male nor female friends. *She* was his best friend, and that made her feel very secure. They did everything together. The only other people he talked about were people he knew at work. He was very proud of his job.

One thing he did not tell her about were the unexpected encounters he had had with King County sheriff's detectives a few years before they met. That was another part of his life that had nothing to do with her, and he meant to keep it that way. Most of them happened before he even knew her, so it wasn't really as though he was lying to her.

Judith had no idea that her lover had been stopped on the highway two or three times. Port of Seattle police officers had talked to him on August 29, 1982. Parked on a dead-end road, he had been only a hundred feet from sites where bodies were found a long time later, and he hadn't been alone. Randy Mullinax had talked to him on February 23, 1983, and Jim Doyon had questioned him in April 1984 in front of the Kentucky Fried Chicken on Pac HiWay, when he appeared to be soliciting favors from a prostitute. He felt comfortable because he had been so agreeable with both detectives, and candid. Yes, he'd admitted, he did sometimes hire prostitutes, and he said he knew Kim Nelson aka Tina Tomson. But a lot of guys paid hookers on the Strip for sex.

The cops had all let him go, so he was serene in his belief that they didn't suspect anything. He knew there wasn't enough evidence to hold him. He'd been single then, a guy with a good steady job. What he did was his own business. Judith wouldn't understand, so why even bother telling her now?

But then Ralf McAllister from the Green River Task Force had gone out and picked him up again in February 1985, the same month he and Judith met. That was after Penny Bristow got brave enough to file a complaint against him three years after the fact. That was a little dicier, but he'd explained it all away when Matt Haney questioned him about the 1982 attack on Penny. He readily admitted that he had tried to choke her, but it had only been a reflex action when she bit him during oral sex. Most men would have reacted the same way. It hurt like hell, but he had quickly come to his senses.

And the girl named Penny didn't want to charge him formally. Without a complaining witness, they had no choice but to let him go. Actually, he was right in assuming they didn't have anything concrete on him. But he didn't know the third incident had elevated him to the level of an "A" candidate.

"He was certainly one of the primary people we had," Frank Adamson said. "We followed him, and surveilled him, watching him stop and talk to prostitutes. We watched him staring at them. We talked to them, and we found no one he was hurting at that time. But he was certainly interested. Later, we were able to connect him to a number of prostitutes by talking to their girlfriends. We knew he had quite an involvement with prostitutes, but we didn't think he was killing them."

In the 1985 incident, Judith's new boyfriend had even agreed to take a lie detector test and Norm Matzke gave him a polygraph. Matzke, who had long been the sheriff's department's polygrapher, following in the footsteps of his father, didn't think this man was responsible for the Green River deaths. His pulse stayed even, he didn't sweat a drop, and his blood pressure didn't waver.

He himself was pretty sure he could always fool their fancy polygraph, but he decided that the next time they talked to him, he would refuse to take a lie detector test. There was no sense being foolhardy.

SOMETIME in either May or June of 1985, Judith agreed to move in with him. He was still living in the small house that backed up to the bank above the I-5 Freeway. Built on a good-size lot with room for their camping rig, it was a nice little house. Judith was thrilled to be living in her own home again. She was with a man who had perfect attendance at his job and who always came straight home to her. If he had to work overtime, he called her, and she appreciated that. He would go almost three decades without being late for work more than a handful of times, and that was only a matter of two or three minutes.

He was so considerate that he didn't even ask Judith to get up and cook breakfast for him when he worked the early shift. He told her he'd stop at Denny's or some other twenty-four-hour restaurant on his way to work. He handed his paychecks over to her and she would take care of the bills, but she always made sure he had enough money with him when he left for work to buy breakfast and lunch and fill up his gas tank.

When Judith's younger daughter and her boyfriend and their babies needed someplace to live until they got back on their feet, he agreed that they could stay with him and Judith. She realized that not many men would have done that. He was someone she could count on even though he didn't seem anxious to get married again. She figured that would happen some day.

In the meantime, theirs was a very comfortable relationship. They went camping, watched television together, and indulged a mutual passion: collecting, restoring, and selling things that other people had either thrown away or sold cheap. "We're pack rats," Judith said. "We like to save stuff. We don't like to see stuff go in the landfill. We'd always go to the swap meet. We'd have yard sales. Oh, it was great because my ex-husband never let me have yard sales. We have so much fun doing that together."

Both of them were amazed at some of the things other people threw away at the landfill, and by the "free piles" left behind at the Midway Swap Meet at the end of a weekend. "Chad and him would look at the free piles," Judith said fondly, "and maybe find something that needs to be fixed. We'd take things home and fix 'em, and so . . . like a bicycle. We got all kinds of bikes. He'd fix a bike after getting it for free, and sell it to a little kid who'd be happy for getting a bike for five or ten dollars. And a toy. He'd pick up a toy and maybe the grandkids would like to play with it."

They found that they could make more profit by having frequent garage and yard sales at their house than they could by renting a space at the swap meet. Their neighbors grew used to seeing the "Yard Sale" sign out when the weather was good.

Pat Lindsay, who worked for the U.S. Postal Service, had sold him his house in 1981 and still lived close by. Although something about him always gave Pat a weird feeling, she liked Judith and often chatted with her as she presided over a yard sale. "They always had sales going, and baby kittens. Judith loved her cats and kittens," Pat recalled. "I think the funny thing about him was that he didn't seem to remember me at all. I'd sold him his house, but he didn't recognize my face or connect me to that when I stopped by during a yard sale. I could have been a complete stranger as far as he was concerned."

Once, before Judith moved in, Pat recalled that he had approached a couple of men in the neighborhood and asked them for help ripping out a carpet in one of his bedrooms. "He said he'd kicked over a can of red paint or spilled it somehow, and he needed to get it out of there and replace it. They helped him get it into his truck, but he never explained how he could have spilled so much paint."

Once he had the carpet in his pickup, he wouldn't have trouble getting it out at the county's Midway landfill off Orilla Road. The men noted that he had a kind of hoist with cables and a "come-along hitch" bolted to his truck.

Despite all the things they found "Dumpster diving" or scanning other people's sales for free "stuff," he never bought Judith any presents. She didn't mind. She had her rings from her first marriage melted down and redesigned. As far as any jewelry purchases, that wasn't something he would buy to surprise her.

"We did all of that together," she said, explaining that he never brought gifts home for her. He just wasn't like that. "We went shopping together."

There were so many things she did with him for the first time in her life. She went on her first plane trip when he took her to Reno. She loved the camping, either at Leisure Time Resorts campgrounds, where they split a membership with his parents, or roughing it. "At the very beginning of our relationship," she recalled, "we went camping up on the Okanogan 'cause he had a week off. That was just so [much] fun and delightful. He was so nice and gentle—I hadn't known him for very long."

They came back from the largest county in Washington and the Pasayten Wilderness that led into Canada via the North Cascades Highway, and she was thrilled by the grandeur of the view and the Ross Dam, with its clear blue water. "I never got to go camping before," Judith explained.

They visited several Leisure Time locations, mostly the site up past Ken's Truck Stop off I-90, but also those at Ocean Shores on Washington's Pacific Coast; Crescent Bar in Concrete, Washington;

and Grandy Creek. At Leisure Time, they could pull their camper in and have electricity and water hookups, and cooking grills.

They finally got married in their neighbors' front yard on June 12, 1988. Judith was the one who gave him an ultimatum about making a permanent commitment. "I told him after three years, he's not getting rid of me. 'We're getting married!' He said okay."

The Bob Havens hosted the event, and most of the people who lived along their street attended. Everyone liked Judith. She was a sweet woman, and he was a good enough neighbor.

They soon bought a bigger house down in Des Moines, and Judith went to work to help pay the mortgage. She sewed on a commercial machine for a SCUBA equipment company there, and later worked at the Kindercare day care, both Des Moines businesses. He kept his job as a painter. He took great pride in his work, but he was always careful about cleaning up before he came home. He didn't have a spot of paint on him when he left the plant and he even combed his mustache to be sure all the paint flecks were gone.

They were definitely moving up in the world. Judith was happy in her marriage, and she enjoyed being with her husband's parents and brothers. She worried a lot about her daughters, especially her oldest, who had gone off to the East Coast, but she knew she could count on her husband.

37

THE FIRST HALF OF 1985 continued to be a fallow period in Seattle as far as new disappearances in the Green River case were concerned and that was one positive sign. The headlines slowed to a crawl, and they were mostly rehashes of earlier stories now. Almost everyone believed that the dread killer had moved on, and some people hoped he was dead. The task force investigators didn't, however. If he was dead, so many questions would go unanswered forever. There was a good chance, however, that he had changed his base of operations—to at least one neighboring state, Oregon.

It looked as if the Green River Killer had thrown the task force a curve. At twelve seventeen PM, on June 13, 1985, a worker was operating a bulldozer on Bull Mountain Road near the Tigard/Tualatin area in Oregon, clearing the land so that a tree farm could be planted there. Tigard is about eight miles south of Portland, a quick exit off the I-5 Freeway. As the dozer operator looked idly at the dirt he had just turned over, he drew in his breath sharply, seeing what could only be human bones. He had uncovered skeletal remains.

Washington County sheriff's deputies responded to the scene and found a skull, what appeared to be two pelvises, and some rib bones. The skull had an obvious defect, a hole left either by a bullet or a surgical procedure. The Multnomah County Medical Examiner's Office said that the hole was from surgery performed many years earlier.

The remains of one of the bodies belonged to a black female who would have been five feet one to five feet four inches tall and had been in her early twenties. Forensic anthropologists estimated that the bones had been buried there for at least a year. A day later, she was identified as Denise Darcel Bush by the Portland-based M.E., in cooperation with the Oregon Health Services Dental School, Division of Forensic Science, and Dr. Don Reay's M.E.'s office in Seattle. Only her upper jaw was available, however. Although her upper teeth were enough to make the identification, it seemed odd that none of the searchers could locate her lower mandible.

There was only the calvarium (the upper rounded part) of her skull. But this was the skull of the only victim who had once had brain surgery. Denise Darcel had been missing since October 1982, almost three years earlier. Where had she been for two years?

(Bizarrely, her lower mandible had been left near Seattle, although that would not be discovered for five more years. In 1990, her lower jaw and the shunt that had carried excess fluid from her brain were found near Tukwila, not far from the Strip. Why had her killer separated her skull into two parts and placed them two hundred miles apart? To confuse the detectives who hunted him?)

The killer was playing macabre games with the task force. There could be no doubt of that. More bones were located a week later. Four detectives from the Green River Task Force drove to the Tigard field as the search for remains continued: Frank Adamson, Dave Reichert, Frank Atchley, and Ed Streidinger.

Adamson agreed to meet a Washington County, Oregon, deputy at the site of the body discoveries. "He hadn't been out to the site, and he wasn't sure where the location was, but he had the number of the closest telephone pole," Adamson recalled. "But I knew. The area was new to me, but so similar to the sites in Washington. I saw the turnout spot on the road. It looked familiar. It was the Green

River Killer's favorite kind of spot. And then I saw the number on the pole. I knew this had to be where the remains had been found. I pulled over and waited for the local deputy."

It would take a week for absolute identification to be made of the second body, which had apparently lain undiscovered for two or three years. They had found a complete skull, one rib, a part of a pelvis, an arm, a tooth, and a partial section of vertebrae. When the name was announced, it was shocking. This was Shirley Marie Sherrill, who had not disappeared from Portland at all, but from Seattle. Her killer had driven her—alive or, most probably, dead— all this way to bury her.

Even more puzzling was the discovery two days later of more remains. As the soil in the Tigard/Tualatin fields was turned over, then raked, sifted, and searched, they found two more skeletons. They had located yet another "dump site." These last two girls could not be identified.

When night fell, a neon sign nearby blinked on and off: Jiggles. It was a club for men, a club not unlike Sugar's in Seattle. Its significance wasn't obvious in June of 1985.

The official toll of Green River victims was twenty-six. Eighteen of them were identified; the rest only "Bones." On June 28, 1985, the F.B.I. officially came aboard the investigation. Victims had been taken across the state line between Washington and Oregon. No one knew if they were dead or alive when that happened.

The summer of 1985 was quiet, as if everyone in Seattle and Portland who cared about the Green River Killer's victims—and, admittedly, some did not—was holding his or her breath, waiting.

And then something happened near Portland that made investigators wonder, even more than the Tigard/Tualatin body discoveries, if the man they tracked had moved his center of operations to Oregon. It would make sense. Things had probably gotten too hot for him in Seattle. A couple of the johns they had stopped on the Strip were repeat offenders, even though the task force hadn't been able to gather enough evidence against them to make an arrest that would stick. Maybe he was really gone.

On September 4, 1985, two young women boarded a Greyhound bus for Portland. The two, Moira Bell* and Kitty Cain,* had met at a drug rehab program in Seattle, and when they got out, they decided to head south. They were very young, fifteen and sixteen, but far too familiar with the seamy side of life even though their pretty faces were dewy and almost childlike.

They had barely arrived in Portland before local officers picked them up and radioed in a Wants and Warrants request. Kitty Cain was kept in jail, but Moira Bell's name brought forth no outstanding warrants and she was driven back to the bus station. She was tired and broke and she made several collect phone calls to Seattle to men she knew there. With no help forthcoming, she struck up a conversation with a man she knew only as "B.B." They both indulged in cocaine, enough for Moira to go out on the street for three hours to make motel money. With enough to pay for a room, Moira slept all night and most of the next day.

On September 5, she was working Union Street at about ten PM with another girl she knew. It wasn't a good night. About midnight, one john pulled a knife on her, but she managed to get away. At three in the morning, she got into an argument with B.B. She didn't have enough for a room, so she was still out on Union an hour later.

A blue taxi, a station wagon with a company logo on the door and a light on top, pulled up to the curb near Moira, and the driver said, "Do you want a date?"

She asked what he wanted and they agreed on oral sex for $20. She studied the cab's interior as they drove: a navy blue dash, navy vinyl bench seats with headrests, automatic transmission, an old-fashioned meter with a white flag, and a package of Benson & Hedges on the dash. She wasn't afraid. It was just her habit to memorize her surroundings. What she was doing to survive was dumb and dangerous, but Moira herself was very smart.

The cab headed south, and then the driver parked under a bridge. He handed Moira a twenty-dollar bill and she slipped it into her right boot. She didn't use birth control pills, but she always carried condoms with her. As she bent over to put one on her client's erect penis, he suddenly grabbed her hair in his right hand and produced a knife with his left.

"Do as I say or I'll kill you." He breathed.

She took him seriously, letting him tape her wrists together behind her back with masking tape. Then he taped her arms to her body at her elbows. She was helpless. The driver forced her to the floorboard where she had to kneel. He headed toward the freeway going north, and then west.

"Excuse me," she asked, "but what are you going to do with me?"

"Whatever I want. Do as I say and I won't kill you."

As they drove through the darkness just before dawn, the cabdriver alternately threatened her with the knife and checked her bonds to be sure they hadn't loosened. Finally, she heard the sound of gravel as the station wagon pulled off the road and parked. The driver leaned over and felt in her boots—he wanted his money back.

"It's in my right boot," she whispered.

"Shut up! I didn't tell you to talk."

Next, he walked around to the passenger door and pulled her roughly out into the chilly air. He grabbed the front of her sweater dress, pulling it down to her waist. His efforts to get her dress off detached the tape where her elbows had been pinned to her body. But her wrists were still tightly bound together and she couldn't fight him as he tore her panties, panty hose, and bra away, leaving her naked, except for the sweater dress at her waist.

And then he forced her onto the hood of his vehicle and raped her violently. As he pulled her off the hood, he punched her twice in the face, making her dizzy and she started to fall. That angered him and he socked her twice more, this time in her spine.

She was bleeding now, and the rapist was furious that he'd gotten her blood on his hand. He climbed into his cab, grabbed a rag, and wiped it off. She lay very still on the ground, hoping he would just drive away and leave her there, wherever she was. But he sat quietly in the driver's seat for what seemed to her "a very long time." She hoped against hope that he wouldn't come back.

But he did. When he headed toward her, she could see that he'd changed his clothes; he now wore a blue nylon jumpsuit with an angled pocket that was zipped closed. Methodically, he tore the tape off her wrists, and finished ripping her dress off. He grunted as he used her panty hose to strangle her, but they tore in two. He reached into his back pocket for a blue bandanna. Once again, he placed a ligature around her neck and tightened it, but even though the bandanna was stronger, it broke, too.

"I pretended I was dead," Moira later told a female F.B.I. agent. "He went back and sat in the driver's seat again. After a while, he came back and checked my pulse and my neck. He said, 'Sorry, but I'm going to have to kill you. You might tell.' "

She lay as still as death, offering no resistance at all as he grabbed her ankles and dragged her backward over rocks and sharp weeds for about seventy-five feet to the edge of a steep embankment. "It was about thirty-five feet down, but he pushed me over. I stayed limp and kept playing dead. I rolled only about halfway down because something, maybe a tree or something, caught me."

The rapist waited at the top of the bank, smoking a cigarette and watching her. Then he clambered down to where she lay still, "dead." Once more, he checked her pulse under her arm and in her neck. He must have felt her heart because he pushed her again until she landed at the bottom of the embankment in a fetal position, still not moving. She saw that he was smoking another cigarette, deciding. And he came back again.

"He stabbed me in the chest—straight in. I took both my hands and pulled the knife out, but then I went completely limp. This time when he checked for a pulse, I held my breath and I guess he didn't feel anything."

He climbed the hill to smoke. And then, for the last time, he crawled down to where she lay, sending rocks and dirt ahead of him. She was getting good at not breathing, and she wondered if she was dying. He evidently felt no sign of life, and he pulled a big oil drum in front of her body as if he was trying to hide her from the road above. Then he changed his mind and moved it away, but he pulled up handfuls of tall grass and threw them on top of her.

She never heard his car engine start or the crunch of gravel. She figured he was up there, waiting to kill her. As the sky turned to pink and then blue, she heard three train whistles, the last one heading west. She realized now that she was in the Columbia Gorge, somewhere near Horsetail Falls.

When it was full daylight, Moira painfully inched her way up to the road. There was a car in the turnout, but she thanked God that it wasn't the blue taxi. She staggered toward it and gasped, "I've been stabbed and raped and the taxi driver did it!"

After several days recovering in a Portland hospital, Moira Bell worked with police artists and the F.B.I. to create a sketch of the man who had been so determined to kill her. The sketch that resulted looked very much like one of the Green River composite drawings done in King County.

The problem was that the four most widely circulated drawings were nothing like one another. One showed a phantomlike face with a long chin and "hippie-length" hair, another had a broad face with very curly short hair, one had short hair combed forward around his face and acne, and the last had a disproportionately long neck and hooded eyes that squinted.

Moira estimated that her rapist was probably between twenty-five and thirty, five feet nine to six feet tall, thinly built, with sandy shoulder-length hair, blue eyes, and a ruddy or acne-scarred complexion. He had had a thin mustache.

Were any of the drawings really like the GRK?

Maybe he was a master of disguise, or at least using wigs to change the way he looked.

Moira's ordeal struck a chord in my memory. One of the many women who had called me, her voice trembling even though it had been decades since her own encounter with a man she would never forget, had told me a very similar story, only it had happened ten years before Moira hid at the bottom of a ravine, six years before the Green River cases surfaced in Seattle.

"I was only nineteen," Cheryl told me, "and it was 1975. I felt I had no other way to make a living after my divorce. I was working in downtown Seattle for a place called Artists and Models. I was 'outlawing'—that means working without a pimp. I didn't know the city very well then, but I was living near 23rd and Cherry Street. I was probably working on Pike Street.

"This man, who seemed about my age, called me over to his car and he asked, 'Can I pay you for sex?' I said, 'Yes.'

"Before I got into his car, I checked the door handle to be sure it flipped up from the inside—I always did that. It seemed okay, so I got in. We drove for about twenty minutes, and he was strange. He didn't say a word to me, and he didn't even turn on the radio. My radar was working at about 150 percent, but there was nothing to pick up on. I thought to myself how 'spiritless' he was, and I knew I'd made a terrible mistake.

"We were on a two-lane road, not on the freeway, and we were in the country before I knew it. I don't know if we were north or south of Seattle. I'm still not sure. He turned off onto a sort of path, not really a road, but it looked as though a few cars had driven down there. The minute he stopped, I was out of the car and running, and I leapt over this embankment. It was steep, but I slowed myself a little by grabbing onto grass and weeds. There was nothing below my feet, so I know I didn't fall all the way to the bottom— I was probably only about ten feet down.

"I could see him up there, trying to spot me. He was backlit by the moon. His foot was on the car fender, and he was smoking a cigarette—not nervously, just standing there, smoking, trying to spot me."

She was still terribly afraid of him, but she was also frightened of slipping farther down the bank and dropping she didn't know how far. She could see part of his car and him.

"After a long time, he said, 'Come on up here. I won't hurt you.'

"I was so scared, but I climbed back up and I got in his car. He didn't ask for sex again. He didn't talk at all on the way back either, but he drove me to a corner close to where my apartment was, and he let me go."

Twenty-five years later, she would see the photograph of a much older man, and recognize him immediately. He had the same build, medium to thin, just an average-size man, and the eyes were the same, the lids so heavy that his eyelashes didn't show. When a photograph showed him in profile, her heart really convulsed. This was the view she'd had of him as they drove silently through the night.

One question keeps running through Cheryl's mind: "Why didn't he kill me?"

She had survived, and she began to straighten out her life the way many people who believe absolutely that they have had a near-death experience often do. She returned to Portland, where she had lived most of her life, finished college, and found a profession in which she worked for twenty years. Even so, the memory of the man outlined against the moon never really went away.

Cheryl's recollections of her terror would be reflected many times over the years ahead as women called or wrote me. I became absolutely convinced that there were probably twenty to forty women who had come close to death at the hands of the Green River Killer, but their will to survive or perhaps pure luck had saved them.

One more girl who didn't get away was found four days after Moira Bell escaped her rapist. A teacher accompanying a class on a visit to Seattle's Seward Park on September 8 found something that had to be shielded from the students' gaze. This is a huge wooded park that extends like a thumb into Lake Washington a few miles east of the Rainier District. A human skull, long denuded of flesh, was hidden there. It was a much more urban site than most of the places where remains had been found. The search crews, long since expert at outdoor scenes moved over the park, and they discovered an entire skeleton in the shadows at the base of a fir tree. There were no clothes at all in the vicinity.

It was Mary Exzetta West, who had been pregnant at seventeen and scared about what she was going to do. She hadn't come home to her aunt's house on February 6, 1984, and had probably been in this lovely park for all of the eighteen months she had been missing.

38

THE GREEN RIVER TASK FORCE continued to be alternately hammered and ignored by the media. It received a million-dollar federal grant in November 1985, and everyone had expected an arrest would surely follow soon after. When it didn't, taxpayers and politicians began to grumble. The King County executive who had backed the task force, Randy Revelle, was out of office and it didn't look as though the new man, Tim Hill, would be nearly as supportive of a very expensive investigation that had yet to net any rewards.

The F.B.I. wrote a summary of the cases to isolate patterns that might have escaped detection. Amina Agisheff was still deemed to be the first victim, taken on July 7, 1982; Cindy Ann Smith, the final young woman abducted, was seen for the last time on March 21, 1984. There were twenty-six Caucasian victims known dead, ten African American, and one American Indian. Of those still missing, five were Caucasian, three African American, one Hispanic, and one Asian.

"All victims are believed to have suffered from either manual or ligature strangulation, the ligature being that of the killer or the clothing of the victim," the F.B.I. summary read. "One possible victim who survived her attack, Moira Bell, from Oregon, was stabbed with a knife in combination with being strangled."

The cluster the Green River Task Force was focusing on during the holiday season of 1985 was not new; the Mountain View Cemetery site appeared to have held almost as many victims as the Star Lake cluster. Another partial skull had been found on December 15, unidentified bones on December 30, and more on January 3 and January 4, 1986. Not only was the GRK still free, it appeared that there would be no end to the rising death toll. Dr. Don Reay and Bill Haglund believed two of the sets of remains belonged to a twenty- to thirty-year-old black female, who had been five feet one to five feet four, and a fourteen- to seventeen-year-old white female who'd been five feet four to five feet eight.

Only a fluke had led searchers back to the Auburn graveyard. A cemetery worker had discovered a battered Lincoln Continental in a woods below the actual grave sites. It proved to be a stolen car and it had been pushed into a ravine where it was almost invisible beneath a blanket of fallen leaves. In investigating the auto theft, the bones were found, too.

It would be poetic justice if the owner of the Lincoln turned out to be the killer. But he wasn't. The luxury car had been stolen from the street in front of a Tacoma tavern owned by the car's registered owner, and the Green River investigators found no evidence at all to connect him to the dead girls in the cemetery. The car thief himself was never found.

Some of the smartest detectives in the Northwest had worked on this thankless case for three and a half years. Almost $8 million had been spent, and still there was nothing to show for it. Now, the task force swelled even further. Ten additional F.B.I. agents were assigned to the Green River cases. This could mean that something big was about to happen, or it could mean that the task force was about to make one last massive effort to bring their quarry in.

Frank Adamson, who wasn't given to making statements that might come back to bite him, seemed almost optimistic that 1986 was going to be the year when the Green River Killer would be brought to ground.

I myself believed that the "fox"—actually "the wolf"—would be penned up and punished. Because of the increased manpower on the task force, I was a lot more likely to wax positive, and I can remember telling a large audience at a seminar in the early months of 1986, "I'm sure he'll be caught before Thanksgiving—maybe even by Easter." And just as I had to do several times before, I would have to eat my words.

I wasn't that sure, and I had no inside information, but the law of averages convinced me that no one could escape the eye of this hurricane of top cops. Moreover, forensic science seemed to have "gone about as far as it could go"—in my mind, at least. The $200,000 computer was humming along, and criminalists were routinely matching hair and fiber profiles and solving other cases. Forensic anthropologists could establish race and sex from bare skulls, and odontologists could match bite marks to attackers and teeth to dental charts. Blood enzymes could already be isolated to show racial probability.

Even though it had been less than a year since DNA blood comparisons had solved the first homicide case in the world, DNA testing for all police jurisdictions was on the horizon. The Green River Task Force had a contingency fund of around $5,000 for DNA testing if it seemed feasible.

Ed Hanson, a task force member on loan from the Washington State Patrol, had an idea that made the job of triangulating measurements at a body site much easier. Given the steep hills and deep ravines and the hundreds of yards the detectives had to traverse over and over in order to mark a body location, Hanson thought it would be far more cost-effective and productive to employ professional surveyors to do that part of the job. And, of course, he was right.

It had to be only a matter of months now.

Having fully recovered from the meningitis that had almost killed him a few years earlier, John Douglas updated his profile of the Green River Killer and was one of the F.B.I. agents on hand in Seattle in January and February 1986. At this point, Douglas claimed a 77 percent success rate in the 192 criminal cases he had personally evaluated "after all leads had been exhausted."

His second look at the Green River Killer was very close to the first profile he had drawn up. Douglas was quite sure that the GRK was in good physical shape, an outdoorsman, although probably both a drinker and a smoker. "He is not very neat," Douglas said. He would be a nocturnal cruiser who drove conservative vehicles. Souvenirs and trophies would be important to him, along with newspaper clippings about his crimes. With those things, he could relive the emotional thrills of his murders.

How old was he? Douglas said "mid-20s to early 30s. There is no burnout for this type of murderer though." He added, "These homicides reflect rage and anger. . . . He will not stop killing until he is caught."

Every detective on the task force still had a favorite suspect—or two or three. Frank Adamson continued to watch three men who seemed to him to be the most likely candidates for being the Green River Killer. Whenever Adamson had "command duty," he made it a point to drive by the houses where these men lived. All three lived close by the Green River or the Pac HiWay Strip. One was the wealthy and eccentric farmer who had held the young prostitute captive and collected photos of young women, albeit pictures the task force had never been able to find in his huge barn. Another was a man who was a familiar visitor to the Strip and had been stopped and questioned at least three times, and who had grown up near the highway. The third was a fur trapper, an outdoorsman, who also lived close to the highway.

Adamson never saw anything suspicious when he drove slowly by their homes, but he thought about them a lot. He wanted to be sure they were still around. "The Green River Killer was extremely active during 1982 and 1983," he commented. "Out of control, really, with two or three victims a month. And then he appeared to stop—at least around here. I wondered why."

In early 1986, Adamson had reread Douglas's profile as well as profiles done by John Kelly, a New Jersey counselor who was also known to be on-target with his evaluations of suspects. Adamson needed to know which of his three main suspects fit most neatly within the parameters of the profiles.

John Kelly quickly dismissed Ingmar Rasmussen, the older man with a barn allegedly full of women's photos. "I believe him to have been a lonely, elderly man who wanted a woman to live with him and take care of him," he wrote. "He [once] even advertised for such a woman. His house was important to him; he felt secure behind the heavy wooden door. I believe his house was much more important to him than the river or woods. . . . He was too conservative and concerned about his wealth and success and would not endanger that by being in the river or woods with corpses or transporting them long distances. If [he] was the [Green] River Killer, that girl would never have escaped from his house."

The second suspect profile was of the meek man the Pro-Active Team detectives had encountered several times on the highway as he talked to prostitutes. He had admitted, of course, that he tried to choke the girl who "bit him." But Kelly didn't think he was viable as a suspect either, despite Sergeant Frank Atchley's strong belief that he was, along with Adamson's more tentative suspicions.

"He had a full-time position . . . with which he was satisfied," Kelly wrote. "I believe that the [Green] River Killer could only have a job that consistently took him to or past [the] dump sites. The amount of energy and time involved in stalking and singling out, picking up and controlling, killing, transporting and staging these hookers could not have been done by someone who had to keep a scheduled full-time position.

"It also seems that he had an overbearing, perfectionistic mother. However, it seems that she showed him enough attention to prove that she cared about him and did not abandon him."

And this man had passed a lie detector test.

John Kelly's favorite pick of the trio of "A's" was the fur trapper. He based this on the man's early years when his mother allegedly cared more about alcohol than she did about him, alternately abandoning him to be raised by others and behaving in an inappropriate way by letting him sleep in her bed and be aware of her sexual relationships with a series of men.

The trapper, who was also a fisherman and hunter, was completely at home in the woods and water, and Kelly drew a comparison with the way he stuffed and mounted his animal prey and the way the body sites were staged. While Kelly had devoted a paragraph or two to the old man and the man with the steady job, he wrote quite convincingly for three single-spaced pages about the reasons he had selected the trapper as the prime candidate to be the Green River Killer.

Adamson had been led to the fur trapper by a ranking officer in the Bellingham, Washington, Police Department who thought he should be considered a likely suspect. His name was Barney Tikkenborg,* a middle-aged man and an avid trapper who was very familiar with the areas where the Green River victims had been found. Other trappers had commented that Tikkenborg was obsessed with killing dogs and took pleasure in using different methods to kill them: traps, rifles, garrotes, knives, and ice picks.

Task force records in the computer were checked, and Adamson had been surprised to find that two other people had called in their concerns about Tikkenborg. One informant had worked with him as a cement finisher, his other occupation. During the eight years the informant worked with him, Tikkenborg spent most of his time off in the woods, trapping animals for their fur. "He's extremely strong and athletic—he can run as fast backward as he can forward—but it's just that he loves to kill things," the informant said. "Once he bought this doctor's surgical kit with different scalpels. He told me he was going to try to cut the unborn babies out of the pregnant animals he'd caught."

Tikkenborg had also shown off his macabre library, which had books and magazines about human anatomy and various methods of killing people. Moreover, other workers kidded him about the prostitutes he picked up, and he seemed to view all women as merely objects. Ten years earlier, he had been furious because a local college student had allegedly given him a venereal disease.

Tikkenborg cruised in his truck at night and kept a red police bubble light in it. He also had displayed a pair of handcuffs and a police badge shaped like a star. He said he'd stolen it and a gun from a police car in Auburn. He often came to work after being out all night "trapping," and both he and his truck had "a foul odor."

The most bizarre thing Tikkenborg's co-worker recalled, however, was the time Tikkenborg showed up with a mannequin he said he'd found in the woods. He kept it in his truck after that, covered with a tarp, and often slashed at it with his scalpels.

In November 1985, task force investigators had interviewed a Washington State Wildlife Control Agent who worked for the Department of Game. He recalled Barney Tikkenborg very well.

His trapping activity peaked between 1976 and 1981, but after that it had dropped off. During his most active years, Tikkenborg had run as many as 125 registered traplines. Moreover, he'd been one of only four trappers who frequented the Green River area during that time.

The wildlife agent said that Tikkenborg's other trapping areas were around Enumclaw, North Bend, and the Seattle-Tacoma area. He was required by law to keep records on every animal he killed, and he was "a fanatical record keeper. His tally sheet for the 1979–1980 trapping season showed he'd killed 103 cats and seventy dogs."

In 1978, the trapper was arrested on Mercer Island where trapping was illegal. He had once put homemade decals on the doors of his green Ford pickup truck apparently to create the impression that he was a wildlife agent. That gave him the chance to trap out of season. When the real agent talked to the task force detectives, he said that he had advised Tikkenborg that his animal skins were obtained out of season and would be seized by authorities, to which Tikkenborg had a surprising reaction: "He broke down and wept."

Ever since Barney Tikkenborg's name had leapt into the "A" category for the task force, detectives had located and interviewed people who had known of his activities, and a sickening image grew more and more detailed. His cruelty to animals and his preoccupation with sadism and death had been noted by many people.

In early January 1986, Frank Adamson read yet another report of an interview with an acquaintance of the trapper. It said he killed animals with an ice pick shoved into the spinal column at the base of the skull. This acquaintance also said that the trapper was obsessed with sex and was drawn to danger.

The Green River investigators learned that Tikkenborg had been a hyperactive child who ran around the neighborhood and had once come close to drowning. His mother, who had been divorced four times, chose an odd way to keep him indoors. She made him wear a dress. That had embarrassed him so much that he never went outside. According to a police officer who knew Tikkenborg, he had heard from one of the trapper's siblings that his mother had once tried to kill him when he was a child because she didn't want him.

Silently and carefully, task force officers and F.B.I. agents spread out to talk to a half dozen or more witnesses who knew Barney Tikkenborg. They would try to conduct concurrent interviews so the word that they were homing in on the trapper wouldn't reach him or the media.

Another fur trapper recalled that Tikkenborg had taken him into the woods to show him trapping methods. He had watched as Tikkenborg pulled his set lines. He agreed to go with detectives into the areas where Tikkenborg had placed his traps. He wasn't sure if he could find the exact spots again, but he said he would try. Tikkenborg had always used natural landmarks and milepost numbers along the roadways to locate his traps and he kept a loose-leaf notebook listing each trap's position.

For the entire day of January 23, 1986, detectives traversed roads that were all too familiar. They went first to the Enumclaw area, coming within several miles of where the bodies of Debbie Abernathy, Mary Bello, and Martina Authorlee had been found. Their potential witness also took them to the Green River, to within four hundred yards of the spot where Wendy Lee Coffield's body had been found floating. Next, they went to the Mountain View Cemetery, and to Star Lake Road where the informant said Tikkenborg had set his traps at both the bottom and the top of the ravine.

Finally, they went to areas near Jovita Road and Soos Creek, and the novice trapper pointed out the exact spot where Colleen Brockman, the girl with braces on her teeth, had been discovered. Yvonne Antosh's remains had been left directly across the road.

Tikkenborg matched both John Douglas's and John Kelly's profiles more closely than any other suspect. The circumstantial evidence was piling up, and for the first time in many months, Frank Adamson felt excited that the long hunt might be over. That excitement increased when one of the F.B.I. agents assigned to the case, who had come from a family familiar with trapping in his home state of Florida, explained about "drowning rocks."

He said it wasn't unusual for hunters or trappers to submerge their game in cold water to preserve it. To keep the carcasses below the surface of the water, logs and large rocks were placed on top of them. "Sometimes they place smaller rocks inside body cavities to be sure they don't get carried downstream," the agent said.

TIME was growing short. A reporter for a Seattle all-news radio station had been watching the Green River Task Force for months and had picked up the focus on Barney Tikkenborg. By following police units, he saw who *they* were following, and it was Tikkenborg, who was himself visiting the areas of some known body sites. When the reporter approached Adamson and asked why Tikkenborg was under such heavy surveillance, Adamson beseeched him not to break a story about the trapper. Yes, they were looking closely at him, but if it hit the media, the suspect would have an opportunity to get rid of evidence before the task force could obtain a search warrant.

The reporter said he would sit on the story, but only if Adamson let him have the first interview if they arrested Tikkenborg. Caught between a rock and a hard place and having, once more, to dodge the swarm of the hovering media, Adamson promised the reporter he would get the first word that an arrest had been made.

"I said *arrest*," Adamson recalled, "and he took it that I would alert him before we served a search warrant. I never promised him that—I couldn't. I wasn't even sure when we'd get a search warrant. He called me and told me he was going out of town and asked if that was a good idea. I couldn't tell him. As we got closer, the media was buzzing."

The newscaster, sensing that something was about to come down, decided to stay in Seattle, just in case.

On February 6, F.B.I. special agents Duke Dietrich and Paul Lindsay, and task force detectives Matt Haney and Kevin O'Keefe set out early in the day to talk to Barney Tikkenborg's mother and stepfather. Back at Green River headquarters, Frank Adamson was writing an affidavit to obtain search warrants for Tikkenborg's house, his mother's house, his two pickup trucks, and another truck located at his mother-in-law's house, which had been cut in two with an acetylene torch and then burned.

The specific items the task force searchers were looking for were women's clothing, shoes, jewelry and purses, notebooks and other documentation of Tikkenborg's trapping activities, weapons such as ice picks, knives, garrotes, scalpels and guns, newspaper clippings or photographs of the Green River victims, trace evidence like hair, fibers, blood or "particles," latent fingerprints of the dead and missing women, and implements and solutions that would commonly be used to clean up the evidence of the crime of homicide. Adamson also listed control samples of carpeting, fabrics, and paint chips from various surfaces, floors, furniture, drapes, and clothing—all to be compared to fibers and particles found with the victims' remains.

As it turned out, there was no need for a search warrant at the home of Tikkenborg's mother and stepfather. Mick and Ruthie Legassi* readily agreed to sign a Consent to Search form. They had no objection to detectives looking around their house. And they were quite willing to be interviewed. Paul Lindsay and Kevin O'Keefe interviewed Tikkenborg's mother, while Dietrich and Haney talked to his stepfather.

Mick was Ruthie's fourth husband, and he admitted that her son had resented his marrying Ruthie at first. Young Barney Tikkenborg had lived with his father until he was about fifteen. Subsequently, he lived with the Legassis and other relatives. He wasn't the kind of person to show his feelings, except when he was talking about hunting and fishing, so his stepfather never knew if moving from one relative to another had bothered him.

Early on, Barney had gotten in trouble for stealing things, and he'd had a brush or two with the law over thefts and burglaries that he had told Legassi he committed for "the thrill of it." He was tossed out of the service after he was convicted of theft from a footlocker in his barracks.

Initially, Barney Tikkenborg hadn't had much luck with women. His first marriage lasted only a year, and he was "shook up" when his bride left him for another man. He'd gone off to Alaska to hunt and fish for a year, but when he came back, he married again—a Canadian girl. She was the daughter of his father's current wife—not a half sister but a stepsister. When he got arrested for burglary again, she left him, too.

Tikkenborg made a third try at marriage. He had a daughter by that wife, and the three of them lived in the Seattle area where he worked as a cement finisher. But periodically, he would be arrested for burglary and have to serve time. His third wife left him while he was in prison.

Duke Dietrich worked hard to keep up with this very complicated family tree, convoluted because so many of them had had multiple marriages. In the late seventies, Tikkenborg's stepfather said that Barney had dated a checker at the Piggly Wiggly super-market located near the Jovita Canyon. She had grown up on a farm in Enumclaw, and while they did not marry, she did introduce Barney to his fourth, and current, wife. They had lived first inside the city limits of Kent, off 192nd Street. And they seemed to have had a good marriage. If Barney teased his wife by talking about other women, she came right back at him.

"They're pretty much equals," Legassi said. "She doesn't take any shit off him."

Tikkenborg's stepfather didn't recall that Barney had ever commented on prostitutes one way or the other. Yes, he'd mentioned the Green River murders once or twice, but only in passing. "One time he said that there was a screwball on the loose. We talked about it a little."

The closest Tikkenborg had ever come to showing his feelings about loose women was when he had put a sticker on his truck that read "Good Girls Go to Heaven; Bad Girls Go Everywhere." But that was only a joke.

Legassi said that Barney hadn't seen anything wrong with his trapping activities, and he'd made good money at it—running three hundred traps at one time. "He said that we'd be overrun with them critters if nobody trapped them." He recalled that Barney trapped muskrats, beavers, and bobcats in the deep woods, raccoons in the airport area, and coyotes near Enumclaw.

"How does he kill them?" Dietrich asked quietly.

"By sticking ice picks into the back of their brain or stepping on their chests," Legassi said. He added that Barney had once used a small pistol, but had stopped that because it made too much noise. Yes, he knew that sometimes his stepson had shot dogs in the woods so they wouldn't get into his traps and tear up his animals. But he'd always had pets at home, both dogs and cats. "He told me that shooting dogs in the woods is 'purely business.'"

Mick Legassi confirmed that Ruthie had once put a dress on her son because he'd disobeyed and gone down to a creek, and she was afraid he was going to drown. But it was only that one time. He couldn't remember that Barney had ever had mood swings or acted crazy.

All in all, Legassi thought his stepson was a good guy. "If he's the Green River Killer—and I don't think he is," he said firmly, "well, he would say so!"

■

FRANK ADAMSON got his search warrant, and later that Thursday evening, February 6, 1986, detectives and F.B.I. agents swarmed over the Tikkenborg house, which was located on a short private street a block from Pac HiWay. Neighbors watched in shock as a hooded figure, whom they assumed to be Barney, was taken away in a police car, and detectives and agents carried out items to be tested.

The hooded figure was not Barney Tikkenborg. He had been detained on his way home from a cement finishing job near Snoqualmie Pass when the car he was riding in was sandwiched between unmarked police units that suddenly flashed blue "bubble lights" on their dashboards. With guns drawn, several task force members and F.B.I. agents ordered him out of his boss's car.

His wife, Sara,* was being picked up at her job at the same time. Both were transported to F.B.I. headquarters in downtown Seattle.

Several of the Tikkenborgs' neighbors were coaxed to comment on-camera by television crews. Their words sounded like every neighbor's in every shocking murder, fire, natural disaster, or tragedy in any neighborhood in any city. "I can't believe it. They're such a nice couple. Such good neighbors . . . This just doesn't happen in a neighborhood like ours."

If ever a police operation was compromised by a determined army of reporters and photographers, this was it. Helicopters hovered overhead with floodlights illuminating the scene and reporters got in the way of the task force investigators. Over at task force headquarters, Fae Brooks did her best to placate the reporters who surrounded her. "We have made no arrests. We are talking to a person of interest."

The public's right to know, and to know immediately, was obviously tantamount in the media's minds and conflicted with the task force's urgent need to do what it had to do.

Given the information the Green River Task Force had gathered on Barney Tikkenborg, surely the probable cause for a search warrant had been met. But the Tikkenborg incident was to be a major public relations disaster. And there was no reason that had to happen. Without the glare of strobe lights and the intrusion of microphones, the search warrant could have been served quietly without undue attention on the family that lived there.

Tikkenborg was questioned for several hours by Jim Doyon of the task force and an F.B.I. agent. He denied having any knowledge whatsoever about the Green River murders, which wasn't surprising. Of course, they had expected that. No suspect was likely to say, "I did it! I killed them all!" the first time he was questioned. Tikkenborg was angry and his wife was angry. He volunteered to take a lie detector test.

And he passed. Absolutely passed. It was a major blow to the task force and to Frank Adamson personally. He had been so sure, and his expert advisers had concurred. They had believed they had the right man. And now it seemed that all their deductive reasoning had been wrong. They had no choice but to release Tikkenborg.

Criminalists continued to evaluate possible evidence taken from his home: all the bloodstained items, which they had expected to find, of course, all the hairs and fibers. But, in the end, Barney Tikkenborg was eliminated as a suspect in the Green River murders three months later.

By reading the next day's papers and tuning into television, it had certainly looked as if the long investigation was over. Headlines blazed; the entire front pages of both Seattle papers trumpeted the news, and smaller local papers echoed the story. Some printed Tikkenborg's name and address, while others did not. Some featured a picture of his house with the address clearly visible on a shingle outside.

Frank Adamson faced the wrath of the reporter who had agreed to hold back his scoop. Adamson met with him and explained the truth—he had promised only to give the man first chance for an interview *after* an arrest was made. As it was, it had been completely out of his hands anyway as the feeding frenzy of the press and airways proliferated.

"I met him in a restaurant in Fremont and he was mighty upset," Adamson said. "But as it turned out, we ended up arresting the suspect, took him to the F.B.I. office and he passed the polygraph. That became my downfall. We made the search, we got bad publicity, and it was an opportunity for the politicians to plan to get rid of me because it was a low point. We'd focused a lot of our energy and the press's energy on the wrong guy. I felt like I was standing on a board when someone was sawing through the other end."

Technically, Adamson would be on the task force from December 1983 to January of 1987, but he sensed which way the wind was blowing. He had begun with the belief that he and his detectives would surely solve the murders of the dead girls, but he was worn down, battered on every side. It was ironic. A public and press that had shouted that the task force must "*do* something" was now eager to condemn them because they *had* done something, and it proved to be wrong.

As the task force members had expected, Tim Hill, the new King County executive, held the opinion that it was always better to "spend less," and the Green River investigation was draining the county's coffers.

"There was publicity about the cases," Adamson said, "but also publicity about the expense of the task force. People complained. After the search on Tikkenborg's house, it got worse. I didn't feel that just because we couldn't prove that this particular person did it, it was the end. There were other suspects."

That was true, but being on the Green River Task Force was hard going now.

Both the media and the detectives were being judged harshly. More than two months after the search of Barney Tikkenborg's house and the abortive probe into his life, the *Los Angeles Times* printed a very long article on the front page of its Sunday edition, tsk-tsking about the "near hysteria" caused by Seattle's television coverage of the detainment of an innocent suspect, and taking swipes at both TV newscasters and the task force. However, the *Los Angeles Times* article also listed the real names of the fur trapper and his wife, perpetuating, it would seem, the attention focused on them.

Proving that Tikkenborg had been in no trouble at all with the law since 1967, the outraged couple sued three media outlets and eventually collected $30,000.

And, all the time, *he* must have been watching the news coverage gleefully. He knew who the real Green River Killer was, and he enjoyed the fact that his persona as an unknown killer was getting so much attention from the media. He especially liked to see the task force members end up with egg on their faces. They *had* talked to him, but he was convinced they didn't have a clue. He had completely snowed them, and they had gone off chasing somebody else.

39

Cottonwood Park is just north of the Meeker Street Bridge on Frager Road, a shabby little stretch of stubbly grass between the road and the river in the eighties, with a few picnic tables gray and splintery from too much moisture and not enough maintenance. It is close to Des Moines, but I never heard of anyone actually going there on a picnic, or to swim for that matter. Beyond that, everyone who lived in the area remembered that Wendy Lee Coffield, Debra Lynn Bonner, Cynthia Hinds, Opal Mills, and Marcia Chapman had been found less than half a mile away in the river. That made Cottonwood seem like a ghost park, and it hadn't been that appealing to begin with.

In March 1986, two Kent Park Department workers discovered what appeared to be human bones at the base of a large tree in the park. There were enough bones to know that it was a young female, but not enough to identify her with the forensic science available at the time. There was no skull, no mandibles, no teeth, just a human torso and spine. It would take thirteen more years to know that this was the only part of Tracy Winston ever found. Mitochondrial DNA, which compares the unknown subject with the DNA makeup of a possible mother, verified in 1999 that the young woman left in Cottonwood Park was the tall, dimpled daughter of Chuck and Mertie Winston, the girl who had vowed to change her life just hours before her death.

Mertie had known for years that her only daughter was gone, but the knowledge that she was absolutely, finally, dead was almost too painful to bear. It always would be. The long wait had probably contributed to Mertie's stroke at a young age, but she fought to re-cover—and she did. When she finally learned the truth, it seemed ironic that Tracy had been so close to home all along, even though her many moves had taken her far north of Seattle.

"I'm not going to second-guess why this happened to Tracy, and to us," Mertie said in 2004. "God had his purpose that we had her for such a short time: nineteen years, eleven months, and two weeks."

The spring of 1986 continued to reveal what the Green River Killer believed he had hidden forever. On May 2, 1986, an employee of Echo Glen, who was looking for a runaway teenager near a pullout off Highway 18 just south of the juncture of 18 and Highway 90, looked down and saw some weathered bones. It was Maureen Feeney, who had disappeared on September 28, 1983. Her family had reported her missing two years and eight months earlier. Maureen had been so thrilled to be living on her own near Bellevue. But she had been enticed into a dangerous life in Seattle. Ironically, her body had been left not far from her first apartment.

In June 1986, Kim Nelson's skull and a few bones were found not far away in a deeply forested area off I-90 at Exit 38. Kim, also known as Tina Tomson, had been only a couple of miles from where Delise Plager and Lisa Yates were found in early 1984. Now her relatives would know why she hadn't come home to Ann Arbor for Christmas. Kim's father had died a few months before she was finally identified, and one of her sisters suffered a nervous breakdown after dealing with too many tragedies. Until there is a formal identification of the remains of a murder victim, relatives cling to a tiny glow of hope amid overwhelming anxiety. Afterward, hope is gone, and there is another phase of grief to deal with.

OFFICIALLY, there were no longer any new disappearances in the Seattle area, and the public seemed to have grown bored with an investigation that apparently had no end and no answers. In November of 1986, I was still convinced that I would soon be writing a book about the Green River murders. Because I have saved every scribbled-up calendar since 1972, it's easy to look back and see what I was doing as long as thirty years ago. And a few words bring back images of events as if they had happened only last week.

That November I accepted an invitation from a King County deputy I had not met before to be taken on a tour of the body sites near North Bend. I figured it was an opportunity to learn the topography and the vegetation of the areas where the Green River Killer had left his tragic victims. I'd eaten many times at Ken's Truck Stop, and each of my children had spent a week in the spring at Camp Waskowitz, but I'd never been into the woods on roads so narrow that they looked like trails.

It was a bleak, sunless day and whatever light there was had disappeared well before four in the afternoon. I must admit that I began to feel nervous, spooked, as the deputy turned into one area that looked more like a moonscape than the forests of the foothills of Snoqualmie Pass. There, I had the sensation that I really didn't know this man at all, and in the back of my mind was the knowledge that many people believed that the Green River Killer was a cop. Wondering if I had been really stupid to drive around with a deputy I didn't know, I told him I didn't want to see any more body sites.

But that was the climate of the times. Every woman in King County was somewhat nervous and all men were suspect.

THERE WAS GOOD REASON to be wary. Hope Redding* was neither a teenage hitchhiker nor a woman who frequented the streets. Her lifestyle was totally different from the victims of the Green River Killer. She was a professional woman, married, and extremely cautious because she had once been the victim of a sexual assault. After that, she vowed that no man would ever do that again, even if she had to die fighting him. She followed every safety guide there was, and under almost any circumstance, she would never get into a stranger's car.

In 1986, Hope was driving home from work along a dark road in the Maple Valley area of King County. Her car sputtered and stopped and nothing she tried got it started again. A short time later, a pickup truck slowed and then pulled over to the side of the road. She watched the driver approach her car and she checked the locks on the doors. Good. All locked. He was saying something to her through the window on the driver's side and she rolled it down only an inch.

"Pop your hood," he shouted. "I'm pretty good at cars."

That might be safe enough. Cell phones weren't common in 1986 and she had no way to call for help. Her husband wouldn't know where to look for her. She either had to trust this man to take a look under the hood, hike miles in the dark to find a phone, or spend a cold night locked in her car. She popped the hood.

The helpful stranger wasn't a very big man; he probably wasn't any taller than she was, and he didn't look muscular. She could hear him tapping and banging on things as he tried to find what the problem was. Time passed and she realized he had spent twenty minutes or more trying to help her. Finally, he slammed the hood down and walked back to her window.

"I can't fix it," he said. "It needs parts I don't have, but I can give you a ride to where you can call someone to come and get you."

Hope felt guilty for having doubted him in the beginning. How many strangers would stand out in the cold rain for so long trying to help someone? She nodded, grabbed her purse, and followed him to his truck.

He didn't say much as they headed toward a crossroads where she knew there was a 7-Eleven, and he didn't even glance at her. He had been so nice that she decided she should give him something for the time he'd spent trying to help her. She opened her purse and began to fish around for her wallet. The driver glanced over at her in alarm.

"He freaked," she recalled. "I think he thought I was reaching for a gun. Since he seemed so nervous, I shut my purse."

Now she began to feel vaguely uneasy as they sped through the night. She figured it was probably because she'd just broken her own rule about getting into a stranger's car. She saw the 7-Eleven up ahead and prepared to hop out of his truck. But he didn't slow down at all, and soon the convenience store was behind them, and the road ahead was even darker and less familiar. She asked him where he was going and he only grunted.

"I started swearing at him," Hope recalled. "And I never swear at anyone. But I was yelling at him, telling him to stop and let me out. I drove my elbow into his ribs as hard as I could."

He glanced angrily at her and Hope realized that he had never intended to stop. He turned corners again and again until she was disoriented about where she was. The road they were on now dead-ended at a junkyard of some sort. "I hit him and fought him and we were struggling inside the cab of his truck," she said. "We fell out the door and I was fighting him on the ground. I was probably in the best condition I'd ever been in in my life—I went to aerobics three times a week—and I was not going to let him overpower me. He kept calling me 'Bitch' and I could tell he was terribly angry."

As they rolled and tumbled on the muddy ground, she saw him sweep his free hand along the ground, reaching for something, a rock maybe, to smash against her head. And he was angling to get his other arm around her throat so he could crush her windpipe.

"I did what I had to," Hope said. "I sunk my teeth as deep as I could into his arm, and he let go."

She ran into the darkness that surrounded them, and hid. She could hear him crashing around, looking for her and she held her breath. Finally, he gave up and drove away. She managed to follow lights and find a phone, but Hope Redding would have nightmares for a long time. And many years later, when she recognized a picture of the man who might have killed her, she called the Green River Task Force.

40

ALTHOUGH Frank Adamson was doing his best to sound optimistic about the Green River investigation, it wasn't easy. Nineteen eighty-six was almost over, and they seemed no closer to arresting the killer than they had ever been. The task force was being downsized, and Adamson had had to give the bad news to a number of detectives that they were being transferred. Twenty-five percent of the task force was gone.

The board beneath his own feet was becoming more and more unstable. He was frustrated, disappointed, sorry about the circus that the search of the fur trapper's home had become, sad because of all the young women who were still unavenged. And he knew his time was coming.

"Vern Thomas called me in and said, 'I don't want any argument. The decision is made, Frank. You can remain in charge, or you can be promoted to major.' "

Thomas, who wouldn't be sheriff much longer himself, offered Adamson the opportunity to command the new sheriff's precinct that would be in Maple Valley. The unspoken alternative for Adamson was that he would be off the task force anyway.

"I took the second option," Adamson recalled, "and Vern said 'You made the right choice.' "

It felt good to get off the hot stove. Frank Adamson would be the longest surviving commander of the Green River Task Force. He had begun in November 1983, and he officially left the task force in January 1987.

Captain Jim Pompey had been with the department since 1972 and was promoted to captain in 1983, making him the highest ranking African American in the sheriff's office. He had been in charge of the county's SWAT Team and its marine unit. Now he moved in to head the much-reduced Green River Task Force amid rumors that it was being absorbed into the Major Crimes Unit where it would quietly evaporate. He admitted that he was not up to speed on the Green River cases, while Frank Adamson, Dave Reichert, Jim Doyon, Randy Mullinax, Sue Peters, Matt Haney, and dozens of other detectives who had lived and breathed the Green River story for years were familiar with every aspect of it.

Matt Haney had joined the Green River Task Force on May 1, 1985, replacing Paul Smith when Smith was diagnosed with leukemia. Sue Peters, the rookie who responded to the second Green River site in August 1982, was a detective by 1986 and had come on board the task force, too. Even though the number of investigators had shrunk, Jim Pompey would be commanding the cream of the crop.

As the Green River Task Force continued to shrink due to budget cuts, King County found money in its budget to "rehabilitate" the Green River itself—partially to take away the onus put upon it by the thirty-six unsolved murders and dozens of missing women. The county's Natural Resources and Parks Division hired artist Michael McCafferty to design a master plan that would change the image of the Green River along its entire thirty-mile course. McCafferty suggested several educational stations, some bronze sculptures, reseeding to "help the fish," and a small memorial of black and purple flowers to honor the murder victims. This last—unsolicited—suggestion from McCafferty alarmed the King County Arts Commission. "It's inappropriate," one member of the commission said. "This [serial killer] hasn't yet been caught. He might think of it as a memorial to him. If he had been apprehended, we might feel differently."

Left unspoken was the hope that the murders would be forgotten and the Green River would once again be known for its rippling waters, salmon runs, great blue herons, and serenity. Honoring the dead would keep reminding people of what had happened.

Linda Barker, speaking for the victims' families, found the thought of a memorial extremely appropriate. "Society and the community need to say these girls were valuable people and their deaths mean something to us."

In the end, the $10 million project went through with a bike and jogging path along the river, a golf course near the Meeker Street Bridge . . . but no remembrance at all of the Green River victims.

JIM POMPEY, the new head of the Green River Task Force, was a great guy with a booming laugh that was instantly recognizable. A graduate of Washington State University's law enforcement program, he was a dedicated "Cougar." A physical training enthusiast, he exercised several times a week lifting weights at a health club near the Burien Precinct. My son, Mike, also a Cougar, worked out with Pompey and another African-American officer, a member of the K-9 Unit.

"I remember him as being very strong," Mike recalled. "And he was always looking to get more hats and shirts from WSU. Every time I went to Pullman, he'd ask me to bring him back something with the Wazzu cougar on it."

Not surprisingly, Pompey was also an excellent swimmer and a SCUBA diver, skills that came in handy when he headed the marine unit. Seattle and King County have water in almost every direction and drowning rescues are common.

Pompey felt he was up to the challenge of catching the Green River Killer, although it wasn't a job he had sought out deliberately. Like each new commander, he came in fresh and enthusiastic even though morale among the detectives still left was running low. Even Dave Reichert, who had been with the investigation since day one, sometimes wondered if they were ever going to catch the man who had eluded them for so long. It would be fair to say that it had become a personal life challenge for Reichert.

SOME of the preeminent suspects from the early days had long since been cleared; others remained in the "A" category, while a few moved up the dubious ladder to a point where it seemed prudent to look at them from another angle. And then there was always the chance that task force detectives might come across an entirely new suspect, a name they had not heard before.

One of the earliest suspects, when reevaluated, began to look much more interesting. The hard-won, state-of-the-art computer that Frank Adamson, Bob Keppel, Sheriff Vern Thomas, and former county executive Randy Revelle had fought for was a new and almost miraculous tool. It had taken time for clerks to enter the thousands upon thousands of tips and field investigation reports, the information about both the victims and possible suspects, into the computer. It continued to scan for connections among victims and connections between victims and possible suspects.

One name that caught the detectives' attention was the mild-mannered man who drove pickup trucks and liked to watch prostitutes on the Strip. He appeared to have been intricately linked to the investigation. Sergeant Frank Atchley had always found him intriguing. Matt Haney noted computer hits on his name were piling up.

- The Seattle Port Authority Police, who patrolled airport property, had listed the "street name" of a pretty woman parked with him in 1982. It was an alias for Keli Kay McGinness, the beautiful blonde who was still missing after leaving the Three Bears Motel.
- He was, of course, the man who had started to strangle Penny Bristow after he said she had bitten him during oral sex. He had admitted that the incident had happened.
- Jim Doyon had talked to him in front of Kentucky Fried Chicken on the Strip near the crossing where most of the dead and missing women had last been seen.
- This same man lived just south of 216th off Military Road. Indeed, he lived in the house where Marie Malvar's father and boyfriend had watched Des Moines detective sergeant Bob Fox question the owner. Fox had walked away, convinced that Marie wasn't in his house, nor had she ever been there.
- He habitually drove older pickup trucks, all of which matched the descriptions given by witnesses or women who had escaped from a man they believed to be the Green River Killer.

At the request of his neighbors, even I had turned in this man's name in early 1987. There probably were other tips about him somewhere in the computer.

Still, in many ways he didn't fit within the parameters of the standard serial killer profile. He was apparently happily married, a homeowner with a young son. In 1984, he had passed a polygraph regarding the murders of young women. And he'd been steadily employed at the same company—the Kenworth Truck Company where he was a custom painter—for more than two decades.

He wasn't the typical serial killer—who was usually a loner without a lasting relationship with a woman. He wasn't a job hopper. He wasn't from a broken home. He'd grown up in the south end of King County and his high school was only a few blocks off the Strip, as was his parents' home.

He'd gotten his hair cut at Don the Barber's ever since he was in junior high school. He'd worked in hotels and surplus stores on the Strip as a teenager, and, as an adult, he shopped there.

His name was Gary Leon Ridgway, and he was thirty-seven years old, a few months older than Dave Reichert. Haney felt there were too many hits on the computer to ignore, but even so, they were all circumstantial. There was no physical evidence to prove that Gary Ridgway was anything more than a slightly creepy guy who had been single during the peak years that the killer murdered the most victims: 1982 to 1984. The Green River investigators had come across a lot of guys who were creepy and, married or single, liked to stare at prostitutes and pay money to have sex with them.

Five years earlier, Melvyn Foster had looked perfect as a suspect. A year before, the fur trapper had seemed like a sure thing when he proved to be totally innocent. And that belief had gotten the task force the worst press yet. There had been a number of other men who seemed more likely candidates to be the GRK than this guy, men the public never heard about. And yet Gary Ridgway warranted a closer look.

When I glanced at the first notebook to tumble out of the file boxes about the Green River killings that I had saved for more than twenty years, I was startled to read my own printing scrawled across a whole page:

Gary Leon Ridgway—Physical Ev? may have ties to GR victim
Went to Tyee
Class of '67 or '68 turn W on 220 21859 32

Half of those notes would turn out to be wrong. But thinking I had something that the task force might want to see, I either filled in one of the tip sheets they'd given me, or, more likely, typed up what his neighbors told me when I met with them after they called me some time in 1987.

Seventeen years ago, feeling truly dumb about playing detective, I put on sunglasses and a scarf, borrowed a car, and drove past Gary Ridgway's house on 32nd Avenue. It wasn't hard for me to get there; I lived then on S. 18th and 240th. There was nothing even slightly unusual about his house. There was no one around and the windows were covered by drapes or blinds. If he had been in the yard, I wouldn't have known it; I didn't even know what he looked like.

I had no idea in 1987 that the Green River Task Force investigators were way ahead of me. They never told me one way or the other whether any of the information I passed on to them was useful. I didn't expect them to.

In fact, the task force investigators and uniformed deputies had been watching Ridgway on and off for months.

Early on, Matt Haney had chosen Ridgway as his favorite suspect, and the more he found out about him, the more enthusiastic he grew. Haney probably worked on more police departments in more assignments than any cop under fifty. Beginning on the Kent Police Department, he investigated a homicide involving the first "government protected witness" in America to be wrenched from his East Coast organized-crime roots. Haney was in his early twenties at the time. He went next to the King County Sheriff's Office where he was first a patrol deputy, then a homicide detective, and would one day be in charge of Special Operations (K-9s and Air Support), as well as training officer.

Haney conferred with Pompey and senior deputy King County prosecutors Marilyn Brenneman and Al Matthews, sharing his convictions that the task force should make a move—obtain a search warrant, if necessary—to find out more about Gary Ridgway.

Brenneman and Matthews were enthusiastic about focusing on Ridgway. Pompey also wanted to monitor Ridgway's comings and goings. So far, their surveillance hadn't netted them much. He went to work and he came home. He sometimes stopped to eat at fast-food restaurants. That was about the extent of it.

41

ON APRIL 8, 1987, Gary Ridgway's sense of invulnerability was severely shaken. He had no idea that he was being surveilled, and he certainly didn't expect the execution of a search warrant on his house, his locker at Kenworth Trucking, and the three vehicles he currently had available to him—his own Ford pickup truck, his father's Dodge pickup, and the Dodge Dart that his wife, Judith, drove. The search warrant drawn up by Matt Haney and okayed by senior deputy prosecutors Al Matthews and Marilyn Brenneman, also specified that there was probable cause for Ridgway himself to give up hair samples.

The search, done discreetly and rapidly, went well. Haney and

Doyon took Gary Ridgway to Kent police headquarters where they photographed him and bagged plucked samples of his head and pubic hair into evidence. While hair is not the optimum source to find DNA, if hair follicles (skin tags) are present it can be done. Almost as an afterthought, Matt Haney asked George Johnston from the Washington State Patrol crime lab to swab the inside of Ridgway's mouth and cheek. The gauze pledget holding the saliva was bagged, labeled, and frozen against a day in the distant future when it might be important.

Sue Peters was a little chagrined to draw only Ridgway's Kenworth locker, which, at the time, didn't seem likely to give up anything vital to the case. She bagged and tagged his white coveralls, stained with myriad paint splotches.

Other searchers took away rope, tarps, paint samples, of which there were many, some carpet threads and fibers.

Gary Ridgway had always been proud of his job with Kenworth and the image he had there, or believed he had. He was a dependable, punctual employee, and he usually managed to follow the computer instructions provided to mix the paint that stylized the big rigs. But sometimes his dyslexia made it difficult for him to remember the numbers on the computers associated with specialty paint jobs. On a bad day, he might ruin a couple of jobs by getting mixed up on a three-color trim, and then he raged at himself. One day he "ruined several trucks" because he got the sequences mixed up. He even had one three-day period when he added the wrong chemicals to the paint. Worst of all, he occasionally painted the wrong truck entirely. The bosses always let him do it over, and he did without protest. One of his nicknames around the plant was "Wrong-Way" and he hated that. But he couldn't show his anger at work because he feared being fired. In the employee break room, some of his co-workers found him inordinately religious, even a zealot, as he read aloud from the Bible. He was a paradox: Sometimes he was far too touchy-feely with women employees and made them nervous when he crept up behind them. Alternately, he would go through his preaching phases where he spouted his opinion about harlots and loose women until spittle flew out of his mouth.

After the task force investigators searched his locker, Ridgway got another nickname at work. Even though the searches of April 1987 were accomplished with little fanfare and, to Jim Pompey's relief, no media blitz, other employees at Kenworth knew the detectives had questioned him, searched his belongings, and taken pictures of his truck in the company parking lot. Nobody really thought he was capable of killing more than three dozen prostitutes, but there was the similarity of his initials that begged for jokes at his expense: "G.R." for Gary Ridgway, and "G.R." for Green River. He soon became "Green River Gary" at Kenworth.

It was just a joke, but he didn't find it amusing. Even so, the search warrant's execution hadn't damaged his career at Kenworth; he was too dependable an employee.

John O'Leary worked at Kenworth, too, but he was much farther up the corporate ladder than Ridgway could ever hope to be. O'Leary was a finely tuned long-distance runner in the mideighties and early nineties, and he and his running partner were interested in true-crime cases. "In our ninety-minute to two-hour training runs," he recalled, "we would spend a lot of time talking about the Bundy case as we read the various books. We also talked a lot about the Green River case since it was on the news constantly.

"I later became the CFO [chief financial officer] of the Kenworth plants in Tukwila and Renton from 1997 to late 2000. Although I wasn't friends with Ridgway, I certainly knew who he was. It was common knowledge that he had been a Green River suspect, but that he had been cleared."

Jim Pompey was relieved that Matt Haney had managed to keep a lid on the details of the April 1997 searches. Even the media, which dogged the detectives' footsteps, seemed chastened in the aftermath of the Tikkenborg search chaos.

It would take several weeks before all the tests on evidence taken from Ridgway's house, locker, and vehicles were finished and they would know if any usable physical evidence might emerge. In the meantime, Ridgway, albeit with his new nickname, went back to his everyday life. He didn't threaten to sue anyone, and the vast majority of the Seattle public wasn't even aware of his moment in the harsh spotlight.

Al Matthews, the prosecutor who had worked with the task force for four years, was as bitterly disappointed as Matt Haney and Sue Peters were when he had to tell them that there just wasn't enough physical evidence to get an arrest warrant for Gary Ridgway. They had done all they could, but the Ridgway part of the Green River probe had to be shelved until something that would hold up in court should surface.

Haney was convinced it wasn't over for good. When he could,

he kept checking for connections between Gary Ridgway and the Green River victims.

NINETEEN EIGHTY-SEVEN was a big year for forensic science. A September 21 article out of London, England, was headlined "Genetic Sample Leads to Suspect in Killing."

For the first time a police department somewhere in the world had used a scientific technique known as "genetic fingerprinting." In their determination to solve the two-and-a-half-year-old rape murders of two teenage girls in the village of Enderby, Leicester County, English investigators took blood and saliva samples from more than 5,500 adult males who lived in the community. After exhaustive testing and the elimination of all other subjects, they charged a twenty-seven-year-old baker with the crimes.

Geneticist Alex Jeffreys of Leicester University had discovered that DNA—deoxyribonucleic acid—found in the chromosomes of all living beings can be charted as a series of bands, unique to each person. In 1987, the test was effective on dried blood as old as five years, and dried semen up to three years old. The chance that two humans would have identical patterns was between 30 billion and 100 billion to one. It seemed very Brave New World, and DNA testing wasn't perfected yet by any means. Plus, the cost could be prohibitive. But when Gary Ridgway was questioned and searched in 1987, Matt Haney had nothing to lose by taking a sample of his saliva.

UNEXPECTEDLY, and tragically, the Green River Task Force would have yet another commander. Jim Pompey went SCUBA diving with sheriff's detective Bob Stockham, Stockham's brother, and Roger Dunn, who, along with Bob Keppel, were the King County detective partners who had tracked Ted Bundy back in the midseventies. Dunn now ran his own private investigating company.

They were diving off Richmond Beach in the north end of Seattle, where Pompey was going to use a new speargun to catch fish. But almost as soon as they descended to depths close to a hundred feet, Pompey began to have trouble with his oxygen tank regulator. Stockham saw that the Green River commander was on the verge of panicking and tried to help him get to the surface, but they got separated and Pompey rose through the water much too fast.

Coast Guard rescuers took Pompey to a Seattle hospital by helicopter and he appeared to be regaining consciousness. But terrible damage had been done to his lungs. He didn't live to be placed in the decompression chamber.

When "Doc" Reay performed an autopsy on Jim Pompey, he found that he had succumbed to a pulmonary embolism. He wasn't forty yet, and he'd probably been in better physical shape than anyone on the task force, but now he was gone.

Lieutenant Greg Boyle stepped in to pick up the reins, and then Bobby Evans took over in December 1987. The Green River Task Force assignment would take its toll on any number of comparatively young men. Danny Nolan died of a leukemia-like blood disorder and so did Paul Smith. Ralf McAllister had a massive coronary and died in his cabin on Snoqualmie Pass. One detective retired after an emotional breakdown. Homicide detectives live under so much pressure and stress that the attrition rate from sudden death is higher than in most jobs, but the Green River case seemed to be taking an even greater price.

The same is true for the parents of young murder victims, particularly their fathers. Their perceived failure to protect their children eats away at the parents who could not save those they loved the most. It had happened in the Bundy cases and it was happening in the Green River cases. The grief of families is often so profound that they lose their will to live. The death toll caused by the Green River Killer extended far beyond his victim count.

42

AT LEAST four missing women who matched the victim type preferred by the Green River Killer came from the Portland area. Trina Hunter, the woman whose relatives reportedly kept her locked in an attic, had been found in a swamp near Vancouver, Washington, and her murder was still unsolved. Two of the sets of remains in the Tigard/Tualatin area were still unidentified, but Portland detectives doubted that the GRK was operating in their jurisdiction. It was a difficult call, given the constant travels of working girls from Portland to Seattle and back.

If Portland and Multnomah County police were hesitant to accept that they might have to form a task force of their own, no one could blame them. It's an old joke among homicide detectives that, given a "loser" case, they might just drag the body over a county or state line and let some other department solve the crime. With all the hassles the Washington investigators had endured over the past five years with the Green River case, no other jurisdiction envied them.

Meanwhile, prostitutes had begun to disappear from the streets of Vancouver, British Columbia—only a four-hour drive north of Seattle. Indeed, the whole West Coast seemed to be riddled by the newest identifiable scourge known in criminal history: the serial killer. And Portland was having its own siege. By midsummer 1987, more prostitutes were missing in Portland. The incident reports sounded all too familiar. One young woman was picked up as she walked toward a 7-Eleven to buy cigarettes. The male driver looked innocuous and seemed quite pleasant. However, he drove past her neighborhood, and as they left the urban area, he tromped hard on his accelerator and told her that he had always wanted to take a woman into the woods, tie her up, and have sex with her. As he hit speeds near sixty miles an hour, she decided to take a chance. Anything would be preferable to being alone with this man who was clearly dangerous. She brought her elbow down on the door handle and tumbled out of the moving car. She hit the road hard. Although she was badly injured and bleeding from "road rash," she was alive when a truck driver found her lying on the highway and called for an ambulance.

Exactly a month later, on August 7, 1987, a Portland woman who also worked Union Street screamed desperately for help, shouting, "Rape! Help . . . Rape!" Nearby residents rushed to their windows. In the Denny's parking lot far below, they saw a man bent over a naked woman, raising his arm again and again. By the time they reached her, however, she was dying from stab wounds to the chest.

As horrible as her murder was, it was far from the worst of it. Oregon detectives traced the license-plate number one witness was able to memorize and linked it to thirty-three-year-old Dayton Leroy Rogers. Rogers, a well-known auto repairman in the hamlets of Woodburn and Canby (about twenty-four miles south of Portland), was married with a toddler son. But he also had a record for sexual assaults going back many years. He had been in prison and then diagnosed as mentally ill, but he had slipped through Oregon's parole system. He was familiar to prostitutes as a foot fetishist, a bondage fan, and as a client who was stimulated by inflicting pain.

When a decomposed female body was found in the Molalla Forest on August 31, Clackamas County, Oregon, detectives recalled Rogers's sexual penchants. He was a known sadist, and he lived less than fifteen miles away. As deputies and dogs conducted a sickening search of the ninety-thousand-acre timber farm, they found six more female bodies. Four of them were within fifty yards of one another on an almost vertical slope. They had been covered with brush and then "self-buried" as weeds and brush grew over and around them.

Dr. Larry Lewman, the Oregon State Medical Examiner, went through the two hundred dental records the King County M.E. had gathered after the Green River murders, searching for matches to the seven victims found between August 31 and September 5, 1987, in the remote forested area ten miles southeast of Molalla, Oregon. He was able to identify most of them by their dental work, even though some of their charts were more than ten years old. But none of them were missing young women in the Green River files. All but one of these known victims had ties to prostitution. One would never be identified. The worst part, however, was the fact that the killer had cut his victims' feet off, probably with a hacksaw.

The Green River Task Force sent detectives to the Molalla Forest to help in working the outdoor body site, a cluster site like those where the Washington State victims had been found. And of course they wondered if they might find evidence that would link these murders to the Green River cases. Since the man they sought had apparently stopped taking victims in King County, he might well have moved south to begin with a clean slate.

Rogers scarcely looked like a killer. He wasn't very tall, and had a slight build and a baby face. He would certainly appear innocuous to women who stared through a car window at him. He was also an alcoholic who never went anywhere without a supply of tiny vodka bottles—the kind used on airplane flights. Several of the bottles were found close to the bodies in the Molalla Forest.

But could Dayton Leroy Rogers be the Green River Killer? Not likely. Some elements were the same, but some were very different. As far as the task force investigators could tell, Rogers hadn't traveled to Washington. Although most of the King County victims weren't found until they were skeletonized, none of the bones showed signs of nicking or breaking from bullets or a knife. None of the first victims found had been stabbed, they were younger than the Molalla victims, and there was no indication that their feet had been cut off. No, the Portland area had its own serial killer.

After the first flurry of interest on the part of King County detectives, they realized that Rogers was not their man. He was a serial killer certainly, but not the one they'd been hunting for so long.

Dayton Lee Rogers went to trial and was sentenced to life in prison.

43

IT WAS 1988 and the centennial anniversary of the most infamous serial killer of them all. Jack-the-Ripper had stalked unfortunate ladies of the night in London exactly a hundred years before. Oddly, no one interested in the Green River murders appeared to note that. At least, there were no "anniversary" articles or television comments about it. Old Jack was a piker compared to the GRK's toll; he had claimed less than a half-dozen victims, but his fame had magnified exponentially over the years because he was never caught.

The Green River Task Force detectives devoutly hoped that was not going to happen with the man they were tracking.

ANYONE who investigates homicides or who writes about them soon learns that there are things that happen that seem far more than coincidence, events and discoveries that have to be almost unexplainable. It is something more than a victim's hand reaching out from the grave, or, more likely, reaching back from the other side. Certainly murder "will out" is not always true. People get away with murder all the time. But sometimes evidence and victims are discovered through such unlikely means that it seems almost miraculous, and I do not question it.

By May 30, 1988, Debra Lorraine Estes, fifteen, had been gone for almost six years. There had been moments of hope. One of her aunts, who lived in Virginia, was known as a psychic, but the messages she got were far more grounded than something ethereal. She had received two phone calls—one in 1985 and another in 1986. The young woman who called said that she was her niece and she needed help. Debra's aunt could hear background noise and the sound of coins being dropped into a pay phone.

"I need help," the girl said. "I'll come to where you are."

The caller said she was Debra, and she even knew her Virginia cousins' first names, although she had seen them only once and didn't know them very well. She got the names right. But she hung up abruptly during both calls. The second time, she screamed before the line went dead.

Was it Debra? Maybe she was being held captive and had managed to get to a phone twice. But why hadn't she called her parents instead of an aunt she barely knew? Or was it Debra from some place just beyond life, making contact with the one relative she had who was sensitive to ghostly communications?

More likely, it was a cruel practical joker, one of the ghouls who thrive on making the pain of victims' relatives even more acute.

Carol Estes clung to her hope that her daughter was out there someplace. She told Linda Barker that if she couldn't have her daughter back safe and sound, she hoped that Debra could somehow be the one girl who would bring the killer down and lead to his arrest. "I want her to be the one to break the case."

On January 20, 1988, Tom and Carol Estes appeared on the *Oprah Winfrey* show, asking for information from someone—anyone—in the viewing audience who might have seen Debra. Although the show has a tremendous following, only four tips came in. All but one were vague. One caller had seen a girl dancing on a dock in the Southeast, a girl who resembled Debra. Another had seen a girl in passing but could give no specific information. The most likely information came from a rehabilitation facility in New England where troubled youths were helped. Debra might be one of their charges.

But it wasn't Debra.

LIKE ANY CITY with a burgeoning population, Seattle and surrounding King County attracted developers with plans to build houses and apartment complexes in the suburbs where there had been nothing but forests and mountain foothills. Federal Way, more than halfway between Seattle and Tacoma, was deemed a perfect site for putting up apartment buildings, and it could be accomplished with creative financing that leveraged a relatively small amount of cash up front.

In 1981, a company called Western Hill began construction on what was originally to be called The Bluffs at 348th Street and First Avenue South in Federal Way. The land for the complex was literally cut out of a dense fir forest. Work began in 1981 but stopped in early 1982 when the company was forced into bankruptcy.

For Bruce McCrory, a landscape architect, the Western Hill project was memorable in many ways. It was the first time he had ever designed an entire project from site to buildings to landscaping. He called it "my baby," and in an architectural sense, at least, it was.

McCrory was on the site of the apartment complex construction almost every day for over a year. More than two decades later, it would be hard for him to pinpoint the exact year that he came across a stranger in the southeast portion of the site. Panther Lake Elementary School was only fifty feet away at that point, and its playground and ball field abutted the landscaped grounds, making it highly desirable for families with young children. The area had been designated as a "tot lot," where teeter-totters, monkey bars, and swing sets would one day be built.

It may have been a weekend when McCrory encountered the man he didn't remember seeing on the site before. "He was wandering around the recently cleared portions of the southeast quarter, near the school property."

Before the stranger noticed him, McCrory paused, just out of his sight. "I remember him poking at the ground with something," he recalled. "Why was he poking at the ground? That question kept bothering me as I tried to remember. As I annotated brief descriptions on the only four remaining [shots] out of hundreds of photos I took, I remembered. He was in a rage, flailing his arms, beating the ground, kicking dirt. Then he noticed me, and shifted into the poking mode. I guess social norms prescribe that we respect embarrassing, private displays of emotions."

And McCrory did that. "I thought he was the soils engineer, and since his vehicle was near where I stood, he had to pass me. I asked him if he *was* the soils engineer, and he said, 'You might say that.' "

The man brushed by him, obviously not wanting to talk further, walked to his vehicle, which may have been a pickup, although McCrory isn't sure, threw the stick and a backpack into the rear, and drove away.

McCrory would probably have forgotten this strange incident, one that was over in a few minutes, if not for a second memory that came later. His company softball team was practicing on the ball field at the Panther Lake School in either 1981 or 1982. "We were nearly overcome with the stench of a dead animal. At one point," McCrory said, "I wandered around trying to identify the source. The area I thought was the location was the present tot-lot curb on the apartment site. The memory is tied to a reference about Ted Bundy by one of my teammates."

The memory went into Bruce McCrory's subconscious mind, leaving him with a creepy sense of fear about the smell of decaying flesh. He was aware of the Green River murders that allegedly began in 1982 and the investigation that continued over the next twenty years, but he hadn't followed the cases closely.

It would be 1987 before construction at the site began again, and, in the meantime, the cleared land would stay as it was except for some low-growing native plants that dotted the bare dirt. When the complex was completed, it was renamed Fox Run, and the apartment buildings were painted a sunny yellow against the dark green of the fir forests that surrounded them. On May 30, 1988, workmen were using a posthole digger in the corner where a six-foot fence would keep children from wandering into the parking lot. There, a huge boulder sat between two tall fir trees. It seemed the perfect spot for a swing set, if a little shady.

They found something in the small hole meant for the swing set's end posts. It wasn't a rock the posthole digger had struck; it was bones. From the small circumference exposed, it wasn't possible for the workers to tell if they were human or animal bones. All work stopped and the King County police were contacted.

Carefully, tediously, Bill Haglund from the Medical Examiner's Office repeated what he had done so many times before, working slowly to prevent any more damage to the skeleton that had clearly been here just eighteen inches below the surface for many years. He found a left hip, knees, ankles, a scapula, some cervical bones from the upper spine, and a skull. The teeth were intact. If this was one of the long-missing girls, Haglund would soon know it. He had studied the dental X-rays of the still-missing girls so many times and thought he recognized a familiar crown. But he said nothing as he gathered up all that was left of this victim—the bones, faded clothing, fingernails, some hairs and fibers. Indeed, some physical evidence was found with the body: a rotting black V-necked sweater with glittery metallic threads and a dark-colored bra. And on those items, there were paint chips. White paint chips.

Comparison of dental X-rays on file identified the remains. Haglund had been right. It was Debra Lorraine Estes, missing for six years. Had the construction workers dug even a few feet away, the chances of her ever being found would have been slight.

The investigators wondered if there was any way to tell if her killer had just left her body on the grounds of the apartment site where work had been stopped by September of 1982, or if he had actually buried her. The former was more likely; trucks full of dirt and bulldozers had dumped landfill there in 1987 and workmen had probably never noticed the bones, which were probably covered with brush and weeds.

Around seven thirty the next morning, before anyone else could get to Tom and Carol Estes, Fae Brooks and Dave Reichert left their offices for a task they dreaded. At eight ten, they stood at the Esteses' door. Carol Estes smiled, initially glad to see them, and then her face paled. She knew what it must be that had brought them there so early. They had found Debra.

It doesn't matter how long a loved one has been gone. The final shutting of a door on hope is agonizing. Carol Estes talked by phone to Bill Haglund and then asked to be taken to the site where Debra's body had been found. They discouraged her from going, but she was adamant.

Linda Barker, now working in Texas with a foundation set up to aid crime victims, called to be sure a victim's advocate was on the way to help Debra's parents. The family asked Dave Reichert to be a pall bearer at Debra's funeral and he immediately said he would. They also agreed to let the Green River Task Force film the funeral in case the killer showed up.

The scope of the investigation into Debra's murder would have to be wide-ranging. How many hundreds of workers, truck drivers, electricians, plumbers, and carpenters had been on the Fox Run site in the last six years? The detectives obtained master lists from contractors and subcontractors, and then did computer runs to see if they showed up in police files as any of the Green River victims' acquaintances, or the johns questioned on the street.

The paint chips—which were scarcely more than flecks—found on Debra Estes's clothing would be studied by Skip Palenik at his Microtrace laboratories in Elgin, Illinois. Palenik's ability to find vital evidence verged on genius. Other than paint, some of the materials the renowned microscopist worked with were paper fibers, hair, crystals, and minute amounts of industrial dust, combustibles, pollen, soil, cement, drugs, and wood and vegetable matter. With his powerful array of microscopes, knowledge, and experience, Palenik was the definitive expert the task force investigators needed. After being buried for years, could the almost invisible paint spheres on Debra's blouse be identified and compared to a known source? They could. Palenik found matches to an expensive paint—Imron, manufactured by DuPont—that was used mostly on commercial vehicles. He set about winnowing down the companies whose standards of excellence would demand paint of this caliber. One strong possibility was the Kenworth Truck Company.

And how long had Debra Estes lain beneath the tot lot's soil? That was important because it would let the detectives know if she had been buried by her murderer, or accidentally by trucks bringing in load after load of fill dirt. One of the top names in another scientific area that aids criminal investigation was available to help. Professor Fio Ugolini, a soil scientist from Florence, Italy, was currently teaching at the University of Washington, and he agreed to come to the body site with Detective Cecil Ray to take samples from the dirt there. Ugolini was able to assure investigators that no soil had been added after Debra's body was placed in the ground. "She's been there since 1982," he said.

That was a terribly important piece of information. Debra had undoubtedly walked out of the Stevenson Motel on September 20, 1982, met her killer that night, and been taken to the tot-lot location in the unfinished apartment complex. Why her name was added to the registration book at the Western Six Motel, along with Rebecca Marrero's who really *was* there on December 1 and 2 a little over two months later, might have been a sick joke. Or it could have been a cover-up on the part of the Green River Killer.

44

IN THE MID- TO LATE EIGHTIES, there were several areas in the United States and Canada where serial killers were at work. Honolulu police were investigating the murders of four women in their late teens and early twenties, all Caucasian, who had been killed between spring of 1985 and April of 1986. None of them was connected to prostitution. It was a stretch to connect them to the Green River murders.

More likely, the San Diego serial killer or, more probably, *killers,* were deemed to have begun a murderous marathon in the third week of July 1985. San Diego's "strip" was a long stretch of El Cajun Boulevard. Norm Stamper, second-in-command of that city's police department, who would become Seattle's police chief three years later, recalled being asked by the San Diego District Attorney to review the multiagency investigation into a string of perhaps forty-four murders of women of the street in both the city and the county. There were rumors of a rogue cop, and the DA was particularly concerned about the possibility of police involvement in the deaths and/or disappearances of a handful of the victims.

This speculation was fueled by the front-page statements of Donna Gentile, a warm, likable, and truthful prostitute with a passion for justice. She knew cops on both sides of the law and spoke openly about that. Her sense of self-preservation was flawed, however. Finally realizing she had gone too far, she expressed concern for her safety because she was a rabble-rouser who made people nervous.

It was too late. Shortly after Donna Gentile was interviewed on the evening television news, she disappeared. Her strangled body was found in the hills east of San Diego. She had been sexually assaulted, and her lungs were full of aspirated pea gravel, indicating that her killer had purposely jammed them down her throat. Was this a message to other prostitutes?

Stamper read every case file and interviewed every detective working on the San Diego cases. It was clear that the San Diego Metropolitan Homicide Task Force, comprised as the Green River Task Force was of city, county, and district attorney investigators, was woefully understaffed. Working in secrecy in an undisclosed Mission Valley office building, the San Diego detectives weren't sure if they were working homicides or internal investigation. Most were talented but inexperienced. It had taken them a long time, for example, to realize that a diagram drawn by a patrol deputy of a key homicide scene was a bit off kilter. In fact, it was completely reversed. It turned out that the county deputy who drew it was dyslexic and had sketched the whole scene backward.

Since Seattle detectives had more than their share of experience tracking serial killers, San Diego investigators flew to Washington to ask questions about the efficacy of forming a task force and how different police agencies could work well together to solve serial murders.

King County detectives had a lot of hard-to-come-by wisdom to share with San Diego's. Certainly, the "Ted" Task Force had proved that the more agencies involved, the better. But the Green River Task Force could not yet validate that having the King County Sheriff's Office, the Seattle Police Department, the Washington State Patrol, the Port of Seattle Police, and the F.B.I. all working to solve more than forty homicides was the best way. They had never caught their man, but they had learned a lot as they hit one brick wall after another.

Perhaps both jurisdictions were looking for the *same* man with a killer who lived primarily in either Seattle or San Diego choosing to take victims in the West Coast's most northern and most southern major cities. A comparison of the timing between the Green River murders in Washington State and the San Diego serial murders was interesting. The peak time period in Seattle seemed to have been between 1982 and 1984, and the California murders of similar victims began in 1985. By August 1988, San Diego County authorities had discovered bodies and skeletal remains of twenty-six women, most of whom fit the same profile as the King County victims. Eight other female bodies had been left in the city of San Diego.

Faced with more than thirty unsolved murders of prostitutes in less than three years, San Diego investigators were happy to share information with King County, and vice versa. In September 1988, a few weeks after they returned to California, authorities in San Diego arrested a man who had taken a young prostitute working on El Cajun Boulevard to a deserted spot in Mission Valley, and then demanded his $40 back after they had sex. He had threatened her with a shotgun. As she tried to talk reason to him, he reportedly said, "Aren't you going to cry and beg like that little Mexican girl did?"

The only Hispanic victim who seemed to match his reference was Melissa Sandoval, whose body had been found in Rancho Bernardo the previous May. Task force members would say only that she had perished "as a result of criminal means," but had not been shot.

The man was held on $100,000 bail.

After analyzing the San Diego Task Force, Norm Stamper called for two major changes. First, any and all allegations of police misconduct—from fraternizing with prostitutes to criminal behavior—would be investigated by the California State Attorney General's office. Second, since most of the prostitute murders had originated in the city of San Diego, the police department would provide additional resources and manpower to the task force. After exhaustive interviews, Stamper selected six additional detectives to complete the murder investigations.

In the end, Gary Schons, a brilliant attorney from the attorney general's office, was appointed to oversee the investigation into alleged police misconduct. He cleared the San Diego force of any involvement with the prostitute murders.

Dave Reichert was interested in the apparent similarities between the Green River victims and those in San Diego. He made one of the many flying trips he'd taken over the years to other jurisdictions and talked to the detectives in San Diego. If there were only some way to link a King County suspect to San Diego, it might be possible to compare times and dates. But nothing came of the California connection, although Norm Stamper isn't sure that is a closed door.

The man eventually convicted of the murder of Donna Gentile was a former marine and mechanic, a traveler who liked to drive up and down the West Coast. Citing fiber and other trace evidence, San Diego detectives were able to implicate him in almost two dozen of their cases. He is currently serving twenty-seven years to life in a California prison.

No one on the Green River Task Force knew in the late eighties that one of the men they'd talked to a number of times on the highway near the Seattle airport had once been stationed in San Diego. Indeed, that was the first time he'd felt betrayed by his wife and begun patronizing prostitutes. However, that was long before the serial killings began in either state. And a check on the whereabouts of the man arrested in San Diego in September 1988 indicated that he had never been to King County.

CAPTAIN BOBBY EVANS, who had once convinced Ingmar Rasmussen that his Cadillac had broken down so he could get inside the wealthy farmer's house to find some sign of the first missing Green River victims, was now the head of the Green River Task Force. But the torch, handed down so many times, was dimming, and all the detectives working the Green River case exclusively were in danger of being swallowed up by Major Crimes until the task force itself was no more.

ON DECEMBER 7, 1988, in what had all the signs of a last-ditch effort to bring forth vital information on possible Green River suspects from the American public, a television marathon called *Manhunt . . . A Chance to End the Nightmare* was broadcast. The show, in an *America's Most Wanted* format, resulted from the efforts of Myrle Carner, a robbery detective in the Crimes Against Persons Unit of the Seattle Police Department.

It featured interviews with the families of the murdered girls and information on dozens of homicides in other police jurisdictions, all unsolved. Patrick Duffy, who rose to television fame through his role, as "Bobby" in *Dallas*, hosted the special, while scores of detective volunteers answered phones. Duffy's sister was a Seattle police officer, and they shared a tragic connection to the victims' families. Their parents, Terrence and Marie Duffy, were murdered on November 18, 1986, by two teenagers during the robbery of their bar, The Lounge, in Boulder, Montana. Kenneth Miller and Sean Wentz, who was believed to have fired the sawed-off shotgun that killed the Duffys, were sentenced to 180 years in prison in 1987.

Not surprisingly, Patrick Duffy had strong personal motivations for trying to find killers who roved free. The show aired all across America and Canada, attracting millions of viewers.

F.B.I. special agent John Douglas faced the cameras to give the profile of the man they sought, and a somewhat nervous Dave Reichert sat beside him. Reichert warned the Green River Killer that he would have to pay for his crimes and asked him to turn himself in to face his punishment.

A lack of tips and information had never been the Green River investigators' problem. Rather, the mountains of calls, letters, and emails had almost buried them. Still, they had to hope the one vital lead that had eluded them for more than seven years might result from *Manhunt*. Sixteen thousand people called in that night and over the next weeks, offering almost two thousand new suspects. The majority of them were useless. However, the show did result in a possible new direction that left the task force with revived hope.

More than one viewer called in with information about William Stevens II, suggesting that he was "weird enough" to be the Green River Killer. "Billy" Stevens was thirty-eight years old, a student at Gonzaga University's law school in Spokane, and he was about to feel the uncomfortably hot glow of the task force's spotlight. Initially, Stevens seemed the least likely suspect of them all. He was in his last year of law school, and he had twice been elected to the prestigious office of president of the Student Bar Association. He had friends and admirers in that group and appeared to a be a winner, if somewhat eccentric. Even so, his name began to creep into Green River news coverage in January 1989.

On a viewer's tip, Stevens was arrested in his parents' Spokane home after the *Manhunt* program. Spokane County deputies seized twenty-six different license plates and twenty-nine guns from his bedroom. A number of the license plates had been issued to municipal departments and law enforcement agencies. He also had a Snohomish County undercover police vehicle, which he had bought at an auction and equipped as a standard police unit, handcuffs, and a motorcycle similar to those used by police.

Stevens was the eldest of three children, all adopted by a caring Spokane pharmacist and his wife. Billy Stevens was less than a week old when they brought him home, and he grew from a chubby child to a bearlike man, tall and lumbering with a big belly. He wore dark-rimmed glasses and had tightly curled brown hair. Indeed, he looked remarkably like one of the four widely disparate sketches of the Green River Killer as described by witnesses to possible abductions.

Just as Dick Kraske had remembered fingerprinting Melvyn Foster when Foster was first arrested in Seattle, Tom Jensen of the Green River Task Force recalled investigating Stevens in a King County burglary case nine years earlier. When Jensen heard his name, he had no trouble recalling the smooth-talking, overweight burglar he'd once interviewed. In 1981, Billy Stevens was being held in a work release unit in the King County Jail with five months left to serve. One day he was supposed to be carrying garbage out, but he'd just kept right on going.

It was what Stevens had stolen that made him most interesting as a Green River suspect, and where he had stolen it: He had taken a police uniform, Mace, surveillance devices, bulletproof vests, and other police equipment from a store out on Pac HiWay, a business located across the highway from the Blockhouse Restaurant, kitty-corner from the Midway Tavern, and just down the block from the Three Bears Motel. Stevens himself had lived in a nearby apartment at the time.

Now, he'd been arrested with guns, license plates issued to police vehicles, *and* a police car. Because of the constant rumor that the Green River victims had been killed by a policeman, Stevens's collection of police gear and weapons put him quickly into the "A" category. He was not just a "person of interest"; Stevens looked good enough to be a "viable suspect," although the task force was careful to keep that appellation to themselves for as long as they could. Stevens fit neatly into so many facets they sought in a suspect.

And with good reason. The face Billy Stevens presented to the world was only a facade. In truth, he was a con man on the level of "The Great Imposter." Ferdinand Waldo William Demara Jr. defrauded scores of people who believed he really was who he seemed to be. A brilliant con man, "Fred" Demara managed to masquerade successfully as a monk, a Canadian navy surgeon (who actually performed complicated surgeries successfully), a cancer researcher, a deputy sheriff, and a professor. Demara, who never graduated from high school, much less college or medical school, had a thirty-year career, although he was sporadically arrested for fraud, theft, embezzlement, and forgery. Had he chosen to pursue any of his "careers" legitimately, he could have accomplished the necessary education easily. Instead, he was a fraud, a man who some considered to be a true multiple personality.

It was the same with William Stevens II. He had a solid legal education after his years at Gonzaga, but he could never have passed the bar in any state that checked his background. He had a felony police record. He had also studied psychology at the University of Washington in Seattle, and had allegedly graduated in 1979 with a degree in pharmacology. He claimed to have been a second lieutenant and a military policeman in the U.S. Army, and to have applied to the Seattle Police Department to become a patrolman. Instead, for all his years at Gonzaga, and even before that, he was supposed to be in jail.

Stevens's early life seemed uneventful enough. He'd been born in Wallace, Idaho, on October 6, 1950, adopted by William and Adele Stevens, and raised in a quiet neighborhood north of the Spokane city limits, attending Jesuit schools and graduating from Gonzaga High School in 1969. His father owned the University Pharmacy, a block from their home, for thirty years, hoping that his son and namesake would take over the business one day. Young Billy was not particularly close to his siblings by adoption, consumed as he was with his own hobbies and interests. He was a police buff early on, fascinated with the lifestyle and paraphernalia of law enforcement. An inordinate number of serial killers are police groupies, eager to move in the same circles as real cops.

Although he had spent some summers working in the family drugstore, Stevens never really wanted to be a pharmacist. He had tried, unsuccessfully, to join the Seattle Police Department, but he had a lousy driving record.

Stevens was one of the most interesting suspects yet to rise to the forefront in this marathon investigation. His photo first appeared in the media at the end of January 1989, when the handcuffed fugitive was arraigned in a King County Superior Court. His attorneys asked Judge Donald Haley to release Stevens on bail because his elderly parents were ill and needed his help. "Our position," Craig Beles said, citing Stevens's success in law school, "is that Bill is a remarkable example of what rehabilitation can do."

The judge asked somewhat wryly why Stevens hadn't responded to two warrants for his arrest in 1981. Stevens explained that he had given police information on his fellow prisoners and he'd been afraid that, as a "snitch," his life was in danger, so he had walked away from work release and was afraid to go back.

In reality, he had never been a police informant.

Where *had* he been between 1981 and 1985 when he enrolled in law school in Spokane? Stevens proved to have had a lifestyle so peripatetic that it wasn't easy to trace the many places he had lived. For the moment, however, he was safely behind bars again in the King County Jail, finishing the sentence he had walked away from ten years before.

The Green River Task Force found that Stevens had crossed the Canadian border into British Columbia shortly after his 1981 escape. There he lived as a "house guest" of a Vancouver couple for about four months. They had acquiesced to his staying there at the request of a mutual friend. They knew him as "Ernie," and thereafter, he changed his name to "John Trumbull." He explained that he was setting up an import business. He never seemed to have much money, but he explained that, too, saying he was waiting for funds to be released. He didn't pay rent, but he bought some groceries, and helped with the dishes and the housework. They found him an amiable and polite guest.

"He was very organized, tidy, and a good talker," the husband of the couple recalled. "He dressed well and gave the impression of being an army man. He slept on a couch in the den and spent his time watching TV and reading."

Toward the end of Ernie/John's time with the Canadian couple, he made several overnight trips. He said he was going to Seattle. Then, in late summer 1981, their visitor left. They weren't sure where he was going.

William Stevens's/John Trumbull's trail picked up again in a southwest suburb of Portland. He bought a house on Southwest Crestline Drive for $108,000, a Roman brick with a double garage and a daylight basement. To help with the mortgage, he occasionally took in tenants in an apartment in that basement.

The task force looked at an Oregon map and saw that the house was within five miles of the Tigard/Tualatin site where the remains of four young women had been found, and within a mile of the location of Shirley Sherrill's skull and the partial skull of Denise Darcel Bush.

How Stevens supported himself was a question. Whether he was a danger to women was also a mystery. When I sorted through the hundreds of emails and notes I took during phone calls about the Green River Killer, sometimes I found circumstances and tips that seemed to match. I remember finding one that struck me as eerily connected to the time William Stevens lived near Tualatin.

A few years after the Portland area phase of body discoveries and attacks on women by would-be stranglers, I received a phone call from a woman who lived in Washington County, Oregon. She was embarrassed and made me promise I would not reveal her name. I promised.

"I'm married now," she explained, "and I don't live the same kind of life at all. But *then* I did pick up men at bars and taverns, and I was drinking too much.

"I met this one guy at a tavern near Beaverton [a few miles from Tigard and Tualatin]. It seemed to me that he was taller than average, and I do remember that he had one of those great big country-western-style belt buckles. We drove out to a field that was quite a ways from the place where I picked him up. And . . . well, we had sex outside in a field someplace. Afterward, I started walking back to his truck and he suddenly reached out his arm and grabbed me by the elbow. I looked down and saw that I had almost fallen into what looked like an open grave. The worst thing was that there was a woman down in there, and I think she was dead.

"When I got back to my car, I was so grateful to be alive that I just tried to put it all out of my mind. But I know there was a grave, and I know there was someone in it."

The "field" that the woman remembered was close to Bull Mountain Road and she believed that was where the man had taken her.

I turned the information over to the Green River Task Force, just one of more than the thousands of possibles it would document, but I kept her name out of it. If they thought it was worth following up, I could get back to her and see if she would talk to them on the condition that she remain anonymous. I don't know if she ever called them, although I urged her to do so.

When William Stevens's name came up, I remembered another woman who had written to me from Oregon. She told me her name was Marisa, and that she had once been a prostitute in Portland. She had described a shorter, thinner man than Bill Stevens appeared to be, but terror and shock can warp such perceptions.

Marisa's recall of her meeting with a stranger was, however, precise. I don't know her real name, but everything she told me about life in The Camp during the early to mideighties was validated by official police files.

Marisa has lived an entirely straight life for many years, and people who knew her after the eighties as a successful career woman would never guess what her former life was like. She was working the streets twenty years ago because she had been badly burned in an accident in a business she'd started and she was tired of being hungry and behind in her rent.

In 1983, she was thirty but looked about nineteen. "I remember being on Third Ave and Taylor Street about eleven PM in downtown Portland when he motioned to me to get in," she recalled. "I had been out there trying to get up rent money." Marisa usually worked in expensive hotels, but rainy Sundays were always slow, and she broke her first safety rule by going out on the street. Halloween decorations hadn't been taken down, so it could have been early November. She got into a shiny red Ford pickup truck, which was clean and new. "The word on the street was that the GRK was driving an old beat-up van so I figured I was safe. And besides, I told myself the GRK was in Seattle."

She broke her second rule, one shared by most working girls: *never* leave the downtown area. But Marisa was having a lucky night and had made almost all of her rent money. There were no other girls out that night and she decided to turn one more trick. "I asked him what he was interested in. He didn't answer. He stayed quiet and drove with purpose as he headed to I-5. I thought he was just shy. I told him I didn't want to leave downtown. He said he didn't feel comfortable because of the cops and he wanted to go to his house."

She was about to break the third rule of the street: never go to anyone's house. "I thought what the heck. I can break a rule because I am on a lucky streak."

The man didn't even glance at her as he raced along the I-5 Freeway, heading south, and then took an off ramp near Tigard. "He pulled into his garage and the automatic door closed behind us." They went into his small two-bedroom house.

She assumed he would ask for oral sex; most men did. He signed a cashier's check for $80.00 and gave it to her. She saw the name "Robert Thomas" on it. She thought he was probably a truck driver because they often had cashier's checks, but she was puzzled that he remained distant and seemingly disinterested in sex. "In fact he was unable to get it up. I thought well what the hell—you bring me all this way for nothing."

Suddenly, the stranger leapt from the bed, and grabbed a rifle from behind a door, aiming it at her. "My life flashed before me," Marisa recalled. She assumed he was upset with her because he couldn't achieve an erection, so she started talking loud and fast, telling him she would give back the check and she ran into the bathroom, locking the door. She was naked, a fourth rule she had broken. Frantic, she dressed hurriedly, all the time shouting through the door that she was searching for his check.

Dressed now, she opened the bathroom door, only to find him standing there with the rifle pointed at her head. She threw the check at him, saying "Here! Here it is. Now let me go!"

She was trying to snap him back into reality, but it wasn't working, and he had no intention of letting her go. She darted past him to the front door, only to find it had three locks. Why, she wondered, would a man who lived on a quiet cul-de-sac need three locks? As she struggled to turn the bolt, he began to beat her on the head with the rifle's butt.

Marisa turned as he started laughing maniacally. "He looked like a kid on a ride at Disneyland, his eyes all lit up and happy. With every swing of the rifle into my head, he got happier. This guy was psycho," she wrote. "He was getting off on it! This is how he gets off! *I remember his big glasses, the same style he wears today . . . and his hair-do the same . . . and his stature . . . not that big a man . . . not that small either . . . that same dumb sneaky look he has today. With that sly sparkle in his eyes.*"

It was evident to Marisa that he had brought her to this house to kill her, but he was taking his time. "He wasn't slamming the rifle with all his might, just cat and mouse style."

She remembered she had Mace in her front pocket, and she squirted it in his face, but his glasses blocked most of it. "He hit me left, then right, then left, then right, and beat up my forearms pretty bad. He finally pried the Mace from my hands and began spraying it in my face. Then I began to pray. My eyes burned with excruciating pain, but I would blink often to see what he was doing."

Now, she turned her attention to the front door, getting a mental picture of where the locks were. She lunged at the door to try to open another lock—the dead bolt. He continued to spray her with the Mace. "I grabbed a pillow on the couch near the door to protect my face. I kept him thinking he was winning so he wouldn't get even more forceful. That would buy me time for the third lock."

Even so, she was losing strength and felt she was going to die. "I was hurting bad and my eyes were on fire."

Her attacker was clearly enjoying himself. "That part is very scary; seeing him be thrilled over hurting someone who wouldn't hurt a fly—me."

She knew she had to get out because the Mace and her injuries were wearing her down. And then, for a moment, he seemed to tire, too. With her eyes almost entirely swollen shut, she twisted the dead bolt one more time.

"To my surprise, it unbolted and the door swung open. 'GRK' was surprised too." Marisa ran blindly across the street and down four houses where she knocked and called out, "Please help me!" It was about twelve thirty AM, but a woman opened the door for her and led her to the bathroom where she washed her eyes.

The police arrived, and Marisa told them that a killer had a friend of hers hostage in a house nearby. Afraid they wouldn't believe her if they knew she was a prostitute, she lied and said he'd picked them both up at a bus stop in downtown Portland. She tried to show them the house but she could hardly see, and the homes all looked alike. There were no trucks parked outside. As she stood on the porch of the woman who had helped her, Marisa saw a big sign right at the Tigard/Tualatin Exit from the freeway. It blinked on and off: Jiggles. She'd heard of it; it was a topless lap dance place.

The police gave up their search after she admitted that she didn't have a friend in any of the houses in the cul-de-sac.

"Please understand," she wrote to me, "living as a sex worker, I felt I had relinquished my rights as a citizen and that I wasn't worthy of protection. I was doing an unlawful thing even though it was in the name of survival."

The cops drove Marisa back to downtown Portland to her car. Her car keys were missing, and it cost her everything she'd earned earlier that night to pay a locksmith in the wee hours of the morning, but all she wanted to do was go home. Her friend, Tatiana,* who also worked the premier hotels in Portland, took care of her for a few days until her bruises began to heal and she could move without pain again.

Years later, when she watched the news bulletins from Seattle, and recognized the man in handcuffs, she felt sick to her stomach. An artist who remembers details, Marisa has always believed that she escaped from the Green River Killer. "We knew many of the girls who got killed," she wrote. "We never thought they had any family. Most of them were on drugs—methamphetamine and marijuana. Sad to say that those girls didn't have a chance in the world, even at their young age. Many were so hooked on drugs, they would have died of an overdose. I do wonder about the ones who came up missing and are not on the GRK list. Most of them were very sweet girls. They were still children in a way."

Marisa herself went to New Beginnings in 1985, got off the street, and changed her life completely.

45

ONE WOMAN who definitely met Bill Stevens was Sarina Caruso, forty-four at the time, who rented the basement of the house on Crestline Drive from September 1984 to January 1985. She knew Stevens as "John L. Trumbull," and although she found him somewhat odd, she didn't suspect he might be dangerous. Caruso, who had just gone through a divorce, worked as a nursing assistant and considered herself lucky to find an apartment that cost her only $200 a month.

In the time she knew him, she never saw Stevens/Trumbull with a date, although she sometimes heard women's voices in his upstairs quarters in the middle of the night. He was a night owl, though, and would often be barbecuing in the backyard at two or three AM. He had no friends, and she thought he might be an undercover cop or a C.I.A. agent. He wore several different uniforms that made it look as if he worked for the gas or electric company or as a repairman. But he had a gun collection and appeared to be fascinated with crime—to the point that he hung "Wanted" posters all over his house. He wore shoes with crepe soles, which allowed him to move so quietly that he would suddenly be behind her when she hadn't heard him approach. He also owned a lot of telephone equipment, a photocopier, and other equipment that he told her he used to analyze fingerprints. One of his many idiosyncrasies was that he would never allow anyone to take a picture of him.

Caruso wasn't too concerned about his eccentric ways, even when Stevens stole her chain saw and her marriage certificate. She worried a lot more when she saw that he had dressed mannequins in clothes she had thrown away. And even more when he cut the female dummies into pieces.

When she found bullet holes in Stevens's bedroom wall, Sarina Caruso gave notice that she planned to move. Stevens/Trumbull had always told her that he was adept at placing secret "bugs," and he'd offered to bug her ex-husband. Now she wondered if he had secreted listening devices in *her* apartment.

On the last day she saw him, Caruso had returned to pick up the remainder of her possessions and he said to her, "How are your nerves today?" He then began locking all the doors. Nervously, she let him lead her to the basement where he showed her the secret room he had there, a room hidden behind a bookcase that would slide open when he flicked a switch. Although she had occupied most of the basement, he demonstrated how he had been able to open a secret door into her area that couldn't be opened from her side.

That did it. Caruso grabbed her stuff and left, but not before Stevens insisted she take a dozen pornographic videotapes as a good-bye gift.

Sarina Caruso recalled Stevens's high-pitched voice and that he perspired heavily. "There were things I wasn't comfortable with," she told reporters later, "but I just thought he was bizarre and antisocial. I feel dumb now. I certainly didn't think he might be a killer."

Perhaps he wasn't, but William Stevens II was a man with many secrets. Fellow students at Gonzaga were shocked by his arrest for escape and burglary. A lawyer who had graduated a few years earlier and once worked with him on the Student Bar Association recalled Stevens as "very dedicated" to duties for the group, but said he seemed lacking in commitment to his law studies. He often missed class. Even with his law school peers, Stevens was mysterious. They realized later that none of them had a phone number where they could contact him directly.

They had no inkling that most of Stevens's life was a very elaborately constructed lie. To give himself official status, he used a crossroad of a town seventeen miles south of Spokane—Spangle—where he had license plates registered to the Spangle Emergency Services and Rescue Unit. Sometimes he purported to be the director of the EMS in Spangle, and sometimes he said he was the police chief. The town wasn't big enough to support either a rescue service or a police department.

One fellow law student knew Stevens was intrigued at the thought of being somehow involved in law enforcement. "He told me that after he finished law school, he was going to be a motorcycle officer for the Washington State Patrol," the man said. "That seemed bizarre. Why would he bother to go all the way through law school if that's what he wanted to do?"

Other law students had found Stevens gregarious and likable, and always busy. But no one ever thought of him as a threat; he was just different.

All through the spring and half the summer of 1989, Green River Task Force investigators and Spokane County detectives were checking out Stevens's life over the prior eight years. Satisfied that they had more than enough to go on by July 12, they obtained search warrants for two residences in Spokane. One was the home where Billy Stevens had grown up, and where he still had a room in the basement, and the other was a rental home his parents owned. The search warrants were very long and complicated, listing dates and times of the disappearances of the victims, followed by Stevens's whereabouts during those periods. It did appear that his constant sweeps around Northwest highways placed him close by when many abductions took place. The warrants also specified all kinds of police paraphernalia, records, credit card slips, suspicious books and photos, videotapes, and other items they hoped to find among Stevens's possessions.

There were, however, more reasons than just his proximity to the crime scenes. Stevens had made his feelings about prostitutes known to some of his acquaintances. One—perhaps his closest friend and a former classmate at Gonzaga—was a lawyer and a Spokane County deputy public defender named Dale Wells, who was also thirty-eight and single. Wells had acknowledged to Spokane County detectives that he and Stevens were close friends and had often discussed criminal cases, especially the crimes of Ted Bundy. Another topic that interested Bill Stevens was prostitution. He had denounced prostitutes to Wells and said they spread AIDS.

"He talked about them a lot," Dale Wells said, emphasizing that Stevens had demonstrated "extreme hatred" for anyone who resisted him and often said of his perceived enemies: "They need to be killed."

While Stevens appeared to have no romantic relationships with women, Dale Wells was involved with a woman he cared deeply for—and she for him. He appeared to be a sensitive and honorable man, and he was very troubled when Stevens became the top suspect in the Green River murder cases. Wells, whose career was dedicated to representing indigents, many of whom he thought were falsely accused, agonized over betraying his friend.

On the other hand, he was an attorney, sworn to uphold the law, and he felt he had to tell investigators what he knew. He also regretted that he had given Stevens two handguns, one of which was a .45-caliber pistol. That had resulted in federal charges against Stevens for being a fugitive felon in possession of a firearm.

If Stevens berated Dale Wells for turning against him, there was no proof. He may not have even known about Wells's defection from his camp. And he was still possessed of the braggadocio that marked his personality. He had to be placed in an isolation section in the King County Jail after he told a judge that he had two hundred pages of notes from his interviews with another prisoner who was a convicted murderer. Stevens said he planned to use that information in a thesis to help him earn his Ph.D. in psychology. That put him in the "snitch" category, more than enough to make him a pariah in jail.

When asked how he supported himself during his eight years of freedom after his 1981 jail escape, Stevens said he made a good living buying and reselling cars, and that he was currently applying for an auto dealer's license.

Deputies and detectives served the search warrants in Spokane and came away with more than forty boxes and bags, many containing pornographic material, dozens of photos of nude women in sexually explicit poses, some with Stevens, and eighteen hundred videocassettes. Detectives would have to view all of that material, looking for a familiar face. Perhaps some of the Green River victims' images might have been caught in Stevens's massive collection.

No one envied the detectives who drew the assignment of wading through the stultifying XXX-rated material that the seemingly affable law student had managed to hide in his parents' home and rental property. If any of the victims' photos *were* in the boxes and bags, what were the chances they would be recognizable? So many of the dead teenagers had dyed their hair, worn wigs, and changed their makeup, that it had been nearly impossible to spot them in mug shots. Stevens's collection of grainy, amateurish porn videos made it difficult to recognize familiar faces.

Stevens himself, still in the King County Jail on his earlier charges, issued a statement that came exactly seven years after the day Wendy Coffield's body was believed to have been discarded in the Green River. If he knew that date was a grim anniversary, he didn't mention it. Instead, he was outraged and stunned. "I am not the Green River Killer," he said through his attorney. "The Green River Task Force has not treated me or my family fairly. They have made me out to be a very bad person and I am not. People should know the fact that I have never hurt anyone in my life.

"If I knew anything about any of this, I would have told the task force long ago, but now I fear I have become the excuse for the time and money they have spent.

"I will discuss the matter in an orderly and honorable fashion in a court of law.

"The task force has put my family and me through a living nightmare that I would wish on no one. I want to serve out my remaining few months and get on with my life.

"Thank you."

HIS FAMILY *was* going through a "living nightmare," although the task force investigators hadn't caused it. They were only doing their jobs. Bill Stevens's brother had been taking care of their elderly parents. Their mother, Adele Stevens, had died earlier in July, and William Stevens Sr. was suffering from advanced brain cancer. No one could estimate what emotional pain Billy Stevens had caused them over the years.

Everyone who followed the seven-year plague of the Green River Killer had settled on a favorite suspect. And so had I. I was convinced in July of 1989 that William Jay Stevens II was the serial killer the task force had hunted for so long. Everything seemed to match my preconceived ideas of who the killer was: a middle-aged male Caucasian, very intelligent, a sociopath with charisma and cunning, perhaps someone pretending to be a police officer, someone who traveled continually, and who liked playing games with real cops.

I hedged my bets a little when I was contacted by reporters, although I did say I believed that charges would soon be forthcoming in the Green River murders. I had a contract to write about the Green River Killer, and I was finally ready to start my book.

I had even more reason to believe I had chosen the real Green River Killer a few months later. On Friday, September 21, 1989, I drove the three hundred miles from Seattle to Spokane where I was to teach a number of seminars over the weekend for the Washington State Crime Prevention Association convention. Daryl Pearson of the Walla Walla Police Department was in charge of providing speakers for an audience consisting of police officers, attorneys, probation and parole officers, and the media. I had done a phone interview with the Spokane *Spokesman Review-Chronicle* that appeared in the paper just before the convention. Among other subjects, I answered questions about the likelihood that the Green River investigators were heading toward an arrest. I certainly didn't know, but it was a subject readers always wondered about. This time, I felt as confident as some of the task force members did, and said so, although I didn't mention the suspect's name.

The convention was held in a Spokane hotel, and I was a little taken aback to find I was scheduled to give my two-hour slide presentation on serial killers—featuring the Ted Bundy case—*four* times on Saturday and twice on Sunday morning. Although I had expected to speak once on each day, there were so many attendees that every seat was full at each session, even when the folding doors between two meeting rooms were opened to double the size.

I recognized a lot of faces in the crowd, but it was impossible for me to note everyone in the six different audiences. As usual, I started with childhood slides of Bundy, Jerome Brudos (The Lust Killer), Randy Woodfield (The I-5 Killer), and a number of other serial murderers I'd written about, and moved on to their progression from exposing and/or voyeurism to rape to murder. At the end of each session, I answered questions from the audience. I wish that my memory was better, but I can't say if Dale Wells attended any of my seminars. If he was there, there was nothing about him that caught my attention.

By the time I drove home on Sunday, I was exhausted.

On Tuesday morning, Dale Wells's landlady unlocked the small apartment he rented. She hadn't seen him coming or going for a few days, and the woman he dated steadily was very concerned about him because she hadn't been able to get in touch with him.

He was there, lying on his sheetless water-bed mattress, but he was dead. Sometime over the previous weekend, he had killed himself with one blast of a shotgun to his head. No one who knew him had any warning whatsoever that he was depressed or troubled enough to commit suicide.

The next day, I got a phone call from Detective Jim Hansen of the

Spokane County Sheriff's Office. He asked me what I could tell him about Dale Wells. Baffled, I said I didn't know anyone named Dale Wells. Hansen told me that Wells had probably committed suicide sometime on Saturday. He had left no suicide note, but I was shocked when Hansen said, "He left a letter addressed to you, though . . ."

I explained that I had been in Spokane that Saturday and asked Hansen what the letter said. He read it to me and said he would mail me a copy. For the first time, I learned who Dale Wells was, and that he had been subpoenaed to appear before an upcoming grand jury empaneled to decide whether William Stevens II would be tried as a fugitive in possession of a firearm. Hansen said that there was no indication at all that Wells himself had been involved in any criminal activity.

When I received a copy of Wells's letter to me, it was undated, and it looked as if it was a rough draft of a letter he had worked over for some time, scratching out sections and adding inserts to make himself clear. It could have been written months before he shot himself on September 22 or 23, 1989.

"Re Your Green River Killer Project
Dear Ms Rule:
    It is my understanding you are writing a book about the Green River Killer w/a scheduled publication date sometime this summer. It is further my understanding, based on accounts in the press, that you do not believe the GRK is in custody. I believe you are mistaken in this regard in that the man I believe to be the GRK is in custody on unrelated charges.
    The basis of my suspicions regarding the ID of the GRK is somewhat analogous to your suspicions re: Ted Bundy where there was no direct confession, even to intimate friends, but a myriad of suspicious circumstances which would have considerable significance to a perspicacious observer.
    As I have not followed the killings in the press as they have occurred, I would appreciate your sending me an advance copy of what you have written so far so that I can better understand the killer's M.O. & the background of the victims.
                                                        Thank you
                                                        Sincerely, D.D.W."

At that point, some fifteen years ago, I hadn't written anything beyond notes because no one had been charged with the Green River murders. And I had no plans to publish a book in the summer of 1989 or 1990, if that was what Dale Wells meant.

Most of all, I felt sad that Wells hadn't contacted me or someone about his anxiety and his depression. Because my only sibling had committed suicide, and after volunteering at the Crisis Clinic, I have always found suicide the saddest way to end a life. Maybe I could have eased Wells's mind over some perceived guilt feelings about Bill Stevens's situation. Maybe I could have listened to his suspicions. More likely, there was nothing I could have done. It was obvious he believed Stevens was a serial killer whom he had befriended unaware, just as I had befriended Ted Bundy unaware. He may have felt guilty because he hadn't come forward sooner. He may even have felt guilty for telling detectives about Stevens's hatred for prostitutes. None of that should have been enough for him to take his own life.

In the end, all I could do was try to comfort Dale Wells's girlfriend and his landlady when they called me, but I could do so only in general terms because I never knew the man they mourned.

Green River Task Force commander Bob Evans, whom I *have* known since he was a road deputy, told reporters it was clear to him that Wells's letter to me compared Stevens to Bundy, but that his detectives weren't sure what significance to attach to the letter. "It's just another bizarre twist," he said, "in [what is] probably this country's most bizarre case."

The Spokane County Sheriff's investigators and the Green River Task Force carried stacks of papers and files out of Wells's apartment, but they never found anything that connected either Wells or Stevens to the Green River murders.

William Stevens II was transferred to Spokane County a few days after Dale Wells's suicide. He had only another month to serve on his King County sentence. However, he and his attorney had steadfastly refused to discuss the Green River murders with the task force, blocking any progress on his case for months.

Robert Stevens, who was a seventeen-year navy veteran, came forward in defense of his brother with photographs of him vacationing on the East Coast with their parents. The dates on the photos and the credit card slips from several cities seemed to validate that Bill Stevens was not in Washington State for most of 1982, and particularly on vital days in July.

After an exhaustive examination of Stevens's pornography collection, weapons, and police paraphernalia, nothing whatsoever was found linking him to the Green River cases. Reluctantly, the task force accepted that the prime suspect so far wasn't their man either.

Robert Stevens called a press conference to say he was furious with the task force for searching his parents' home, and for the ordeal his family had undergone because of the publicity surrounding that.

Evans countered, "It is not my fault he [Bill Stevens] was a fugitive, that he told his friends he wanted to do things to prostitutes and that he collected police badges and equipment. If I would have walked away from that without checking it out, I should have been fired."

On December 6, 1989, Stevens pleaded guilty before U.S. District Judge Justin Quackenbush to one count of being a felon and fugitive in possession of a firearm. In a plea bargain, two similar firearms counts were dismissed, and U.S. Attorney Ron Skibbie recommended a standard range of two to eight months in prison. The judge accepted the plea but said he would determine the sentence. The maximum penalty was ten years in prison, a $250,000 fine, and three years of supervised release.

In the end, Steven's sentence didn't really matter. He was diagnosed with liver and pancreatic cancer while still in prison and subsequently paroled. Once overweight, he weighed under ninety pounds when he died in September of 1991 at the age of forty-one. He was unrecognizable as the man whose picture appeared on front pages from British Columbia to California, Washington, and Oregon to Idaho. Even so, he had been arrested for theft in the last year of his troubled life. He was a consummate con man who never used his superior intelligence for anything but the next scam.

Was Bill Stevens responsible for any of the sexual assaults or deaths of young women in Washington and Oregon? I don't know. Was he the Green River Killer?

No. He liked to frighten women as he had scared his tenant in Oregon. I wouldn't be at all surprised if he had planned to scare the woman who left the Beaverton bar with a stranger. The "body" in the "open grave" she saw might well have only been one of Stevens's mannequins.

46

By 1990, THE GREEN RIVER Task Force's days were numbered, its manpower and assets siphoned off into the county's Major Crimes Unit, and then the detectives were quietly reassigned. Where Frank Adamson's task force had once had seventy people, including clerical support staff, Bobby Evans had only seventeen, and they were much easier to disassemble without fanfare.

Fifteen million dollars and a tremendous amount of work and dedication hadn't brought the real killer to his knees. Some of the best detectives in America had stepped up to the plate, full of energy and confidence, and struck out. One of the F.B.I. special agents— Paul Lindsay—had been so sure that he would find the man who had murdered at least four dozen women. In the end, Lindsay said to Frank Adamson, "Captain, I am humbled."

The others who had hung in for so long probably felt the same way.

Dave Reichert, the youthful detective of 1982, had some lines in his face now and his hair was shot with gray. He was promoted to sergeant and moved out of the task force. When Mertie Winston, Tracy's mother, met with him and pleaded with him not to give up the search for the man who had killed her daughter and so many others, Reichert tried to explain to her that he wasn't quitting—he never would—but he was in a command position and he couldn't command the people he had worked beside.

Some of the task force investigators had retired, some were dead, and many of them had lost heart. In the prior eighteen months, two of their most likely suspects had been cleared. It was difficult to believe they would ever again execute a search warrant that wouldn't turn out to be a bitter disappointment.

Every so often, another skull turned up in some godforsaken spot, but the public seemed jaded about it now. Even as the possibility that William Stevens might be the GRK still existed in October 1989, the remains of a woman who had been missing since 1983 were found just south of the SeaTac Airport. The skeleton was within fifty yards of the remains of three other victims—Mary Bridget Meehan, Connie Naon, and Kelly Ware. An Alaska Airlines employee found it as he was clearing brush, and Dr. Reay's office tried to establish who the vacant-eyed skull had once been.

Through the long Green River siege, Bill Haglund had become expert at comparing the jaws and teeth of the lost girls to the hundreds of dental records he had gathered. Forensic odontology is a technique that has emerged as a significant tool of forensic science. A human's teeth are unique—not as individual as DNA or the whorls and ridges of fingerprints, but unique nonetheless. Size, shape, placement in the mouth, and chipped, broken, and missing teeth hold a kind of silent history of who that person is, or was. Furthermore, victims of murder and sex crimes often have bite marks that can be used to identify their attackers.

In his job as the chief investigator for the King County Medical Examiner's Office since 1983, Haglund had been called upon again and again to find a name and a life to fit the pathetic bones ravaged first by a killer and then by animals and the elements. Despite his somber job, he was a pleasure to know, a gentle man with a great sense of humor.

One evening each Christmas season, I got together with my neighbor Cherisse Luxa, the longtime task force member who oversaw the records for still-missing Green River victims and did her share of digging and sifting in the wilderness. We looked forward to an invitation to dinner at Bill and Claudia Haglund's north-end home. Bill's pets and avocation usually stayed in his basement, and in their cages. He raised boa constrictors.

While I am afraid of rats and certain big hairy spiders, I've never been afraid of snakes, so one of my oddest holiday rituals was to get my picture taken with Bill Haglund's twenty-plus-foot boa constrictor. Since few of the Haglunds' dinner guests, including Cherie, cared to spend up-close time with his pets, Bill was happy to drape one of the snakes around my neck. It was my third or fourth Christmas when I discovered that while boa constrictors aren't poisonous, they do have teeth. Fortunately, the young snake I was holding bit Bill and not me. He laughed, but I quickly handed his newest pet back to him.

Whenever I look at photographs of a grim-looking Haglund at a body site, I remember how much he cares for the families of victims and what a warm heart he has. Long after the worst of the Green River saga was over, he spent months working for the United Nations in Bosnia-Herzegovina and Rwanda, helping to identify unknown victims of terrorism who had been buried in mass graves. Cheri Luxa also went to Bosnia and even rescued some Croatian kittens and brought them home with her.

HAGLUND had gathered more than two hundred sets of dental charts, mostly from Seattle area women, but some included missing persons from Florida, Oklahoma, and Montana. He had identified Debra Estes because he'd memorized her unique dental characteristic—a stainless-steel crown. Now he reconstructed the jaw of the latest possible victim. A missing nineteen-year-old named Andrea Childers was initially added to the Green River list in April 1983, but she'd been taken off when records at the Canadian border noted that someone with the same name had crossed into British Columbia a year later.

Like Missy Draper's, dark-eyed Andrea's dental records showed a distinct gap between her upper middle teeth. Haglund looked at the teeth in the skull and realized that Andrea hadn't gone to Canada; she had been hidden just off the Strip for six years. She was victim number forty-one.

Even though bloodhounds and searchers had combed the area where Andrea's remains were found years later, they had missed her. "When someone's buried," Captain Bobby Evans said, "unless you know a grave is there, you can walk right over the site and never even know it." Evans believed that there were many more victims yet to be found than anyone realized. "There are at least eight, and I'm convinced there are more."

Andrea had grown up in southern California, but she moved to Seattle when she was sixteen to live with her father and stepmother. She'd been very close to her eighty-five-year-old grandmother who cried as she remembered the last time she saw Andrea. "She wanted to be a dancer. She gave lessons and she was very good, and she taught dance exercise," Helen Koehler remembered. "She came for a late birthday celebration [in 1983]—her birthday was March 29. She was wearing a beautiful dress and a long gray coat. I baked her a chocolate cake. She kissed me, like always, and then she left."

OTHER MEDICAL EXAMINERS' personnel might have thrown out old dental records that seemed no longer to have any relevance, but not Bill Haglund and Dr. Don Reay. "This whole case is so freaky,"

Haglund said, "that I am almost paranoid about getting rid of anything."

None of the Green River Task Force regimes—from Dick Kraske's to Frank Adamson's through Jim Pompey's and Greg Boyle's to Bob Evans's—had gotten rid of anything either. The first computers had been about as modern as a treadle-powered sewing machine, but the newest computer system was a marvel, and it contained photos and text and even images of scribbled notes on matchbooks and torn pieces of paper. Nine thousand pieces of evidence remained in the Green River archives.

Try to imagine your own life, as if you had pressed every corsage, saved every letter, taken photos of each piece of jewelry you ever owned, every garment, dirt samples from the yard of every residence, all your lost baby teeth, locks of your hair, all the artifacts of your days on earth. That may give you some idea of the depth and breadth of the Green River files. Each victim's section was at least two thousand pages long; some were ten times that count. And as anyone familiar with police files knows, so many promising interviews end in disappointment, but the text of each was preserved.

Tom Jensen had joined the Green River Task Force in 1984, and there had once been fifty detectives working on it with him. Now for a long while Jensen was the only "keeper of the flame." Jensen is a friendly, Scandinavian-looking man with dark blond red hair and mustache. There must have been many times when he wished for another assignment, because it was such a tortuous case. But he stayed because he worried about what would happen to the cases if he left. Later Jim Doyon joined him, but the rows and rows of files had to be intimidating. How could two detectives ever hope to follow up on all those tips?

Just because the task force had disbanded didn't mean that new reports weren't coming in. Wives, ex-wives, and girlfriends continued to call me throughout the 1990s, each of them convinced that the men they had once loved were, in truth, serial killers—and probably the Green River Killer. I passed the most credible information on to Tom Jensen, knowing that probably all he could do was feed the facts into the computer on the chance there might be a hit with information someone else had reported.

Despite the intrusiveness of local reporters who had no compunction about publishing information the task force wanted kept secret, the Green River investigators did manage to play some of their cards close to their vests. "We were excited by these microscopic pinkish glass beads the crime lab detected on some of the victims," Frank Adamson recalled. "They looked as if they were very rare. We were feeling pretty good at first, but the F.B.I. lab told us what they were, and that they were really quite common. Almost anyone who drives on highways has some of those on their cars. The beads were from reflector stuff on road signs, or in paint used to paint the center lines."

In February 1988, the F.B.I. had listed the commonalities among the Green River victims in the case they called "Greenmurs: MAJOR CASE #771." Maybe all the dead girls weren't known in very many places in America, but the Bureau recognized their deaths as some of the most important the Behavioral Science Unit had ever helped investigate.

The B.S.U. noted that all the victims were found outdoors, and that there was precious little physical evidence left behind. A few of the dead girls had their clothing scattered near their bodies; most were nude. The public did not know that Opal Mills was the only victim whose body held evidence of a blood group other than her own. Semen in her vagina was from a man with Type O blood; Opal had Type A blood.

Moira Bell, who survived her attack at Horsetail Falls in Oregon, had described the two-inch-wide, beige masking tape that was used to bind her wrists and arms. She also remembered that the knife used to stab her was a French butcher-block type of kitchen knife with a straight wooden handle and a straight edge, approximately eight inches long in a triangular shape, wider at the handle.

Many of the victims had had tiny fibers on their bodies. With a tool called a spinarette, crime lab technicians (like the Western Washington State Police lab's resident fiber expert Chesterine Cwiklik) can find all manner of matches with minuscule fibers. Indeed, some of the strongest evidence against Ted Bundy were five distinctive fibers that could be linked to him found in the van he used in 1979 to kidnap twelve-year-old Kimberly Leach, the murder that he paid for in Florida's electric chair. Rug fibers had also helped convict Wayne Williams, the Atlanta Child Murderer.

In the Green River evidence room, there were: blue acrylic fibers, green acrylic fibers, red acrylic fibers, black polyester fibers, and green carpetlike fibers, all found with the victims' remains. Missy Plager and Alma Smith both had "blue" dog hairs on their remains.

Interestingly, there were also paint particles found on eight of the victims: red enamel, medium brown enamel, medium blue metallic "nitrocellulose lacquer with fragmentary light gray primer," and medium blue metallic paint. "None of the above-described paint particles is typical of—or consistent with—any type of original motor vehicle finish system," Skip Palenik had reported. "A particular source or origin of these particles cannot be determined." And eighteen of the victims had foreign hairs on them, hair that had not come from their own heads or bodies.

There had been at least eight vehicle sightings—five different pickup trucks, a green station wagon, and two blue station wagons: among them a full-size American-made light-colored truck, 1960–64; a 1970–77 (possible Ford) perhaps white over blue; an older 1960s GMC or Chevrolet pickup, turquoise green; a burgundy pickup; a two-toned brown pickup—and on and on. Some witnesses had reported numerous "sanded" spots painted with primer, as if the pickups were in the process of being repainted. There was a definite preference for pickup trucks, and all the vehicles were American made. None of them had been brand-new, and many had campers or canopies on the back.

When it came to describing the man (or men) last seen with the victims, there was even more variation. Witnesses tend to be less observant when they are upset or frightened, of course. They are most often wrong about height. And it would be learned in retrospect that many of the women the GRK encountered, the women who got away, never reported it. They were either too frightened or in a business where their view of the police was not favorable.

All the Seattle-area witnesses had said the suspect was Caucasian with blond to light-brown hair, and between five feet eight inches to five feet eleven inches tall. He was almost always described as being in his early to midthirties. And he usually wore a plaid shirt and sometimes a baseball cap. Most of the witnesses who had seen the dead and missing girls for the last time thought the man they left with had a mustache, a scrubby little mustache. In essence, he was "Mr. Average," driving down a busy highway in a nondescript pickup truck.

But *who* was he? And *where* was he?

Like most people, I tended to believe the Green River Killer was either dead or in prison. Every once in a while the news services would carry stories about a breakout of serial murder in some state far away from the Northwest and I would wonder if he was there now, But usually there was an arrest and it wasn't anyone who sounded like the King County description.

Tom Jensen and Jim Doyon manned the massive Green River Task Force computer, and then the state-of-the-art computers that took over the job as technology moved forward. They stood guard over files stacked to the ceiling that held a seemingly endless outpouring of tips and information, much of it disturbing and macabre. And still they had not found their man.

PART THREE

47

2001. IT WAS A NEW CENTURY, and he hadn't moved away, at least not very far. He liked his life in King County, and he had years of job seniority that he didn't intend to lose. He had a wife who suited him. She was a homebody who took care of things there, paid the bills, kept the house nice, and trusted him.

That gave him a sound base to work from. It no longer mattered that for much of his life people had pegged him as slow or dumb. It was really an added bonus because he had taken on the big boys and beaten them handily. The newspapers were full of stories about how many detectives had tried to catch him, and how many millions of dollars they'd spent—and now they were all gone and he was living in a big new house with a great yard. He had tried to up the ante on the game by writing to them and giving them hints, but they hadn't seemed to connect him to his helpful advice. As far as he could figure it, the time they came snooping around at Kenworth and pawed through his house was just because he had been stopped on the highway too often. He knew he was only one of a lot of men who cruised the Strip. They hadn't been able to prove anything more than that. He had passed their lie detector tests, and that slowed them down. The rest of it was because he studied why other guys had been caught, and he made sure he didn't make mistakes.

They had come so close to him that it had unnerved him a little bit, but they went away with their hats in their hands. So who was dumb now? He could still drive by the places he had left the women and relive what he had done to them any time he wanted. He was hiding in plain sight, going over to Renton to work at Kenworth as he always had, and even though guys at work sometimes still called him Green River Gary, that wasn't so bad. It was a joke to them; nobody knew how right they were.

He had read a lot about Ted Bundy, and knew that Bundy was supposed to be practically a genius. But Bundy didn't last very long, and he didn't have nearly as many "kills" as Green River Gary.

■

GARY and Judith Ridgway had moved several times, and they'd always bought up. By 2001, they lived on S. 348th Street, with an address on the West Hill of Auburn. Their place was nicer than anything his parents ever had. He let Judith decorate it however she wanted. She liked "girly" stuff like dolls and artificial flowers and crocheted afghans and frilly lacy things on the couch and chair arms. They were both acquisitive, and they had about a dozen of everything because of the swap meets and garage sales they went to most weekends. Judith displayed the things she liked, and they stored extra stuff in boxes and bins in their spare bedrooms.

Their yard was showy, with lots of evergreens, rhododendrons, ferns, and flowers. Judith loved her flowers and he kept the lawn looking nice. Inside, she had more house plants than anyone they knew.

Judith's girls were now out on their own and his son, Chad, was in the marines. He and Judith could do pretty much whatever they wanted. They had a very fancy motor home, he had a practically new pickup, and she had a nice sedan. In another ten years, he could retire and they'd be set for life. They had some investments, the company retirement plan, and social security to count on. Judith liked that secure feeling; she even kept cash hidden in the house and in the motor home—stacks of five- and ten-dollar bills—so they'd always have grocery and gas money.

She didn't know everything about him, of course. There was a whole hell of a lot she didn't know. That was *his* life, the things that made him feel good. It wasn't that he wasn't being faithful to her. All men cheated. What she didn't know wouldn't hurt her.

THERE WERE THINGS he didn't know either. The task force wasn't really dead, after all; in computer language, it was in "standby mode." If it had been dead and buried as he thought it was, the room on the top floor of the King County Courthouse would no longer be full of black binders, physical evidence, and hundreds and hundreds of thousands of pages of follow-up information.

Frank Adamson had moved out to the new Criminal Justice Center south of the airport to become chief of the Criminal Investigation Division; Bob Keppel got his doctorate, wrote a couple of well-received books, and taught an immensely popular course called Homicide at the University of Washington all through the nineties. Dave Reichert had moved up through the ranks of the brass in the sheriff's office.

In early 1997, there would be big changes in the sheriff's office.

Sheriff Jim Montgomery was offered the job of police chief in suburban Bellevue, and he accepted. That meant that King County had a vacancy for sheriff. Frank Adamson passed on the offer from King County executive Ron Sims. Adamson was looking forward to retirement, and so were several other command officers Montgomery considered.

Dave Reichert was almost fifty, and his hair, although still thick, was rapidly turning silver. His enthusiasm for higher office continued, and he wanted to be the sheriff of King County. He was happy to accept Sims's appointment in 1997. Adamson supported Reichert, and so did many others in the sheriff's department. Remembering how hard Reichert had worked on the Green River Task Force, I was glad to help raise money for his campaign when the next sheriff's election came up. He proved to be a natural politician; a mature, handsome, and assured man instead of the "Davy" he had been back in 1982. He won the election easily and was, at long last, in a position to reopen the hunt for the man who had evaded him and scores of others for almost twenty years.

Unlike most of the men who had been sheriff, Reichert usually wore his full uniform rather than a business suit. He was still a cop, and he had kept himself in top physical condition, working out and lifting weights as he always had. During the World Trade Organization convention that brought riots to Seattle in 2000, news cameras caught Reichert chasing down looters who had just smashed the window of a jewelry store. It was reassuring in a time of chaos to see the sheriff himself out there in the streets dealing with lawlessness. He admitted with a grin, however, that he couldn't run as fast as he had twenty years ago.

If Gary Ridgway was obsessed with killing hapless young women, Dave Reichert was obsessed with tracking him down and seeing him arrested and convicted. It was really no contest. Throughout the years, I had always believed that Reichert, Randy Mullinax, Tom Jensen, Jim Doyon, Matt Haney, and Sue Peters would one day catch the Green River Killer. As the new sheriff, Reichert sometimes said to me, "Ann, we're going to catch him—and then you can write the book."

And I always said, "I know, and I will."

As the world entered the millennium, the investigators who had worked on the Green River cases for so long had shifted their focus from the men they had suspected most in 1982 to 1984. But some of them were difficult to forget. Tom Jensen kept himself aware of where Gary Ridgway was. "Why doesn't he leave—move to California or some other place," he wondered. "I believe he thinks he's gotten away with it. He has no need to leave." Jensen believed that when Ridgway passed the polygraph he felt he was home free.

After the task force was revived, both Reichert and Jensen suspected they were watching the right man, even though Melvyn Foster was still around and occasionally talking about the case. The people who were definitely *not* talking about it were the Green River Task Force members. If an arrest was imminent, the public had no inkling.

November 30, 2001, was a Friday, and the wind whipped and tore angrily as a pounding rain fell, making commuter traffic at the beginning of a weekend even worse than usual. By late afternoon the storm grew in intensity. It was high tide and the waves of Puget Sound were crashing high over my bulkhead. But there was something else in the air, something almost undefinable. A ripple of rumors, barely distinguishable at first from other whispers that something big might be happening in the Green River case. Such rumors had, of course, boomed to megaphone-like shouts several times over the prior twenty years, and then subsided.

My phone rang often that afternoon, and either reporters or cops I knew asked, "Have you heard that they might have him?"

No, I hadn't. We all knew who they meant by "him" without speaking it aloud. I hadn't heard anything. But something *was* up. By five that afternoon, all three major network affiliates sent reporters and cameramen to my house. I was usually a dependable "talking head" for any story connected to serial murder or the Green River cases when official sources were clamming up. And at the moment, the sheriff's office wasn't saying anything, but reporters had tracked detectives to the Kenworth plant and to Judith and Gary Ridgway's home near Auburn.

My phone rang again around six. The answering machine picked it up. It was Dave Reichert, his voice full of barely contained enthusiasm. "We caught him, Ann," he said. *"We've arrested the Green River Killer!"*

FOR ME, it was one of those moments when I will always remember just where I was when I heard the news. Pearl Harbor. Kennedy's assassination. Ted Bundy's arrest. The explosion of the *Challenger*. And now, after nineteen and a half years: *"We've arrested the Green River Killer!"*

I saved the tape of Dave Reichert's triumphant and yet incredulous voice telling me that what had seemed impossible had finally come to pass.

I had written nineteen books while I was waiting for the Green River story to end in an arrest, always thinking that surely it would be my next book, always deciding not to throw away any of the files of information—just in case. As a crime writer, I was elated. And yet Gary Ridgway's arrest was the beginning of a kind of horror that no one who had followed the Green River story could even have imagined.

In the end, there would be nothing hidden, no hideous detail omitted in what would become the hardest story I ever had to tell.

48

IT HAD TAKEN so long, and yet when it came together, all the ragged segments glided into place perfectly. Even so, the arrest had been precipitous. The investigators weren't quite ready to pounce. Ironically, Ridgway's own actions put a crimp in their plans and the detectives had to move in.

On November 16, 2001, he had told his wife, Judith, that his truck was low on gas and she gave him thirty dollars to fill the tank. She didn't often give him more money than he needed to buy breakfast or lunch. But on this day, the thirty dollars in Ridgway's wallet apparently spiked old appetites.

He slowed down when he spotted an attractive young woman strolling provocatively along the curb on the Pac HiWay. And then he pulled out the money his wife had given him and waved it at the girl. She asked him what he wanted to buy. He told her—and she promptly arrested him. Gary Ridgway had been tricked by a decoy prostitute, an undercover deputy who was working in another unit and was unaware of the task force's plans for him. He was arraigned on a charge of loitering for prostitution, but was soon released on his own recognizance.

HE WASN'T really worried, thinking that it would cost him only the towing charge on his truck. Judith had never doubted his word and he could explain it to her as a case of mistaken identity. She trusted him completely and never questioned his explanations. He was totally unaware that his name had become number one on a dark list.

Not many of the detectives who worked the Green River murders from the very beginning remained to see the ending. Just as the passage of twenty years changes all lives, retirements, transfers, new jobs, illnesses, and deaths had decimated the roster of those investigators who began the quest for justice in 1982. Only those who were in their twenties and early thirties at the beginning were still on the sheriff's department. Despite all the sixty-plus-year-old actors who play detectives on television cop shows, there are precious few sexagenarians who still wear a badge in real life.

As the world entered the millennium, most of the investigators who had worked on the Green River cases for years had shifted their focus from the men they had originally suspected from 1982 to 1984. But some of them were difficult to forget.

There were many detectives who had never found Gary Ridgway a credible suspect in the Green River killings, preferring those with more complicated and sophisticated personalities. And there was just a handful who had always thought the deceptively meek and ordinary-looking man was exactly who they should be concentrating on.

Randy Mullinax, who had been with the first and second task forces, had written Ridgway off after he passed two polygraph tests. Mullinax came to law enforcement almost as an afterthought. One of several brothers who grew up in the south-end Boulevard Park community, he married at twenty and went to work for the Water District in Burien, Washington, but not for long. "I got tired of using my back," he recalled, "and standing outside in the rain, so I went to college."

Mullinax took a few police science courses as electives and soon found himself hooked. He had hired on with the King County Sheriff's Office in January 1979. Sue Peters and Mullinax had joined the sheriff's office within three years of each other and worked together on the Green River investigation in the eighties.

Peters never really thought about law enforcement as a career either. She had always planned to be a physical education teacher, but when she earned her degree in P.E. at Central Washington University, she found that teaching jobs in her field weren't plentiful. She wasn't really disappointed, because another career had been tugging on her sleeve for years. From the time she was a child, Peters spent her summers east of the Cascade Mountains in Ritzville,

Washington, where her grandmother was a deputy sheriff in rural Adams County. In those days, female deputies worked only with women prisoners or as matrons in the jail, but even so Peters was fascinated with the mystique of police work. As a teenager, she hung "Wanted" posters on her wall instead of those featuring rock stars. Peters graduated from the police academy in May 1982, two months before Wendy Coffield's body was found floating in the Green River. As a young deputy, she had joined Dave Reichert on the second river body site, but Peters wouldn't actually be assigned to the Green River Task Force until 1986. After working patrol for three years, she went undercover with a proactive narcotics team investigating drug traffic in high schools—she could easily look like a teenager. She also investigated sexual assault cases.

Ralf McAllister, who had died of a sudden heart attack—and whose wife, Nancy, took his place on the task force—had always been one of those who felt Ridgway was probably the Green River Killer. Frank Atchley was one of the few who shared this conviction. But it was Matt Haney, who had been absolutely convinced that Ridgway was guilty and tracked him doggedly in 1986 and 1987, who was the most disappointed when interest in the truck painter faded.

"Everything fit, when Randy and I went to Las Vegas and, as a last resort, agreed to have Paige Miley hypnotized to see what she could remember about the man who asked her about 'Star' [Kim Nelson/aka Tina Tomson]," Haney recalled. "And her directions to the police artist gave us a drawing that looked just like Ridgway. Randy and I had been assigned to track down the owner of the burgundy red pickup with the white canopy, and we found that Ridgway had a truck like that. That was the one that Marie Malvar's family found in his driveway."

Paige Miley insisted that she had memorized the license number of the red pickup truck, jotted it down on a scrap of paper, and called it in to the first Green River Task Force. Unfortunately, the detective whose name she gave did not recall whether he had followed up the lead, and three years later, even with hypnosis, Paige couldn't remember it. She believed it began with a K and had a 1, followed by four or five numbers. It wasn't enough information to trace. In the first two years, there was such an avalanche of tips coming in that no one could be blamed for inadvertent mishaps that, in retrospect, became important.

Back then, Tom Jensen, keeper of the computer, was one of the detectives who dismissed Ridgway with a shrug. He was adamant that Gary Ridgway's two clean polygraph tests proved that he could not be the Green River Killer, saying that any continued belief that he was the one was only smoke and mirrors.

Haney knew Randy Mullinax was sick of hearing Ridgway's name. "Randy and I were, and are, great friends and he's a good detective, but he didn't think Ridgway was the killer and he couldn't bring himself to investigate him any longer. He left the task force in 1986 or '87."

When Haney lost Mullinax as a partner that year, he got a new one. "Sue Peters transferred in and became my partner," Haney, now the chief of police of Bainbridge Island, Washington, remembered being enthusiastic about that. "Sue's the best homicide detective in the King County Sheriff's Office," he said, "the best interviewer."

Haney had left the King County force after the task force was dissolved and was recruited by two Alaskan police departments, first King Salmon on Bristol Bay and later Homer. Aleut natives were not fond of police officers, but Haney was welcomed. They thought he was an "Outside Native," while in truth he is half-Korean. "I'm a war baby," he said with a smile, "adopted in 1956."

Haney loved Alaska, but after six years he deferred to his family's desire for less snow and more daylight in the winter, and came back to Washington State. He was quickly hired as a lieutenant by Chief Bill Cooper of the Bainbridge Island Police Department. He had only worked for his new department for two weeks when, in mid-October 2001, he got an on-duty phone call from Sue Peters.

"I have to talk to you," she said.

"Good," Haney said. "We'll have lunch soon."

"No, Randy and I have to talk to you *tonight*."

It was nine o'clock, but whatever was on Peters's mind was urgent. Haney agreed to take the ferry to the mainland and meet Peters and Mullinax near midnight at the latter's house in South King County. If Haney had been the type to gloat and say "I told you so," this would have been the time to do it.

"When I got there, Sue and Randy were sitting by the fireplace," Haney recalled, "and Sue said, 'Matt, you were right all along. We're focusing on Gary.' Mullinax nodded. 'It's Ridgway. We have DNA.' "

"It was great just being able to tell him," Peters said later, "because that was someone he 'worked' for a while. Our team would be coming back together, but we didn't have a minute to let it sink in."

Haney recalled a meeting Dave Reichert had called six months earlier for all former task force members to discuss the possibility that an advanced DNA test might work on body fluids and hairs found with Opal Mills and Carol Christensen's bodies. Matt Haney and Jim Doyon had taken Gary Ridgway to the Kent Police Department fourteen years earlier as multiple search warrants, under Haney's direction, were served on the extended Ridgway family properties. Although a superior court judge had felt at the time that it would be too invasive to demand a blood sample from Gary Ridgway, he had permitted the part of the search warrant that sought hairs from his head and pubic area, and added, "Saliva samples will be allowed."

Fortunately, reporters hadn't thought to stake out the police facilities in Kent, and that was where WSP criminalist George Johnston had handed Ridgway the small square of gauze and asked him to chew on it. Haney and Doyon oversaw the pulling and plucking of hair samples, and all this possible physical evidence had remained pristinely preserved in a freezer.

But Haney had heard nothing more after that. Now he learned that in March 2001, Tom Jensen had submitted biological samples from six victims to the Washington State Patrol Crime Lab in the hope that criminalists would find semen and be able to isolate DNA. Forensic scientist Beverly Himick compared the vaginal swabs from Marcia Chapman to Gary Ridgway's known DNA and got a positive match. Pubic hair combings from Opal Mills also carried his DNA.

At the WSP lab, criminalist Jean Johnston had also accomplished a positive match. She reported that a tiny bit of sperm on a vaginal swab from Carol Christensen's body was so consistent with Ridgway's DNA that only one person in the entire world, save an identical twin, would have this DNA profile.

Sue Peters explained to Haney that Dave Reichert was about to start up a secret task force to surveil and hopefully arrest Gary Ridgway. And Haney was the detective who knew Ridgway the best, the one who had always been convinced that he was the Green River Killer.

"We need you back with us," Peters said. "But you can't tell anyone—not even your new chief. He has to loan you to us blind. No questions answered."

Chief Bill Cooper wasn't thrilled about letting Haney go back to King County without a good reason, but Haney just shook his head and said he couldn't tell him why. Cooper finally asked, "Does this have something to do with your past?"

"Yes," Haney said.

"Okay. You can go. Tell me about it later."

IN November 2001 the reborn task force emerged. Haney, Peters, and Mullinax would be as close to the heart of the Green River probe as any investigator ever was—too close, perhaps, for them to ever completely stop thinking about it. It would play like a subliminal song in their brains twenty-four hours a day for month upon month.

There were also a number of detectives on the reactivated investigation who had been teenagers when the seemingly endless stream of murders began. The Green River Task Force became charged with energy again, albeit so quietly that the public didn't realize its vitality, and in mid-November, the probe began to hum. Ironically, the man who was now dead center in their sights obviously believed he was home free. Gary Leon Ridgway, the truck painter, had long since returned to his old haunts and sexual obsessions.

THE PAC HIWAY WAS a far less friendly environment for prostitutes than it had been twenty years earlier. The cheap motels were either cheaper or gone completely, and there were many more upscale hotels constructed close to the airport. Casey Treat, a minister made popular by his television appearances, presided over a huge church complex he had built at the south end of the onetime Strip, and most of the legitimate businesses and stores had expanded.

Even so, there were teenage girls whose purpose for being on the highway was obvious—some of them second-generation prostitutes, the daughters and nieces of the lost young women of the eighties. One of them was Keli McGinness's daughter, who had been adopted when Keli never returned for her. She had grown into a beautiful woman, even lovelier than the mother she couldn't remember. Sue Peters, who was assigned Keli's case, found her daughter instead. The girl was alive and well, but in as much potential danger as her mother once was. Peters did her best to persuade the young woman to contact Keli's extended family.

There were other circular patterns that had emerged in the twenty-year search for the Green River Killer. Was it possible that tracing the similarities would help to build a circumstantial case against Gary Ridgway to add to the positive DNA results the task force had?

It would seem so.

The detectives assigned to the new, clandestine task force pored over all of the earlier information gleaned on Ridgway, looking for anything that might have been missed, evaluating his past in light of what they now knew, and searching for what motivation he could have had to kill dozens of women. He had been married three times, but Green River investigators who located his first two wives were told that his mother never really let go of running his life.

His first wife, Heather, wasn't a "slim blonde" as he'd once claimed. She had been an overweight brunette teenager, and their marriage had been fine for the first few months. She remembered that she and Gary had made some friends in San Diego, playing cards and visiting back and forth.

"Her father and I never could see why Heather married him," Heather's mother said. "When they were dating, he would come to our house and sit there like a stump. He never ate, never said a word. One day, he sat in a chair for about eight hours—and he didn't speak to us at all. He didn't even get up to go to the bathroom, for that matter. But we figured Heather must have seen something in him we couldn't see. He seemed affectionate with her, and when he was in the Philippines, he sent us one of those velvet paintings for Christmas. It sounds strange to say now, but we thought at least Heather would be safe with him as a husband, and we thought his mother was very nice."

Heather had been surprised, though, to see how shocked Gary was by the price of things in San Diego. "He'd never had to pay for anything before," she said. "His mother, Mary, had always bought everything for him. And he was afraid people would steal things from him, too. At night, he didn't just lock our car, he took out the radio and what he said were very expensive parts from the engine because he said somebody might steal them."

Heather's opinion about Mary Ridgway would change radically after the young couple returned, albeit separately, from San Diego after Gary got out of the navy. It was true that Heather didn't drive up to Seattle with him, but that was because she was taking a course in school in San Diego, and Gary wouldn't wait for her to finish. He wanted to get home to his mother.

"When Heather flew up a few weeks later, Mary wouldn't hear of their getting their own apartment," Heather's mother recalled. "She wanted them to live in a camper on her property, and they ended up moving into the house with her and Tommy. Mary ruled the roost—I felt sorry for her husband. She made Gary give her his paycheck, and he and Heather had to go to her to get a few dollars a day."

Mary Ridgway kept Gary's checkbook and she had to okay any purchase they wanted to make. She wouldn't even let her daughter-in-law get her ears pierced without her permission. "Heather saw it wasn't going to change. She just packed her bag and went back to San Diego—she's lived there ever since," her mother said. "Gary held on to everything they had. We'd given them all the appliances you could think of—toaster, Mixmaster, blender, things like that—and he kept them. But Heather had a real nice white bed and her grandmother made her a canopy for it. Heather wanted that. Well, I called Mary Ridgway to ask about it and she just screamed at me. I've never heard anyone so furious."

Gary demanded Heather's rings back, even though the diamond was almost too small to see, and the set had cost only a hundred dollars. Heather remained in San Diego for thirty years, and she never saw Gary again.

Jim Doyon, Matt Haney, and Carolyn Griffin had talked in depth to Gary Ridgway's second wife, Dana, in September 1986. While Heather had only lasted a year with him, Dana stayed seven and bore his only child, their son, Chad. "I was his housekeeper, secretary—I did everything for him—all his laundry. But I never saw his paychecks or anything. I never saw his pay stubs. Most of the times on weekends, we spent at his parents'. He never wanted to have any friends."

Heather had never mentioned any unusual sexual demands, but Gary had apparently been more adventurous with his second wife. Although Dana said she hated it, he insisted on anal sex and he sometimes tied her hands and feet with belts from bathrobes. She didn't mind that so much because it didn't hurt her.

But once he had choked her. They had been out someplace and she'd had too much beer. "I was a little drunk," Dana told the detectives, "and I got out of our van and stumbled. I started to reach for the door and the next thing I knew he had his hands around my neck and he was choking me from behind."

The hands on her throat grew tighter and tighter and Dana said she had started to scream. "I realized it was him and I started fighting him. He finally let go and he kind of pushed me. By the time I got my balance back, he had walked around to the other side of the van and tried to convince me that there was somebody else there who had run off. I tried to get him to call the police, but he wouldn't."

She explained to Jim Doyon that Gary had first put his fore-arm around her neck in a "police-type choke hold," and then had grasped her throat with both hands. That hurt her and frightened her because he was much rougher than usual. "He always liked to sneak up on me and scare me. He would hide around the corner or something and scare me. He was always coming up behind me and taking me in this arm-type hold—not to hurt me, just to grab me. He liked to see how softly he could walk so that he'd be just totally noiseless, and he could do it, too!"

As he would later do with Darla, his hiking girlfriend from Parents Without Partners, Gary had enjoyed having oral sex in his vehicles and particularly liked to have sex outside. Dana remem-bered their spreading blankets in a wooded area near Ken's Truck Stop off the old I-90 highway. And he had other favorite places—Greenwater east of Enumclaw and close by the Green River. They often rode their bikes along Frager Road, next to the river.

"Did you ever stop and have sex along the Green River?" Doyon asked.

"Geez, yes . . . lots of places," Dana answered, a little embar-rassed.

"Where?"

"On the banks, in the tall grass."

NOW MATT HANEY and Jim Doyon revisited the mass of circum-stantial evidence they had uncovered fourteen years earlier, once again incredulous that it hadn't resulted in the discovery of absolute physical evidence during the 1987 search warrants.

That September, Haney and Doyon had picked Dana up early in the morning and they began a long, meandering drive as she di-rected them to various locations where Gary had taken her during their marriage. The hairs had stood up on the backs of their necks as they realized they were being taken on a tour of most of the body-cluster sites, although they hadn't told Dana that. First, they'd headed northeast on Highway 18 until they reached the I-90 junc-tion, then turned toward North Bend and the road near Ken's Truck Stop. Dana had pointed out places where she and Gary had once stopped to have outdoor sex. They'd also come close to unofficial garbage dumps and a spot where Gary had enjoyed sliding down snow-covered slopes in an inner tube. Headed south, they'd reached the area east of Enumclaw along Highway 410.

Dana had even pointed out that the Mountain View Cemetery

Road was a favorite shortcut for Gary, although she hadn't recognized the Star Lake site. New construction made it look entirely different from the way it had a year or two earlier. She'd indicated many spots along Frager Road where she and Gary had made love: next to the PD&J Meat Company, under a large tree near the Meeker Street (Peck) Bridge, and in Cottonwood Park.

When Haney asked if she and Gary had ever gone to any areas near the SeaTac Airport, she nodded. "We used to pick blackberries and apples near the empty houses—close to the runway lights."

Like Heather before her, Dana had quickly discerned that Mary Ridgway "wore the pants" in her family. If Gary wanted to buy a truck with money from his own bank account, Mary wouldn't let him withdraw the cash until he agreed to buy the pickup she and his father had chosen. As for Tommy Ridgway, Gary's father, he'd had little clout in the family. Mary screamed and scolded him much of the time. Once, she got so angry with him that she had broken a plate over his head. Dana had come to feel sorry for her father-in-law.

Although Mary Ridgway often criticized Dana's housekeeping or accused her of neglecting Chad's health, the two women reached an uneasy peace because Gary was very devoted to his mother. He worried about her and sought her approval.

Oddly, just as Dana and Gary moved in together in 1972, Mary Ridgway told her son that she was receiving threatening and obscene phone calls. "Gary would go and give her a ride to her car [at work] and make sure it was okay," Dana said. Gary had even told Dana that some man had exposed himself to his mother.

"You never knew who it was that was threatening his mother?"

Dana shook her head. "No. No. But it went so far that she got a gun and carried it with her. There was somebody—a man—calling and making suggestions over the phone."

Dana didn't mention anything about Gary's alleged jealousy when she went out dancing with friends or stayed until closing at the Eagles' Lodge, and they didn't ask her. According to her, their marriage had ended for more mundane reasons. "There was no communication," she said. "There was no real relationship. I felt that he just wanted somebody to keep a house clean for him and do the shopping and the cooking. He was always in the garage with his cars, working on them, doing something. All he wanted was food and sex, and that was it. Any time we did talk, it would end up in arguments."

Jim Doyon had asked if her husband ever verbally degraded or criticized her. "He ever call you a bitch or a whore when you were having sex? Ever try to slap you around? Knock you down? Keep you under his thumb, so to speak? Belittle you?"

And Dana had shaken her head. "No, no. He liked playing little games. Chased me around the house, and caught me in the hallway and took my clothes off there. You know, things like that."

Whatever Gary Ridgway might have done to strangers, he apparently hadn't carried any grossly perverted fantasies into his home—at least with his first two wives. A lot of men are intrigued with thoughts of bondage, far fewer with choking, and that activity had happened only once with Dana. So far, the investigation into his domestic life indicated that he was somewhat selfish, domineering with wives, but submissive to his mother.

Mary Ridgway had directed a large part of her son's life—his finances, his wives' housekeeping, child care, his clothes, his major purchases—and, not surprisingly, his first two wives had resented it, although each of them acknowledged that his reading skills were those of a third-grader and paperwork confused him.

It had been different with his third wife. Rather than resent her mother-in-law, Judith Ridgway had admired her. And Judith had been with Gary for twenty years. Indeed, Judith had apparently taken over Mary's role as Gary's caretaker. Green River investigators would find that she was anything but domineering, but in many areas of his third marriage, Judith handled their money as if Gary was a child who couldn't cope with the daily tasks of life. While he was a punctual and steady worker at Kenworth, she paid their bills and gave him spending money. They were both frugal people who preferred saving money to spending it.

Mary Ridgway died of colon cancer in the summer of 2001, and by then Judith had taken over the things Gary wasn't able to do well.

49

WHEN MATT HANEY returned to the Green River Task Force on loan from his new position on Bainbridge Island, he fully expected to be part of the team that would arrest and question Gary Ridgway. He was the resident "Ridgway expert." Just as he had carefully orchestrated the search warrants and sweeps of Ridgway's property in April of 1987, he now outlined the questions that he would ask Ridgway when he was arrested. Because Ridgway had solicited sex from the police officer decoy, the task force's time line had accelerated; they feared he was on the prowl for victims again. He'd been arrested before—back in the early eighties—and that hadn't stopped him from killing. Haney worked overtime, wanting to be sure he had an organized approach for his part on the postarrest interview team.

And then, Lieutenant Jim Graddon called Haney in to inform him that he had been removed from the roster of those who would interrogate Ridgway. "You'll be replaced by Jim Doyon," Graddon said flatly.

Evidently there had been a meeting among the brass where the decision was made. Haney had no quarrel with Doyon, and he wondered if the last-minute edict was because he was no longer officially a King County officer. He suspected they had decided it would look better for the department to have someone from inside the sheriff's office make Ridgway's arrest.

It was a bitter disappointment for Haney, particularly after he had taken such an abrupt leave from his new job with the Bainbridge Island police to come back to help in the Green River probe. But he accepted his new assignment from Reichert and Graddon. Haney would not be there to see the denouement of his long held conviction that Gary Ridgway was the Green River Killer. Instead, he would accompany Sue Peters and question Judith Ridgway at the exact time Gary Ridgway was being arrested, and try to get her out of their home before the media trapped her.

Shortly thereafter, Dave Reichert and King County prosecutor Norm Maleng would call a press conference to announce that Ridgway had been captured. All of it would be carried out with a virtual synchronization of watches, as meticulously choreographed as a military invasion.

Ridgway had no idea that the trap he had evaded for two decades was about to slam shut on him. He went to work as usual on Friday morning, November 30. Haney and Sue Peters had already contacted the Kenworth plant supervisors to let them know that there would be police activity that Friday, but there must be no forewarning to anyone at Kenworth.

First, Peters and Detective Jon Mattsen drove to the Kenworth plant to interview Ridgway. He had been under surveillance for weeks, but he didn't know it. When his boss told him someone wanted to talk to him about designing a truck, he walked toward the two detectives with no sign of recognition. He didn't remember Peters or Mattsen from earlier conversations, and seemed surprised to hear that they were from the sheriff's office.

They questioned him about Carol Christensen, telling him that her now-grown daughter wanted to know more about her, and they were following up on her mother's case. Ridgway didn't seem nervous as he looked from one detective to the other in response to their questions, his pale eyes blinking behind thick glasses. Yes, he said he had known Carol Christensen from going into the Barn Door Tavern.

"Did you ever date her?" Sue Peters asked.

He wasn't sure about that. It had been a long time ago. He remembered talking with her at the Barn Door. He seemed to be under the impression that the two investigators were looking for a witness who might be helpful in a trial someday should anyone ever be charged with Carol Christensen's murder. He had always enjoyed offering his theories on unsolved murder cases and now he seemed relaxed, even when their conversation continued for almost two hours. No sweat beaded on his forehead and his body language betrayed little tension.

The next question was very important to Peters and Mattsen. In evidence since May 1983 was the DNA that Carol Christensen's killer had left inside her vagina. "Did you ever have any sexual contact with Carol Christensen?" Peters asked as casually as she could.

He shook his head slightly. "No . . . no. I didn't."

Bingo. That was the wrong answer as far as the truth went, but it was the answer they needed in order to arrest him as the Green River Killer. Still, it wasn't quite time yet. Gary Ridgway smiled at the two detectives as they walked out into the rainy morning. He figured the only thing they could get him for was lying to a judge about propositioning the fake prostitute two weeks earlier.

After they left, he went to the lunchroom where he sat in his usual spot. He liked predictable routines. Changes disturbed him, but he hadn't even detected the slight flicker in the investigators' eyes as he denied having intercourse with Carol Christensen. Even though co-workers teased him a bit about the cops being there and asked if it was more Green River stuff, he was calm when he said "no." He was sure the police believed him.

He drank his usual cup of tea, but his stomach was a little queasy; he ignored the frosted brownie and the bag of peanuts Judith had put in his lunch.

On that last day of November 2001, he was working the seven AM to three PM shift, and he walked out the door a few minutes after three, heading through the heavy weather toward his truck, unaware of a camera clicking silently, frame after frame. Randy Mullinax and Jim Doyon were waiting just out of his line of sight, and they noted that he looked over his shoulder and around the parking lot, almost as if he expected someone. Even so, he jumped when they walked up to him and told him he was under arrest for murder, and read him his rights under Miranda.

Detective Paul Smith hadn't lived to see Gary Ridgway arrested; the marrow transfusion procedure to fight his leukemia had left him vulnerable to the infection that claimed his life when he was barely past forty. But now, Doyon and Mullinax placed Smith's handcuffs around Ridgway's wrists in a symbolic gesture that acknowledged Smith's dedication to the Green River cases. Later, they would give the cuffs to Smith's widow.

Mullinax and Doyon drove Gary Ridgway to the Regional Justice Center in Kent, where he was photographed wearing a plaid shirt and jeans—the attire so many witnesses had described. His face was expressionless. He was medium height, medium build, totally average-looking, a man who scarcely resembled what they believed him to be—the most infamous and prolific serial killer ever known in America.

Standing on the porch of a large house on a quiet street in Auburn, Sue Peters and Matt Haney were at Judith Ridgway's door at the same moment her husband was being arrested. It was a little after three on Friday afternoon when she let them in and led them through her crowded living room past Gary's exercycle. She seemed slightly surprised to see the two detectives, but certainly not shocked. She thought they were there to discuss Gary's recent arrest on the highway. She knew that was just a mistake because he had told her it was.

"We wanted to tell her that Gary was being arrested for some of the Green River murders before reporters got to her," Sue Peters recalled. "And we could see she didn't know why we were there."

On a normal Friday, Gary would have been home within a few minutes, asking about her day, telling her about his. Instead, he was in an interview room at the Regional Justice Center being questioned by Randy Mullinax and Jim Doyon. She didn't know that yet.

Judith had no objection to being interviewed and agreed to let Haney and Peters tape their questions and her answers. Sue Peters began by asking her if she knew that detectives had spoken to her husband earlier in the day.

"Yes," Judith said with a nod, but she didn't know why.

"And what we'd like to do is verify some information that he's provided," Peters said, "as well as ask you some questions about your background with Gary, and go from there. Okay?"

"Okay." She was a sparrowlike woman nearing sixty, neither fat nor thin, with blondish brown hair and little makeup. Matt Haney found her almost a cookie-cutter image of Gary's first two wives, none of them with his late mother's flair for makeup and fashion.

At Peters's request, Judith recalled the first time she'd met Gary at the White Shutters and their subsequent courtship. They had been together since 1985.

"What type of man was he [then]?"

"Oh, the best. Nice, sweet, gentle. . . . He comes home, and we're still best friends." She explained that Gary had few friends, just some men he talked to at work, although he didn't socialize with them. He would rather be with her.

"What about female friends—female acquaintances, not a relationship-type thing, but a friendship?" Peters asked.

"No. I don't know of any."

"So you pretty much keep to yourselves and do your own thing?"

"Yes. If I'm at the grocery store I'll, you know, notice what time it is. I know he's coming home and I want to be here when he comes home every day." Judith could not remember any trouble in her marriage or his prior unions, nothing more than slight arguments he might have had with his son's mother, Dana. When Chad was a little boy, Gary's mother had picked Chad up from his day care to bring him to Gary and Judith for his weekend visitations.

"Do you know why they broke up?"

"Oh, she [Dana] used to be a country-western singer and stayed out late with the band and groups, and he would be home babysitting. I don't know all those details," Judith said.

"He has mentioned that she was unfaithful to him. Do you know anything about that?"

"She was probably with some of the band people, maybe. I have no idea."

As for Gary's first wife, Judith knew virtually nothing about her. She had heard about some fight over furniture, but she thought that might have been Gary's brother's ex-girlfriend. Now that she thought about it, she didn't think it was Heather who had demanded her furniture.

"Was there anything in particular you can think about any of his ex-wives that made him angry about them?"

"*Real* angry? Not real bad anger. He's never been mad."

"Okay. Does he have a bad temper?"

"No."

"Have you ever seen him just out-of-control angry . . . or violent?"

"Not violent—he's raised his voice to me one time. It was just something minor. I don't remember exactly what it was."

"Has he ever struck you, ever grabbed you? Have you ever had the police respond to any of your residences on a domestic violence?"

"No! Heavens, no. No." Judith seemed shocked at the very idea of that.

"I'm just trying to get a better understanding of your relationship," Sue Peters explained.

"He's the best," Judith said firmly. She still hadn't asked them why they were questioning her. She and Gary got along just fine, always had.

"What's Gary's relationship with Chad?"

"Oh, it's wonderful. He's the best," Judith said. "They shake hands, give each other hugs. When it's his birthday, I'll send him some money. We forgot his birthday [this year] because so much was going on with Gary's mom, when she was sick. Chad is just like his dad. He's in the marines, eight years now, in Pendleton, California."

Judith said that the current year—2001—had been a difficult one for Gary. His mother had died of cancer and, at the end, he and Judith had taken turns caring for her so she could stay in her own home. His father had died in 1998 after a battle with Alzheimer's. After his father passed away, she and Gary had chosen their current house because it sat on a shy acre and had extra bedrooms. "We thought we were going to take care of his mother because his daddy died and his mother got sick."

"Did he [Tommy Ridgway] stay at home, or did he go to an outside facility?"

"He stayed at home mostly, and I would go and help his mother, help take care of his daddy. And Gary would stop by to see his father every single day after work. And his mom would have a glass of juice or coffee or a cookie on the table for him, and say 'Hi.' After his daddy died, he'd still stop by every day to make sure his mom was okay and to comfort her." But then Mary Ridgway was diagnosed with cancer. "They gave his mother ten months, and she died ten months to the day."

Judith spoke rapidly and breathlessly as if she were afraid of an empty spot in their conversation where they would tell her something she didn't want to hear, all the while adding positive strokes to her word portrait of her perfect husband, the perfect son. Gary and his two brothers were in the process of selling their parents' house. Judith felt that Gary's younger brother had always gotten more attention from their mother, but hastened to add that Mary was the "sweetest mother-in-law."

Mary had made the major decisions for the family, as Tommy, Gary's father, had been a quiet man. Gary's older brother was in charge of their parents' estate, but Judith wasn't sure what he did— he was a businessman of some kind who worked in a "big building" in downtown Seattle, while his younger brother was more of a "mountain man."

Peters asked about Gary and Judith's hobby of seeking out yard sales, swap meets, and discarded items they could use. "You don't have any particular areas where you'd go constantly, where, you know, people dump things—there was one on Highway 18 and I-90. . . ."

Puzzled, Judith shook her head. "Oh, we never go to places like that. If we went in that direction, we'd go to the campground, Leisure Time Resorts."

They both loved to camp out and had steadily upgraded their trucks and campers to the twenty-seven-foot Class-C Coachman that Peters and Haney had seen in the yard. Where their bathroom facilities had once been only "a coffee can," Judith said with a laugh, they now had the $22,000 motor home with its own bathroom. They spent long weekends and vacations in campgrounds in many spots in Washington and along the Oregon coast. They had gone to Canada a long time ago.

Peters changed the subject. "You were upset when we came to the door, and you mentioned that there had been something that just recently happened to Gary—out on Pacific HiWay. What do you know about that, Judith?"

"He told me that he stopped and had to close the window on the door on his truck—the back one—and that's why they came over and arrested him."

"Did he tell you what he was arrested for?"

"Well, he didn't exactly, but the officer that called and talked to me said it was 'soliciting.' I said, 'That can't be.' It didn't sound like him."

"What did the officer actually tell you?" Peters and Haney could see that Judith was either truly naive and trusting, or was trying to shade the truth.

"That some people's husbands go out and do things—" She fought now for composure.

"That the wives don't know about?" Haney asked.

"Um-hum."

"Did that upset you?"

"Well, yes. I got a little shook, but he wouldn't do anything like that. He's friendly. He's a friendly person. So he probably just looked at somebody and smiled."

"And you think the officer might have just arrested him because of that?" Peters asked.

"He's always friendly. Even when you're walking by somebody, like in a store or you're shopping, and, you know, he'll smile and say 'Hello.' "

Judith recalled that Gary had called her from jail, and she had asked him if he was okay and he said he was and that he hadn't done anything. She had gone at once to pick him up when he was released. He had jogged down to the Kmart from jail and together they'd picked his truck up from the impound lot.

"Did you have any conversation when he got home about the situation? I mean, did he tell you?"

"No." Gary's wife seemed incredibly passive and accepting, and Peters pressed a little. But Judith insisted she could understand completely why his back window might have been open and he would have had to stop to close it. "He drives through Sea-Tac every day, but he can't now."

"Would it surprise you," Peters asked carefully, "if he was trying to date a girl on the highway, a prostitute?"

"Yes, it *would* surprise me. It would hurt me, and, you know, I'd wonder what did I do wrong or—"

"Or what *he* did wrong. Not necessarily you, right?"

Judith was very nervous now. Asked if Gary had been arrested in the past for picking up a prostitute, she vaguely recalled something like that years earlier, just before they got married. "He was on his way home and someone would see the same truck driving by, and they stopped him and arrested him."

Peters turned to Matt Haney and asked him to remind Judith about the time in April 1987 when he had obtained search warrants for Judith and Gary's house just off Military Road, for the Kenworth plant, and Gary's locker, and even for his parents' home.

Haney nodded, reconstructing some details of that day. Judith had been working at the day-care facility in Des Moines then. Finally, she allowed that memory to come back. The first house she shared with Gary *was* searched, and deputies picked her up at work on that day. But she had never believed Gary had done anything wrong, and she didn't think about it afterward.

"Do you remember him ever telling you, before the search warrant, that he'd been arrested earlier in his life?" Peters asked. "In the early eighties—that he'd been arrested for picking up prostitutes?"

"No. What eighties?"

"May 1982," Matt Haney said.

"I didn't know him then."

"So that's new information that you've never known?" Peters asked. "Is that correct?"

"Yes."

"Has he ever said anything to you about prostitutes, like, you know, they're garbage, or he likes talking to them, or they're just ordinary people, or 'What's *your* feeling?' What do you think he thinks of prostitutes, or what has he told you he thinks of them?"

"We've never talked about them." Judith's absolute trust in her husband had been badly shaken, but she was still doing her best to describe him as a good man.

"Does he have any [feelings] about someone's particular race. Does he treat blacks and whites the same, do you know?" Peters asked. "How does he feel about blacks . . . or Filipinos?"

"It doesn't matter what color somebody is, or—"

"That's *your* opinion," Peters pointed out. "What do you think Gary's opinion is?"

"Well, he works with all kinds of different people at work, and he talks to them and all."

The woman before her was in complete denial, struggling to hold her world together even as it broke into shards and began to slip away, but Sue Peters knew she had to ask certain questions. "I'm asking you questions to find out what type he is, because I don't know him and you do."

"He's understanding. He's gentle. He's soft-spoken—and he's always smiling."

Matt Haney asked Judith about the area where she was living when she first met Gary, and the detectives realized that she'd been only a block or two from where most of the dead girls had vanished. Judith described their dates in fast-food restaurants on the Strip, and their camping trips to bleakly familiar areas.

But she was unshakable in her insistence that Gary rarely, if ever, went anywhere by himself except to work. "We talked earlier about your relationship with Gary," Haney began, "and I know that all marriages have their ups and downs."

"He makes me feel like a new woman every day," Judith cut in quickly. "That's how I feel. He just makes me feel good."

"How does he do that?" Haney asked.

"Just by being himself. He'll come through the door and say, 'Hello, I'm home,' with a big smile and give me a hug and a kiss, and [say] 'What's new?' Or years ago, he'd always ask me what needs to be fixed, and, you know, I'd say, 'The faucet's leaking,' and he'd fix it or the washer." She spoke faster and faster, afraid to let Matt Haney interrupt her. "He's just always made me feel so good, 'cause he's always smiling and happy and pleasant."

"So for sixteen years, you've never had a ripple?"

"No, just a couple of little ups and downs, you know."

"Did you go to court with him the other day?" Sue Peters asked.

"No, it was early in the morning."

"Did he plead guilty or not guilty?"

"He said he pleaded guilty," Judith said softly.

"Why would he do that?"

"Because," she said with a trembling voice, "it would've cost a whole lot for lawyers."

"How much did it cost him to plead guilty? Did he have to pay court fees?"

"He had to pay a fine. It was $700. He said the lawyers would have cost more than that. [He paid it] so that he wouldn't have to have the lawyers and pay all that, and have all that kind of money going out."

"So as far as you're concerned," Matt Haney asked, "that incident is behind you now?"

"I believe him and I trust him."

Haney had talked with Mary and Tommy Ridgway a few days after the 1987 search and they had formed a solid wall against the police. In their opinion, their son was being singled out unfairly. But when Haney pointed out lies Gary had told them, their attitude changed. Still, they, like Judith, remained in denial, and when the task force found no solid evidence to arrest Gary, the unpleasantness was all "put in the past."

Judith said now that she had never asked questions that might have upset him, or, perhaps more frightening, whose answers would have destroyed her perfect marriage. They had been talking for half an hour when Sue Peters asked Judith about her sex life with Gary. Somewhat discomfited, Judith described it as quite normal, although Gary desired intercourse a little more often than she did. No, he wasn't kinky and he didn't watch porno movies. Maybe, early in their relationship, they might have watched movies like that once or twice. She thought she might have borrowed some from a relative of hers, but that was mostly out of curiosity. Gary didn't buy off-color books or magazines. He had never tied her up to have sex, and Judith seemed surprised to be asked such a question. As for "outdoor sex," why would they want to do that when they had comfortable beds at home and in their motor home?

"All right," Sue Peters said. "Has he ever done anything that made you feel uncomfortable?"

"No, *never.*"

Finally, Haney and Peters asked Judith if she remembered that there had been a lot of circumstantial evidence in 1987 to lead detectives to believe Gary might have been responsible for the deaths of the Green River victims. "Are you familiar with the Green River [cases]? Have you followed it through the years?"

"I've seen the pictures, and how many vic— And, you know, it's sad."

"Is there any information in your house about Green River?" Peters asked. "Any books, or reading?"

Judith's answer was surprising. "Yes. I've kept it, and tucked it away, you know, in the bottom of a drawer, put away. It's not Gary's choice. It was my choice. I just kind of kept them and folded them up and stuffed them away."

They were just at the point in their questioning when it seemed as if Judith Ridgway was going to tell them something important, when the doorbell rang, followed by the phone. All three of them tensed. It was eighteen minutes to four when they had to pause the tape. Haney and Peters knew the media must have discovered Gary's arrest, and they would all be trying for a scoop for the five o'clock news.

Judith answered the phone. Luckily, it was one of her sisters-in-law, and, without letting her speak, Judith quickly said "I'm busy" and hung up. But then she moved to the front door where someone pounded insistently. Sue Peters managed to step in front of her before she could be blasted by a zealous reporter's question. Judith didn't know yet that Gary had been arrested, and having a microphone stuck in her face to hear her initial reaction would be a cruel thing. News cameras caught just a glimpse of Judith's startled face at the door, then cut fleetingly to Peters before she firmly closed the camera out. What she had to tell Judith was going to be overwhelming. The woman deserved some time to absorb what would change her life forever.

They were back on tape, and back to discussing Green River, but the phone rang constantly, until Matt Haney asked Judith if they could temporarily disconnect it.

"What's going on?" Judith asked, suddenly suspicious. "Don't I have a right to know?"

Haney and Peters said they were trying to tell her. "Gary was a Green River suspect back then," Peters said, speaking of April 1987, "and we recently sent a lot of samples from these women to the crime laboratory for DNA purposes. It turns out that we have three cases now—confirmed—that Gary's DNA was left inside them, meaning he had sex with them. His DNA was left on three of the prostitutes. So, again, he is the focus of the investigation by the Green River Task Force. And now we have the recent incident on Pacific HiWay on the sixteenth, and it was an undercover police decoy and Gary was trying to meet up with her again for sex—for thirty dollars. I know this is probably shocking to you—"

"Um-hm," Judith said, her face paling.

"Can you even— Is it feasible that he had sex with these women? I mean, do you believe that?"

Judith shook her head, crying now. But she admitted that Gary had saved some of the articles written about the Green River Killer. Shocked almost silent, Judith agreed to continue to answer questions on tape. She didn't know that the task force investigators had been following her husband, and she clearly had no idea that he had been driving side roads and making detours on his way to work. She thought he got up before four AM just to be sure he was on time for work at six thirty.

He didn't shower in the morning, only shaved, drank tea or coffee, and left. She assumed he'd been at Denny's having pancakes. She was sure Gary had never rented storage space, and nothing in their homes had ever been off-limits to her. She kept repeating that he had no secrets from her. But there was so much about her husband that she obviously hadn't known. She was stunned.

The floodgates had opened and Judith answered their questions now, flinching at the meaning behind them. No, he had never tried to choke her. He'd never frightened her, beyond coming around the side of their house and saying "Boo!"

"I know you care a lot about him, and you didn't know him in the early eighties," Sue Peters said now. "If this ever comes to trial, how would you feel about testifying to what you told us. About the man you know."

"The man I know is wonderful," Judith said quietly.

"So would you mind testifying to that in court—the things you know about Gary?"

"I would tell them everything is good about him. He's been the best. I love him."

"She was in shock," Sue Peters recalled. "I don't think she had any idea that this could happen. She was upset and kept denying that it could be true."

It was hard not to feel sorry for Judith Ridgway. Gary had come along and brought love into her life when she was crushed by the tawdry end of her first marriage. More than anything, she had clung to the haven of her own house and yard, the husband she trusted. Now, Peters and Haney told her that she would have to pack a bag because a search warrant would be served on that house and property.

"We're going to take you to a hotel," Peters said.

"My cats . . . the kittens . . . ," Judith protested.

"We'll see that they're fed and taken care of," Matt Haney told her. And they were.

Judith wouldn't be able to come home for more than a week, hidden from a rabid press in a hotel room. And when she did come home again, it would never be the same. It would never really be her house again. Without Gary to bring in his paycheck, there was no way she would be able to keep it.

50

GARY RIDGWAY might never come home at all. He was now fifty-two years old, and the photographs Randy Mullinax and Jim Doyon took of him at the Regional Justice Center showed an almost expressionless man, save for a vertical crease that had deepened over the passing years so that it bisected his forehead. Combined with the heavy hooding of his upper eyelids, the crease gave him an almost evil mien. In some photos he wore blue jeans and the familiar plaid shirt. In others he wore only white jockey shorts. One picture, given the suspicion that this was the weapon used to take dozens of lives, was chilling; it was his right arm from the elbow down. It didn't appear muscular and the hand itself showed fingers gnarled by the beginning of arthritis.

Brought to earth at last, the man they had considered a preying wolf had a meek presence. But at that point he refused to answer Mullinax's and Doyon's questions and he seemed determined not to do so. He wanted to talk to an attorney.

Ridgway was placed in an "ultra security" cell in the King County Jail, high up on the hill behind the courthouse and the Public Safety Building, where guards would check on him twenty-four hours a day. His mug shot was on the front page of every newspaper from Vancouver, British Columbia, to San Francisco by morning, along with speculation that he might be guilty of scores of unsolved homicides in those areas.

I looked at the picture in the Seattle papers on December 1, 2001, wondering if I had ever seen this face before, and I cannot say that I recognized it. But my daughter did. Leslie called me and said in a hushed voice, "Mom, remember how I told you about that man who came to our book signings? The one who leaned against the wall and just watched you? The one who never said anything and never bought any books?"

"Yes," I said.

"It was him."

"It was who?" I asked.

"Gary Ridgway. He's the man I saw." She paused. "He was even in the audience one time when you were giving a talk at a bookstore and you said 'Nobody knows who the Green River Killer is or what he looks like. For all I know, he could be sitting here tonight.' I guess he was."

People usually chuckled when I said that. It was a way to put an audience at ease and, at the same time, make them realize that serial killers didn't look like monsters. But it certainly gave me pause as I realized Ridgway must have been sitting in a darkened high school auditorium in Burien or Auburn or Tacoma as I showed slides of other serial killers I'd written about.

DESPITE THE ELATION that Dave Reichert voiced during the news conference he'd called, his media spokesman, John Urquhart, was cautious, as he always was. "What we're saying is we have not caught the Green River Killer," he told reporters later. "What we're saying is we've arrested a suspect in the deaths of four women who happen to be on the list of Green River victims. We don't know who killed those other forty-five women. Period. We're up to our eyeballs in police work."

And, indeed, they were. It wasn't over by a long shot. Every single case, each dead girl, most of whom would have been in their late thirties and early forties by 2001, would be scrutinized again. Authorities currently had only enough evidence to link Ridgway to four murders, and even those might be squeakers. But Norm Maleng's King County prosecutor's office had been with the task force every step of the way as they planned the arrest, skillfully fortifying any weak spots. They would continue to do that. It was a matter now of one step at a time.

First, there would be massive searches for possible new evidence. When Ridgway was arrested, crime scene specialists were already primed to employ their expertise in forensic science. "We knew a couple of days in advance that he was going to be arrested, and so we were prepared to search four homes, including the one where he'd lived for so long on Military Road," one of the technicians said.

They would have precious little daylight; in Seattle in December, the sun sets before four PM. The weather was miserable as rain fell heavily and relentlessly, and fierce winds blew branches from evergreens, closing some streets and knocking out power lines, but the dark skies couldn't quash the jubilance of the task force. There was a huge break in an investigation that almost everyone had given up on. At the same time, it brought back the memories of so many young women long dead, some of whose bodies had yet to be found.

Members of the Crime Scene Response Team from the Washington State Patrol were assigned to do thorough searches of houses where Gary Ridgway had lived over the prior twenty years. The forensic technicians hoped to find links between the suspect and many more than four victims. He had lived in the small house near the Pacific Highway all during the peak years of disappearances; they suspected that it might hold the most secrets.

It had been a long time since Ridgway occupied the now blue-gray house off Military Road, and the family who lived there in 2001 barely spoke English. They were cooking dinner when the WSP team arrived, surprised to find a crew of crime scene technicians about to swarm over their two-bedroom home.

"We had to convey to them that they would have to leave," Cheryl Rivers, a technician recalled. "That's the way it has to be."

Wearing coveralls, latex gloves, and "booties" to cover their shoes so they would not inadvertently shed evidence themselves, the WSP team moved in. Back in the eighties, Ridgway's old neighbors had been mystified by how he could have spilled enough red paint to destroy a carpet. There was an air of expectation as the crime scene experts pulled up the current carpets. They could see fibers from various old rugs below, but when they tested the layers beneath for signs of blood or body fluids, they got negative results.

That was disappointing. Green River investigators suspected that Ridgway had taken his victims to one of the bedrooms, probably the spare bedroom. But they knew that he shared his house from spring to late fall in 1982 with a couple to help pay his mortgage. He had fashioned a space for himself—a combination bedroom/storage area—in the garage, living there weekdays and disappearing each weekend. It would have been difficult, if not impossible, to bring girls to his house during those months. Still, he had lived there alone for two years before Judith moved in.

Even though the crime scene technicians worked their way down to the underlying carpet pads, bare floors, and baseboards, they found nothing of evidentiary value. They looked at the walls for signs that they had been repainted, but whatever had happened here had taken place long ago. It seemed impossible that there was no sign of the hapless girls trapped alone with a killer, their screams—if any—drowned out by the constant roar of the freeway just beyond the edge of the backyard. Even the crawl space beneath the house was empty of clues.

Finally the crime scene technicians were done, and the bewildered family who currently occupied the residence were allowed to come back in. Did they even know what might have happened in the house where they lived? With their tentative grasp of English, it was hard to tell. The county would, of course, replace and repair the torn carpets and baseboards, restoring the house to the way it had been.

Next, the state patrol teams moved several miles south to the Ridgway's interim home in Des Moines near Salt Water State Park and the big house in Auburn. Each move had been to a better neighborhood, and their current house was a much larger and more expensive home. In both the Des Moines and Auburn searches, they looked for souvenirs, photos, hairs, fibers, prints or blood, mementoes from the victims, hidden jewelry, bloodstained clothing, weapons, anything that might link Ridgway to the victims with hard physical evidence. He had been married to Judith for a long time, but she was not a suspect, even though she had lived with him in all these houses.

Most serial killers cannot resist keeping a cache of items to remind them of their crimes. And Judith never questioned her husband about anything. It would have been comparatively easy for him to hide something from her, stowed up in rafters or behind insulation.

They found nothing like that.

Ridgway was in jail, and Judith hidden away in a hotel, still dazed by the way her life as she had known it had come to a halt. The only remaining occupants of their house in Auburn were feline. There were cats and kittens all over, playing and dashing around, and the criminalists had been instructed, "Don't let the kittens out!"

They were careful to shut the doors so that the animals were safe. The team's goal was to find as much as they could without doing damage to the house itself. If need be, there were techniques to X-ray the walls later. "My impression was that it was a very nice home," one of the forensic searchers said, "but its decor was old-fashioned, outdated, and it looked like it had been decorated with things from the seventies, even though it wasn't that old. It was so feminine. There was no indication at all that a man lived there. It was cluttered with plants, knickknacks, dolls, crocheted doilies, and things some women like. Every flat surface was covered with collectibles and 'stuff.' There was nothing at all of him there."

Most of the decor did smack of another era, but it appeared to be a comfortable home where an average American family might live. There were multicolored crocheted afghans with the familiar zigzag pattern draped over the backs of couches and recliners, flowered pillows, life-size ceramic cats on the floor, a fully equipped oak entertainment center, arrangements of artificial flowers, wood stacked by the fireplace, and framed prints of angels, flowers, and ships. One frame held twenty family pictures. Mary Ridgway was in several, wearing harlequin glasses with her black hair teased into a high bouffant style. There were photos of Chad as a child, and some that were probably of Gary and his brothers in their early years.

The furniture was plush and solid. None of it seemed brand-new, but it looked cozy. "They were major pack rats, though," one of the searchers said. "There was too much of everything in that split-level house, but it was clean, dusted, and reasonably neat in the living room and kitchen area."

The master bedroom had a lovely floral bedspread and its double closet was filled with his and her clothing, ironed and carefully hung on hangers that all pointed the same way, shoes lined up neatly beneath.

When the crime scene team moved to the other bedrooms, however, they opened doors and stood back, stunned. "Oh, man!" one breathed.

Every available space, except for pathways, was filled with towering stacks of *things*. These rooms obviously weren't to be lived in, but were only for the storage of items that had been packed tightly and saved, or possibly resold. Both of the Ridgways appeared to be consumed with a desire to squirrel things away, possibly just for the sake of having them. The forensic searchers had heard that they were regulars at swap meets, but this was bizarre. The rooms were orderly enough, but chock-full. The couple must have spent hours arranging and stacking their obviously secondhand possessions.

The living-dining area and the kitchen were sprinkled liberally with knickknacks, but these rooms were packed so tightly that the Washington State Patrol technicians couldn't begin to process them for possible evidence, and they were grateful that that wasn't part of their assignment; the task force detectives would have to go through the boxes and bins.

Although Judith had said she was rarely away from Gary, she

had visited relatives from time to time. The WSP technicians knew there were often spots suspects didn't think about wiping clean. In each house they processed, the team members looked for latent fingerprints and flecks of blood under protected surfaces, along edges of shelves and on the undersides of tables. Picture frames were often a good source for partial prints.

They lifted several for comparison, but these, too, would prove to be disappointing.

Outside the Auburn house, investigators were carefully turning dirt over around rhododendrons and other bushes, lifting up sod and leaving excavated squares and rectangles in an organized grid dig. Judith had been upset at the thought that her beloved poodle might be dug up from its grave, so they were careful to rebury it. "They were digging the heck out of the yard," one state technician commented, "but really trying not to kill the stuff that was growing there."

Even in gray December, anyone interested in gardening could tell that this was a carefully tended yard, and the Ridgways' neighbors told detectives and reporters that gardening was one of Gary's main topics during over-the-fence chats. He kept his lawn in top shape, and he and Judith spent a lot of time working side by side in their garden spots. All of the earth moved in the massive digs was replaced, but no buried bones were found. Wherever the bodies of the still missing victims were, they weren't hidden within the sanctity of Gary Ridgway's properties or former homes.

After she was allowed to move back into her house, Judith Ridgway went to the sheriff's department's Burien precinct and waited patiently to see someone. She seemed so lost and timid that a Community Service Officer and a volunteer who often helped out with clerical tasks approached her to see if they could help her. They were surprised when they heard her last name.

"She had come to find out how she could file for damage compensation for her house after it was searched," the volunteer recalled. "She seemed bewildered by everything that had happened. She told us that the police wanted her to testify against her husband, but that she couldn't do that—she was too frightened at the thought of getting up in front of all those people in the courtroom. We felt sorry for her."

From jail, Ridgway wrote to Judith in his cramped, misspelled style. Trusties Xeroxed his letters, hoping to sell them as collectors' items, perhaps on eBay, unaware that, legally, the contents belonged to him and not to them. He told Judith that his years with her were the happiest of his life. And while that may well have been true, investigators were not at all convinced that he had stopped his stalking and prowling during the many years they had been together.

Predictably, he had been denied bail when his case came before a judge. Gary Ridgway did not appear in person but waived that right and let his attorneys Mark Prothero and James Robinson, from the Associated Counsel for the Accused, speak for him. As for the information that the public waited for avidly, there wasn't much. They weren't even afforded a glimpse of Ridgway being led down the marbled halls of the courthouse in the custody of several armed deputies.

On December 5, Gary Ridgway was formally charged with four counts of aggravated murder in the deaths of Marcia Chapman, Opal Mills, Cynthia Hinds, and Carol Ann Christensen. Every corpse but "Cookie" Hinds's had provided DNA that matched Ridgway's, but the circumstantial evidence linking Hinds to the other cases was overwhelming. Again, Ridgway remained in his ultra-security cell, perhaps afraid to face the public's rage. Legally, he wasn't obligated to appear at these early hearings, but, at some point, he was going to have to come out and enter a plea.

Prosecutor Norm Maleng announced that he would not plea bargain with Ridgway. If convicted, he would face either the death penalty or life in prison without possibility of parole. He said that senior deputy prosecutors Jeff Baird and Marilyn Brenneman would represent the prosecutor's office in the marathon legal procedures that lay ahead.

Without a defendant to film, the media turned to the usual interviews that accompany every high-profile crime. The Ridgways' neighbors and co-workers voiced their shock that someone on their street or in their workplace should be arrested for such heinous crimes. They recalled a quiet man who had seemed anxious to make friends, their reactions very much like those Matt Haney had evoked when he canvassed Gary's former neighborhood in 1987.

The only thing Ridgway had done to annoy any of his neighbors around his Auburn property had been to cut down many of the towering firs on his large lot, but that was his choice. And back on 218th and 32nd Avenue South, neighbors who had lived there in the eighties recalled how he had tried to organize a block watch targeting prostitutes, telling them that he suspected sex workers and their johns were parking nearby, leaving needles and condoms in the street. He had appeared to be obsessed with the wickedness of prostitutes, even though it seemed unlikely that their quiet street would attract sex for sale.

At the Kenworth plant in Renton, Ridgway's co-workers realized how on target they had been when they referred to him as "G.R." and "Green River Gary." Aside from his tendency to invade the personal space of female employees, he had been a somewhat pathetic fixture at Kenworth, a rather slow man who tried to be gregarious. "He'd go out of his way to be friendly," one co-worker said. "You'd see him coming down the hall and he'd be smiling and all happy. If he didn't know your name, he'd still say, 'Hi, friend!' If he was standing by the coffee machine and you walked by, he'd stop you and buy you a cup. In the cafeteria, he'd sit with groups and join in the conversation, but he wouldn't contribute much. He just wanted to belong real bad."

Other Kenworth employees remembered Ridgway's bizarre transformations from a Bible-quoting fanatic to a man who made obscene sexual remarks as he sat in the cafeteria. In either mode, his actions had been inappropriate, but not ominous. A few people who had known him said "I told you so," but not many. Most were flabbergasted to see the man nobody had paid much attention to at the top of the nightly news.

THERE WERE RUMORS that Ridgway's wife and brothers had come to visit him in jail, but they weren't substantiated.

Jon Mattsen interviewed Ridgway's younger brother, who was currently living on their deceased parents' property. Although Gary had once helped him get a job at Kenworth, it was obvious the brothers weren't close to one another or to their older brother. Younger than Gary by two years, Tom Ridgway appeared to know virtually nothing about him, his life, his motivations, his fears, or what hobbies he might have. "I know he always had a girlfriend, somewhere," Tom told Mattsen, but he didn't know anything much about Gary's three marriages beyond what Mary Ridgway had told him.

There was a strange disconnect among the Ridgway brothers, almost as if they had been raised in a vacuum where family ties meant little. The last times Tom and Gary had been together were at their mother's funeral and a few years before that, at their father's funeral. Pressed to recall any other interaction, Tom remembered that he had asked Gary to find a part for his Suzuki Samurai, a

4x4 truck designed to drive off-road. "My life revolves around that Samurai," he said, and Mattsen looked up sharply to see if he was serious. He seemed to be.

Tom said Gary had to be pretty well set financially because he had thirty-five years at Kenworth, "and he's a penny-pincher and a Dumpster-diver. . . . He'd go down to Levitz where they throw [broken] glass-top tables into the Dumpster at night and pick it up. 'Oh, it just needs a sheet of glass. I'll just [get] glass and set it on there' and he's got a brand-new table. So for a freebie, he's making thirty bucks."

Gary's younger brother was adamant that Gary was always with Judith, and read only free magazines you could pick up at the grocery store like *Little Nickel* want ads. As far as Gary's arrests for approaching prostitutes, he'd never heard of them. Tom hadn't the faintest idea about Gary's sex life. Indeed, he knew so little about his own brother that an interview with a stranger on the street might have elicited more information.

"What do you think about everything that's going on?" Mattsen asked, referring to the Green River arrests. "Do you think he could be responsible for—"

"Well, anything is possible, but I just can't picture it. 'Cause he's opposite of what I am, you know. I was always the wild one."

Tom said that Gary had taken their parents' deaths hard, but that was because Gary hadn't been the one looking after them— Tom said he and his wife were the caregivers, so Gary seemed surprised to find out how close to death they'd been.

GARY RIDGWAY would be a curiosity in jail, but not a popular inmate. Some of the men in nearby cells recalled that he was pleasant enough and didn't cause any trouble, but none of them had any respect for a man who had reportedly killed dozens of young women. Later, those who could get close enough urinated outside his cell so that the yellow puddles would flow toward him.

He received a visit from one of Seattle's venerable criminal defense attorneys—Tony Savage, a gentle and rumpled bear of a man whose signature brown beard of the sixties was now white. For decades, Savage was known for taking on any number of infamous cases where the death penalty seemed sure to be invoked. He was a strong voice for the defense, and one who had always been against the death penalty. Savage had defended dozens of Washington's most loathsome clients—clearly not with the hope of acquittals but to save their lives. He was a brilliant and kind man who seemed worn down by the decades of dealing with defendants accused of ghastly crimes, but he was good, and if he consented to represent him, Ridgway could not do better.

Asked about Gary Ridgway's state of mind during the days after his arrest for murder, Savage said, "I think he's doing very well, considering the pressure he's under."

Could Ridgway afford someone like Tony Savage? Probably not, unless Savage did it pro bono or was appointed as a public defender. It was difficult to imagine how any attorney could prepare for a trial where the victim toll might swell to almost four dozen. How long would it take in trial? Years, certainly.

If Savage was going to take on Ridgway, he would need help, a whole phalanx of lawyers and legal assistants. Gary and Judith Ridgway had some equity in their house, though no one knew how much, and several vehicles. There was the house left by Mary and Tommy Ridgway, reportedly for sale for $219,000. But any sale proceeds had to be split three ways, and allegedly the three brothers had already squabbled over that division of property. Even millionaires could go broke paying for the best criminal defense attorneys for years.

It seemed ironic now that Ridgway hadn't wanted to pay an attorney to defend him on the loitering for prostitution charge. Realistically, the trials that lay ahead were going to cost an estimated $12 million. And most of it would probably come from King County taxpayers.

51

NOW THAT Gary Ridgway had become the defendant and not merely the suspect that many detectives and leaders in the sheriff's office had long since dismissed, their recollections changed. Everyone from the sheriff on down had jumped onto the "Ridgway Did It" bandwagon, most asserting that they had been convinced of his guilt all along.

Critics pointed out discrepancies and mistakes, a phenomenon in every high-profile murder case. Although Dave Reichert was hesitant about giving away too much about the continuing investigation, he often commented that he had been the "lead detective" in the Green River probe since the beginning. He had, indeed, been the first King County detective to be designated to a lead position, but only in the Debra Bonner, Opal Mills, Cynthia Hinds, and Marcia Chapman cases. No one questioned that he had worked doggedly alongside his fellow task force members on the dozens of cases that followed until he made sergeant in 1990. But, of course, no single investigator had been the sole "lead detective," and many others had been assigned as "leads" as the unsolved homicide cases grew in number over the years.

Matt Haney had written the 1987 search warrants for Gary Ridgway's vehicles and property, and assigned Reichert to handle the sweep of the first, most suspect, house off Military Road. Jim Doyon and Ben Colwell had been in charge of investigating Carol Christensen, Kimi-Kai Pitsor, Yvonne Antosh, and the woman known only as Bones #2. Rich Battle and Paul Smith were the leads in the murders of Giselle Lovvorn, Shawnda Summers, and Bones #8. And Port of Seattle investigators Jerry Alexander and Ty Hughes had traced the movements of people connected to Mary Bridget Meehan, Constance Naon, and Bones #6.

Early on, Sergeant Bob "Grizzly" Andrews and Randy Mullinax were responsible for women still missing. Mullinax was probably the most diligent in keeping families informed and comforting them. Sue Peters handled Keli McGinness's investigation. And, of course, there had been numerous Green River Task Force commanders— from Dick Kraske to Jim Graddon. Dave Reichert had been away from the Green River cases for almost eleven years when, as sheriff, he reactivated the task force in the fall of 2001.

Although Reichert was a natural focus for the media—the first deputy ever to rise through every step in the department to become sheriff—he could take neither the credit nor the blame for all that had happened over the previous twenty years. As could be expected, there had been great gains and ignominious mistakes made in the hunt for one man among at least forty thousand suspects. Reichert and Tom Jensen had not been in the Ridgway camp, but the DNA tests had convinced them. Now, Reichert appointed Bruce Kalin, who had worked on an earlier Green River Task Force to head the further investigation of Gary Ridgway.

Two items of actual and circumstantial evidence that might well have added to the case against Gary Ridgway had, unfortunately, been lost. When Opal Mills's clenched hand was unfolded in

August 1982, investigators had seen a straight, brown Caucasian hair—a hair undoubtedly yanked from her killer's head—just like Gary Ridgway's. It had been bagged, sealed, marked . . . and lost. In 1982, the root tag couldn't have been matched to Ridgway with DNA, in any case. Fifteen years later, it might have been possible.

The license plate number that Paige Miley, Kim Nelson's friend, had given to an early task force member had also been lost. That might very well have led to Gary Ridgway nineteen years earlier, but by the time Paige was hypnotized, she could not find it in her subconscious mind.

Matt Haney was disappointed that two task force members hadn't questioned Mary and Tom Ridgway in any depth when their house was searched in 1987, nor committed their conversation, if any, to a written report. Now, of course, both of Gary's parents were deceased, and anything they might have contributed about the way his mind worked was lost forever.

The harshest critics of the Green River probe were DNA experts who decried the sheriff's department's long wait to employ the newest forensic science to pinion Ridgway. With the task force long disbanded, there was apparently no one in Reichert's office who realized that the saliva sample Matt Haney, Jim Doyon, and WSP criminalist George Johnston had retrieved from Gary Ridgway in April 1987 and frozen could have been tested by 1996. While the new technique known as STR-PCR (short, tandem repeats polymerase chain reaction), requiring only minuscule amounts of test material, had been in place since then, the sheriff's office didn't submit suspects' test samples to the WSP crime lab until March 2001, and the state lab had been using STR-PCR for almost two years.

A single cell from a fragment of sample could now be amplified exponentially, producing billions of DNA copies within hours. It does, however, take a "rocket scientist" or the equivalent to understand DNA, and there was quite possibly a three- to five-year lag in isolating Gary Ridgway's DNA profile.

Unfortunately, not only was Jensen's request several years late, the state patrol laboratory was overwhelmed with backed-up requests from other agencies. The state lab, of necessity, prioritized samples for cases that already had trial dates.

Howard Coleman, CEO of GeneLex, a Seattle-based DNA testing corporation, said his lab had been using the new technique for the Indiana State Police crime lab for five years. Had Jensen and Reichert thought to send the Green River DNA to a private lab, it would have been expensive but Ridgway might have been arrested much sooner. "There's no one answer why we didn't [request the tests earlier]," John Urquhart said. "It's a confluence of factors. To begin with, the Washington State Patrol crime lab is our primary lab." Urquhart went on to say that the expense of a private lab wasn't the main reason for the delay; it was more that Tom Jensen had been working as the only Green River detective. "He's had a lot to do."

Any investigative team faced with the challenges of at least four dozen serial killings would have made mistakes and misjudgments. All Reichert could do was hope that there had been no new victims during the years when the DNA tests could have been carried out. But hindsight is always twenty-twenty, and the rejuvenated task force investigators moved into 2002, confident that they would uncover evidence that would convict Gary Ridgway in the trials to come.

The important thing was that they finally had a suspect in custody and charged with four counts of aggravated murder. If things worked out well, the task force could hope to increase those charges to include several more victims. County Executive Ron Sims announced some positive financial help on December 8, 2001. The federal government would contribute $500,000 to help pay for DNA tests on the forty-five victims' cases where there were no charges yet filed.

Back at the Ridgways' home in Auburn, two Christmas stockings still hung from their fireplace mantel, the names "Gary" and "Judith" embroidered on them, but the couple wouldn't be sharing the holiday. Instead, Ridgway appeared in court for arraignment on the four aggravated murder charges. Court watchers and television viewers were somewhat surprised to see the meek-looking man in white scrubs with "Ultra Security" stamped on the back of his shirt. Was this the infamous Green River Killer? He looked more like Caspar Milquetoast.

He pleaded "not guilty" and was led back to his cell.

CAPTAIN BRUCE KALIN now commanded the newest Green River Task Force and Sheriff Reichert added a sergeant, D. B. Gates, and two more detectives to bring the number of investigators up to ten. He would soon beef up the task force even more. The command officers in the sheriff's office, the task force members, and the prosecution team held frequent meetings to discuss how they would proceed. Matt Haney recalled that he admired the attitude in the task force where everyone, no matter the rank, was encouraged to say what they thought and to suggest ways to proceed. And everyone listened. "We tried to think 'out of the box,' " Sue Peters said. "It didn't matter how odd or strange a suggestion sounded. We weren't going to proceed according to the way it was always done— always had been done. This was a very unusual investigation, and we were going to do whatever it took."

And they were going to do it as secretively and cautiously as they could. One of their first goals was to try to locate the scores of vehicles once owned by Gary Ridgway. His frequent sightings in pickup trucks suggested that some of the victims might have been killed or transported in those trucks. They found one of them, a 1977 black Ford pickup, in Johnstown, Pennsylvania, where its current owner, a soldier formerly stationed in Washington, lived. They paid $2,500 to buy it back. A number of Ridgway's vehicles had long since been crushed into squares of scrap metal, but some still existed and could contain telltale physical evidence.

Every possible item that might become useful evidence—garbage at body sites, the contents of the boxes and bags in the Ridgway house—was photographed, bagged, and labeled: thousands of pieces of jewelry, beads, buttons, hair samples, scraps of cloth, matchbooks, cigarette butts, intact and broken bottles, bone fragments found in envelopes in Ridgway's houses, a possible skull bone from his vacuum cleaner, empty cans, and torn and rotten clothing. The list went on endlessly, and so did the photos that were downloaded onto DVDs. Judith and Gary had bought hundreds of cheap rings, pins, earrings, and bracelets at swap meets and yard sales so that it would be difficult to find out if any of them had come from the victims.

OVER the past thirty years, I have read more than a thousand homicide case files. Most of them could be contained in a single binder or perhaps two binders, albeit each four or five inches thick. And those were cases that required a great deal of detective work. *Each* Green River victim's file contained both important information and minutia. To grasp the work that early investigators had done and what the last task force would still do was akin to counting all the changing patterns of glass fragments in a kaleidoscope.

The effort put forth by so many detectives and forensic experts was amazing.

In early March 2002, the Green River Task Force moved into new offices in a glass-and-concrete building owned by King County. It was near Boeing Field, Seattle's smaller airport, and not many miles from the Strip or Kenworth, for that matter. It was impossible to estimate how long they might be there. There were now fourteen investigators. No one outside the task force knew what avenue of investigation was being pursued, even though Dave Reichert held an open house to show off the new Green River headquarters. Beyond that, there wasn't any information on the progress of the cases where no charges were pending.

Detective Graydon Matheson was in the process of organizing the evidence they had gathered. Kevin O'Keefe was loaned back from the Seattle Police Department and Detective Katie Larson was the media spokesperson. From time to time, I talked to Katie and Sue Peters, but not about the Green River case. I knew I couldn't ask and they couldn't tell, so I didn't even try. One of the many things Sue didn't tell me was that the coveralls she had retrieved from Gary Ridgway's locker at the Kenworth plant in the 1987 search had proved to be a gold mine of irrefutable evidence. They held tiny, tiny dots of paint that Skip Palenik had found to be microscopically identical to those found on three additional victims: Wendy Coffield, Debra Estes, and Debra Bonner.

On March 27, 2002, Ridgway was charged with three more counts of aggravated murder because of what was found on those coveralls. Sprayed paint often dries in midair, leaving infinitesimal spheres that the naked eye can barely see. Many colors of paint that were once used in Gary Ridgway's custom truck assignments were detected on the jeans knotted around Wendy Coffield's neck, the black sweater buried with Debra Estes, and on Debra Bonner's clothing. The paint's chemical composition was identical to the DuPont Imron paint used at Kenworth in the eighties. It was very expensive paint and few other companies used it at the time.

The passage of time and tremendous advances in forensic science were an enormous boon to the Green River investigators. As the years went by, one group of detectives built upon the work of those who preceded them. As Matt Haney said, "If it hadn't been for the initial great work of the first detectives and the King County Medical Examiner's Office, the evidence that trapped Gary Ridgway might have been lost—and we needed that. Fortunately, the DNA was preserved and the crime scenes were handled very professionally."

AND NOW THERE WERE seven counts of aggravated murder against Gary Ridgway. But when would he go to trial? By late 2002, I hesitated to plunge into a book on some other case because I didn't want to be away from Seattle when Gary Ridgway's trial began. Practically, it seemed unlikely that it would be soon because his star team of defense attorneys, which now included not only Tony Savage and Mark Prothero, but also Todd Gruenhagen, David Roberson, Suzanne Elliott, and Fred Leatherman, wanted discovery of the endless files the Green River Task Force had amassed before arresting their client. That could take years. So far, they had been given 420,000 pages of files, and that was only the beginning.

Moreover, there were rumors that they would ask for a change of venue. I wondered if there was any courtroom within the borders of Washington State where Ridgway and the Green River murders weren't well known, and if moving the trial would make it any easier to find jurors who hadn't formed an opinion.

By June 2003, it looked as if Ridgway would be tried in King County. King County public defender Ann Harper said that her office was using the Ted Kaczynski "Unabomber" case as a model for allocating personnel for the defense. Ridgway would pay for one attorney, but he would be provided in total with 8 lawyers, 7.5 investigators, 2 clerks, and 6 paralegals.

As for the trial, Paul Sherfry, King County Superior Court's chief administrative officer, expected to face a courtroom situation very much like the O. J. Simpson trial, juggling families, media, and spectators. Jury summonses would be sent to ten thousand registered voters in the county, a huge roster that would then be winnowed down to five hundred prospective jurors. Covering Ridgway's trial wouldn't be like the scores of others I'd observed in the old courthouse, where I could arrive at nine twenty AM and expect to find a seat on one of the hard oak benches with enough elbow room to write in my lined yellow legal tablet.

Still, the trial didn't appear imminent. The first tentative date to begin was said to be July 2004. Once more, I kept the Green River Killer book on a back burner while I wrote two more books, and went on a book tour around America.

52

A TIGHT LID was being kept on what was happening behind the scenes. Not long after Gary Ridgway was arraigned on the three additional charges of aggravated murder in the deaths of Debra Estes, Debra Bonner, and Wendy Coffield, his attorneys had contacted Prosecutor Norm Maleng to ask if Ridgway might avoid the death penalty if they offered a proffer that he would plead guilty to the original counts *and* show the task force investigators where the bodies yet undiscovered were located.

It was a difficult decision for Maleng and the five deputy prosecuting attorneys, Jeff Baird, Patricia Eakes, Bryan McDonald, Ian Goodhew, and Sean O'Donnell. The State could move ahead to trial and seek conviction and the death penalty on only seven of what Maleng suspected were more than fifty victims. The rest would go unavenged and their families would never know for sure what had happened to them. Given the lengthy appeals process, the now-fifty-four-year-old prisoner might very well die before he could be executed.

If Maleng's office accepted the defense proffer, the case would be over, there would be no trial. But, after all the years, there would be answers. "The community's most enduring nightmare would be over, the families and survivors of the victims of the uncharged killings would find a measure of justice and resolution at last," Jeff Baird recalled in his summary. "Ridgway would be held accountable for all the murders he committed, not just a select few."

Part of the agreement would block any chance that Ridgway could appeal his four dozen life sentences without possibility of parole, and he would die in prison. An acceptance of this proffer would, however, cover *only* King County, and would be automatically void if Ridgway failed to include every single victim within its borders. It would not apply to any murders he might have committed in other counties or other states.

In many ways, it was an agonizing choice for the State to make. Everyone who had seen the agony and tragedy of a twenty-two-year series of unsolved murders of young women wanted to see Gary

Ridgway face a jury of his peers, to watch him sit in court and face the terrible evidence of what he had done. But he would only be prosecuted for seven murders; there was simply no way to find further physical evidence linking him to all the dead girls.

On June 13, 2003, the prosecutors' office and the defense team entered into an agreement. The State would not seek the death penalty, but Ridgway would have to plead guilty to aggravated murder in the first degree for all the homicides he'd committed in King County. And this didn't mean only the forty-nine victims on the official list. If he had killed before 1982 or after 1985, he had to admit those murders, too.

The agreement was not revealed to the public. Norm Maleng's prosecution team, Sheriff Dave Reichert, and the task force would have to meet with the survivors before they did that, and even before they talked to the victims' families, they needed to pursue interrogation of Gary Ridgway to see if he meant to keep his promises.

It was mid-June of 2003 when the rumors began. Where was Ridgway? One thing was certain; he was no longer in the King County Jail. Katie Larson, speaking for the task force, acknowledged that he had been moved from his cell there, but said any information on his whereabouts had been sealed by a judge. She acknowledged that she knew where he was, but she wasn't at liberty to say. Larson assured the public that Ridgway was in a secure facility and there was no need to worry that he might be able to escape. "He has a right to privacy," Larson said, although most citizens didn't much care about Ridgway's privacy.

His most likely hiding place was Western State Hospital in Steilacoom, a state mental institution. Someone who was in a position to know told me that Ridgway required treatment for mental illness, and authorities had spirited him to the Steilacoom high-security wing late at night, but that wasn't true.

Reporters had attempted to find him by checking to see if Ridgway was an inmate in the Pierce County Jail, the Snohomish County Jail, or in the State Hospital. If he was, he was listed under another name.

Something seemed to be happening, however. Green River Task Force members and Search and Rescue teams were spotted in rugged areas where victims' bodies had been found and in similar regions around King County. It had been a long time since Green River investigators had been a staple on the nightly news, but suddenly they were a familiar sight again. Had they simply gone back to look for something they might have missed earlier, or was it possible that the prosecutor's office had struck some kind of a deal with the defense team—Ridgway's life for information the task force needed to find more victims?

Larson said they were only doing "routine searches," based on reviewing cases and following up tips that had come in from the public. And yet it seemed that every weekend, they were spotted somewhere in some woods. However, the seven or eight hours the searchers spent each day clambering up and down deep ravines apparently netted nothing at all.

But something had to be going on. Throughout July and August, and into the fall, the Green River teams were visible in the south county area or near North Bend. They wore jeans and shirts, civilian clothes with baseball caps or other hats to protect them from an unusually hot summer sun. Most of the areas they searched were dry as dust, but, on occasion, they had to dig into thick mud— the most difficult digs.

Katie Larson, who was a pretty, slender blonde, worked double-duty; she joined the diggers during the day and then faced the cameras, but she declined to be specific about what they were looking for, or who, if anyone, had directed them to a particular site. Barred from getting as close as they would like, television cameramen used telephoto lenses to show the men and women working with shovels, trowels, rakes, buckets, and screens. I recognized a lot of the task force members, but the rest were strangers to me. That was to be expected—I'd been away at trials in Texas and Florida and didn't know most of the younger investigators. Two local newspaper reporters who had haunted the task force for years tried to cross the yellow "crime scene" tape on a site near Des Moines and were turned away. I admit that I was tempted to drive down the hill and watch, too, but I didn't because I didn't want to get in the way and it would have been embarrassing to be asked to move on.

Privately, the new task force had dubbed Seattle police detective Kevin O'Keefe the official "bone man." He had an unerring talent for discerning immediately whether a bone was animal or human. "We found so many bones from dogs, cats, and wild animals," Sue Peters said. "We'd toss them to Kevin and he could tell us at once what we had. But one time we threw what we thought was an animal bone to him, and he said, 'Whoa . . . hand these to me gently. This is human.' "

On August 16, 2003, they found human bones in the woods near Enumclaw. They were identified as belonging to Pammy Avent, Keli McGinness's closest friend in the Camp in Portland. Both of them had come back to Seattle in 1983, only to disappear. Keli was still missing; the last sighting of Pammy was on October 26 of that year. For Pammy's family, it was both a closure and the end of all hope.

On August 23, the task force detectives revisited a four hundred by one hundred–foot lot off the Kent–Des Moines Road, ground they had checked in June only to be stymied by a morass of ten-foot-tall Himalayan blackberry vines. Now the prickly vines had been cleared with machetes and they were able to divide the lot into a grid pattern.

And here they found nineteen human bones. They had no idea whom they belonged to, or if they had come from one person or several people. It would take a while to get the results from mitochondrial DNA tests, and many of the victims' mothers had died over the twenty-two years since the killings began. All the years of changing seasons had covered the lost girls more deeply than their killer had buried them. It seemed a miracle that any of their poor bones had been found.

In September 2003, the Green River Task Force investigators located more bones in Snoqualmie, near North Bend and I-90, another familiar body-cluster site over the years. On September 16, the King County Medical Examiner's Office identified them as belonging to April Dawn Buttram. She was the seventeen-year-old girl from Spokane whose mother had caught her crawling out the window, running away to a more exciting life in Seattle. She hadn't found what she was looking for. She had found only death. April had vanished almost twenty years to the week that her bones were discovered.

Marie Malvar had been gone a few months longer, snatched by the stranger in the burgundy red pickup truck driving off into the night, even though her boyfriend tried to follow. The trauma of her disappearance, exacerbated by her father's certainty that he had found her killer's house but couldn't go inside, had pretty much destroyed her family.

Ex-commander of the task force Frank Adamson believed that Bob Fox of the Des Moines Police Department should have taken the concern of Marie Malvar's father and boyfriend more seriously in 1983 when they took him to the house where Ridgway lived. They were sure the dark red pickup parked in his driveway was her abductor's vehicle. Had the Des Moines police gone inside, they might not have saved Marie, but it was possible they could have found evidence of a crime and stopped further killings.

For a long time, the Malvars had gathered on April 1 to celebrate Marie's birthday and pray for her safe return. No longer. Marie's parents were long-divorced and her father was living in the Philippines and remarried with a young daughter he'd named after his missing Marie. Her mother was in California, ill and suffering from dementia, with Marie's only sister, Marilyn, caring for her. Her four brothers were scattered.

But at last the searchers had found Marie's earthly remains, only bones now, in a deep ravine near Auburn where someone had thrown her away. With each new discovery of partial skeletons secreted in the wilderness, the rumors grew stronger. Ridgway had to be telling the task force searchers where to look; they couldn't be so unerring in their discoveries unless someone had mapped it out for them.

The rumors were correct, of course, but they didn't go far enough. Gary Ridgway's attorneys had successfully plea-bargained in their fight to save his life. But it would be months before anyone officially announced that.

There was shocking news yet to come. All through the summer months of 2003, the mystery about where Gary Ridgway was being housed remained. He wasn't in any jail, any hospital, any prison. At least there was no record of his being there, and it seemed impossible that someone as infamous as a suspected serial killer could be hidden for months. There were new reports that were disquieting: Ridgway was said to be housed in a two-bedroom apartment under secure guard. Surely, that couldn't be. How could he be living in comparative luxury after what he was alleged to have done?

Finally, when the gossip swelled, Katie Larson was instructed to announce where he was. Gary Ridgway wasn't residing in any comfortable apartment. Not at all. He had been living, quite literally, *with* the Green River Task Force investigators—in the office complex where they worked each day. It was the last place anyone thought to look. No police agency had ever taken such a bold step. During their frequent brainstorming sessions, someone had come up with the idea and the detectives and prosecutors who first scoffed at the idea began to toss it around. At that point, Ridgway had been in custody for six months and hadn't given up any secrets, protected as he was by his flying buttress wall of attorneys. In the county jail, other inmates watched what went on, and they were quick to tell each other and their visitors what Ridgway was up to and who was coming to see him. But now everything had changed.

In order to get inside the head of the one person in the world who could tell them whom he had harmed, why he had done it, and where he had secreted their bodies, the Green River Task Force investigators decided to do something off the charts. Although he didn't appear to care about the lives of anyone else, Ridgway wanted to live. That's true of most serial killers whose own survival is paramount. Behind closed doors, the prosecutors and the defense team had come closer to a decision everyone might be able to live with.

It was difficult for the detectives. No investigative team had ever agreed to spend so much time with a cold-blooded killer. But there he was, thirty feet from Sue Peters's desk, sleeping on a mattress in a barren, closely guarded room. He was a constant, malevolent presence. When Peters came to work, Ridgway called out "Hi Sue!" and she forced herself to answer back cheerfully. He learned the names of most of the personnel in the task force office, and he seemed to think that it would be like his days back at Kenworth, where he was always smiling and trying to make conversation with people.

It was like having the fictional Dr. Hannibal Lecter living down the hall, albeit a far less charismatic "Lecter." Cocooned, however sparsely, in terms of the amenities of life, Gary Ridgway was a captive—but he had a captive audience, too. As Ted Bundy had once delighted in the attention paid to him by Florida detectives after his 1978 capture, Ridgway would now be able to discuss the ghastly details of his crimes. He was a macabre champion of sorts. He held records that no one else would want to brag about.

Up to the moment of his arrest, Ridgway had been a nonentity, a boring little man of meager intelligence, a joke, someone to tease, and, worst of all for his ego, someone to ignore. But beginning in mid-June 2003, he made himself available as a subject who was quite willing to participate in long hours of questioning, day after day after day. He loved it. He had always found pleasure in demonstrating his expertise in the art of murder, and he was talking to his ideal audience—the very detectives who had faced his deadly handiwork for so many years. He knew that psychiatrists and psychologists, homicide detectives and F.B.I. agents were curious about him, and he enjoyed being the center of attention.

For his questioners, it was exhausting, disgusting, shocking, frustrating, and horrific work. And sometimes, yes, boring, as Ridgway often repeated himself or stumbled awkwardly as he searched his memory in vain.

After the public found out where he was living, and that he was admitting his crimes, there would be yet another shocking revelation about Gary Ridgway. One of the faces in the telephoto shots of the cars full of investigators that turned into the woods and mountains should have been familiar. Anyone who watched television or read the papers knew that face. Gary Ridgway accompanied the task force investigators on what they called "field trips." *He had been hidden in plain sight.*

Except when they were in deep woods, Ridgway was never allowed to get out of the police units; that might have allowed someone to recognize him. But he was there, an interested spectator as well as a guide who led detectives back to where he'd left the bodies of his victims more than twenty years earlier. In order to learn what they needed to know, detectives had to allow him to revisit these sites that he had returned to often over the years of his freedom. He brightened, smiling in anticipation, as they got closer to his trophy areas.

And no one outside the investigation ever suspected.

Ridgway was guarded on every side and hampered by handcuffs with chains attached to a chain on his waist, along with leg irons. There was no chance he could escape. He rode in a locked police vehicle with two detectives accompanying him and two more in a car following. Prosecutors and his own attorneys were also in the search parties.

"He never knew when we were going," Sue Peters recalled. "We might wake him up before the sun rose, or take him in the middle of an interview. He had no forewarning. He liked the field trips, but we couldn't help that. Whatever he was reliving, it was something we had to know."

For the most part, the interviews themselves were handled by four Green River detectives: Randy Mullinax, Sue Peters, Tom Jensen, and Jon Mattsen. Occasionally, psychiatrists spent hours with Ridgway, and Dr. Mary Ellen O'Toole from the F.B.I.'s Behavioral Science Unit flew in to talk with him in her soft, feminine voice, her eyes unblinking as he spoke of his perverted fantasies. "We were relieved when the F.B.I. or the doctors talked to him," Peters remarked. "It gave us some time away from him."

That was understandable. A long time later, it was hard enough for me to watch the interviews, caught on DVDs, without having to have been there, masking the revulsion that came with his unfeeling recitation of his crimes. The questioning was usually accomplished in an hour-and-a-half to two-hour segments.

A team of two detectives sat at a round, Formica-topped table across from Ridgway, who was manacled even inside the task force headquarters, although he could move his hands enough to take notes or drink from his bottle of artesian water. He wore jail "scrubs," usually bright red, sometimes white. At a rectangular table, just out of camera view, members of Ridgway's defense team listened and watched. A wrinkled gray painter's tarp covered the wall behind the prisoner, although other detectives could observe and hear what was going on through the closed-circuit television system.

"We quickly learned how to deal with him," Peters recalled. "He would have enjoyed talking for sixteen to eighteen hours a day, but none of us wanted to listen that long. At first he seemed to think he was running the show. When we gave him a choice of what he wanted for breakfast or lunch, he got the wrong idea and thought he was in some kind of control, so after that he ate whatever we decided he should get."

If he was particularly forthcoming, Ridgway realized small rewards—a salmon dinner, or extra pancakes, something he wanted to read—although his dyslexia made that difficult for him.

They established a routine. Most of their morning interview sessions began shortly after eight with a recitation of what the prisoner had eaten for breakfast: "Pancakes, an egg, sausage," Ridgway would say with a smile. And then he evaluated the quality of his sleep during the night while the detectives feigned interest. He appeared to be sleeping remarkably well, given the ghastly imprints laid down in his memory. But since this was all about *him*, the memories of the dead didn't disturb him.

They never had.

WATCHING the videotapes that caught every word of the interrogations of Gary Ridgway during those four months of 2003 would have been an unsettling experience for anyone, hundreds of hours of grotesque recollections from a man who looked totally harmless as he described killing dozens of women in a halting, dispassionate voice. Like all criminals, he minimalized his crimes initially, only slowly admitting the monstrous details. While he had ample motivation for telling the truth—his life—he said he knew he was a pathological liar.

"Ridgway also suggested another reason why he would lie or minimalize his conduct," Jeff Baird, the chief trial deputy, wrote in the prosecutor's summary of evidence. "He believes that a popular 'true crime' author will write a book about him, and he wanted to portray himself in the best possible light."

In the beginning, Ridgway denied any premeditation to murder, claiming that he killed when he was in a rage. It was the victims' fault because they didn't seem to be enjoying sex with him or they made him hurry. "When I get mad, I shake. Sometimes I forget to breathe and things get all blurry," he said.

Of course, the anger wasn't his fault either; he blamed his failure to be promoted at Kenworth on women, who got the best and easiest jobs. His first two divorces were his ex-wives' fault, as were the child support payments he'd had to make for Chad even though *he* hadn't wanted a divorce in the first place. Small things enraged him; when he bought his house, the sellers were so cheap they had taken all the lightbulbs. All these things made it difficult for him to sleep, and he said the only way to release the "pressure" had been to kill women.

That wasn't true, and his specious reasoning soon faltered. He had wanted to kill for the sake of killing, although even he may not have known why. Again and again, he would repeat, "All I wanted to do was have sex with them and kill them."

It was obvious early on that Ridgway could remember neither his victims' faces nor their names. His memory wasn't all fuzzy, but it was compartmentalized. He recalled every vehicle he'd ever owned, houses he'd lived in when he was a child, his various shifts at Kenworth—basically inanimate objects. (Ted Bundy had been like that, too. He could cry over a dented Volkswagen or an abandoned bicycle, but not a human being.)

Gary Ridgway had maps in his head and sharp recall of where he had left bodies, but the dead girls were apparently interchangeable in his mind. Who they were or what they might have become made no difference to him. They had existed only to please him sexually for a short time and they were then disposable.

Some he had deliberately let go, saying, "You're too cute for a guy like me." But that, he explained, was only so he would have witnesses, if he should ever need them, that he was a good guy.

"A couple of times the urge to kill wasn't there. It could have been where I had a real good day at work. Somebody patted me on the back, 'You did a good job today,' which was a rarity. It could have been maybe on my birthday . . . or maybe I just didn't have time to kill them and take them someplace."

The detectives worked out ways to stimulate Ridgway's memory. They did their best to keep him on track, and to recall one victim at a time. When his train of thought began to wander away, they brought him back. Sue Peters often showed him photographs of the living girls, and he shook his head. They didn't look familiar to him. He had never really bothered to look at them in the first place. He recognized photos of locations, however, saying that fences, trees, or road signs helped him pinpoint them.

The investigators used innovative ways to reach the stuttering, expressionless prisoner. He seemed cowed by the strength of the male questioners, perhaps more responsive to the female interrogators, but there wasn't a vast difference in his response from one to the other. He may have felt powerful with his victims, but they were such pathetically easy targets. He seemed a mouse now.

"Think of it as a paint job," Tom Jensen said, as he attempted to trigger Ridgway's recollection of his crimes. "What do you do first?"

"Well, you prep it. Do the taping and all."

"So, how did you prep taking the women?"

"I asked if they were 'dating,' and told them what I wanted and I waved money at them, and we decided that." He said he offered them more than they usually got, but that didn't matter because he knew he wouldn't have to pay them anyway.

Some of the victims were killed out of doors on the ground after he had spread a blanket he carried in his truck. Some died in the back of his truck. During the times when he lived alone in the little gray house off Military Road, his preference had been to take the women, whom he ironically referred to as "ladies," to his house. He set their minds at ease in different ways. "A lot of them asked me if I was the Green River Killer when I picked them up," Ridgway said. "I told them 'No, of course not. Do I look like the Green River Killer?' And they says, 'No, you don't.' They always thought it was a big tall guy—about six three, 185 pounds."

There were women who refused to "date" Ridgway because they were afraid he was an undercover cop. He alleviated their concerns by keeping beer in his truck and offering it to them, and they relaxed because a police officer wouldn't do that.

He had most of his bases covered. To allay the fears of the frightened girls, he kept some of Chad's toys on his dashboard. He wanted to appear as an ordinary Joe, a good guy who was a single father. He kept cartons of cigarettes to give away. Sometimes he groomed girls by dating them a few times, offering to help them get jobs, to become a regular customer they could count on, or let them use his car. "And they think, you know, 'This guy cares,' and . . . which . . . I didn't. I just wanted to get her in the vehicle and eventually kill her."

Even when he had the girls in his house, he showed them his son's bedroom with its toys and souvenirs, keeping up his pretense of normalcy. Once in his house near the Pac HiWay, Ridgway said he usually asked the women to go into his bathroom to wash their "vaginas" while he watched through the open door. Aside from crude slang, he didn't know how to describe the female anatomy. He used the word *vagina* when he meant *vulva*. He insisted that none of the young prostitutes objected to his watching them through the open bathroom door.

He also urged them to urinate before sex. That way they wouldn't be as likely to wet his bed when he killed them. Indoors or outside, he had discovered that having intercourse "doggy style" gave him a physical advantage. Entering them from the rear—but never, he insisted, for anal penetration—gave him a physical advantage. After he ejaculated, he sometimes told them "I hear someone," and they lifted their heads to listen. Or they tilted their heads back as they reached for their clothing. With their throats exposed and extended, it was easy for him to press his right forearm against their larynxes and cut off their breath, choking them.

"If we were outside near the airport, they would look up as a plane went over, and that was when I did it," he said matter-of-factly. "If my right arm got tired, I used my left, and if they really fought, I would put my legs around them. I told them if they stopped fighting, I would let them go. But I was always going to kill them."

It was an eerie experience for anyone watching and listening. Ridgway's voice was tight, as if it was emerging under great pressure, and his words came out in bursts. Even so, he seemed quite comfortable about answering probing questions.

Because the victims meant nothing at all to him, he apparently had no preference about race or body type. He had "dated" some of the women before, but knowing them made no difference to him. "I just wanted to kill them. If they told me to hurry, that made me angry. And I would kill them."

Many of the girls had pleaded for their lives, telling him they had children at home, a family to take care of, or, quite truthfully, "I don't want to die." Of course, it didn't matter to him. Nothing that the hapless women could do dissuaded Ridgway from his goals. "Some went easily," he recalled, "and some fought hard, but they all died." He estimated that even the most violent struggle didn't last longer than two minutes.

He had never used a gun to kill, or a knife. "It would have been messy, and they still might be able to scream."

"Why did you choke them?" he was asked.

" 'Cause that was more personal and more rewarding than to shoot her."

He was indignant about the young women who had fought him, leaving bite marks or scratches. He had switched to ligatures that gave his arms more protection—anything that was handy or something he had prepared: towels, belts, extension cords, ropes, his necktie, socks, jumper cables, even his T-shirt.

Only one of the girls Ridgway brought to his house had fought him hard enough to escape his bedroom, managing to reach the front door. She was inches away from freedom when he caught her and killed her in his living room. Although it was impossible to know which victim that had been, it was likely that it was Kim Nelson, who was also known as Tina Tomson.

Had they not been attacked when they were completely off-guard, some of the women he killed might well have bested him. Tina Tomson was many inches taller than he was and weighed as much. Marie Malvar was small but she had hurt him badly, scratching him until he bled and leaving scars that he'd had to pour acid over to hide. Marie had made him very angry—so angry that he said he decided to leave her body all alone in a different place from the other girls. Later, he had tried to find her but he'd been consumed with such blind rage when he left her that he couldn't find her again for a long time.

Even though Ridgway claimed his anger was a natural reaction to having been cuckolded by his second wife, his interviewers knew that during the time after his divorce from Dana, he had had many consensual sexual partners. It hadn't mattered. He'd still roved along the highways, continually looking for prostitutes.

He described how he planned in advance how he'd get rid of the still-warm bodies of the victims he choked in his bedroom, protecting his mattress with plastic in case they urinated or evacuated their bowels as they died. "If that happened, then I would have to clean up," he said mildly, "and do laundry. I never closed their eyes or touched their faces. I dragged them out of the house on plastic or an old green rug I had, and put them in my truck. I got rid of them right away."

Once, he'd put a small woman into a blue metal footlocker that belonged to his son, Chad.

"What did you do with that trunk?"

"Afterward I sold it at a swap meet."

Wherever he had formed his ethics—or lack of them—about sex, he was alternately lewd and prim. He explained that he considered masturbation a greater sin than going to prostitutes. Sometimes, he'd had no choice but to seek out the women on the street. He didn't like "labels," and took offense when any of his questioners called him a serial rapist. "I'm not a serial rapist," he complained. "I'm a serial *killer.*"

Ridgway's stalking hours depended on what shift he was working at Kenworth, his vacation time, or whether Kenworth employees were on strike. He could verify dates by checking his job schedules. His own memories were precise only in his recall about whether the weather was warm or cold, wet or dry, when he picked up his prey.

53

ONE MORNING a few days after Gary Ridgway began his confessions to Green River Task Force detectives, Jon Mattsen and Tom Jensen were puzzled to find a man whose attitude was much changed. As if by rote, Ridgway gave them his breakfast menu, but rather than smiling at them and saying good morning, he turned away and sat with closed eyes, his back to them.

It was June 18, 2003, and his voice was tinged with anger as he said he'd awakened in the night and begun to think. "The *Other Gary* came into my mind," he said.

They wondered who the "Other Gary" was, but it soon became obvious that he was referring to a stronger, angrier persona than he had demonstrated so far.

The *Other Gary*, he told them, was enraged because of the power and control the detectives had over him. "You guys are trying to control me, but I never slept with a dead woman. Sure, I screwed them a couple of times. The 'New Gary' wants me to candy-coat this."

It was apparent that the man they had talked to until this morning was the "New Gary," a reasonable man who was pleasant and cooperative. The "Other Gary," who was also the "Old Gary" didn't want to talk about the murders and resented being controlled.

"I killed them because I wanted to," the Old Gary said. "I was mad. I killed forty-nine or fifty people between 1982 and 1985. I killed a lot of them because of my rage and anger at my ex-wife."

Now the Old Gary wanted to go out and find the bodies of his victims. *He* would call the shots about where they would go. The man with closed eyes stuttered as he said, "I hated 'em—hated 'em."

It had started, he said, with Wendy Coffield. "I don't give a shit about where I killed 'em. I didn't give a shit about them or their jewelry. Carol Christensen meant nothing to me. The fish I put on her were to attract animals. I dragged 'em by their feet. All of them didn't piss me off. Some I wasn't mad enough to kill."

Either this was another personality fighting its way out of the "New Gary" of 2003, or it was a clumsy attempt to present himself as a multiple personality. "I had sex with them afterward. They weren't human, I guess. I didn't give a shit. I bit [one of them] on the breast. I didn't know Mary was pregnant. The New Gary is a wimp."

Ridgway seemed genuinely angry as he spouted out filthy admissions for half an hour, his eyes squeezed shut. Jensen and Mattsen picked up on the dual method of interrogation the prisoner was suggesting. Perhaps even he couldn't tell them everything he had done unless he could hide behind "the Old Gary." That was fine with them. They pretended to respond to this angry man.

"The man who talked to us yesterday, the New Gary, was a real man," Tom Jensen said, but the personality now onstage wasn't buying it. The Old Gary was in charge and he insisted that he didn't let women control him. "I had sex with every one of them but the pregnant one. I dumped a bag with cans [off the bridge] on 216th. Maybe they had prints on them."

He continued to talk about how much he hated women, interspersing his monologue with details about evidence. "I left some jewelry by a tree near IHOP. I'm in charge now and I'm not gonna take it. I took three or four pictures of women under the Red Lion, and then I tore them up. I did write to the *Times* or the *P.I.* Don't waste your time looking under my houses.

"I killed two ladies after I met Judith."

Ridgway, whichever version this was, swore frequently although his grasp of scatological words wasn't very extensive. "Old Gary" or "New Gary," he had a limited vocabulary. He recalled killing one victim on the floor of his white van, using a cord pulled tight. "They're all pieces of trash to me—garbage."

"*Why?*" Jensen asked.

"Women always had control of me. They used me. I did cry after sometimes, but that was the good part of me. I'm the Old Gary now. The jewelry's gone. I left it at Kenworth or in the airport and some Laundromat. I left some in a covered part of a light pole, and in a seam in some concrete beside the Safeway, and then I peed in a corner by the fence."

They let him vent as he jumped from one subject to the next, not sure if this was an act. "That 'burn' on my arm isn't acid," he said. "It's where Marie Malvar scratched me. I had scratch marks on my back. . . . Once I dropped [a victim] on her head off the tailgate."

Jon Mattsen asked him about the cluster site near Exit 38 near North Bend, but Ridgway wasn't sure. "I did roll one down the hill at Star Lake," he said. "I didn't kill no damn dog. I had control of those bitches. I didn't have no love. Nobody loved *me*. So fuck 'em all! The New Gary is too soft. He's not gonna hurt anyone."

"What's the Old Gary gonna tell us?"

Still turned away from the detectives questioning him, Ridgway's eyes remained closed. "I killed a black lady in Ballard and one by a hospital. I took two to a graveyard by Washelli, and there's one by Kmart, one by Leisure Time. I did take a head to the Allstate parking lot in Oregon. There was blond hair on the head. There's three separate parts of bones on that funny-sounding road [Bull Mountain Road in Tigard], but I had a head that I lost."

This seemingly furious Ridgway told them that he'd worn gloves and switched his shoes from tennis shoes to his Kenworth shoes in an effort to throw them off. He'd replaced the tires on his 1975 Ford pickup so they couldn't be traced. He'd cut out some newspaper clips for information on what the task force was doing, and said he'd read four pages of a book that had information on evidence. He'd given two earrings to a girlfriend's daughter. Now he moved on to the girl who got away: Penny Bristow.

"There was one lady I strangled without killing—on 188th. Nice lady. Dark hair. I left her there, naked, and took her purse, but she didn't have any money. Sometimes I took their wallets and put their money in my pockets."

He mentioned a woman he'd talked to near the airport, and had "motel sex" with. "I picked her up later and I took her someplace and I killed her. I know that for sure."

He was probably referring to Keli McGinness, who had never been found. It may have been her severed head he took to Oregon with him, losing it in a culvert near the Allstate building.

The Old Gary was on a roll of rage, but it was sporadic now. "I didn't hug 'em and kiss 'em at all. I didn't give a crap about 'em. I had sex with a dead body [near where Connie Naon was found]. The other Gary's [the New Gary] all screwed up. If you want to know what I did, talk to me. I'm the one who did it. Sometimes I tore up I.D. on the highway and threw it out. For that short time, I was in control. I'm the one with the devil in my head. The New Gary didn't want me to come out. I don't have rage anymore, but I got mad last night. I don't have no rage no more.

"I'm in control now. You put words in his mouth. I didn't give a shit about sleeping with them. The numbers of victims came from *me*. I don't know if the New Gary can get back in. I killed 'em at S.I.R. [Seattle International Raceway], Green River College, 410, Riverton, Highway 18. I didn't shoot no women. Two on Black Diamond Road, Carnation Road . . ."

He faltered. "The old one . . . The new one just flipped back in."

Gary Ridgway's voice was softer, tired sounding, but he hinted he had more to say. Mattsen and Jensen tried to bring the Old Gary back, but he wouldn't come out. It was doubtful that Ridgway was a multiple personality. It seemed more believable that he had seen too many movies about multiples. And, in the Northwest, there had been massive coverage of the tapes of the "Hillside Strangler"— Kenneth Bianchi, arrested in 1980 for serial murders of young women in Los Angeles and Bellingham, Washington. Bianchi had done a very convincing double-personality. Ridgway's acting wasn't even in the ballpark.

Still, the session was very productive, if repugnant. Whether it was the Old Gary or the New Gary, he had admitted countless murders provoked by his fury at women in general. He had planned the murders and the disposal of the victims' bodies.

It wasn't yet nine thirty in the morning and he had filled the interview room with ugly admissions. The man Mattsen and Jensen had encountered at first seemed to have had his say, but the New Gary wanted to tell them things. He wanted to talk about the death of Giselle Lovvorn, the seventeen-year-old genius whose body was found at the south end of the deserted airport property.

"Chad was with me when I picked her up," he said. It had been on a weekend, and his son was staying with him.

Jensen and Mattsen exchanged a quick glance. This seemed so far outside the pale of what any father would do. But Ridgway went on talking, and he was currently "the New Gary," at that. But he assured them that he had left Chad—eight or nine at the time—in his truck while he walked the woman he called "LaVerne" well out of sight. The sex was over quickly, he explained, and then he had choked her with his forearm as a plane flew over.

"To be sure, I tied my black socks together and around her neck, and twisted the knot with a twig until it broke."

"Did she fight you?" Mattsen asked.

"I can't remember."

"How could you kill a woman right in front of your son?" Jensen asked.

"I was in charge," Ridgway said, but in the New Gary's mild-mannered voice. "We were out of sight."

"How long were you gone from Chad?"

"Probably five or ten minutes. When I came back, Chad asked where did the girl go. I just told him she lived nearby and she'd decided to walk home." He remembered that he took his son someplace, then came back alone to move the girl's body deep into the weeds.

They took a break. If Ridgway didn't need one, the two detectives certainly did.

Facing his questioners, the regular Gary was still with them. He apparently didn't get that whatever persona he affected, his confessions were odious. They had to convince him that nothing shocked them, but that wasn't true. However experienced Ridgway's questioners were, it was virtually impossible not to be taken aback by the complete and utter lack of feeling he demonstrated.

He did seem uncomfortable about giving the details of his intercourse with the corpses of the women he'd killed, and, for once, talked around his perversions, avoiding questions he seemed to anticipate.

"We have evidence of necrophilia," Mattsen said calmly. "You wouldn't be the first person, or the last, who did that."

"Yes . . . I did lie about that. I had to bury them and take them far away so I wouldn't go back to have sex with them. I had an urge to do that. It was a sexual release that I didn't have to pay for. Maybe it gave me power over them."

Ridgway admitted to returning to the bodies of about ten of the women he had left close to the Strip. "That would be a good day, an evening when I got off work and go have sex with her. And that'd last for one or two days till I couldn't—till the flies came. And I'd bury them and cover them up. And then I'd look for another. Sometimes, I killed one one day and I killed one the next day [and] there wouldn't be no reason to go back."

He had returned to one victim to have intercourse with her body even though his eight-year-old son was asleep in his truck thirty feet away. When he was asked what would happen if his son remembered that and threatened to tell, he wasn't sure.

"Would you kill him?"

"No . . . I might have."

Penny Bristow, the one girl who got away from Gary Ridgway, had always felt that he only wanted her dead, and that live sex hadn't mattered. Even though he'd demanded fellatio, he had no erection. "I don't even know why he took his clothes off," she said. "His face looked white, clammy, cold. His arms and everything were cold. His hands. He was a totally different person and he kind of made me think that, if he did kill me, since he wasn't interested in me sexually before that, he probably would have tried to have intercourse if I was dead."

DR. MARY ELLEN O'TOOLE may have come the closest to uncovering the early childhood events that had the devastating impact on the way Gary Ridgway viewed women and why he developed the aberrations that consumed him. O'Toole had initially explained that the F.B.I.'s Behavioral Science Unit didn't have time to consider the cases of every serial killer referred to them, and they didn't even care about how many victims a man might have taken. "They're not all equally interesting to us," she said. "I would need to put you through what I refer to as a 'verification process.' "

It was a challenge Ridgway could hardly have resisted. He had always wanted to be interesting, and he'd been anxious to present his perversions to her.

"At what age did you realize that there was something wrong with you?" O'Toole asked.

He thought it was when he was about ten. His "red flags" were his forgetfulness, his breathing, his allergy problems, and his depression. Dr. O'Toole said that was not what she meant; she was more interested in his paraphilic behaviors, a term she had to explain to him, starting from "personality disorders," which he seemed to grasp, and linking that to the abnormal sexual desires he had practiced: frotteurism, exposing himself, stalking, voyeurism, rape, murder for sexual release, and, finally, necrophilia.

Although he would deny it for a long time, Ridgway felt that the bodies of his victims "belonged" to him. As long as they weren't discovered and removed by the Green River Task Force detectives, they were his. "A beautiful person that was my property—uh, my *possession,*" he told O'Toole, "something only I knew, and I missed when they were found or where I lost 'em."

"How did you feel, Gary, back in the eighties when the bodies were found and taken away, those times they were discovered," O'Toole asked. "How did it feel?"

"It felt like they were taking something of mine that I put there."

That was, he explained later, why he had taken some of the skeletons or partial skeletons to Oregon. It was to confuse the task force detectives because he didn't want them to find and remove any more of his possessions. He'd often wished he could find some of the old "bottomless" mine shafts that still existed in southeast King County so he would know he had a secure place to leave the corpses of his victims. The bodies were both a burden to get rid of and treasures he wanted to keep.

O'Toole was particularly interested in his relationship with his late mother, and it proved she had good reason to be suspicious. Gary Ridgway had, indeed, had an inappropriate relationship with Mary Ridgway. When he was thirteen or fourteen, she had both humiliated him and sexually stimulated him after he wet his bed, something that happened at least three times a week and sometimes every day. "She said to me, 'Why aren't you like [your brothers]— they don't wet the bed. Only babies wet the bed. Aren't you ever going to grow up?' She degraded me. I didn't feel much love at that time."

But his mother spent fifteen minutes or more soaping, washing, and drying his penis and testicles, even though he often became erect when she did that. She had also appeared half naked in front of him, and even though he felt depressed and ashamed, he admitted to O'Toole that he had been sexually aroused. "Well, here's a woman like the ones out of the dirty magazines—she's got smooth legs, smooth figure, and breasts, tight skin. . . . She had breasts and a flat stomach and I probably saw her, maybe walked into the bathroom [when she was] on the toilet. She didn't have a penis or anything like that. [She was] someone that could turn somebody on, turn me on a little bit."

Ridgway admitted that he had peeked at his mother's breasts when her robe fell open, looking down far enough to see her nipples. He had also developed a "hard on" when she measured his inseam so she could buy the right size pants from Penney's, where she worked. He didn't know if she knew or not, but his mother often told his father and her sons about measuring male customers at work the same way, and feeling their penises become erect.

He insisted he had never touched his mother, although being so close to her physically when he was naked and she was partially undressed had made him want to touch a female. Nor had she ever caught him masturbating. He accomplished that after school in a locked bathroom before she got home from work at six. "I don't think she even talked about masturbating. It's like nasty to her to talk about it."

He didn't remember resenting his mother, although he admitted that he sometimes thought about stabbing her.

Quite probably stimulated by his mother's inappropriate touching, Ridgway admitted that he had begun to stalk girls and women when he was about twelve, hiding as he watched them in his neighborhood or in class, then following them and peering at them from across the street. "I'd have a hard-on, and think of the woman as a goal, find out where she lived. And then in the morning, I'd go the same way and watch her."

He admitted his compulsion not only to kill women but to have intercourse with them after they were dead. He pointed out he had not revisited all of his victims after death. The ones who had fought him and hurt him made him angry, and he punished them by leaving them in some deserted spot by themselves.

"Blondes were special," Ridgway said. "And I think there were at least four or five blondes. I don't remember having sex after I killed them. I always liked blondes with big breasts. They were the high-priced hookers and they were my special goal—to go out and get a blond lady and have sex with her and kill her. She was at the top of the list."

Keli McGinness, who had never been found, had been the most beautiful, the blonde who fulfilled his fantasy. Detective Sue Peters had looked for Keli for such a long time. Ridgway insisted that he had picked up six or seven hundred women, and despite studying pictures of the forty-nine known victims, he often claimed he just couldn't remember which ones he had killed or where he killed them.

"Did you take her to your house," Sue Peters asked. "Did you kill her in your truck, or did you kill her out in the woods someplace on a date?"

"I had to kill her in the back of the truck."

"That's what you originally told us."

"Well, I probably told you at my house, if I could have got her to my house."

Peters persisted. "Do you remember getting Keli McGinness into your house. . . . This is the one with large breasts. Do you remember lying with her on your bed?"

"No, I don't." His vagueness was ultimately frustrating.

"Where do you remember her?"

"In the back of the truck—the maroon Dodge."

"And when you picked her up on Pac HiWay—I don't even care *where* on Pac HiWay—where did you take her to date her and kill her?"

He sighed as he searched his unreliable memory. "Over in the airport area where I killed—" He knew he had played volleyball near where he had killed her, but he couldn't place the murder itself in his mind. "I remember vaguely killing somebody in that area—at least one or two."

"Where's her body?"

"Her body's up at Leisure Time."

"Are you a hundred percent sure, because before you gave her a fifty-fifty percent chance of being there at Leisure Time."

"I'll give her seventy-five, at least. The blond lady I took up there. It couldn't have been April because now I know where April was."

"Where was April?"

"I figure April was probably over at Lake Fenwick."

And so it went in a seemingly endless series of dialogues. He had said he left Keli McGinness in the middle of a cleared field near Auburn. He had said he took her head to Oregon and lost it in a culvert in the Allstate parking lot. If he really knew, he wasn't telling.

It was so mindless and so cruel.

Ridgway knew that he had picked up a small, thin black girl in the Rainier Avenue area, although, of course, he could not say when that was nor could he remember her face. "She had something wrong with one of her feet," he commented. "It was thinner than the other and it turned in funny."

"Did she have difficulty getting up into your pickup truck?" a detective asked.

"Yeah."

"Did you help her up?"

"No."

That would have been tiny Mary Exzetta West, sixteen, who was newly pregnant and scared in 1984. He didn't remember her face, but he remembered that he left her body in Seward Park after he killed her.

He gazed at the investigators day after day, sipping from his bottle of water, jotting notes on his yellow pad, his face as bland and unthreatening as the Pillsbury Doughboy's. But the investigators sensed the evil energy behind his eyes, and it was always good to walk out of the Green River Task Force headquarters, smell clean air, and realize that he was an aberration, unlike the vast percentage of human beings.

And he was caught, trapped so he could never kill again.

54

ALTHOUGH Gary Ridgway said he had left all of his victims lying on their backs, he added, "I didn't look in their faces. It was dark."

"Were their eyes open?" Jon Mattsen asked him.

"No. I don't know. I never closed their eyes," he said again. "I undressed them after they were dead, but I never touched their faces."

He recalled one woman whom he'd choked in the back of his truck. He had tried to bring her "back to life" with closed chest compressions. "But I couldn't."

Sometimes, in his house, he said he'd put plastic bags over the dead girls' heads to see if he could detect any breath left in them. "But I never had one wake up on me."

"Why did you try to resuscitate the one woman?" Tom Jensen asked.

"I panicked. I don't know why. It was daytime."

"Who was it?"

"I don't know. A white woman."

Ridgway admitted to killing Linda Rule, the blond girl whose skeleton had been found near Northgate Hospital, a homicide that had not been attributed to him. For some reason, he said he had set fire to her hair after she was dead, but he had become alarmed that someone would see or smell the smoke and put it out.

There were so many young women who had died, most of them with no forewarning. Gary Ridgway didn't care about them, but the task force detectives knew them as well as anyone they'd known in their lives, and they cared deeply about each victim. As Ridgway described their last moments, other faces flashed in the four investigators' consciousness—all the parents, sisters and brothers, even children of the lost girls. Each detective dealt with memories of the victims in his or her own way; some allowed themselves to remember the details of the lost lives, and some had to keep emotional distance for their own equilibrium.

And yet, day after day, they went back into the stuffy room to listen to Gary Ridgway spew out more venom and, almost worse, to hear him discuss his crimes with completely dispassionate recall of what he had done.

The interviews had to be accomplished, and they went on with little respite for more than a hundred hours. Outside, it was an unusually nice summer in Seattle, people were sunbathing along Puget Sound and flowers were blooming. For the task force detectives, and their prisoner, most of their ventures outside were the grim field trips to body sites.

"The one I covered with a bag was special," Ridgway admitted, as he spoke of Carol Christensen. He had known her, he had liked her, and she had been nice to him. He knew she had a little girl and that she was excited about her new job, but in terms of her chance for survival, it didn't matter. He recalled picking her up near her job at the Red Barn Tavern, and taking her to his home. According to him, she had enjoyed sexual intimacy with him, but on May 3 she was in a hurry to get home. "I wasn't satisfied," he remembered. "It made me mad. I got behind her and choked her with my arm."

Afterward, he had redressed Carol Ann, realizing that he had her bra on backward, but it didn't matter to him. He took time, he said, to drink the Lambrusco wine. Then he took the empty bottle, the trout that someone had given him, and the sausage along when he drove Christensen's body to the woods at Maple Valley. In the first ten days of questioning, he stressed that he wasn't "staging" a body scene as the F.B.I. agents deduced. "I left the fish and sausage to attract animals. I didn't want that stuff because I didn't cook."

For the first time, Ridgway showed a bit of remorse. "I laid her faceup, put the grocery bag over her head, and lay down with her," he said. "I cried because I killed her."

By all that was holy, he should have been caught that afternoon. As he drove out of the road to the woods where Carol Christensen's body lay, he said he saw a WSP patrol car coming out of the next road down. "I stopped at the first stoplight, and put on my signal to turn. I checked in the mirror to see if he had turned into the road I'd just left, but he didn't, and he didn't pay any attention to me."

Through sheer coincidence, Matt Haney, who was a King County new hire at the time, had stopped his patrol unit to talk with another officer a fraction of a mile away when the call about the body in the woods came from the sheriff's dispatcher.

But Gary Ridgway had slipped away. Given the chances he took and the degree of police activity hunting for him, he was diabolically lucky. Or perhaps, despite his initial protests, he'd been very careful. He'd been afraid of being caught after the first murder. But not since. Although he couldn't remember Wendy Coffield, he recalled that he had redressed her, and that the buttons on her blouse were the size of "dimes." Christensen was only the second victim he redressed.

Twenty years before, Ridgway figured he would never be caught. He'd learned to cut their fingernails so he wouldn't leave any of his skin beneath his victims' nails. He took their clothing away and threw it in Goodwill bins so the detectives wouldn't have any semen stains to test. He didn't understand DNA but he knew they could figure out something that way, and it might help them catch him. And although he claimed at first that he only put the fish and sausage with Carol Christensen's body to attract predatory animals, he had really done it to make the body scene look different. That would throw the police off, and it would taunt them, too. He thought the police wouldn't connect him to a body that was in a different place, with different clues.

In the beginning, he was right. But he *had* left his DNA behind, his semen in her body. And that was one of the bigger mistakes he'd made. He didn't realize that it was a ticking time bomb, albeit one that wouldn't explode until 2001.

His research to perfect his crimes continued. He had not only taken great pains, he said, to remove all traces of himself from the victims, his house and trucks, but he had begun to plant "evidence." He scattered cigarette butts and chewed gum at the cluster sites. (He didn't smoke or chew gum, but he gathered it in other places.) He took motel pamphlets and car rental agreements he'd found around the airport and threw them around the body sites to make the detectives believe they were looking for someone who traveled. He even left a hair pick used to groom Afros, thinking the investigators would suspect a black pimp. And it was Gary Ridgway who left Marie Malvar's driver's license at SeaTac Airport so people would think she'd taken a flight of her own accord. And, of course, he admitted he had written letters to the *Post-Intelligencer* and Mike Barber and others with false tips about who the Green River Killer might be.

Perhaps his smartest move in avoiding suspicion was that he talked to no one about what he had done. He had no close friends, and he didn't feel the need to brag about it. Most killers eventually feel compelled to talk about their crimes, if only to point out how cleverly they have avoided detection. Not Ridgway. He got enough gratification out of checking the sites where he'd left bodies years before. He was fascinated, he told detectives, that he found some skeletons virtually intact in areas where he had expected animals to dismantle them, and others, left in wide open fields, completely gone.

Later, Ridgway would say he lied to the task force detectives for the first ten days of the summer interviews in 2003. It was hard to tell sometimes if he had forgotten the truth, genuinely confusing the victims with one another, or if he was overtly lying. Sometimes he hinted that Wendy Coffield wasn't the first murder at all, that when he told the woman he was dating in PWP in late 1981 or early 1982 that he'd "almost killed a woman," he really had killed a woman. He even had vague feelings that he might have murdered a woman in the seventies, but he could not be sure.

Gary Ridgway had reasons to keep his interviewers on the hook. The longer he could delay making a formal guilty plea in court, the longer he could stay out of prison. His accommodations weren't lavish, but they were a lot better than a stark prison cell. And, here, he was still able to talk about murder and pontificate on all aspects of homicide.

Ridgway wasn't crazy—his attorneys hadn't even suggested a

multiple personality defense—and he certainly wasn't a genius. In fact, his I.Q. tested at low normal. He may, however, have been an idiot savant, someone of very low intelligence who shows remarkable brilliance in one area. (For instance, an idiot savant may be a musical prodigy or able to memorize the numbers on the side of every freight car on a long train as it passes by, but developmentally disabled in every other area of intelligence.)

Violent thoughts appeared to have been part of his thought processes for most of his life.

From the time he was in his early teens, Ridgway had studied murder, twisting and turning it in his mind. In some of his interviews with Mary Ellen O'Toole, he spent hours discussing motivations for murder, about his thoughts on how someone other than he had murdered a female neighbor forty years before, and offering his insights. It left the question: Did he kill that woman? There was no way to tell.

He did describe stabbing the six-year-old boy when he was fifteen or sixteen. Remarkably, one of the task force investigators had located that child—now a man of forty-six living in California. He recalled the incident well. The man remembered being dressed in cowboy boots and hat, wearing toy pistols on his belt, when a much older boy asked him if he wanted to build a fort. He had agreed and followed him into the woods.

"Then he said, 'You know, there's people around here that like to kill little boys like you.' " He'd grabbed the youngster's arm and led him farther into the trees. Suddenly, the teenager had stabbed him through his ribs into his liver.

"I asked him why he killed me. I watched too many cowboy movies, you know," Ridgway's early victim said, "and I saw all the blood pumping out of me. It was [bleeding] profusely—already running down my leg into my boots. With every heartbeat, it was just pumping out. The whole front of my shirt was soaked. And he started laughing, and had a smile on his face. He stood there for a minute, and he had the knife in his hand, and I didn't want him to stab me again. But he reached toward me and just wiped the knife off—both sides of the blade—once across my shoulder and twice across my shoulder on the other side. He folded [the knife] back up and he says, 'I always wanted to know what it felt like to kill somebody.'

"Then he started walking down that knoll and he was laughing, kinda putting his head in the air, you know, and laughing real loud."

■

RIDGWAY told his interrogators that he had read a lot of crime magazines and books in the past. I was jolted to learn that he had read *True Detective* magazine and other fact-detective magazines that I wrote for early in my career—even more discomfited to hear my name come from his mouth as Ridgway talked with Dr. Robert Wheeler, a psychologist who asked him what books he'd read.

"I read so many of 'em that they all come together. I read quite a lot," he said. "*Zodiac,* two or three of Ann Rule's, and a bunch. But I don't want to tell something that I haven't learned from them." He explained that he had read my books to learn how not to act in court. He was studying all the mistakes other defendants had made by jumping up in court when they should have kept quiet. He didn't want to do that.

I didn't want to be part of Gary Ridgway's thought processes. There is always the chance that disturbed and obsessed individuals may read something I have written, and I accept that as part of being a true-crime writer, but writing about Ridgway was the most difficult endeavor I would undertake, and I had no desire to be inside his head or hear him say my name. The sheer cruelty that consumed him and his total inability to empathize with any living thing is unfathomable, a black cloud of evil that was so hard to erase from my own memory.

WHEN—IF EVER—Gary Ridgway had stopped stalking and killing women was an obvious question. Nineteen eighty-two to 1984 were undoubtedly the peak years, but it is almost unheard of for serial killers to simply stop. They usually accelerate.

In talking with Dr. Robert Wheeler, Gary Ridgway said the last time he killed was in 1985. He insisted that his period of extreme rage, anger, and frustration only lasted for three years. "After 1985, I had a new wife that cared for me," he said. "I did yard work and stuff to help out with the anger."

"All of a sudden, in 1985," Wheeler asked incredulously, "when you got angry, you raked the lawn?"

"Yes."

He explained that he and Judith were having a nice life, vacationing in Las Vegas or Reno, gambling a little bit. They also went to Disneyland. He was trying to forget all about the bad time when he was alone and killing women. But he'd been angry again when the investigators from the task force served their search warrants in

1987. He was upset because they came to his work and said they were from the Green River Task Force. At that point, he was trying to forget all the murder stuff.

Ridgway's biggest fear in the summer of 2003 was that he might not be able to lead detectives to the bodies of his victims who were still missing, that his memory might fail him. If that happened, he felt he would probably be executed because they would think he was lying and failing to keep his part of the plea agreement.

He had thought a lot about the death penalty. He figured it wouldn't happen for seven or eight years, and he'd read about lethal injections. "It's a process that you just go to sleep and your heart stops, so there's very little pain."

Wheeler asked if he worried about being dead. Ridgway said he did, but he figured that if he told the truth and prayed, he would go to Heaven. Other prisoners had told him it would be worse to go to prison for the rest of his life. Still, all things considered, he wanted to live.

He was afraid of dying, he told Dr. Wheeler, and he wanted to get all the killings off his chest. "Confessing, and trying to help the families, and to give the best I can on that."

"And why do you want to help the families?"

"Because they'd like closure. They want to have a place for where their daughter or wife is buried."

"I don't mean any disrespect, Mr. Ridgway," Dr. Wheeler said carefully, "but why didn't you help the families in 1985?"

"Because I didn't want to go to jail."

Gary Ridgway's thoughts always circled back to himself. He said that he cried a lot, at first attributing that to the number of lives he had taken.

"You took a lot of lives mostly sometime before 1990. . . . Why are you crying about it now, rather than then?"

"Well, because I screwed up. How I screwed up on killing them. Maybe leaving too much evidence at the time."

Ridgway said he never thought about escaping, although he fantasized about there being an earthquake where he could just walk out of jail. But he knew there would be a price on his head and no one would care if he was dead or alive to collect "$100,000" reward. And where could he go? He didn't speak any foreign languages.

The only thing he had to look forward to were the "field trips" to look for bodies, even though the detectives wouldn't let him out of the car very often. He still liked the experience of going out on the same roads he took to deposit the bodies of his victims.

OF COURSE, one of Gary Ridgway's greatest anxieties was alleviated during those field trips, when he was successful in leading the task force searchers to the remains of Pammy Avent. Tips had said Pammy was living in Hollywood, or Denver, had given birth to a baby girl, and even that she was still working as a prostitute in a motel in the Seattle area. But she hadn't been in any of those places. Ridgway took the investigators to Highway 410 just east of Milepost 26. After six days of digging and raking, they'd found Pammy next to the fallen cedar log, the passing of seasons had buried her six inches beneath the forest floor.

Unerringly, again and again, he had led the task force detectives to isolated locations where Green River victims had been discovered over the years since 1982. To test his truthfulness, some of the sites they took him to were "false sites" where no women had ever been found. He never missed. There was no question that Gary Ridgway was the Green River Killer. He knew bleak facts that no one else could know, and his very life depended on his finding the truly lost victims. And now it looked as if he would, indeed, never have to enter either the gallows room or the fatal injection chamber at the Washington State Penitentiary in Walla Walla.

What he would face might be worse than the gallows. In November 2003, Gary Ridgway would have to plead guilty to aggravated first-degree murder in the deaths of forty-eight young women, and do so in the presence of those who had loved his victims. And, in December, his punishments would be meted out. Sentencing might be easier than listening to the words of those same survivors.

55

GARY RIDGWAY was expected to plead guilty on forty-eight murder counts on November 5, 2003. Prosecuting attorney Norm Maleng and Sheriff Dave Reichert and their staffs held a meeting that almost all of the victims' families attended. So there would be no surprises in the courtroom, they wanted the families to know why they had chosen the path they were taking, and to discuss their reasons for accepting Ridgway's guilty plea. The State had agreed to the Defense's proffer way back in June, but absolute secrecy was maintained. Accepting a guilty plea to aggravated murder in the first degree where the death penalty can be invoked violates statutes because, essentially, it allows a defendant to commit suicide. *This* plea bargain would save Ridgway's life, effectively eliminating the possibility of his being executed. For five months, he had allegedly been cooperating with the Green River Task Force, although some investigators thought he was still minimalizing his crimes.

The majority of the survivors accepted Norm Maleng's choice to plea bargain; some did not. They wanted to see Ridgway dead. They always would.

It had not been an easy decision for Maleng to make, nor a popular one with some voters, but politics had never driven him. In the end, he knew that he was doing the best thing for the most people. If his office had proceeded to what would be endless trials and appeals, Maleng doubted many questions would have been answered for those who still grieved for their children. He knew the pain of losing a child. One wintry day in 1989, his daughter, twelve-year-old Karen Leslie Maleng, was killed in a sledding accident on a snowy public street. Seattleites remembered that and the prosecutor's quiet courage in the face of such tragedy.

On that first Thursday in November, Superior Court Judge Richard A. Jones's courtroom was filled with families and friends, investigators and the media, all of whom had passed through heavy security. Ridgway shuffled in wearing his jail scrubs, his back to the gallery, a harmless-looking little man with thick, dark-rimmed glasses.

Gary Ridgway's voice was calm and emotionless as he acknowledged that he fully understood that he had signed away his rights to a trial in return for avoiding execution. He said, "Yes, I did" when Jeff Baird asked him multiple times if he had signed one clause or the other with his initials. Yes, he knew he would have no jury, no appeals, no new trials, no hope of ever walking free again. But he would live. He was an automaton now, carefully keeping his back to the gallery behind him, and he seemed no threat.

But the depth of his perversion would soon destroy that illusion. Although the defense quickly waived Baird's reading the entire sixteen pages of the charges, the gallery would hear enough.

Judge Jones had asked Ridgway to state, in his own words, why he was pleading guilty to forty-eight counts of murder, and he complied, although his confession had more legalese in it than he might generally use.

There was no way for the prosecution team to describe what Ridgway had done in "an antiseptic manner," Baird warned the judge and observers. The language would be graphic and disturbing, just as the hundreds of hours of taped interviews had been. Now, the public heard some of the worst of the acting out of Gary Ridgway's fantasies.

As Baird read Ridgway's statement aloud, there were muffled gasps and grief-stricken faces in the crowd on the other side of the courtroom's rail. "I killed the forty-eight women listed in the State's second amended information. In most cases, when I murdered these women, I did not know their names. Most of the time, I killed them the first time I met them and I do not have a good memory of their faces. I killed so many women I have a hard time keeping them straight. . . .

"I killed them all in King County. I killed most of them in my house near Military Road, and I killed a lot of them in my truck, not far from where I picked them up. I killed some of them outside. I remember leaving each woman's body in the place where she was found. . . . I picked prostitutes because I hate most prostitutes and I did not want to pay them for sex. I also picked prostitutes as victims because they were easy to pick up without being noticed. I knew they would not be reported missing right away, and might never be reported missing. I picked prostitutes because I thought I could kill as many of them as I wanted without being caught."

The entire summary of evidence would be released later. Baird and the other prosecutors had brilliantly winnowed down thousands of pages of police follow-ups and statements into a horrendous document recounting the crimes of a man consumed with cruelty and killing for more than forty years.

It didn't seem to trouble him; Ridgway answered "Guilty" in a monotone voice forty-eight times as the names of the dead girls— and four who had no names—were read aloud. Either he didn't care about them or he had no affect at all. It was probably the former. Never once in discussing his crimes had Ridgway appeared to have any remorse or regret as he talked with detectives about the murders he had committed; any emotional pain he'd felt was for *his* losses. There was no way to describe it verbally, but now they saw what he was, a roving predator who had perfected his techniques for luring the vulnerable with the same bland vacuity he demonstrated in court, killing them efficiently as he robbed them of air, allowing himself no more than an hour to load them into his truck—headed for the wilderness where he would throw them away.

Any living creature deserved better, and these were human beings sacrificed to fulfill his sexual appetite and assuage his rage, a rage the cause of which seemed unclear even to him. Gary Ridgway demonstrated a seemingly endless capacity as a killing machine.

As the charges were read, it was apparent that there were some unexpected and heretofore unknown victims who came after the young women who had become familiar to those who followed the Green River cases. In the months of interrogation, Ridgway's questioners had discovered that the murders had not stopped in 1984 or even 1985. After Judith moved in with him, the fires of his rage had been somewhat banked but not extinguished. He continued to patronize prostitutes and sit in dark spots along the Strip, watching the girls, seeking prey. On weekends, he had attended swap meets and garage sales with his trusting wife, gone camping and gardened. And he'd rarely missed work. But he had still found time for his favorite hobby: killing.

And killing was what he was all about. The spontaneous erections of his teenage years were long since gone even in the eighties. The women who went with him had had to perform oral sex to harden his penis enough so he was able to get behind them for intercourse. More important, he'd needed that position so he could choke them with his forearm. If they didn't die from his throttling them, he stood on their necks to finish the job.

He had perfected the murder part, and he got better over the years at hiding the dead girls. It must have been a matter of some pride for him that it had taken so many years to find some of the victims from the 1982 to 1984 spate of killing. He had apparently varied his master plans to throw the detectives off as the years rolled by—into the nineties, probably past the turn of the century.

THE BODY OF CINDY SMITH, the "Punky Brewster" girl who had just come home from California happily betrothed, hadn't been found for thirty-nine months. Children playing in a ditch near Green River Community College in June 1987, took a stick to poke at a pile of debris. They screamed and ran home when a human skull rolled out. With dental records, Cindy had been identified almost immediately. Ridgway had been confident that he could lead task force investigators to where he had left the rest of her body, but he faltered. He was confused because he was certain he had left Cindy as a beginning focal point to start another cluster site, and failing to locate the bodies he considered his property upset him. Finally, it became obvious that new roads had been built, changing the topography of the area. He could only place Cindy's resting spot from aerial photos. Once he did that, he visibly relaxed.

 THE SECOND VICTIM he'd disposed of in that general area fit his description of the S.I.R. auto race way site, but she hadn't been on the Green River list. Patricia Barczak was nineteen when she was last seen on October 18, 1986. A pretty, bubbly young woman with thick, frosted brown, shoulder-length hair, she had just completed a course in a culinary school and was on her way to fulfilling her dream of becoming a baker of wedding cakes. Like most girls her age, Patty was somewhat gullible when it came to men. Just before she disappeared, she was dating a man who'd led her to believe he had a successful career working at the Millionair's Club. Because she lived in Bellevue, she didn't know that the club, spelled without the usual *e,* wasn't an exclusive social spot but rather a shelter for down-and-outers, a longtime Seattle fixture that provided meals and day jobs for men on the streets. After she discovered that her boyfriend had grossly exaggerated his status, she had trouble getting him out of her house and out of her life. To avoid him, she had to meet her girlfriends someplace else, just to get a breath of fresh air, hoping in vain that he would be gone when she returned. But he had no home to go to, and he had staked out a claim on the couch of the apartment Patty shared with her roommates. He became an early suspect in her case.

Her worried mother told Bellevue detective Jim Hansen that Patty hadn't picked up her paycheck at the Winchell's Donut Shop where she worked. When Hansen found many of her things, including her backpack filled with personal and religious items that mattered to her, in her "boyfriend's" possession, he was on the hot seat, though the detective couldn't absolutely link him to her disappearance.

So Patty Barczak wasn't placed on the Green River victim list. When her skull was found in February 1993, two hundreds yards off Highway 18, near the entrance to the S.I.R., sheriff's captain Mike Nault was doubtful that she could be a Green River victim. The timing was off; the profile for the GRK said he liked to leave the bodies of his victims in the wilderness where he could revisit them and fantasize. Patty's skull was out in the open, near a freeway.

Even so, the girl who hadn't called her frantic mother for seven years shared certain characteristics with the other victims. Animals might well have moved her skull from where it had been originally. There was a remote, but possible, chance she had met the Green River Killer. But it was impossible to determine the cause of her death because no other bones were found. Her skull was buried in an infant's casket.

Ridgway had missed the news stories in 1993 when Patricia's skull was found, and that disturbed him. He had meant to surprise the task force investigators by giving them this new cluster, offering up at least one new victim. Although he cared nothing for their names, faces, or lives, he prided himself on keeping track of their bodies. And he was slipping. He was finally able to verify that he'd left Patricia Barczak close to the S.I.R. exit from the freeway, and within a half mile of Cindy Smith's skull. He referred to her as his "S.I.R. Lady," just as he called other victims things like "the Log Lady" and "the Water Tower Lady." He remembered that Patty had been a little overweight, and had dark hair, which, for him, was a detailed description. Only he knew if he'd left complete bodies or just their heads. Toward the later years, he had apparently decapitated many bodies, leaving the heads many miles apart from the torsos to confuse the task force.

 ONE OF THE PREVIOUSLY UNKNOWN VICTIMS that Gary Ridgway presented to his questioners was Roberta Hayes, twenty-one. She was "Bobby Joe" to her family. She had rounded cheeks and a wide smile, resembling Sally Field in her *Flying Nun* role. Despite her hard life, Bobby Joe looked younger than her years. But she had lived and lost so much in two decades, always seeking love and a permanent place that would be home to her. She was raised by her father and her stepmother, but she struck out on her own at the age of twelve, ill equipped for the challenge of the streets. Bobby Joe may have been running away from housework and child-care responsibilities at home. And yet she would give birth to her first child at fifteen and to four more in the next six years, all of them released to state agencies to be adopted.

Bobby Joe could be counted upon to show up at her maternal grandparents' house for Christmas and her birthday. She said she wanted to live with them, and while she was there, things were fine. But the lure of the streets always took her away. She was two people, really, trusting and almost naive when she was with her aunts, uncles, grandparents, and brothers, but flinty and obstinate when they ran into her on the streets somewhere, even though they pleaded with her to walk away from that life. No one in her family could totally convince her of how much they loved her. It was as if the time to be loved had passed her by and she could no longer accept it without question.

Bobby Joe had close companions in "the life," and she was drawn to them, too. She was a good and faithful friend. She usually worked the Aurora Avenue red-light area, a petite blond, blue-eyed girl who looked totally out of place. She didn't hate cops, and often stuck her head into a police unit to say "Hi" to the patrol officers who were trying to clean up the street. They tried to reason with her, too, but no one could warn her convincingly enough that she was playing with danger.

Sometimes Bobby Joe Hayes was far from home—in Sacramento, California, or in Portland. The last time anyone recalled seeing her she was in Portland, and it was February 7, 1987. Police in the Rose City had picked her up for prostitution and released her when she said she intended to go back to Seattle.

For some reason, she was never on the Green River victim list either. Looking back, February 1987 was a period when Gary Ridgway felt very confident that he would never be identified. Matt Haney's April 8 search warrants wouldn't be served for two months, and Ridgway had no idea that he was under surveillance.

At some point, he slid under the radar and killed Bobby Joe Hayes. As usual, he remembered very little about her. He thought she had had blondish brown hair and been "skinny." In 2003, he was able to draw an accurate map of the dead-end road off Highway 410 where he had left her body and, later, lead detectives to the site.

All the sixteen years Bobby Joe had been gone, her family had hoped that she would pop in at Christmas or for her birthday, yelling "Surprise!" Of course, as time passed, that possibility waned. But they didn't know what had happened to her—not until the investigators called them in the first week of November 2003 and told them that Ridgway had confessed to killing Bobby Joe. It was both a gift and a heartbreak. They no longer had to worry if she was lost, trapped, or in pain, but they knew she was gone forever.

Marta Reeves was a delicately featured brunette woman of

thirty-six, estranged from her husband and her four children, and seriously addicted to cocaine. Her only way to live and to feed her habit was to prostitute herself, and she worked the Central Area in Seattle, caught in an increasingly downward spiral. She called her husband asking for money sometime in March 1990, and he told her no. "Okay," she said wearily, "then I'll have to work all night."

That was Marta's last contact with anyone who knew her. In April, her husband received an envelope with the U.S. Postal Service's return address. Inside was Marta's driver's license, which had either been found and turned in to a post office or dropped into a mailbox. By the time her husband took it to the police, it was smudged with dozens of fingerprints superimposed upon one another, making it impossible to find even a portion of a clear print large enough to feed into the AFIS computers.

Six months after Marta's last phone call, mushroom hunters found scattered bones and some rotted clothing near the Highway 410 body cluster east of Enumclaw. That was in late September 1990; but it would be January 1991 before they were identified as Marta's.

Marta's body lay in a familiar woods that Gary Ridgway had described often during his almost daily interviews. He remembered the loop road off Highway 410 and pinpointed on the map where he had left Marta. As usual, he could not remember where he had picked her up, how he had killed her, or whether she was black or white. Six years after the height of his murder rampage, he was apparently stalking and killing less frequently, but the victims' humanity was still meaningless to him.

ONE MURDER Ridgway admitted would never have been known had he not told the detectives about it. Originally, it had been written off as an "accidental death." Patricia Yellow Robe was a tall, very thin woman, quite lovely when she wasn't using drugs. She was a member of the Chippewa-Cree nation, registered at the Rocky Boys Indian Reservation in Montana. She'd grown up in Havre and then Great Falls as the oldest of ten children who had complicated connections because their parents had married and remarried. They were a handsome family—all of them—and many of Trish's siblings were professionals, but she had struggled with drug and alcohol addiction for most of her life. In 1998, she was thirty-eight and living her usual precarious existence.

"She was always fun," recalled a younger sister who did legal work for a prosecutor. "She was ten years older than I was, and she took care of me—I could talk to her. She took me to the fair and on shopping sprees, and she taught me how to drive."

The Yellow Robes' grandmother was blind, and it was Trish who had been her "eyes," leading her gently wherever she needed to go. But later, Trish's lifestyle was unpredictable and she would take off on a whim. She had hooked up with men who took care of her for a while, but, inevitably, those relationships ended and her family worried about her. And then she would show up like Auntie Mame, sweep up her nieces and nephews and take them for ice cream or on some adventure. Trish had three children of her own: Diamond, Emerald, and Matthew. They were raised by their fathers or her mother, who saw they needed some stability.

"We'd lose track of Trish," her sister said with a sigh. "We asked her just to check in with us every two or three months so we would know she was okay, and usually she would. We sat together on the porch once toward the end of her life, and she told me how much she wanted to get clean and sober. She said she was sure she could beat it. She wanted to live."

"And I told her she was going to die if she didn't," her younger sister said. "I told her she was stronger than that, but then bad things happened and she would be gone again."

If Trish Yellow Robe had a new boyfriend or something else she wanted to show her siblings, she would come sweeping into their offices unexpectedly. They didn't mind because they loved her, and when she was happy, she *was* fun to have around. In August of 1998, the family was planning a dinner to celebrate one brother's birthday on the eighth. "We'd just heard from her on August 4," her sister said, "and she was due to come for dinner on his birthday. She was planning on it."

Trish Yellow Robe didn't make it. On the morning of Thursday, August 6, the owner of All City Wrecking, a business in the South Park area of Seattle, moved toward his locked cyclone fence and saw a woman lying just outside that fence in a gravel parking lot. At first he thought she was sleeping or had passed out, but she was dead. She was fully clothed in a T-shirt, jeans, underwear, socks, and boots.

It was Trish Yellow Robe. An autopsy revealed no possible cause of death beyond what was indicated in a tox screen of her blood, and the pathologist concluded: "The cause of death is acute, combined opiate and ethanol intoxication. The circumstances, scene investigation and postmortem examination, did not reveal evidence of significant injury. The manner of death is probable accident."

Her family viewed her body, saddened that Trish had died so young. "We thought it was an overdose," her sister said. "We could accept that. But she was bruised on her eye. The [prosecutors] told us that was postmortem lividity. We didn't question that because we all knew that Trish would be the first to go."

The task force detectives had never included Trish Yellow Robe as a possible Green River victim, and they had no information on her during the summer of 2003 as they questioned Gary Ridgway. Still, he had brought up South Park three times in June and July, all the while insisting he hadn't killed anyone he dated in the nineties.

As they drove him around on field trips, they used the South Park parking lot as a "false site" to test him. And despite new construction over the prior decade, Ridgway recognized the site, and it stirred something in his memory. He was able to describe Trish Yellow Robe's body placement perfectly, although actually killing a woman there was foggy in his mind.

It had taken a forensic psychologist to dredge up what Ridgway clearly did not want to remember. He was more at ease talking about the women who had died way back in the early eighties. Now it was apparent that he had murdered at least one woman fourteen years after he claimed to have stopped killing.

He didn't recognize a photo of Trish Yellow Robe in life, but he did identify a photo of her body. Again, there was a coincidence of dates that so often happened in the Green River probe. It was August 8, 2003, when Ridgway's memory of killing Trish popped up, five years and two days after her murder.

"I remember that one," he said. "The one at South Park. She wouldn't let me get behind her and screw her, and so I got madder and madder. And when we got out of the back of the truck, I opened the door for her and started choking her."

It had been her own fault, he pointed out. "She didn't want to spend an extra three or four minutes to have me climax and be a customer. She just said, 'You're over with'—something like that, and [she] got dressed, and I was still angry with her and choked her and after that I panicked. I didn't put her in the back of the truck and take it some place. I just left it there."

A reporter called Trish's sister, Alanna, in late October 2003, and blurted out that Trish had just been added to the Green River list. "I thought it was a bad joke," she said. "We had grieved for her, thinking she had died of an overdose. I told the reporter he was wrong, but he said he'd already talked to my father and it was true. Now we had to start a different kind of grieving."

With tears marking his face, Dave Reichert read all the lost girls' names aloud. They meant a great deal to the Green River Task Force even though they appeared to be negligible to the man who had just pleaded guilty.

Families watching and listening in the gallery would have their turn to speak, but not for weeks. Judge Jones set Ridgway's sentencing for Thursday, December 18, 2003, exactly a week before Christmas. In thirty years of covering murder trials in Seattle, I had attended many trials that had their denouement during the holidays, always aware of the dichotomy between the decorated tree in the lobby of the King County Courthouse and the grim proceedings on the upper floors. And yet this time it seemed right. All those families who had endured so many Christmases with a hollow spot that would never be filled, an empty place at their table, or around their tree would at least have a modicum of justice.

IT WAS OBVIOUS from the time the interviewing process began that Gary Ridgway considered Dave Reichert the "Man," the leader of all cops, the most daunting of opponents, and that he was tantalized by the idea of meeting him personally. He was, after all, the "High Sheriff," the boss of the detectives who questioned him every day. On some of his field trips, Ridgway thought he'd glimpsed Reichert in a car driving by and asked hopefully if it was him, only to be told "No."

They had met earlier that summer when Reichert, dressed in his perfectly pressed uniform with hash marks and gleaming brass, had come into the interview room at task force headquarters. Their first encounter had been a bit bizarre. Virtually nose-to-nose, Reichert stared at Ridgway, leaning further in toward the prisoner as his quarry shrunk back until it seemed they would both lose their balance and tip out of their chairs. They appeared not unlike a cartoon cat and mouse, with Reichert having the advantage. Minutes went by without his saying a word. Although Ridgway was clearly sweating, he had seemed unable to look away from Reichert's piercing blue eyes. Whatever he had expected to happen if they were ever to meet, it was obvious that this silent stare wasn't it.

The sheriff hadn't presided over the daily interviews, but he had monitored many of them. His personal animus toward Gary Ridgway was palpable, but when he finally spoke, Reichert played with the prisoner, seemingly almost genial at first. Ridgway was too dense and too intimidated to catch on.

Reichert remarked upon their many similarities—in age and in the region where they were both raised. He even confided in Ridgway that he, too, had suffered from dyslexia when he was a boy, and could understand why Ridgway had been worried that he would have to ride the "short bus" to Woodside School, the Highline School District's designated school for developmentally disabled students. It was a classic "You and me together" technique, and Ridgway, still wary, relaxed a little.

The sheriff commented on the irony of their ending up here in this interview room—one of them a confessed serial killer and the other the sheriff. He dangled a carrot. Wouldn't it be something if the two of them went on the road together, giving talks and seminars to law enforcement groups and psychiatrists and psychologists? He suggested that many people would be fascinated with what each of them had to say. There had never been anything like it, but he said he figured there was a huge potential audience for a man who had killed as many victims as Ridgway had.

Ridgway nodded nervously. He didn't know what to expect. He smiled tentatively as if he believed that Reichert was really going to take him on buses and trains and planes on some macabre dog and pony show. That would, of course, be the pinnacle of his life—to stand shoulder to shoulder with this man he clearly both admired and feared, and they would both discuss how successful he had been as a serial killer.

Sue Peters and Randy Mullinax, Jon Mattsen, Tom Jensen, and Jim Doyon had asked him questions, brought him up short and urged him to tell the truth, to stop "bullshitting" them, Drs. Chris Harris, Robert Wheeler, and Mary Ellen O'Toole had asked him the most intimate questions, and Ridgway had managed to look back at them with some shred of self-confidence. But the sheriff kept him off-balance. Reichert smiled at him, but not with his eyes. He seemed to be offering him the world, but he might jerk it back if Ridgway reached for it.

Their conversations had eventually turned into interrogations, of course. But it was much easier for Ridgway to give up secrets to the detectives with whom he felt more at ease. He could call them by their first names; Reichert was always the man in charge.

56

TWO DAYS BEFORE Ridgway's sentencing, Dave Reichert visited him again. As always, he was in full uniform, which gave him a distinct psychological advantage over the prisoner in his bright red jail scrubs over a long-sleeved maroon T-shirt. Reichert hitched up his chair and stared disconcertingly at Ridgway.

"How long you been here?" he asked.

"Six months, I guess. I came here on Friday, the thirteenth—in December."

He was wrong. Six months ago it had been June. He had lost track of time.

Reichert baited Ridgway: "How do you think things have been going?"

"Pretty good," Ridgway said, summing up what he had told Peters, Mullinax, Jensen, and Mattsen. "We're up to seventy-one victims, but there's six sites where we haven't found the bodies." He seemed to consider himself part of the team. It was not "they"; it was "we."

"Do you think we should call in the F.B.I.?"

This was obviously another carrot, with Reichert feigning ineptitude, tacitly admitting that his department couldn't carry out a search as well as the feds. Ridgway pondered that and answered that an organization as prestigious as the F.B.I. might have new search devices that could pick up some minerals in bones. Despite their last encounter, he appeared to be at ease, facing the sheriff man to man, discussing a mutual problem.

"What are some good things that have happened in the time you've been here?" Reichert eased the point of a hook in, tantalizing him, but Ridgway didn't get it yet.

"Well, sometimes we find an extra body, one they didn't account for," Ridgway said. And it was "good" that each find took more pressure off him, releasing a tightness in his chest. "I celebrate that I found another person."

"Why?"

Ridgway clearly flailed around in his mind to find an answer that would show he cared about the victims' families. But his answers were self-serving and completely off the point. And Reichert kept responding with "Why?" to everything he said.

Ridgway spoke of some of the clever things he had done to fool the Green River Task Force. "I didn't lick the letter I sent to the paper," he said.

"Why?"

It was DNA that had trapped Ridgway, but he would not say that term. He only repeated that he had not licked the flap of the envelope. He pointed out that he had typed the letter instead of writing it in longhand. He thought that had been smart.

"You did a good job in court," Reichert said suddenly.

"Thank you." Ridgway explained that he was concerned, though, about the sentencing. He was afraid he might trip walking in, given the restriction of his leg shackles, or that he would cry or the families would yell at him. He wanted them to know that some of the victims had "touched" him.

Disbelief in his tone, Reichert asked him just how they had done that, and the prisoner reached into his memory and pulled out Debbie Abernathy's name.

Reichert wanted to know in what way.

"Because it was on Chad's birthday," Ridgway said. It was obviously almost impossible for him to connect with the women he had murdered, or to see them as human beings. He had to connect any sadness to something or someone involved with himself. He said he felt bad about Colleen Brockman because he killed her on Christmas Eve. And he was sorry because "Meehan" had been pregnant, and he hadn't noticed that. He felt bad, he said, about Connie Naon "because she was beautiful."

But all in all, he thought that the session where he had pleaded guilty "went real good."

"What about Thursday?" Reichert asked, referring to the sentencing date.

Ridgway said he'd read some of the letters the families had sent—the ones who couldn't be there—but he didn't want to discuss them much. The families had called him evil, and he thought that was probably true, but he hastened to point out that it wasn't his fault if he was. He had done it all from "lack of love." He figured it might take five or six hours for the families to say what they wanted to say.

"But I have remorse—sadness in my heart. I'll answer their questions," he said confidently.

"You won't have a dialogue with them," Reichert said. "Would it matter to you if someone killed your son, what they said to you? Would it matter if they said, 'Sorry, I'm the devil and I'm evil'?" And then in a conversational tone, Reichert asked, "Why *did* you [kill them]?"

"I had a craving, because they were prostitutes. I wanted to kill them. . . . Wanted to control them."

"You can control people without killing them."

Reichert kept pelting Ridgway with "Whys?" as he searched hard to find reasons for his killing rampages.

"I was mad at them," he finally blurted. He had tried to impress the task force investigators all along with his explanation that he had actually killed the "hookers" to help them keep the streets clean. The detectives had never appreciated what he had done for them.

There was no disguising Dave Reichert's profound hatred for the man in front of him. It seeped out of his pores. It had gone beyond a contest between a lawman and a killer, and he probably had to fight an impulse to put his hands on Ridgway.

Reichert believed Ridgway was withholding information, and he hoped to find more answers. He pointed out that Ridgway was still making all kinds of excuses, even though there was no way to justify what he had done. "They were 'garbage' all along; they had no meaning to you," the sheriff said.

"They have meaning now." Ridgway speculated that he should go back to Woodside School, that he needed to go back in time to cure the "learning disability" that had caused him to lack "caring" for others. That made little sense, but it still would allow him to take the stain of his crimes off his hands.

He told the sheriff that he could not recall killing anyone in the sixties or seventies, only the time when he stabbed the neighborhood kid, and, after all, he hadn't died.

"We were looking forward to six months more with you," Reichert said. "But you shut down after you pleaded guilty. Why should you talk to us now? Don't you have a nice place to stay back there?"

"Yeah. My stay here has been good. They've treated me really good." Ridgway agreed that the little room in the task force headquarters was probably a lot nicer than his prison cell would be. He knew that he would need to have his "back to the wall," because other inmates would try to kill him. He'd listened to advice from inmates at the King County Jail and they had warned him about that.

Reichert reminded him that once he went to prison, he wouldn't have all the benefits he currently enjoyed, and urged him to give up the rest of the secrets he held on to so tightly. But everyone had noticed that he had changed. He wasn't telling them all he knew. "You're cocky now."

The sheriff said that Sue Peters, Randy Mullinax, Jon Mattsen, and Tom Jensen were walking out of interviews angry because Ridgway had stopped giving them information. He had only two more days to tell them what he knew. Then he was going away, headed for prison. "My detectives are pissed, tired of your lies, your crap, your bullshit," Reichert said. "You're still hiding secrets. All the souvenirs that would give you credibility. I'm going to find them. We're going to X-ray your houses— But we're not going to come over there [to prison] to talk with you."

Ridgway wasn't concerned about that. He planned on detectives from other counties—Snohomish, Pierce, and maybe San Diego—visiting him to ask questions. What he couldn't recall right now, he figured he could spend his time in prison trying to remember—*if* there were murders he'd forgotten.

For the first time, Ridgway bridled at Reichert, telling him firmly that he would not find any evidence in the houses he and Judith had lived in. "There are no souvenirs—the jewelry was at Kenworth, and the other places I told you. Your X-rays won't find them—that's a major quote. I'm one hundred percent sure you're not going to find anything."

"I don't believe you," Reichert said, and then asked, "Are you mad at me?

"No." But it was clear that he was. Reichert had managed to get under Ridgway's skin. Whatever he remembered, he would have to walk a geographical tightrope, aware of county and state boundary lines. He admitted that he was worried that he may have forgotten some of his murders, and that would mean he had broken the agreement. He said he expected to be back in King County within a year on new charges. He didn't mention that there could be other counties and other states involved. He wanted to live, but he knew the death penalty was hovering over him. That was what was scaring him.

He was clearly holding back. Earlier in this last interview, Ridgway had mentioned seventy-one victims, and yet he had admitted to only forty-eight. Kase Lee, Keli Kay McGinness, and Patricia Osborn had never been found. And there were still unidentified bones, and probably undiscovered bones, of some of the women who had never been reported missing. Who were the others? And what proof did any of the agencies interested in him have that there weren't eighty-one or ninety-one? He had sometimes said he had killed right up until 2001.

Ridgway's eyes darted, showing that his mind was racing, searching the dark corners of his memory to be sure he didn't reveal something that would break his deal with the prosecutor.

"You're a coward," Reichert said scathingly. "You're an evil, murdering, monstrous, cowardly man. You got behind sixteen-year-old girls and choked them."

"They died slow," Ridgway said, accidentally giving new information in his anger. "I never had one wake up on me. I counted to sixty to be sure. I used a ruler to twist the knot to be sure they were dead. That's why there was a tourniquet mark. That was after they were dead."

"You're a rapist."

"I had sex for money."

"Isn't that rape?"

"No, it's robbery."

"A rapist is lowest on the totem pole in prison."

"I'm not a rapist. I paid them for sex and I killed them."

"No, it's rape, robbery, *and* murder," Reichert countered. "You're a coward. That's why you chose women. You chose weak, young women because you're a coward." He reminded Ridgway that he hadn't killed the witness in the raft in the Green River because he was a man.

"I might have," Ridgway objected. "I might have."

"Judith and Chad won't visit you," Reichert said. Why would Chad visit his father now that he knew he might well have killed him?

Ridgway said he thought Judith was going on with her life, and seeing other men. "I have to suffer now," he said mournfully.

"You think *you're* going to suffer?"

Dave Reichert gave Gary Ridgway one more chance to tell the task force everything he knew. If he did that, the sheriff would try to buy him another six months outside prison walls. He wouldn't have to watch his back all the time, the food would be better, and there would be more field trips. Eventually, of course, he was going to the "joint," but he could stave it off if he told them the truth—*all* of the truth.

"Right now, give me something?" Reichert asked, mentioning the name of an unsolved case.

"I can't."

"Then you're on your way," Reichert said in disgust. "I hope, Ridgway, for your sake, you've told us everything you know. Well, this is it. I can't say it's been a pleasure because it hasn't. I don't like you. I don't like what you did. No one does. You don't even like yourself. . . . This will end the interview process."

The scene froze on a room empty save for Gary Ridgway. It *was* the end of the interview process. But he still had to face a courtroom full of people who had every reason to hate him.

THE WEATHER on December 18, 2003, was unseasonably warm and the sun shone brightly on the self-contained satellite television trucks parked along 4th Avenue and Yesler Street, and even on the scrubby grass of City Hall Park next to the courthouse. The moment the sentencing was over, local stations, Court TV, and CNN would go on-air. Media seats for December 18, 2003, were at a premium. Reporters would sit where juries usually sat, our names thrown into a "hat" to be drawn, hopefully, by Gene Johnston, the designated Associated Press correspondent. Because I was neither fish nor fowl—not a newspaper, radio, television, or wire service correspondent—I first had to establish that I was a journalist, albeit one whose coverage of legal proceedings came out months after verdicts and sentences were announced. I managed to do that by listing my twenty-two books and hundreds of articles on actual criminal cases. I was relieved to see my name on the list of those who would be allowed into the courtroom. My assigned seat was in the middle of the front row of the jury box, between Liz Rocha from KOMO, the ABC affiliate in Seattle, who had covered the Green River murders for almost as long as I had but in more depth in recent years, and a *Washington Post* correspondent.

I'd won the draw, but was I lucky to be there? As a journalist, yes, but the pain in that courtroom was pervasive, clinging to everyone, except, perhaps, the man who would be sentenced. I had never witnessed a more intensely compressed period of grief, fury, hopelessness, or, in a few surprising instances, forgiveness.

Before Judge Jones handed down Ridgway's sentences, each family member who wished to speak directly to the man who had murdered a daughter, granddaughter, sister, mother, niece, or best friend would be allowed ten minutes to tell him what they thought of him. That broke down to less than thirty seconds for every year they had waited to see the nameless, faceless Green River Killer caught. It had to be that way, or the proceedings could go on endlessly.

The families filled the benches from the front of the courtroom to more than halfway back, some just behind the rail where it looked as if they could have leaned forward close enough to touch Gary Ridgway, although court security would have stopped them. Most of the detectives who had worked the Green River cases since 1982 sat in the rear, or off to the side. Many of those who had retired, including Dick Kraske, had come back to see the ending of it all for themselves. Frank Adamson had decided he couldn't stand the pain of it. Some detectives were long dead.

Court security was no-nonsense, and everyone had passed through very sensitive metal detectors outside the courtroom in addition to those at the entrance to the courthouse itself. I hugged Mertie Winston, a friend as well as Tracy's mother, and was told the press was not allowed to talk to anyone. When Sue Peters said "Hi" to me, it was the same. No conversation. Everyone in the courtroom was to take his or her seat, entering and exiting as we were directed. This was, of course, understandable. Despite the court deputies' vigilance there was great potential for violence. Ironically, Gary Ridgway had to be protected from harm.

Once everyone was seated, Ridgway was brought in through a door on Judge Jones's right, surrounded by armed guards and his six attorneys. Although he had claimed he was five feet ten inches tall, he appeared to be five feet six at most, a pallid little man in white scrubs that advertised his ultra-security status. Beneath that, he wore his usual wine-colored long-sleeved T-shirt. The central crease in his forehead had deepened since his arrest, and there were several half-moon-shaped wrinkles above his eyes, all of which made his face appear to be made of immutable clay or plastic. Six feet away from me, he sat looking down, both hands flat on the table in front of him.

There were no empty seats at all. No room for the regular court watchers. The tension in the room was palpable, the air itself difficult to draw in. Someone coughed and an infant wailed.

Deputy Prosecutors Sean O'Donnell and Ian Goodhew took turns reading the sentence guidelines for each victim's murder, and what was over quickly in an ordinary hearing took a long time for this one. "The defendant has pled guilty and agreed to a mandatory sentence of life in prison without the possibility of early release or parole."

O'Donnell repeated the phrases forty-eight times, naming each victim. It was only fair. Each victim had died her own death at Ridgway's hands. Each deserved to have her life matter. His sentences would run consecutively, not concurrently.

Ridgway would be in prison for eternity, and Goodhew said that he would also face a fine of $50,000 on each charge. The families would be allowed to submit their claims for restitution at a future time, although there would be little reason for doing that. He had no money. With her greatly reduced income and attorneys' fees, Judith had had no choice but to sell their home at a loss.

The Son of Sam law would be invoked, preventing Ridgway from profiting from his crimes. Under no circumstances would he ever be allowed to contact his victims' families.

Deputy Prosecutor Patty Eakes acknowledged the family members in the courtroom who had chosen not to speak to Ridgway, and also those who could not be there but who had sent letters to Judge Jones to be passed on to Ridgway. Then she introduced each family member as they approached the lectern next to the jury box to speak directly to Gary Ridgway. At the Court's direction, he had turned in his chair so that he had to look into their eyes. As the survivors stood at the lectern, they were, perhaps, fifteen feet from the killer.

Those who still mourned deeply were from all backgrounds, all races, all ages, all demographic groups. Although it was probably the first time most of them had spoken in public, they were remarkably eloquent as they stared at the man who had taken the lives of the young women they loved. No one else could have scripted what they needed to say. All of their stories were different and yet, in some ways, the same.

They told Ridgway what the girls he had called "garbage" and "trash" were really like, and about the sadness and loss he had caused their families: the premature deaths caused by grief, the suicides, the memories that crowded back, especially at holidays or when babies were born who would never know their aunts.

Garrett Mills recalled his lonely memorial to the little sister he had promised to protect forever. He had visited the junior high where he and Opal had their last happy times, and he'd left roses in the dirt beneath the swings where they used to play. He'd also eaten a doughnut—something Opal always enjoyed—in her memory, remembering how she worried continually about losing weight. At the Green River, he had sat and cried for Opal. He recalled two fishermen who had paused as they tossed beer cans into the water, staring at him and clearly wondering "what kind of fool I was." They were unaware that Opal's body had once lain there. Garrett said he had left roses and doughnuts on the riverbank, too.

One woman said that her sister had "met her first monster" in her own home, enduring a family member's abuse until it drove her out to the streets in a desperate escape. And there, the teenager had met her second monster: Gary Ridgway.

Many family members wanted Ridgway to "burn in hell," or wished him a long and miserable life behind bars. They warned him of what lay ahead and said they would rejoice in the news that a guard had been distracted just long enough for an avenging prisoner to attack him. They called him a disposable man consumed with evil, "garbage" and "trash" himself, the spawn of the devil, and almost every epithet known in the English language. And yet they did it with a dignity born of years of suffering. They were not out of control; they had waited so long to face an unknown terror but their words were measured and well thought out.

I never saw Ridgway change his expression. He seemed incapable of grasping any emotion at all. Their words bounced off his "plastic" face, and only rarely did he even blink behind his thick glasses.

Beyond seeing their limitless pain, I was most impressed by how many of the dead girls' survivors said they refused to remain hostage to Gary Ridgway. They had come to realize, they said, that if they continued to despise him, he would win. And they would not allow it. He would not be part of their thoughts any longer, not even as an object of hatred.

Many of those who spoke thanked the Green River Task Force, specific detectives who had helped them, Sheriff Reichert, and the prosecuting team for bringing justice to their loved ones. One even thanked the defense team for doing a job that must have been onerous for them. Original poems had been written and classics were quoted, and the ghosts of the long-dead victims were somehow present in the courtroom, silent and invisible witnesses. Almost all of us had tears in our eyes.

And still Gary Ridgway's facial expression remained the same. Untouched. Removed. It wasn't until three survivors forgave him that his eyes filled. Opal's mother, Kathy Mills, thanked him for the fact that there had been no trial. She didn't think she could have gone through that. "You have held us in bondage for all these years," she intoned, "because we hated you. We wanted to see you die, but it's all going to be over now. . . . Gary Leon Ridgway, I forgive you. You can't hold me anymore. The word of God says I have to."

Ridgway blinked at that. He was as he always had been. If something directly affected *him,* he reacted. He had always felt sorry for himself.

Linda Rule's father, Robert, was a large man with a snowy beard, and I jotted down "Santa Claus type" next to his name. As it turned out, he did work as a store Santa Claus during the holiday season. But he, too, got a reaction from Ridgway. "Mr. Ridgway," he began, "there are people here that hate you. I'm not one of them. I forgive you for what you have done. God says to forgive all so you are forgiven, sir."

At this, Ridgway took off his glasses so he could wipe the tears that coursed from his eyes with his handkerchief. He had told Dave Reichert that he hoped he wouldn't cry during the sentencing, but he appeared touched by forgiveness in the face of so many who had not forgiven him, and probably never would.

I didn't believe his tears. It was obvious that they weren't for his victims—they were for himself. As Green River investigator Kevin O'Keefe said, "I think he's got all the emotions of a reptile."

Trish Yellow Robe's sisters were the last to approach the lectern. When they had spoken, committing her to "The Great Spirit," it was time to hear any remarks the killer might choose to make. He did have words, and he shuffled up to stand before Judge Jones and haltingly read his statement, stumbling over what he had printed. He did not look at his victims' families, however, the group to whom he should have directed his "apology."

"I'm sorry for killing all those young ladys," he said, choking up a little as he read the short sentences he or someone else had printed on a single sheet of paper. The words were mostly spelled correctly in this document, unlike the letter he had once sent to the newspaper. There were commas and periods.

> I have tried hard to remember as much as I could to help the detectives find and recover the ladys. I'm sorry for the scare I put in the community. I want to thank the police, prosecutors, my attorneys and all the other, that had the patience to work with me and

help me remember all the terrible thing I did and to be able to talk about them. I know how horrible my acts were. I have tried for a long time to get these things out of my mind. I have tried for a long time to keep from killing anymore ladys. I'm sorry that I've put my wife, my son, my brothers and my family through this hell. I hope that they can find a way to forgive me. I am very sorry for the Ladys that were not found. May they rest in peace. They need a better place than where I gave them. I'm sorry for killing these young Ladys. They had their whole life ahead of them. I am sorry I caused so much pain to so many families.

Gary L Ridgway.

Judge Richard Jones, appointed to the bench nine years earlier, had maintained a relatively serene courtroom despite the incendiary possibilities in the hearings of such a high-profile offender. Jones was an outstanding jurist who had lectured often to attorneys at Continuing Legal Education classes and to bar associations. The brother of music legend Quincy Jones, he was very accomplished in his own field.

Judge Jones had read the letters from the anguished parents thoughtfully, and he recalled one. "There is a hole in my heart," a mother had written. "A vacancy that only my child can occupy. The emptiness is deep and it hurts."

He also quoted the poet John Dryden: "Murder may go unpunish'd for a time, but tardy justice will oertake the crime." And, indeed, it had. Now he ordered Gary Ridgway to turn toward the gallery and look at the faces of those who grieved, suggesting that these tearstained faces should be the last memory he had of the free world. "The remarkable thing about you," Judge Jones commented, "is your Teflon-coated emotions and complete absence of genuine compassion for the young women you murdered."

And that was, indeed, what anyone who observed Gary Ridgway would remember—the automaton, the robot, the true animal who appeared to operate from the limbic system of his brain with no censoring from the frontal lobe. He had admitted to detectives and psychologists that he might have killed his own son, his wife, his mother, anyone who interfered in his survival and his continuous pursuit of sadism and pleasure.

Judge Jones honored the memory of the victims as he prepared to sentence Ridgway. He asked for forty-eight seconds of silence before he pronounced the sentences.

Gary Ridgway was sentenced to forty-eight life sentences without possibility of early release or parole, sentences that will, indeed, run consecutively. He will be liable for all the fines the prosecution had mentioned. Judge Jones added a final, somewhat bizarre, punishment. Ridgway had to give up his permit to carry a firearm. That seemed to be the least of his worries.

As former deputy prosecutor Al Matthews observed the final denouement of the Green River murders case, he was ambivalent. Like all of the others who had worked for decades to convict a killer, he felt a sense of triumph for the final resolution.

He didn't regret that he hadn't gone ahead in 1987 and pushed for a State case based on a great deal of circumstantial evidence. "I felt strongly that he was the one. If I filed the case and tried it, I [believed] I could get past a half time motion for dismissal. The problem was that with no physical evidence, there was no telling what a trial would bring. And, of course, we would only get one shot at him."

He meant that double jeopardy would attach if Ridgway was acquitted, and he could have walked away, knowing that he could not be tried twice for the same crimes.

"Only one thing bothers me," Matthews would recall. "It was all a matter of a savage who had to be in control. At the very end, he still was. He avoided the death penalty by controlling the situation and providing the information to keep himself alive."

AND AT LAST it was over. The sun was still shining and the air smelled good as I walked out of the courthouse to be interviewed by Nancy Grace of Court TV. Shell-shocked family members were all around me, negotiating their way past construction barricades around the aging courthouse, ducking the microphones thrust into their faces, hurrying away from what must have been one of the worst days of their lives.

I saw a familiar face from the eighties. Melvyn Foster, no longer a "person of interest," had come to watch the sentencing. He wore a jacket advertising the popular forensic detective series of the day: *CSI*.

And then I saw Dick Kraske standing off to one side, watching new, young detectives being interviewed. Dave Reichert stood in the center of the media's lights, but he wasn't a young detective any longer either. So many years had passed.

It was the end of a terrible era.

AFTERWORD

THE GREEN RIVER TASK FORCE, much diminished, continues to follow up unsolved crimes and unidentified bodies that may be linked to Gary Ridgway. The consensus is that there will be more corpses surfacing in the months and years to come. In the meantime, the world moves on without him.

Dave Reichert is still the sheriff of King County, but perhaps not for long. Ridgway's capture made Reichert a media star. For two years, rumor had it that Reichert would run for governor. Instead, he set his sights on Washington, D.C., and, in 2004, became a Republican candidate for Congress representing the Eastside of King County. If he should go to Washington, it is likely that Tom Jensen and John Urquhart will go with him.

Sue Peters went to Africa on safari in early 2004, about as far as she could get from the cloistered interview room at Green River headquarters where she spent six months in 2003. She continues to work on the Green River cases, hoping, especially, to find an answer to Keli McGinness's fate.

Some years ago, Peters and Detective Denny Gulla, determined to save as many young women as they could, put together a program called the Highway Intelligence Team (H.I.T.). With detectives Jesse Anderson and Christine Bartlette, they go back once a month, to the Strip and other locations where prostitution is rife, looking for the working girls of a new generation. They are not there to arrest them but rather to check on their welfare.

"I give them my card," Peters says, "and tell them they can call me twenty-four hours a day if they need help. I do my best to put them in touch with services they need and, hopefully, to get them off the street."

Peters and the other three detectives are available all the time, and she has received phone calls from desperate girls at all hours of the day and night. "When I get to know them, I ask for the names of the motels where they usually stay, for their dental information, and if they have any significant scars," Peters says. "Sometimes they ask me why I need to know that, and I tell them the truth: 'So we can identify your body if something happens to you.' That shocks them and makes them realize how dangerous it is to be out there."

A few of Peters's and Gulla's "regulars" call once or twice a week just to check in. It gives them a lifeline and a connection to someone who cares about them. Although gathering information is definitely not the primary purpose of H.I.T., many of the young women report "bad dates" and their license plate numbers. Some of their warnings have led to the arrests of serial rapists.

Randy Mullinax has put together a comprehensive seminar on the Green River investigation that is much in demand with law enforcement agencies all over the country.

Bob Gebo, Ed Streidinger, and Kevin O'Keefe have returned to the Seattle Police Department. Frank Adamson has retired. Richard Kraske has retired. Cherisse Luxa has retired. Ben Colwell has retired. Medical Examiner Dr. Donald Reay has retired, and lives on an island in Puget Sound where he recently completed a class on repairing boat motors—as far from forensic pathology as he could get.

Bill Haglund continues to aid in identifying victims of terrorist slaughters in foreign countries.

Danny Nolan, Paul Smith, Ralf McAllister, Jim Pompey, Dr. John Berberich, and Tonya Yzaguerre are deceased.

Matt Haney is the chief of police of Bainbridge Island, Washington. Robert Keppel is a professor at Sam Houston State University in Huntsville, Texas, teaching criminology and investigative techniques.

Judith Ridgway lives in seclusion, but has told friends that she plans to write a book about her marriage to Gary Ridgway.

Chad Ridgway is in the marines in California.

Judy DeLeone, Carrie Rois's mother, broke her ankle a few years after Carrie's remains were found. An undiagnosed blood clot formed, and she died suddenly from a pulmonary embolism.

Mertie Winston suffered a stroke shortly after Tracy Winston's remains were identified, but has fought her way back to complete recovery.

Suzanne Villamin lives with her little dog in an apartment in downtown Seattle, surrounded by memories of her daughter, Mary Bello.

Looking through a two-foot-high stack of emails, letters, and phone notes I received over twenty-two years, I was once more amazed at the diversity of Green River Killer suspects: doctors, lawyers, psychologists, cops, pilots, writers, blue-collar workers, students, cultists, salesmen, cabdrivers, bus drivers, parolees, ministers, teachers, politicians, actors, and businessmen. In the end, it came down to the realization that the Green River Killer could have been almost anybody.

Almost anybody but a boring little man of seemingly predictable habits, a penny-pincher, miser, a collector of junk, and a target for jokes and demeaning nicknames. And yet it was Gary Ridgway's protective coloration that let him stay free for more than twenty years. That and his uncommon ability to mask what lay beneath his bland facade and to hide his rage and frustration from his ex-wives, numerous girlfriends, his family, and even the woman who became his third wife. Judith Ridgway appeared to have truly believed that she and Gary "did everything together." She was confident that neither of them had a need for friends or other diversions.

Gary Ridgway was good at only one thing. He was an efficient killer who was so inept at everything else that it was easy for him to hide in plain sight. In a way, he achieved what he had sought for most of his life. At last, people noticed him and he got his name and picture in the paper and on television.

For six months, he spent his time with detectives who, although they were much smarter than he, were obliged to come to him for answers. He got to go on field trips, and if their body site searches continued over a mealtime, he got to order fishwiches or hamburgers and french fries at fast-food drive-throughs.

In January 2004, when Ridgway was transferred, secretly of course, to the Washington State Penitentiary in Walla Walla, he fully expected that he would continue to be a celebrity. He was taken first to the M.H.U.—the Mental Health Unit—where he would stay until May undergoing various tests.

"He had a cocky attitude," an observer said. "You could tell that he thought he was superior to the other prisoners—that he was special."

He soon learned that he was not. The stream of detectives he had expected to visit him did not appear, although he was flown once to Snohomish County, just north of King County, to go on field trips there. Nothing significant was found. The media was unaware of the quick trip.

Ridgway is considered prey in the Walla Walla prison for several reasons: most prisoners despise him for his crimes against women—rapists and child abusers are on the very bottom rung in the penitentiary; some convicts are related to the victims or their friends and would jump at the chance to wreak vengeance. Perhaps most of all, the prison hierarchy would reward any man who killed Ridgway. It would be a real feather in the cap of the con who managed to accomplish such a difficult feat. Wisconsin serial murderer Jeffrey Dahmer didn't survive long in prison; he was murdered in the shower room. In 2003, a Catholic priest convicted of child abuse was strangled shortly after he entered the General Population.

During Ridgway's first few months in the M.H.U. in Walla Walla, one prisoner managed to get very close to him before he was spotted, quickly restrained, and hustled away. Ridgway will, indeed, have to keep his back to the wall—even when he is in solitary.

In May 2004, Ridgway was transferred to the I.M.U.—the Intensive Management Unit—where the most dangerous and difficult prisoners are housed in single, boxlike cells, shut off from the General Population of the prison. There, he is confined to his cell twenty-three hours a day. His accommodations are spartan, and it is rare to see a woman in the I.M.U. He is housed with the worst of the worst: women killers, sexual perverts, convicts whose crimes once made sensational headlines but who have long since been forgotten—shut off from the world with no hope of parole.

One of the other inmates on his tier laughed as he told a visitor about Gary Ridgway's first night in the I.M.U. He had activated the emergency signal. When a guard responded, Ridgway complained loudly that there was a "hole in my blanket."

"Then put your toe in it," the guard responded. "And never ring that alarm again unless you have a real emergency."

Just before Ridgway was sentenced to forty-eight life terms, he said that his worst fear was that he had forgotten some of his victims and the places where he left them. There is every likelihood that he has not yet revealed everything he has done. He knows full well that his plea bargain will be voided if it can be proved that he purposely held back information. And he has no plea bargains with other jurisdictions; he has admitted to leaving bodies or parts of bodies in Oregon, but insists that he committed all his murders in King County, Washington.

The geographical location of murders still undiscovered may yet see Gary Ridgway die in the death chamber.

ACKNOWLEDGMENTS

OVER the past twenty-two years, scores of people have helped me with various aspects of my research, writing, and preparing this book to go to the printer. I am so afraid I will forget someone, but I'm going to try to go back to July 1982 and thank everyone who played a part. In some instances, I will use an alias or only a first name. The reasons, I think, will be obvious, and I know readers will understand.

It hasn't been easy for grieving families to answer some of the questions I asked them, and I am forever grateful that they were willing to talk to me about the good days and the sad days of their lives.

Bill Aadland, Frank Adamson, Mike Barber, Linda Barker, David Bear, Brook Beiloh, Moira Bell,* Bren and Sharon, Marilyn Brenneman, Darla Bryse,* Lorrie C.,* Lynne Dickson, Gerald "Duke" Dietrich, Val Epperson, Families and Friends of Violent Crime Victims, Gene Fredericksen, Betty Pat Gatliff, Bill Haglund, Matt Haney, Ed Hanson, Jon Hendrickson, Maryann Hepburn,* Edward Iwata, Robert Keppel, Jean Knollmeyer, Dick Kraske, Katie Larson, Pat Lindsay, Lorna, Cherisse Luxa, Rebecca Mack, Norm Maleng, Josh Marquis, Al Matthews, Bruce McCrory, Dennis Meehan, Garrett Mills, Randy Mullinax, Kevin O'Keefe, Princess Oahu, John O'Leary, Sue Peters, Charlie Petersen, Barbara Potter, Don Reay, Barbara and John Reeder, Dave Reichert, Robert Ressler, Elizabeth Rhodes, Cheryl Rivers, Ruby, Mike Rule, Austin Seth, Paul Sherfry, Norm Stamper, Anne Stepp, Tenya, Kay Thomas, Kevin Wagner, Don White, Don Winslow, Mertie Winston, Chuck Wright, Suzanne Villamin, and Luanna Yellow Robe.

I APPRECIATE my friends who have forgiven me for staying glued to my computer these past six months: my always dependable first reader Gerry Brittingham Hay; my organizer Kevin Wagner; Betty May Settecase and the rest of the "Jolly Matrons," a secret—but friendly—society who have known each other since we were seventeen, Joan Kelly, Sue Morrison, Sue Dreyer, Patricia Potts, Shirley Coffin, Gail Bronson, Alice Govig, Shirley Jacobs, Joyce Schmaltz, and Val Szukovathy. To my fellow writers Donna Anders and Leslie Rule, and all my old pals with whom I'm going to go out to lunch again: Shirley Hickman and Rosalie Foster, Claudia House, Chirlee House, Margie McLaughlin, Cece Coy, Jennifer Heimstra, Marnie Campbell, Bonnie Allen, Elisabeth Fredericksen, Janet West, Patty Greeney, Gretchen DeMulling, Dee Grim, and Maureen Woodcock.

I am very lucky indeed that I still have my editorial and publishing team at Free Press/Simon & Schuster/Pocket Books as we work on our seventeenth book together. Authors need editing and more editing, a clear legal head to advise them, production people, proofreaders, designers in the art department, an enthusiastic marketing department, creative publicists, and accurate printers. This is my *writing* home, and I am glad I found it! Thank you all for so many years of support and friendship: Carolyn Reidy and Martha Levin (publishers); Fred Hills and Burton Beals (editors); Kirsa Rein (editorial assistant); Isolde Sauer, Jane Herman, Betty Harris, and Eva Young (copyediting); Jennifer Weidman (legal); Carisa Hayes and Liz Keenan (publicists); Karolina Harris (text design); Hilda Koparanian (production); and Eric Fuentecilla (cover design).

I chose the best literary agents in the world—at least for me—thirty-five years ago, and Joan and Joe Foley are, happily, still with me. Thanks to Ron Bernstein of International Creative Management for representing my theatrical rights.

There is also an irreplaceable team in Seattle who never let me down as the deadlines creep up: Roadrunner Print and Copy, Entre Computer, and the FedEx folks at the SeaTac Airport who hold the door open as I come racing up with finished manuscript pages due in New York City overnight.

And, finally, to my "writing dogs"—Lucy and Willow—and the cats who sit on my warm computer—Fluffbutt, Beanie, Bunnie, and Toonces. They all keep me from getting lonesome when days go by without my seeing human beings.

ABOUT THE AUTHOR

ANN RULE is the author of twenty-one *New York Times* national bestsellers, all of them still in print. A former Seattle police officer, she has a B.A. in Creative Writing from the University of Washington, an A.A. in Criminal Justice from Highline Community College, and a Ph.D. in Humane Letters from Willamette University. She is a certified instructor for police, probation, and corrections officers, and for CLE and CME, and has taught seminars to many law enforcement groups, including the F.B.I. Academy, for many years. She has been an active advocate for victims' rights organizations for three decades. She has testified before U.S. Senate judiciary subcommittees twice, and was one of the five civilian advisers on the VICAP (Violent Criminal Apprehension Program) Task Force to set up its program to track and trap serial killers. Ann is currently at work on two new books. She lives near Seattle, and can be contacted through her website pages at www.AnnRules.com.

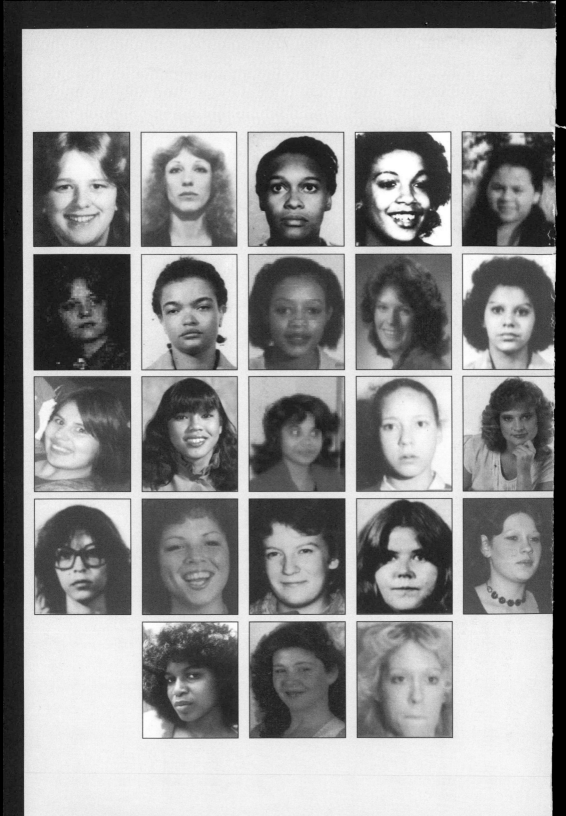